Autoroute with Junction
	Autoroute (under construction)
	Dual Carriageway
	Main Road
	Secondary Road
	Minor Road
	Track
	International Boundary
	Province/State Boundary
	National Park/Reserve
	Ferry Route
✈ ✈	Airport
✝ ⸸	Church (ruins)
✝	Monastery
	Chateau/Castle (ruins)
∴	Archaeological Site
∩	Cave
★	Place of Interest
	Mansion/Stately Home
☀	Viewpoint
	Beach
⊖	Border Crossing
	Autoroute
	Dual Carriageway
	Main Roads
	Minor Roads
	Footpath
	Railway
	Pedestrian Area
	Important Building
	Park
❶	Numbered Sight
	Bus Station
❶	Tourist Information
✉	Post Office
	Cathedral/Church
☾	Mosque
✡	Synagogue
⚐	Statue/Monument
▯	Tower
	Lighthouse

INSIGHT GUIDES

PROVENCE
AND THE
FRENCH RIVIERA

East Baton Rouge Parish Library
Baton Rouge, Louisiana
4449 0927

⚜ INSIGHT GUIDE
PROVENCE
AND THE
FRENCH RIVIERA

Project Editor
Carine Tracanelli
Picture Editor
Tom Smyth
Series Editor
Tom Stainer

Distribution

UK & Ireland
Dorling Kindersley Ltd
(a Penguin Group company)
80 Strand, London, WC2R 0RL
sales@uk.dk.com

United States
Ingram Publisher Services
1 Ingram Boulevard, PO Box 3006,
La Vergne, TN 37086-1986
customer.service@ingrampublisher
services.com

Australia & New Zealand
Woodslane
10 Apollo St, Warriewood, NSW 2102,
Australia
info@woodslane.com.au

Worldwide
Apa Publications GmbH & Co.
Verlag KG (Singapore branch)
7030 Ang Mo Kio Avenue 5
08-65 Northstar @ AMK
Singapore 569880
apasin@singnet.com.sg

Printing

CTPS-China

©2014 Apa Publications GmbH & Co.
Verlag KG (Singapore branch)
All Rights Reserved

First Edition 1989
Sixth Edition 2014

ABOUT THIS BOOK

The first Insight Guide pioneered the use of creative full-colour photography in travel guides in 1970. Since then, we have expanded our range to cater for our readers' need not only for reliable information about their chosen destination but also for a real understanding of the culture and workings of that destination. To achieve this, we rely heavily on the authority of locally based writers and photographers.

How to use this book

The book is carefully structured both to convey an understanding of the region and its culture and to guide readers through its myriad sights and activities:

◆ The **Best of Provence and the French Riviera** section at the start of the book gives you a snapshot of the region's highlights, helping ʸ prioritise what you want to do.

◆ The **Features** section, indica▮ by a pink bar at the top of each pa▮ covers the region's people, his▮ and culture in lively essays writ▮ by specialists.

◆ The main **Places** section, i▮ cated by a blue bar, provides a ▮ rundown of all the attractions w▮ seeing. The main places of inte▮ are coordinated by number with ▮ colour maps. Margin notes pro▮ background information and tip▮ how to save time and money.

◆ **Photo features** illumin▮ aspects of the region's rich art▮ heritage, flora and festivals.

◆ The **Travel Tips** listings sec▮ with a yellow bar, provides infor▮ tion on transport, hotels, shopp▮ festivals and outdoor activities▮

took a fresh look at fast-changing cities like Marseille and Toulon, and provided coverage on lesser-known inland areas and beauty spots. Edwards also penned many new features on a wide variety of topics, from the new breed of chefs, wine and truffles to tropical gardens, perfumes, and the latest on the Avignon festival. She also planned and wrote the routes on the touring map that accompanies this guide.

Past contributors include: **Rosemary Bailey** (author of the chapter on Provençal Artists) and **Anne Sanders Roston**. Additional features on *Wild Provence* and *Architecture* were provided by London-based writer and editor, **Roger Williams**, who is knowledgeable on all things Provençal. He also co-wrote the *Provence Today* chapter and expanded the history section to bring it up to date. Thanks also go to **Peter Capella, Peter Robinson, Ingrida Rogal** and **Caroline Wheal**.

Production work on this new edition was carried out by **Rebeka Davies**. The majority of pictures were taken by regular Insight photographers **Sylvaine Poitau** and **Wadey James**. They have captured the timeless beauty of the Provençal landscape and its historic towns.

The book was indexed by **Penny Phenix**.

◆ Photographs are chosen not only to illustrate geography and sights but also to convey the moods of the region and the life of its people.

The contributors

This new edition of *Insight Guide: Provence and the French Riviera* was commissioned and managed by **Carine Tracanelli** and completely revised and reshaped by **Victoria Trott**. Trott is a passionate Francophile who has updated several guidebooks on France and has travelled extensively in the country. She has also contributed articles to magazines *Living France, France Magazine* and *French Entrée*.

This edition builds on the excellent foundations laid down by contributors to previous editions, notably **Natasha Edwards**, who

CONTACTING THE EDITORS

We would appreciate it if readers would alert us to errors or outdated information by writing to:

Insight Guides, P.O. Box 7910, London SE1 1WE, England.
email: insight@apaguide.co.uk

NO part of this book may be reproduced, stored in a retrieval system or transmitted in any form or means electronic, mechanical, photocopying, recording or otherwise, without prior written permission of *Apa Publications*. Brief text quotations with use of photographs are exempted for book review purposes only. Information has been obtained from sources believed to be reliable, but its accuracy and completeness, and the opinions based thereon, are not guaranteed.

www.insightguides.com

LEFT: the harbour
at Menton.

Travel Tips

*Château
des Papes*

THE BEST OF PROVENCE AND THE FRENCH RIVIERA: TOP SIGHTS

Unmissable attractions range from a marvel of engineering to marvels of nature. Add a balmy climate, plenty of art and fine cuisine, and Provence and the Riviera cannot fail to enchant

△ **Pont du Gard, Nîmes**. This astonishing triple-decker aqueduct shows the Romans' technical genius. *See page 160*

▽ **Gorges du Verdon**. Enjoy adventure sports in this dramatic canyon. *See page 163*

△ **Beaches**. From supervised family beaches to wide sandy expanses, Provence is a sun-worshipper's delight. *See page 207*

◁ **Marseille**. The rejuvenated 2013 European Capital of Culture is one of the Med's most vibrant cities. *See page 105*

◁ **The Van Gogh Trail**. See where the artist painted his most famous works in St-Rémy-de-Provence. *See page 132*

▽ **Promenade des Anglais, Nice**. Bike or just stroll along one of the world's great promenades. *See page 244*

△ **Markets.** Provence's markets are a treasure trove of local produce and a feast for the senses. *See page 313*

▽ **The Lubéron**. Oak woods, vines and the quintessential hill villages of Bonnieux, Gordes and Ménerbes. *See page 89*

▽ **Monte-Carlo**. This tiny part of Monaco is one of the world's most glamorous locations. *See page 279*

△ **Palais des Papes, Avignon**. Thanks to a new audio-video guide, experience how the popes lived in their 14th-century palace. *See page 66*

THE BEST OF PROVENCE AND THE FRENCH RIVIERA: EDITOR'S CHOICE

Setting priorities, saving money, unique attractions...
here, at a glance, are our recommendations, plus some tips
and tricks even Provençals won't always know

MUSEUMS AND GALLERIES

● **Musée International de la Parfumerie (MIP), Grasse.** Scents and smells in the perfume museum. *See page 224*

● **Musée Jean Cocteau Collection Séverin Wunderman, Menton.** Architecturally interesting new museum showcasing the artist and writer's work. *See page 270*

● **Musée de la Préhistoire, Quinson.** Ultra-modern museum of prehistory. *See page 167*

● **Musée Picasso, Antibes.** Works by Picasso in the castle where the artist had a studio. *See page 257*

● **MuCEM, Marseille.** Shimmering new Museum of Civilisations from Europe and the Mediterranean on the regenerated waterfront. *See page 107*

● **Musée de l'Annonciade, St-Tropez.** Superb collection of Post-Impressionist paintings displayed in an atmospheric old chapel. *See page 205*

NATURAL SITES

● **The Camargue.** Mysterious wetlands of flamingos, cowboys and wild horses. *See page 146*

● **The Calanques, Marseille.** Dramatic limestone cliffs and coves between Marseille and Cassis. *See page 116*

● **Colorado de Rustrel, Luberon.** Colourful rock formation, man made and natural. *See page 100*

● **Mont Faron, Toulon.** Great views and walks overlooking the beautiful bay of Toulon. *See page 184*

● **Ile de Porquerolles.** Silver sand and pine woods: Robert Louis Stevenson's Treasure Island. *See page 202*

● **Parc National du Mercantour.** Wild mountains with prehistoric scratchings. *See page 229*

TOP: flamingos in the Camargue wetlands. **ABOVE LEFT:** a classic exhibit in the Musée International de la Parfumerie, Grasse. **RIGHT:** the stunning Calanques, southeast from Marseille.

PERCHED VILLAGES

- **Gourdon.** The quintessential Provençal hill village and star of many a film. *See page 223*
- **Mougins.** Immaculate houses, great restaurants and a couple of interesting museums. *See page 254*
- **Eze.** Spectacular fortified medieval village with a tumultuous history and two luxury hotels. *See page 267*
- **Peillon.** Arguably the most beautiful of all the perched villages, high up among olive and pine trees. *See page 229*
- **Les Baux**. Imposing fortified hill village, complete with historical reenactments, in the Valley of Hell. *See page 133*
- **Ramatuelle.** Escape the crowds of St-Tropez in this chic hill-top village with summer music and theatre festivals. *See page 208*
- **St-Paul-de-Vence.** This village was 're-discovered' by artists in the 1920s and has some spectacular modern art. *See page 217*

ABOVE: the perched village of Eze. **BELOW LEFT:** tackling white water in the Gorges du Verdon. **BELOW:** the Cours Saleya in Nice is perfect for fresh produce as well as people-watching.

PEOPLE-WATCHING

- **Cours Mirabeau, Aix-en-Provence**. The focus of Aix's chic café society.
- **Vieux-Port, St-Tropez.** For celebrity-spotting and yacht-gawping.
- **La Croisette.** Cannes' essential promenade with designer shopping.
- **Cours Saleya, Nice**. From market traders to gay partygoers, there's all walks of life here.
- **Bar de la Marine, Marseille**. The city's most famous portside bar attracts young and old.
- **Place du Casino, Monte-Carlo**. Watch the supercars pulling up outside the luxurious casino and Hôtel de Paris.

OUTDOOR ACTIVITIES

- **Water sports**. From windsurfing in Hyères to white-water rafting in the Gorges du Verdon, there's 'water, water, everywhere'. *See page 163*
- **Hiking**. Take a gentle stroll along the coastal paths or lace up your boots and head into the 'back country'. *See page 310*
- **Horseriding**. The perfect way to explore the saltmarshes of the Camargue or the Massif des Maures. *See page 148*
- **Winter sports**. Just an hour inland from the French Riviera a snowy playground awaits. *See page 232*
- **Cycling**. Enjoy a leisurely ride along the seafront or follow in the wheel tracks of Sir Bradley Wiggins up Mont Ventoux. *See page 310*
- **Golf**. There are 70 courses spread across the region including the ultra-exclusive Monte-Carlo Golf Club. *See page 310*

PROVENCE AND THE FRENCH RIVIERA TODAY

'It was a pleasure to feel one's self in Provence again, the land where the silver-grey earth is impregnated with the light of the sky.' – Henry James, A Little Tour in France

Provence and the French Riviera, also known as the Côte d'Azur, form the ultimate pleasure zone. No other region of Europe conjures up such familiar, enticing images, and few places live up to such continual hype. The region's unique combination of romance and glamour mixes a Mediterranean climate and a timeless Latin lifestyle with youthful dynamism and French chic. From beach resort to hill village, big city to nature park, it manages to embrace all these things.

France's sunny south is also a magical, mythical land where the ancient soil never seems far from the Romans who gave Provence its name. Long a poor, predominantly rural economy, it was not until it was 'discovered' in the 18th century, first by foreign aristocracy and then by artists, that other Europeans, Russians and Americans began to turn their envious gaze towards this corner of the Mediterranean that was so benign in winter and so frolicsome in summer. They brought their millions with them and made it the world's most expensive coast.

A hard life

For the people of Provence, however, life is not one long holiday. Inland, in the hills and the sparsely populated mountain areas of Mont Ventoux and the Alpine foothills of the Alpes-Maritimes, the soil is thin and the living hard. Here, the people are conservative and cling to

traditions. This rural landscape is imbued with a romantic quality, as immortalised in *Jean de Florette* and *Manon des Sources*, the books of Marcel Pagnol turned into haunting films.

Keeping traditions

The deep conservatism of the countryside, and the refusal to allow traditions to die, can nowhere better be seen than at Arles, where the cowboys of the Camargue don their bright Provençal print shirts, and tenaciously traditional women pull on their shawls and full skirts at every festival.

Conservatism extends to food, too, and people coming here year after year will wonder why

PRECEDING PAGES: lavender field in Viens; boats in Sanary-sur-Mer's harbour. **LEFT AND RIGHT:** pavement cafés and beaches: the social hubs of Provence.

the menus so seldom change. Many will be glad they don't. Even the new generation of talented young chefs remain faithful to authentic Provençal ingredients and seasonal produce.

Some parts of Provence seem to live in a nostalgia for lost glory, trying to keep a pre-industrial spirit alive, and for many visitors, this is how they want Provence to be. Many like to come on courses, to cook in the traditional Provençal way, to paint as the artists before them have done. But they should not forget to look out for the active cultural scene, which includes prestigious festivals and a dynamic creativity that can spring from anywhere. There are adventurous dance and theatre companies

has just over half a million. In between, with around a million, is Nice, the silicon valley of France, where opinion polls consistently reveal that French people would like to live more than anywhere else in their country.

Many other people not born in France would like to live here, too. Marseille, Nice, Toulon, Nîmes and Avignon are big multicultural cities with large immigrant populations, especially North and West Africans from former French colonies, as is evident in the local markets and street culture. Lying at a trade crossroads, Provence has long been multicultural, but this did not stop trouble flaring in towns and cities throughout the region during the civil unrest

in Marseille and Aix, theatre and opera in Nice, and a lively, often controversial annual festival in Avignon.

This creativity is propelled by a high student population. There are around 50,000 students in Marseille, and many of the foreigners who come to study in Provence inject a demand as well as a supply of new diversions.

Population

The population of Provence-Alpes-Côte d'Azur (PACA) is 4,900,000. Marseille, the administrative capital and a great Mediterranean port, is the largest city, with around 1.5 million inhabitants; Toulon, the naval port,

in 2005 that provoked long debates about immigration and integration.

Italians are also a large immigrant group, though they only come from next door and feel quite at home, owning many of the properties and restaurants around Nice and Menton, a municipality that has cross-frontier administrative agreements with its neighbour Ventimiglia. Nice's most famous son is Garibaldi, founder of the Italian state, and the Italian flavour of the city is distinct.

In the 1980s the oil boom brought Arab money to the coast. Now it's the turn of the Russians, and Cyrillic script frequently appears in the menus of restaurants looking for a share of the wads of dollar bills that spill from the pockets of nouveaux riches Russians. In the restaurants of the Côte d'Azur, particularly in Nice and Antibes, English is frequently the majority language, as Britons make up the largest foreign resident population on the coast.

Immigration of retirement populations in search of warm winters, both from northern Europe and the rest of France, has given towns like Menton and Beaulieu the reputation of being France's "costa geriatrica". But it also means that hill villages that were deserted half a century ago have come back to life and there is at least some work – building, maintenance, gardening – in the quieter months of the year.

Provence being home to a number of food and drink groups, including Pernod-Ricard, Nestlé and Coca Cola. As well as fruit and vegetables, Provence is an important producer of wine in the Vaucluse and the Var – the Côtes de Provence is one of the few areas of French wine production that is actually flourishing. Other less expected industries include salt in the Camargue, perfumes and food flavourings in Grasse, bauxite around Brignoles, nuclear research at Cadarache, and oil refining and petrochemicals companies around the Etang de Berre. People like to do business in Provence, and the large congress centres in Cannes and Nice are always popular.

Economy

The services industry is by far the largest employer, but technology companies, with a turnover of around four billion euros, now bring in the same amount of revenue as tourism. The high-tech industries are centred on Sophia Antipolis near Cannes, and there is a burgeoning electronics industry near Aix-en-Provence, where a quarter of all France's components are produced. The pharmaceuticals sector is expanding, too. Agriculture and the food and drink sectors are major employers,

Zaha Hadid's 33-storey glass CMA-CGM tower for a French shipping container company (2011) dominates the waterfront in Marseille's Euroméditerranée development zone.

Marseille, France's second city and the Mediterranean's largest port, has been undergoing a dramatic revival. This boom city of the 19th century that suffered so badly in the war, and long held a reputation as France's crime capital,

Left: girls about town in St-Tropez. **Above:** village life in the Provençal hinterland.

is now a lively cultural focus and a magnet for service industries and advertising and creative agencies. These are moving in to replace the traditional port industries. Marseille's massive Euroméditerranée urban renewal programme, intended to create 35,000 jobs, includes the Joliette port district, with new passenger terminal, offices in converted warehouses, museums and cultural facilities, and the Belle de Mai Media Park, dedicated to film, TV and hi-tech media industries. Other large urban development projects are happening in Nice and Toulon.

Marseille may no longer be the crime capital of France, but it is not entirely redeemed. In fact, this whole region is spotted with dark areas where reputations are not always squeaky clean. Municipal corruption surfaces now and then in allegations, prosecutions and occasional shootings. Greedy property developers have been suspected to be behind the outbreaks of summer fires. Monaco continues to resist efforts by France to eliminate money laundering by making its banking rules more transparent. Its 35 banks produce a third of the nation's revenues, and fears have been voiced that these may fall under mobsters' control.

There are gangland killings over drugs and prostitution in the cities, and racketeering reverberates around slot machines. There are rich pickings for burglars along the coast, while the Cannes Film Festival and other glamorous events attract conmen and assorted small-time thieves. The gentlemen burglars of the Riviera are a breed that has passed.

Urbanisation

One would have thought that the authorities had learnt the lessons of *bétonisation*, the concreting-up of the coast at the risk of ruining the environment and the special beauty of the Riviera – along with the region's tourist potential. But judging from the number of hoardings announcing new developments of 'Grand Standing', it still seems as if nobody cares if all the land is cluttered up by unsightly apartment blocks, villas and garages, as long as everyone can have a glimpse of the sea.

Incessant urbanisation threatens to make the coast between Cannes and Menton one continuous conurbation. It puts up prices and excludes locals who can no longer afford the rents. Elsewhere the demand for holiday homes and second residences has seen a new sprawl around rural villages, while villas in the tinderdry woods of the Var add a further fire risk to an already charred landscape. Fire is aided when there is little water to quench it, and the risk of drought increases as expanding urban areas tap the finite reserves.

Sun and wind

One thing that all the *départements* share is dazzling light from a potent sun. There is twice as much sunshine here as in Paris, even if out of season the climate is not always perfect. Winter has its share of cool or cold days,

FILM SET PROVENCE

Provence has proved ripe material for cinema. The gritty urban underworld of Nice and Marseille provide the backdrop for such gangster movies as *Borsalino* with Jean-Paul Belmondo and Alain Delon, *The French Connection* with Gene Hackman and the stunt-packed *Taxi* series. The romance and excitement of the Corniches between Nice and Monaco inspired Hitchcock in *To Catch a Thief*, with Cary Grant and Grace Kelly. St-Tropez epitomised glamorous sea, sex and sun with Brigitte Bardot in Roger Vadim's *Et Dieu créa la femme*, but is also the setting in a cult French series of comic films starring inimitable Louis de Funès that began with *Les Gendarmes de St-Tropez*.

and there are often spectacular thunderstorms at the end of August.

The months of hot weather appeal not only to tourists; farmers and gardeners delight in the long growing season, and painters revel in the magical glow that surrounds the land. Another unifying characteristic is the infamous mistral. This wild, indefatigable northern wind sweeps across the region between late autumn and early spring, although the western and central sections, particularly down the Rhône valley and between Marseille and Toulon, are generally the worst hit. Its violent, chilling gales, often lasting days

Tourism

Coastal resorts and picturesque hill villages swing between seasonal extremes, from the summer, when populations increase tenfold, to winter, when it's quiet and there's little to do but watch the birds fly by. This has created a seasonal pattern of employment and many who come here to work cannot afford to stay all year round.

The growth of cheap flights, high-speed TGVs and the French 35-hour working week all help to extend the tourist season. Aix, Avignon, Marseille and Nice are ideal for out-of-season breaks. There have been efforts, too, to tempt visitors away from the crowded sea-

at a time, are created whenever a depression develops over the Mediterranean.

High winds and a dry, hot climate mean forest fires are a real hazard, and access routes and walking paths are closed at times of high risk. Every summer thousands of hectares are destroyed by forest fires, making them especially susceptible to erosion from the mistral. The valuable top soil, rich in nutrients, is then lost, making the land less fertile and therefore less productive.

side hotspots and lead them towards cultural centres and the developing 'green tourism'. The latter comprises activity holidays, often involving hiking, climbing and white-water rafting, in the less frequented inland areas, such as the Var, the Gorges du Verdon and the Parc National du Mercantour. Monaco is trying to regain its reputation as a cultural centre with its new art museum (two villas comprise the Nouveau Musée National de Monaco), and even along the crowded coast, in the Calanques, Cap Bregançon or along the Corniche des Maures, you can still find glorious unspoilt natural beaches. ❑

LEFT: Forville market in Cannes. ABOVE: French veterans in St-Tropez. RIGHT: glass maker in Biot, the medieval hill village renowned for its bubble glass products.

Comment monss saint lois prist la second fois la cruv pour
aler oustremer z de son testms. vl.e chapitre.

l'annee dessus
mil Et. lois
le bon roy Et
lois qui toute sa vie auoit

este aueru et ententif de
auoir z de prise de huir
adieu Aduen que la tie
sainte auoit besoing de

THE MAKING OF PROVENCE

Like most regions of France, Provence is a well-defined area with a history of independence and a strong identity. The Romans gave it shape by establishing Provincia, and it drew its colour from Renaissance troubadours, alternative popes, a cosmopolitan seaport and a dazzling coast

Through the ages, Provence's strategic position and climate have drawn wave upon wave of settlers and colonisers. Ligurians, Celts, Greeks, Romans, Visigoths, Franks and Arabs have all left their mark here.

Prehistoric rock carvings in the Grottes de l'Observatoire in Monaco, made over a million years ago, provide the earliest evidence of human habitation in the region, and are among the oldest carvings of their kind in the world. For thousands of years, Neanderthal hunters occupied the area, until modern man (*Homo sapiens*) made an appearance in 30,000 BC. Ancient sites all along the coast show significant traces of primitive settlements in the form of skeletons, rock carvings and paintings, standing stones and drystone dwellings. Among the most fascinating of these are the thousands of Bronze Age petroglyphs of the Alpine Vallée des Merveilles at the foot of Mont Bégo.

Between 1800 and 800 BC the area was inhabited and cultivated by Ligurians, an extremely tough people, who lived in small, disparate settlements and enjoyed a considerable degree of autonomy until the arrival of the Greeks.

Greeks and Romans

It could be argued that Marseille was the birthplace of Western civilisation on the European continent. It was to this marshy bay that Greeks from Phocaea in Asia Minor set sail in the early 6th century BC. The peaceable Phocaeans

formed a happy alliance with the locals and quickly set up a successful trading post. Their new colony, Massilia, soon became the most important commercial centre along the coast and a flourishing republican city-state in its own right. During its heyday in the mid-4th century BC, the Phocaean presence spread throughout the area. Among the cities founded were Nikaia (Nice), Antipolis (Antibes), Citharista (la Ciotat), Olbia (Hyères) and Athenopolis (St-Tropez). The Greeks introduced the olive tree and techniques for cultivating vines.

By the 3rd century BC, however, the indigents' ties with Greece were weakened, as a budding relationship with Rome developed.

LEFT: scenes from the life of saintly king, Louis IX.
RIGHT: the founding of the town Massalia (Marseille) by the Phocaeans, c.600BC.

The friendship with Rome initially proved beneficial. The warlike Celts, Ligurians and Celto-Ligurians in the north of the region had been watching the prosperous Phocaeans with envy, and banded together in 125 BC to seize the Massilian riches. Overwhelmed, the Phocaeans turned to the Romans for help, and, in response, the warrior Caius Sextius Calvinius brought in an entire Roman army. After a vicious three-year war the victorious Roman consul established the city of Aquae Sextiae (Aix-en-Provence).

Before long, the Romans had replaced the Phocaeans as lords of the region, which they called 'Provincia Romana'. Massilia, however, continued to thrive and to operate with a fairly high degree of autonomy. Now no longer just a trading post, the city became famous as an intellectual centre, with universities rivalling those of Athens.

During Rome's civil war though, Massilia made the fatal error of siding with Pompey against Caesar. After Caesar's victory, in 49 BC, the dictator punished the city by making it a Roman vassal. He further crushed the colony by strengthening the port of Arelate (Arles), strategically located on the Via Aurelia – the Roman road linking Italy with Spain – and recruiting its inhabitants to besiege Massilia. With the fall of Massilia, Arelate became capital of the

COUME VAI?

Today there are few speakers of Provençal, the language bequeathed by the Romans to this corner of their empire. In various dialects this Occitan language developed right across southern France from the Atlantic into Italy, unaffected by words from visiting Saracens or northern tribes.

The earliest surviving complete works in Provençal are poems designed to be sung, written by William IX, duke of Aquitaine (1071–1126). In fact, most of our knowledge of the development of the language comes through song, particularly through the ballads of troubadours who gathered at courts such as Les Baux *(see page 133)*. This medieval period saw the flowering of the language.

Although few people speak Provençal today, it has been making something of a comeback. It is possible to study Provençal for the baccalaureat, while various associations offer courses in the language, songs and traditional instruments. Street signs in old towns are often bilingual: look for the Nissart *carrièra* or Provençal *carriero* meaning *rue* or street, and *castelét* or *castelar* for *château* or castle. Troubadour revivalists continue to reinterpret the medieval music, and world music performers have even tried mixing it with reggae.

In answer to the question *coume vai?* (how are you?), you might say *balin-balan* (so-so).

Roman province, with a secondary city, Cemen-elum, at modern Cimiez, just north of Nice.

The Romans remained in Provence for a further 600 peaceful and prosperous years, uniting the disparate trading posts and building roads, temples, bridges, aqueducts, baths and amphitheatres. One sign of this growing unity was the emergence of a regional language, Provençal, which was derived from Latin and is still spoken in the region (*see panel, page 22*).

The arrival of Christianity

According to legend, Provence was converted to Christianity in the 1st century after the miraculous landing of the boat from Judaea –

Invaders and marauders

With the fall of the Western Empire, chaos reigned once again. The territory was invaded and occupied by Vandals, Visigoths, Burgundians, Ostrogoths and finally the Franks, who took control of the territory in 536. For the first two centuries under Frankish rule, Provence fared pretty well commercially. But the Franks ruled with an iron fist. Anti-Frankish rebellions in Marseille, Arles and Avignon between 732 and 739 were brutally quashed. Great numbers of Provençals were slaughtered, and whole cities, including Avignon, were razed.

In the 8th and 9th centuries more marauders came from across the sea. The Saracens,

the so-called Boat of Bethany – carrying, among others, Mary Magdalene, Martha and Martha's resurrected brother Lazarus. This saintly company landed at Stes-Maries-de-la-Mer. Mary Magdalene found a cave up in the hills of Ste-Baume where she lived as a hermit until her death 30 years later. When the Western Roman Empire fell in AD 476, the entire region had been converted to Christianity, with important centres of monasticism at the Abbaye St-Victor in Marseille and the Iles de Lérins.

LEFT: Pont du Gard, Nîmes. **ABOVE:** early 19th-century painting on glass of Mary Magdalene. Legend has it that she lived in a Provençal cave and was fed by angels.

originating from North Africa and the eastern Mediterranean coast, appear to have been exceptionally violent, and devastated great swathes of the Mediterranean coastline. The terrified inhabitants were forced to flee to the hills, where they set about building the *villages perchés* – fortified hill villages – Provence is so famous for. Not until 974 did Guillaume le Libérateur drive the Saracens from Provence once and for all, beating back the Arab forces at their fortress in La Garde Freinet. The providential hero took the title of marquis, thereby inaugurating the first Provençal dynasty, and at the same time marking a new era of prosperity for the region.

Architecture

From Roman arenas to modern art galleries via Renaissance elements in hill towns – Provence contains a veritable multitude of architectural styles

I t was the Romans who set Provence's building style. Nowhere outside Italy is there such a collection of Roman remains – arenas, theatres, temples, cemeteries and triumphal arches. The

great gladiatorial arenas at Nîmes and Arles, the theatre at Orange and the Pont du Gard demonstrate how the Romans displayed their power through their buildings. They also invented the arch, and nowhere can its function be better appreciated than in the three tiers supporting the vast Pont du Gard aqueduct.

From the Romans' rounded arches and barrel vaults came Romanesque, the style of medieval church architecture that combines spaciousness with bulk. Great

ABOVE: grand-scale buildings: the Pont du Gard aqueduct and Le Corbusier's Unité d'Habitation.

ecclesiastic buildings were constructed in this style, some in secluded surroundings like the Abbaye du Thoronet. Others were highly ornamented; the figures on the façade of St-Trophime in Arles and the abbey church of St-Gilles-du-Gard are exquisite examples. Gothic style arrived late in Provence but can be seen at the Eglise St-Jean-de-Malte in Aix or the cathedral in Grasse.

A Renaissance flair embellishes the streets of many *villages perchés*, fortified hill towns, where from the late 16th century onwards, mansions were built side by side. An additional flourish was the ironwork belltower, a speciality of Provence. Castles, too, such as the Château de Lourmarin, Château Grimaldi at Cagnes-sur-Mer and the Palais des Papes at Avignon, were built in, or adapted to, the Renaissance style.

The modern era

Grand classical town houses in the 17th and 18th centuries were built where life prospered, notably in the Cours Mirabeau in Aix, while wealthy parliamentarians erected country bastides. In the 19th century, Marseille and Toulon gained Parisian-style apartment blocks. The Belle Epoque resulted in a lavish casino and hotels in Monaco and the Côte d'Azur, injected with a touch of fantasty in the mock castles, neoclassical mansions and Mauresque villas built by wealthy aristocrats.

The early 20th century saw the construction of avant-garde villas such as Mallet-Stevens' Villa Noailles in Hyères and Eileen Gray's villas at Cap Martin and Menton, while Le Corbusier's Unité d'Habitation in Marseille marked the beginnings of modern architecture for the masses.

Adventurous design is rare in a region where strict planning laws are in force, but Norman Foster has snuck in with a glass art gallery in Nîmes, and the world's largest museum of prehistory in the Gorges du Verdon. Provence has its own star architect in Bandol-based Rudy Ricciotti, who, after rehabilitating the Abbaye de Montmajour, is behind the radical Pavillon Noir in Aix, the MuCEM in Marseille (2013) and the Cocteau museum in Menton (2011). ❏

Feudal Provence

The lack of a strong central authority in the region promoted the rise of the feudal system. Towns such as Arles, Avignon, Nice, Grasse, Tarascon and Marseille became independent, self-governing forces. Grandiose castles were built, and the church started a major expansion campaign. The construction of Romanesque churches and chapels was also inspired by Roman building techniques. The arts found patronage within the various courts, and cultural creativity reached unprecedented heights.

Agriculture developed and trade increased, and through the interplay of expedient marriages, control of the area was divided between onwards, the destiny of Provence was linked to that of the Angevins and, increasingly, to France. Two years later Louis IX (St Louis) set out from Aigues-Mortes on the Seventh Crusade, which bolstered economic activity back home.

The popes in Avignon

In 1274 Comtat-Venaissin on the lower Rhône (roughly Carpentras and its Vaucluse hinterland) was ceded to Pope Gregory X in Rome. In 1309, Pope Clement V, a native Frenchman, decided that he had had enough of the anarchy that had gripped Rome, and when King Philippe the Fair of France invited him to return home, he transferred the papal court

the counts of Toulouse, who ruled the north, and the counts of Barcelona, who ruled the southern area stretching from the Rhône to the Durance and from the Alps to the sea, known as the Comté de Provence. Raimond Bérenger V in particular did much to unify the province, and took up residence in Aix, by now the regional capital. After his death in 1245, his daughter Béatrice was married off a year later by the cunning Blanche of Castille to ambitious Charles of Anjou (brother of the French king, Louis IX), who became Count of Provence. From that day

ABOVE: Giovanna, heirless queen of Naples, visits Pope Clement VI in Avignon, to surrender her lands.

> *In 1297 a new dynasty was born when François Grimaldi seized the rock of Monaco disguised as a monk.*

to Avignon. What had been a small provincial backwater suddenly swelled into an important centre for diplomats and pilgrims, holy ecclesiastics and very unholy courtiers, who brought with them a sophisticated and *mondaine* way of life. Six more popes were to follow, and a period called 'the second Babylonian captivity of the Church' began. The third Provençal pope, Benedict XII, had a reputation for being avaricious, egotistical and uncharitable. He instigated the construction of the vast Palais des Papes, as a symbol of the absolute power of the Church. Benedict's successor, Clement VI – who had bought Avignon from the reigning Countess Jeanne of Provence for 80,000 gold florins – added a more ornate section to the palace, and had the Pont d'Avignon built in 1350.

The popes stayed in Avignon for almost 70 years. In returning to Rome, however, they started the 'Great Schism' (1378–1417), when there were two popes: one in Avignon and one in Rome. This bitter rivalry continued for several decades. The popes in Rome and the antipopes

in Avignon excommunicated each other with monotonous regularity, and each of the powers in Europe chose their papal champion according to their current interests. The Schism was finally brought to an end in 1417 by the Council of Constance, which deposed the antipopes.

Good King René

Meanwhile, the rest of Provence had degenerated into a state of constant civil war. The area was already reeling from the devastation of the first great plague in 1348. A semblance of peace and order was restored by Louis II, a capable ruler. Louis fathered the most beloved count of Provence, René d'Anjou, popularly known

as Good King René. René ushered in a new era of prosperity. A self-styled philosopher and humanist, he devoted himself to promoting the economic revival of Provence and its ports and to reinstating interest in the arts. He was a tolerant, amicable leader, whose steady control allowed cultural life to flourish.

After René's death in 1480, Provence passed to his nephew and heir, Charles III du Maine, who in 1481 bequeathed the entire region to Louis XI, king of France – a distant cousin – although the Savoy-controlled Comté de Nice remained outside France. The River Var thus became an important frontier, marked by a line of fortresses. The conditions the count attached for Provence's independence were confirmed by the Constitution Provençale in 53 'chapters', which the central government in Paris increasingly ignored. This caused constant friction between Provence and the French government, and there were numerous rebellions and attempts to secede. François I further curtailed the region's independence by strengthening the control of the hated Parlement over the local judiciaries and declaring French the official language, supplanting the native Provençal dialect. Although the ancient dialect was not wiped out, the new law initiated its decline.

The Provençals fight back

Despite the repression by France during the early 16th century, noble Provençal families continued to thrive. Numerous chateaux were built, and small fortunes were amassed. Concerned that these wealthy inhabitants might try to rival the French nobility, the Parlement turned its Gallic eye towards their belittlement. Deciding that the chateaux, with their rounded corner towers, were potentially aggressive as well as presumptuous, they commanded that all towers be truncated to the level of the main roof. The stunted leftovers are still visible, dubbed *poivrières* ('pepper pots') by the locals.

However, the arts continued to flourish. There was a revival of native literature, mostly in the form of religious mystery plays; the period is sometimes called the 'Provençal Renaissance'. Many of the writers were scientific pioneers. Among them was the physician and astrologer Nostradamus *(see panel, page 27)*. A less sensational Provençal was Adam de Craponne (1527–76). Born in Salon-de-Provence amid the dry plains of the Crau, de Craponne designed the irrigation canal that diverts water from the Durance River through the Lamanon gap, bringing water to the region.

War, rebellion and plague

The brutal Wars of Religion between the Catholics and the Protestants, brought on by the Reformation, lasted much of the mid- and late 16th century. A particularly bloody campaign was wielded against the Vaudois sect in the Luberon (see page 92), which was disbanded in 1545. Countless other atrocities took place in the region, notably in Orange; Nîmes, where three-quarters of the population was Protestant; and Vence, where the people threw out a reformist bishop. However, in 1598, the first Bourbon king, Henri IV, issued the Edict of Nantes, which granted religious tolerance to Protestants and calmed the situation. Under Richelieu, the Catholic church fought back with Counter-Reformation Baroque churches. When the Edict was subsequently revoked by Louis XIV in 1685, thousands of Huguenots emigrated from Nîmes.

New dissension against the French emerged in the form of the Provençal Fronde, which pitted itself against royal absolutism. The Fronde was suppressed in 1653, but discontent persisted in Marseille. The defiant city revolted in 1659,

only to be stripped of all its remaining rights after its defeat the following year.

In 1660, Louis XIV made one of his rare visits outside the royal palace, coming with great pomp to Marseille, whose strategic importance he recognised. His objective was to win over the opposition and anchor Marseille on his side. He ordered the construction of Fort St-Nicolas, from which both the town and port could be closely monitored, expanded the urban area threefold and encouraged the

NOSTRADAMUS

Michel de Notredame – Nostradamus – was born in St-Rémy-de-Provence in 1503. He studied medicine and developed a remedy against the plague. Expelled from the medical profession for keeping the cure secret, he turned to astrology. In 1555 he produced *Centuries*, a book filled with predictions of the world's future, which was banned by the papal court. Interpreters claim that he foretold World War II and the Holocaust, Kennedy's assassination, the Industrial Revolution and even global warming. Numerous other predictions, especially those relating to the end of the world, continue to tantalise his readers. He died in Salon-de-Provence in 1566.

LEFT: Good King René (1409–80). **ABOVE:** carts laden with the dead, outside Marseille town hall, during the plague of 1720.

growth of maritime trade by making it a free port. In a period of constant wars with Spain, Louis XIV's military engineer Vauban also built new star-shaped fortifications at Toulon and Antibes.

In all likelihood, it was the expansion of Marseille port which caused the third and deadliest of all the plagues to hit Provence. The epidemic that struck in the early 1720s was carried on trading vessels from the east, and more than 100,000 people – 38,000 from Marseille alone, some 40 percent of the population – died. Traces of a vast wall built in the desperate effort to contain the disease can still be seen near Fontaine de Vaucluse.

The French Revolution

The people of Provence embraced the Revolution with open arms and an extraordinary excess of blood-letting. Their interest in the new constitution stemmed not so much from a desire for social reform as from the hope that it might offer a chance to regain lost powers. A revolt against the established church as well as monarchy, churches as well as chateaux were ransacked and confiscated as state property. Marseille was an enthusiastic adherent. Before long, a guillotine graced la Canebière,

ABOVE: *The Marseillaise*, by Gustave Doré, 1870.
RIGHT: La Croisette, Cannes, in the 1920s.

the city's main street, and the cobblestones ran red with spilt blood.

On 11 April 1789, the Société Patriotique des Amis de la Constitution was formed on the rue Thubaneau in Marseille, and it was there that Rouget de Lisle's *Le Chant des Marseillais* – now the bloody national anthem for all of France – was sung for the first time. It was from the small nearby town of Martigues that the *tricolore* (now France's national flag) originated. Martigues consists of three boroughs, each with its own standard. Ferrières's is blue, Ile St-Genest's white, and Jonquières's red. United, they form the red, white and blue flag adopted by the Revolutionaries.

The Revolution did not, however, restore the autonomy Provence had enjoyed in earlier centuries. Instead, the region lost what little independence it had been able to retain. The local government was completely dissolved in 1790, and the region was divided into three *départements*: the Bouches-du-Rhône, the Var and the Basses-Alpes. The Vaucluse was added in 1793, after the French annexation of the papal territory in the Comtat-Venaisson, as was Nice, conquered by revolutionary troops.

Napoleon

Although the Provençals had embraced Napoleon the military genius, they were much less enthusiastic about Napoleon the emperor. This same people, such eager participants in the early years of the Revolution, soon became staunch supporters of the returning Bourbon monarchy. Blood flowed again in the streets, as those suspected of being anti-royalist were slaughtered with the same intensity as the anti-Revolutionaries had been under Jacobinism.

The Provençal antipathy towards Napoleon proved to be justified, for his ever-escalating wars resulted in the ceding of much of the eastern territory (including Nice and the land as far north as the Var River) to Sardinia during the Congress of Vienna in 1814–5, after Napoleon's defeat. It was not until 1860 that these lands were returned to France.

The 19th century

Nonetheless, the 19th century was probably the most peaceful period Provence had ever experienced. The French revolutions of 1830 and 1848 and the new regimes they heralded aroused little interest in the southern regions. With the Second Empire (1852–70) came a Provençal revival, led by Nobel Prize-winning poet and local hero, Frédéric Mistral. With a group of Provençal poets, he founded the Félibrige, a cultural and literary organisation that encouraged the local language and traditions. He used his Nobel Prize money to found the Provençal museum in Arles.

Agriculture remained the economic mainstay, but the Industrial Revolution, which came fairly late to France, did not leave Provence untouched. Between 1876 and 1880 alone, the rural *département* of the Vaucluse lost some 20,000 inhabitants to the cities.

Aix-en-Provence languished through most of the 19th century as a provincial, if distinguished, backwater. Marseille, on the other hand, grew dramatically in size. Almost all trade with the French Maghreb (Algeria, Tunisia and Morocco) passed through the city, and the new industries it engendered drew waves of immigrant workers from Algeria, Armenia, Spain and Italy.

Another thriving new industry came in the form of tourism. A small community of English aristocrats had begun wintering on the Côte d'Azur in the late 1700s, but it wasn't until Lord Brougham took a fancy to the town of Cannes in 1834 that tourism on the 'French Riviera' really took off *(see page 249)*. The area became very

THE BLUE TRAIN

In the early 20th century the only way to travel to the Côte d'Azur was on the Calais–Mediterranean Express, popularly referred to as Le Train Bleu from 1922, when blue-and-gold-painted sleeping cars appeared. This luxurious palace on wheels, whose carriages each only catered to 10 passengers, would leave Calais at 1pm and arrive in Monte-Carlo at 9.30am the following morning. It became known as the 'millionaires' train', with some justification. The American James Gordon Bennett, owner of the *New York Herald* and famous for his profligacy, once, to the horror of his valet, tipped the conductor 20,000 francs; the conductor used the money to open a restaurant in Boulogne. When Charlie Chaplin came

to stay with Frank Jay Gould, he arrived on the Blue Train. The Duke of Windsor had a carriage with a specially designed bathroom. The fame of the Blue Train has been enshrined by the arts: Agatha Christie set a Hercule Poirot story on it, *The Mystery of the Blue Train*; Diaghilev directed a musical called *The Blue Train*, which was written by Jean Cocteau, with bathing costumes by Chanel and curtain by Picasso. The Blue Train stopped running in 2003 but its name endures: Monte-Carlo Casino has a restaurant called *Le Train Bleu*. But it is still possible to travel in great comfort overnight by train through France, half-waking at dimly lit stations and rising to the golden sunlight glinting off the Mediterranean.

> *In the 1890s, Queen Victoria stayed several times in Nice, travelling as Lady Balmoral and visiting the town with a donkey and trap.*

popular with the aristocrats of Victorian England and European royals. Rich French, American and Russian tourists followed. Railway lines and roads were extended along the coast, and grand neoclassical buildings mushroomed.

The extraordinary quality of the light and intense colours of the landscape were captured

on canvas by Monet, Renoir and Van Gogh, who were drawn to Provence, and by Cézanne, a native of Aix *(see pages 39–43)*.

Between the wars

Although thousands of soldiers conscripted from the south were killed in World War I, Provence was far from the battlefields of the north and remained unscathed. Post-war recovery was rapid. The period between the wars saw a boom in the tourist industry, particularly along the coast. In the 1920s and 30s Cannes and Nice became the playground for the rich and famous. The Scott Fitzgeralds, Noël Coward, Wallis Simpson and Gertrude Stein all made

their mark on the Côte d'Azur, their hedonistic and liberal lifestyles centred on the casinos, jazz clubs, villas and outdoor pools. Sunbathing had been famously introduced by Coco Chanel, and the first nudist colony opened on the Ile de Levant. With the introduction of paid holidays in 1936, the south of France was no longer the preserve of the rich. French workers began flocking to the south, many of them to see the sea for the first time.

Provence continued to flourish as a centre of the avant-garde. Matisse, Picasso, Le Corbusier and other cutting-edge artists and architects continued to find inspiration here.

World War II

The Depression and World War II brought this carefree period to an end. Occupation by Italy in 1940 was followed by German occupation in 1942–3. When the Allies landed in North Africa in the winter of 1942, the Germans marched on Toulon and Marseille. Eager to get in on the deal, the Italians took over the Côte d'Azur. After the collapse of the Italian regime ten months later, the Germans took possession of the entire area. The Provençals were swept into the thick of things. Those who had not already been conscripted into the French army banded into fierce local Resistance groups. Particularly active in the mountainous regions, their guerrilla tactics brought relentless reprisals from the occupying forces. Meanwhile, the US Air Force began to mount counter-attacks against the Germans, causing additional damage to once peaceful towns and destroying many historical monuments.

Finally, General de Lattre de Tassigny's 1st

SCANDALOUS

Political scandals are part of life in Provence. Most infamous was Jacques Médecin, mayor of Nice from 1965 to 1990, who was imprisoned for financial corruption. Throughout the region, mayors and public officials have been indicted and imprisoned for underworld dealings. Hyères became known as the 'Chicago of the Côte' after a series of bomb attacks and the assassination of a local official campaigning against corruption. The mayor of Cannes was brought to trial over a casino scandal, and the mayor of Fréjus was investigated for financial irregularities. In 2005 officials in Nice were accused of accepting bribes for contracts on the new tramway.

French and General Patch's 7th US armies landed on the Dramont beaches just east of St-Raphaël on 15 August 1944. By 15 September, most of Provence had been freed from the occupying forces, and by April the following year, the enemy had been totally eliminated.

Post-war Provence

Glamour and optimism returned to the Riviera soon after the war. The first international film festival at Cannes in 1946 delivered Hollywood to the sunny Mediterranean shores, as the arrival of the likes of Clark Gable, Humphrey Bogart and Rita Hayworth heralded a return to the star-spangled tradition of the Côte d'Azur. Artists and writers continued to take up residence in the area. Picasso moved to Antibes in 1946 and spent the rest of his life in Provence. Parisian bohemian stars like Juliette Greco and the writer Françoise Sagan followed in the footsteps of Colette and Anaïs Nin, and basked in the simple, sunny pleasures of the little port of St-Tropez. By the late 1950s, with the arrival of the bikini and the Brigitte Bardot phenomenon, the quiet fishing village had been transformed into a 'metropolis of illicit pleasures'.

Until the war Provence's economy had been almost entirely based on agriculture. After the war, farmers were encouraged to modernise their operations. The small-scale Provençal farms tried to adapt, going into debt to invest in modern machinery, but without any form of government support many were unable to survive. By the early 1980s only 10 percent of locals worked the land, compared to 35 percent 40 years earlier.

The 1960s were characterised by industrial expansion and the embracing of new technologies. Nuclear power stations developed along the Rhône and at Cadarache. Hydroelectric plants were built on the banks of the Durance, and the area around the Berre Lagoon was turned into a huge petrochemical zone and industrial port with tanker docks and oil refineries. The traditional jobs of boat-building and fishing available to the locals were replaced by less interesting jobs in the industrial plants.

In 1969 the high-tech Sophia-Antipolis Science Park, north of Cannes, was inaugurated.

Hailed as Europe's answer to California's Silicon Valley, this centre for new technologies has been expanding steadily since its foundation. It now has around 1,200 companies occupying an area a quarter the size of Paris, and is one of the most sought-after business locations in Europe. More traditional heavy industry continues on more than 7,000 hectares bordering the port of Marseille and Fos, which remains the country's main chemical and petrochemical centre.

Immigration and the far right

Following the creation of the Fifth Republic, General de Gaulle, its first president, set about tackling the unrest in the French colonies,

negotiating independence with Algeria in 1962. Algerian independence was followed by a wave of immigrants from North Africa. Tens of thousands of *pieds noirs* (literally 'black feet') – French settlers from Algeria – flooded into France, many settling in the large southern cities like Marseille and Nice. A steady flow of immigrant workers (legal and illegal) from the former colonies added to the ethnic mix, creating significant Muslim communities in towns across the region.

With economic recession and growing unemployment at the end of the 20th century, the extreme right Front National party gained enormous popularity in the region among those less

Left: an Allied soldier and local demoiselle.
Above: Roger Vadim's *And God Created Woman*, shot the director's then wife, Brigitte Bardot, to fame.

than content with the growth of a multi-ethnic society. Its xenophobic leader, Jean-Marie Le Pen, was not born in Provence, nor does he embody any particularly Provençal attributes, yet he found a remarkably large following in the region, polling 22 percent in the elections in 2004.

After losing popularity for a few years, the far right gained significant ground in the 2012 presidential elections with Marine Le Pen (daughter of Jean-Marie) of the Front National coming second in the overall results for the PACA region.

The 21st century

It has taken a while for Provence, which for so long has been deeply rooted in agricultural life,

flights is bringing more and more visitors to Provence – and not just to the big cities and coast. The more rural, further-flung corners are attracting increasing numbers of tourists looking to escape the crowds. The rural economy is experiencing a significant boost, with foreigners buying and renovating run-down farmhouses and other properties. Whole villages have been rejuvenated as a result of well-to-do British and German tourists buying holiday homes in the countryside, while multi-millionaires, particularly Russian oligarchs, have pushed up prices so dramatically in the Côte d'Azur that a lot of old French money is moving out.

to come to terms with modernisation. However, prosperity in the region is now growing, and unemployment continues to fall. The European Fund for Regional Development is currently involved in supporting scores of minor rural enterprises and agricultural projects which benefit the regional economy. The TGV has been extended to Avignon, Nîmes, Marseille and Aix-en-Provence, making Provence only a comfortable three-hour journey from Paris. Property prices in the region have boomed, and plans have been confirmed to extend the track to Nice (due to open in 2025).

Tourism continues to dominate the economy. An increase in the number of low-cost

Provence also continues to be the most popular holiday spot for the French themselves. They make up 80 percent of the 34 million visitors who bring 14 billion euros to the region's economy and account for 12 percent of its GDP. Such an influx obviously creates ecological problems, both on land and in the sea. Global warming brings the increased risk of summer fires, and many hiking trails are now closed during high-risk periods, but by and large the region continues to look after its visitors very successfully. ❏

ABOVE: the marina in the Baie des Anges, the 'Bay of Angels' which lies between Nice and Cannes.
RIGHT: Saint Martin de la Brasque backstreet.

Shaping the Coast

In the beginning the Riviera's mild winters attracted foreign visitors, from invalids and artists to royalty. Then the railway brought the masses, and in the 20th century came the hedonists

Cannes is for living, Monte-Carlo is for gambling and Menton is for dying – such was the Victorian popular wisdom on the French Riviera. By

Until the railway arrived In the 1850s, getting to the Riviera took three weeks by coach and about the same time by steamship. Then within 10 years, Hyères, Cannes and Nice had large foreign colonies in winter. Hyères was the first Riviera resort to be patronised by the British and Queen Victoria wintered there before favouring Nice, which already had a large British community who lived in the grand hotels. The Victorian obsession with standards and public works made a big impact on the city; the promenade des Anglais was built as part of to a philanthropic scheme to give work to the impov-

the 1850s, the South of France had become the home from home for well-to-do Brits and began to attract visitors from all over Europe.

The Côte d'Azur was first noticed in the 1760s by Tobias Smollet, the Scottish doctor and writer who pioneered sea bathing as a cure for consumption; consumption was the main killer disease in Britain until the 1870s, and the only remedy was believed to be a warm climate. Visitors in search of health were soon followed by social climbers and pleasure-seekers with the wherewithal to migrate south in autumn and north in spring.

erished locals – as well as to make a pleasant stroll for the visitors. Eventually Nice was eclipsed by Cannes, which, after being discovered by the British in the 1830s, flourished under the patronage of the Prince of Wales, and later by Menton, which by the 1890s had the largest British colony on the Continent thanks to its perceived health benefits – it has its own special microclimate, making it the warmest of any of the Riviera resorts.

ABOVE: La Promenade des Anglais, and the old Palais de la Jetée in the 1890s. The pier was destroyed by the occupying German troops in 1944.

International appeal

Before World War I, the Russian community was second only to the British in size and influence. In 1856, Alexandra Feodorovna, the widow of Tsar Nicholas I, bought Villa Acquaviva on the promenade des Anglais and forged the early Russian links with Nice. French was the language of the Russian court and the Riviera made a welcome change from the harsh Russian winters. Non-European royals, including the Princess of Siam and the Aga Khan, were also drawn to the area. The grand hotels they stayed in have now mostly been converted into apartment

of the Mediterranean appealed to jaded tycoons, who built beautiful villas and gardens and collected art. After World War I, only the Americans had the money to live out their fantasies, and summer, rather than winter, became the fashionable season.

Not for nothing were the 1920s known as *les années folles,* but amidst the wanton partying creativity seemed to flourish. Colette, Scott Fitzgerald, Somerset Maugham and many others found inspiration for their writing on the Côte d'Azur, while modern art flourished in the hands of masters like Picasso and Matisse, who

blocks, but their architecture has been preserved, and with it, the Riviera's period feel.

While the flow of royal visitors continued during the inter-war years, a new elite emerged: the American dollar kings. Dr James Bennett's *Winter and Spring on the Shores of the Mediterranean* had been published in the USA in 1870 and provoked a new wave of wealthy visitors. The simple yet sophisticated pleasures

both spent their most creative years here. After World War II and the creation of Cannes Film Festival, Hollywood stars arrived and Grace Kelly's marriage to Prince Rainier III of Monaco once again established the Riviera as the world's most glamorous destination, although at the same time the introduction of paid leave for workers was bringing ordinary holidaymakers down to the south too. Still, thanks to its sumptuous villas, luxury hotels, gourmet restaurants, international airport and hot summers, the South of France remains a draw for the glitterati and, as a result, the rest of us. ❏

ABOVE: the train en route to La Turbie and Èze, 1890s. The arrival of the railway in the 1850s dramatically reduced the hardships of travel to the Riviera.

Decisive Dates

Prehistoric times
Evidence of human habitation in the Gorges de Verdon, the Vallée des Merveilles, Terra Amata, Nice, and caves near Cassis and Monaco.

1800 BC
Ligurians occupy the Mediterranean coast.

600 BC
Marseille is founded by Greek traders.

121 BC
Romans conquer southern Gaul and establish Aquae Sextiae (Aix-en-Provence).

27 BC–AD 14
Reign of Caesar Augustus. Provence flourishes.

AD 3rd–5th centuries
Christianity spreads.

476
Fall of the Western Roman Empire. Vandals, Visigoths, Burgundians, Ostrogoths and Franks invade.

8th–10th centuries
Provence becomes part of the Frankish Carolingian Empire. Arabs from Iberian peninsula invade, but are expelled 200 years later in 974.

1032
Provence annexed to the Holy Roman Empire.

1178
Frederick I (Barbarossa) is crowned king of Provence in Arles.

1297
François Grimaldi, disguised as a monk, takes the Monaco rock.

1316
Pope John XXII moves papacy to Avignon.

1348
Pope Clement VI buys Avignon. Plague strikes.

1377
Papacy returns to Rome.

1388
Eastern Provence (Comté de Nice) now ruled by the House of Savoy (Italy).

1409
University of Aix is founded.

1471
Good King René (1434–80) moves to Aix.

1481
Provence becomes part of the French kingdom.

1501
The founding of the parliament in Aix.

1539
French replaces Provençal as the official language.

1545
Massacre of the Vaudois heretics in the Luberon.

1598
Under the Edict of Nantes, the Huguenots are granted the right to worship in freedom, ending the Wars of Religion.

1660
Pilgrimage by Anne of Austria to Apt and Cotignac in thanks for the birth of her son, the future king Louis XIV.

1685
The Edict of Nantes is revoked, and thousands of Huguenots emigrate, especially from Nîmes.

1691
The French conquer Nice, but the town is handed back to Savoy in 1715 after the Spanish War of Succession.

1718
Nice becomes part of Sardinia.

1720
Plague spreads from Marseille into Provence and more than 100,000 people die.

1789
Start of French Revolution.

1790
Provence is divided into three *départements*: Basse-Alpes, Bouches-du-Rhône and Var.

1791
France annexes Avignon and the Comtat-Venaissin.

1793
End of the siege of Toulon, which sparks Napoleon Bonaparte's rise to glory.

1815
Napoleon lands at Golfe Juan on escaping from Elba; the English aristocracy begins to winter in the south of France.

1854
Mistral founds the Félibrige, a cultural association to promote Provençal.

1860
Nice votes to return to France.

LEFT: detail from the *Burning Bush* triptych, showing Good King René and his wife. Painted by Nicolas Froment, it can be found in Cathédrale St-Sauveur in Aix-en-Provence. ABOVE: Napoleon.

1869
Suez Canal opens. Marseille gains in importance as a Mediterranean port.

1887
The term Côte d'Azur is coined by the writer Stephen Liégeard.

1929
Monaco holds its first Grand Prix.

1939
The Cannes Film Festival is inaugurated but World War II causes the first festival to be delayed until 1946.

1940
Italians annexe Menton and occupy Alpes Maritimes.

1942
German troops occupy southern France.

1944
The Allies land between Toulon and the Estérel in August, recapturing Toulon and Nice.

From 1945
Mass tourism. The coastal strip no longer attracts only the rich and famous.

1956
American film star Grace Kelly marries Prince Rainier III of Monaco. Brigitte Bardot hits St-Tropez, starring in the film *And God Created Woman*.

1962
Many French Algerians settle in Provence after the Algerian war of independence.

1972
The Provence-Alpes-Côte d'Azur region is created with the reorganisation of local government.

1990
Jacques Médecin, mayor of Nice for 25 years, flees to Uruguay to avoid trial for corruption.

1999
The Front National is split by internal feuding and an extreme-right breakaway party forms.

2001
High-speed TGV rail network reaches Marseille, cutting journey times to the Riviera.

2003
Heatwave and fatal forest fires create major problems for the region.

2005
Prince Rainier of Monaco dies, and Prince Albert II enthroned. Avignon and Nice affected in nation-wide riots.

2010
Marseille wins French football championship. Floods in the Var cause 25 deaths.

2011
Prince Albert of Monaco marries former Olympic swimmer Charlene Wittstock.

2013
Marseille-Provence is European Capital of Culture. New venues opened to stage events.

ARTISTS IN PROVENCE

'The whole future of art is to be found in southern France,' Van Gogh told Gauguin. He was right. With such intense light, inspirational landscapes and azure bays, no other part of the world has had such a dramatic effect on modern art

Our image of Provence has been largely created by modern artists, and they in turn have given the history of modern art a distinctly southern flavour. Familiar images include Cézanne's *Montagne Ste-Victoire*, Van Gogh's tortured olive trees, Picasso's nymphs and sea urchins, the iron tracery of Matisse's balconies and Bonnard's red-tiled roofs and palm trees, typically seen through an open window.

Today Provence and the Côte d'Azur are among the best places in the world to see modern art in the setting in which it was created, whilst enjoying the sensual pleasures and luminous light that inspired Cézanne, Van Gogh, Matisse and Picasso.

Van Gogh

Vincent Van Gogh (1853–90) was one of the first artists to be inspired by the intense bleached

'The Midi fires the senses, your hand is more agile, your eye sharper, your brain clearer...' wrote Van Gogh to his brother.

light and brilliant colours of the south. Today his image and work are slapped on everything from wine bottles to ash trays, but few people wanted to know him when he arrived in Arles in 1888 at the age of 35. Yet this was where, in

Left: *Café Terrace, Place du Forum, Arles,* by Van Gogh, 1888. **Right:** Renoir painting in his garden, c.1910.

just three years, all his great paintings were executed. Here he found a power and vitality that inspired him almost beyond endurance.

'The Midi fires the senses, your hand is more agile, your eye sharper, your brain clearer...' he wrote in one of his many letters to his brother, Theo. Interiors, sunflowers, irises, night skies and the harvest fields all charged his brush with colour – 'The olive trees look like silver, at times bluer, at times greener, bronze-coloured, whitening on a soil that is yellow, purple or orange pink or even deep ochre red.'

Van Gogh had been painting for only six years before he arrived in Arles. He was born in the Netherlands, the son of a Protestant pastor, and although he began work as an art dealer, he became obsessed with evangelical Christianity. Determined to become a preacher, he spent a year living in poverty in a mining community in Holland. Slowly the inspiration to paint took over, and after training in Antwerp, he went to Paris where Theo worked as an art dealer at Goupil & Cie. Inspired by what he saw of the Impressionists, he then headed for Provence and immediately began working furiously. Wanting to share his experience, he wrote to his friend Paul Gauguin, saying 'The whole future of art is to be found in southern France.'

In preparation for Gauguin's arrival, he rented four rooms in the Yellow House at 2 Place Lamar-

tine in Arles as a studio and began painting sunflowers. Impoverished, his health was deteriorating and he was drinking excessively. When Gauguin arrived he found Vincent impossible to tolerate and they fell out. This was the cause of Van Gogh slicing off part of his ear lobe, which he wrapped in newspaper and gave to a prostitute in the local brothel, asking her to keep it safely.

A series of mental breakdowns followed as epilepsy and syphilis took their toll, exacerbated by heavy drinking and a meagre diet. Finally he entered the Asylum for the Alienated in St-Rémy-de-Provence, and although he suffered further breakdowns, he continued to paint, producing more than 150 works, among them

THE SCHOOLS OF AVIGNON AND NICE

The patronage of the papal palace helped to establish a school of Avignon painters led by Simone Martini of Siena, who arrived in 1335, and his successor Matteo de Giovanetti from Viterbo. They worked on the palace and in surrounding secular buildings, and some of their frescos can still be seen. One of the finest works to emerge from the school is the *Avignon Pietà* (1457) by Enguerrand Quarton, now in the Louvre; there are more works of his at Villeneuve-lès-Avignon and the Musée du Petit Palais in Avignon. Nicolas Froment (1435–86), another member of the Avignon school, was court painter to Good King René. He came from northern France, where he had been

a follower of Jan van Eyck, and both he and Quarton are credited with infusing French art with Flemish naturalism. Froment's major surviving work is the triptych in the cathedral of St-Sauveur in Aix, which depicts René in the left-hand panel.

In the 15th and 16th centuries a painting school flourished in the county of Nice, where many churches and even the humblest chapels were decorated with murals. The school's principal painter was Louis Bréa (1450–1523), the 'Provençal Fra Angelico', who provided the altarpiece for Monaco cathedral and three fine works for the Franciscan monastery in Cimiez.

some of his best paintings. He then travelled to Auvers-sur-Oise just outside Paris to consult a physician recommended by Pissarro. Here he ended his life by shooting himself, even though by this time he was becoming appreciated as a major talent. The only original Van Gogh to be seen in Provence is in Avignon, but around the Asylum *(see page 132)* you can follow a trail to see the scenes that he painted. The landscape that inspired him remains largely unchanged, and it is hard to see it all without feeling moved.

Cézanne and Braque

Although many painters came to Provence, one of the most famous was born there. Paul

that the Impressionists' work lacked an understanding of the 'depth of reality'.

In 1870 Cézanne returned to Aix, where he lived until his death in 1906. He painted the Provençal landscape, the park and gardeners at the family home Le Jas de Bouffon (now open to the public) and, above all, countless versions of his beloved Montagne Ste-Victoire, determined to capture the structure of nature on canvas. 'To paint a landscape well,' he wrote, 'I must first discover its geological characteristics.'

You can tour Montagne Ste-Victoire and, in Aix, visit Cézanne's atelier *(see page 127)* and the Musée Granet *(see page 126)*, which shows 10 of his works including *Les Baigneurs (The Bathers)*.

Cézanne (1839–1906) was the son of a banker from Aix-en-Provence, where he went to college with his friend the novelist Emile Zola. In spite of a desire to paint he struggled for a while to become his father's successor. Eventually his family realised that it would be better to allow him to pursue his painting, and in 1863 he went to join Zola in Paris. Once there, Cézanne's distaste for the 'old school' led to his association with the revolutionary group of painters now known as the Impressionists. But he eventually went his own way, believing

Cézanne was highly influential. His paintings of the bay and sea at l'Estaque, just outside Marseille, inspired Georges Braque (1882–1963) to visit the port in homage to the master. The Cubist's key painting *Les Maisons de l'Estaque (Houses at l'Estaque*, 1908) was the result. Although the port is now overwhelmed by industry, the little houses that were transformed into revolutionary blocks and planes of colour can still be seen.

Renoir and Bonnard

The Impressionists came to Provence and the Côte d'Azur, fascinated by what Claude Monet (1840–1926) described as 'the glaring, festive

Left: *Avignon Pietà*, by Enguerrand Quarton, 1457.
Above: *Montagne Ste-Victoire*, by Cézanne, 1900.

light', which made colours so intense that he claimed no one would believe that they were real. In 1883 Monet brought Pierre Auguste Renoir (1841–1919) on his first visit to the area; Renoir returned increasingly often to paint the filtered golden light, the olive trees and the soft terracotta roofs that are characteristic of Provençal villages.

Suffering from arthritis, he settled in the south for his health, buying up a 500-year-old olive grove and building a house, Les Colettes, at Cagnes-sur-Mer for his family. This proved the ideal setting for Renoir's final period; he had a glassed-in studio built among the olive trees, with curtains to control the light, providing a

perfect solution to the choice between working from nature and in a studio. He even found the strength, with the help of an assistant, to sculpt. 'Under this sun you have a desire to see marble or bronze Venuses among the foliage', he said.

By 1910 Renoir was using a wheelchair and his paintbrush had to be wedged between his fingers, which had become too painful to move. Day after day he continued, in his Arcadian wonderland of brightness and colour, to paint naked girls bathing in shallow ponds, washed by the Mediterranean light. 'I'm still making progress', he said a few days before his death on 3 December 1919. As an assistant arranged a still life for him, he uttered his last word, 'Flowers'.

THE APPEAL OF ST-TROPEZ

Although many of the ports and coastal towns beyond Marseille, such as Toulon, La Ciotat, Cassis and Hyères, became favoured destinations for artists, St-Tropez had the greatest pull. Paul Signac (1863–1935), a keen sailor, was one of the first artists to move here, although the place was then only accessible by sea. In 1892 he bought a villa just outside St-Tropez, which at that time was no more than a tiny fishing port. He invited many of his fellow artists, including Georges Seurat (1859–91), Maurice Utrillo (1883–1955), André Derain (1880–1954) and Raoul Dufy (1877–1953), who all painted the little harbour, the ochre cottages and the shimmering sea. Henri Matisse visited

Signac in St-Tropez in 1904, producing his own experiment with pointillism – *Luxe, Calme et Volupté (Luxury, Calm and Delight)* – and the liberation from traditional techniques that led him to Fauvism. In 1909 Pierre Bonnard (1867–1947) also rented a villa in St-Tropez. He too was stunned: 'Suddenly I was hit with a Thousand and One Nights; the sea, the yellow walls, the reflections which were as brightly coloured as the lights...'

The work of many of these artists, including Signac's *St-Tropez au Soleil Couchant (St-Tropez at Sunset)* and Matisse's *La Gitane (The Gypsy)*, is on show at the Musée de l'Annonciade in St-Tropez *(see page 205)*.

And here among the olives you can still see his bronze *Venus Victrix*. Today Les Colettes is a museum *(see page 260)*, reopened in 2013 after total renovation, surrounded by the magnificent shady olive grove. Inside the house are 14 original paintings as well as the master's studio, with chair, easel and palette just as he left them.

Like Renoir, Pierre Bonnard (1867–1947) had grown up in Paris. He was one of the founding members of the 1890s art movement Les Nabis, a group of Post-Impressionist Symbolist artists who worked with a range of media. In the summer of 1909, he took a villa in St-Tropez, returning most years before set-tling in Le Cannet, a small village on a hill now engulfed by Cannes.

> Cagnes became known as Renoir City after the artist and his family came to live here. Young, local women, employed as servants for the house, often became models for his paintings and sculptures.

Picasso and his influence

The south of France belongs in large part to Pablo Picasso (1881–1973), and nowhere is his presence more palpable than the Musée Picasso *(see page 257)* in Antibes.

In 1925, shortly after marrying his model, Marie Boursin, star of many of his domestic interiors, he bought a small pink house called Le Bosquet, nestling high among the trees on avenue Victoria. He delighted in his garden, which was filled with birds and blossoming mimosa, almond and fig, and he painted the views from his window out across the red-tiled roofs and palm trees of Le Cannet to the bay and surrounding mountains. You can see some of these works at the Musée Bonnard, which opened in 2011 in the village *(see page 253)*.

Picasso's love affair with the Riviera began in 1920, when he spent the summer in Juan-les-Pins, and he became a frequent visitor to the coast over the following summers. When World War II broke out in 1939, he was in Antibes, painting *Pêche de Nuit à Antibes (Night Fishing at Antibes)*, a luminous nocturnal seascape inspired by watching the fishermen and their boats illuminated by white acetylene lamps. The painter returned to Antibes in 1946 with Françoise Gilot, whom he had met in 1943, and he was given a floor of the Chateau Grimaldi – then the local archaeological museum – to use as a studio by the curator, who was struggling to fill the space.

LEFT: *The Harbour at St-Tropez*, by Paul Signac, c.1905.
ABOVE: Picasso's *Joy of Life*, 1946.

In return, Picasso donated all the works he painted there to the museum, which became the Musée Picasso.

After the grim war years in Paris, Picasso was inspired by the light, colour and antiquity of the Mediterranean; his nymphs, centaurs, goats, sea urchins and monumental women running on the beach have a pagan innocence that expresses the inspiration the painter derived from the hard shadows and bright colours of sea, beach and mountains. These paintings and drawings resulted in a major work, *Joie de Vivre (Joy of Life)*, the gem of a collection that includes paintings, drawings, sculpture, engravings and ceramics. The Musée Picasso

In Vallauris Picasso single-handedly revived the town's pottery industry *(see page 255)*. In Cannes he painted the *Las Meninas* series (1957), comprehensively reinterpreting Velázquez's painting of the Spanish court. The pleasure he took in the environment is particularly evident in the wonderful dove paintings, *Els Colomins* (1957), which feature exuberant yellows and oranges with views of turquoise sea and black-and-purple palm trees.

Droves of painters followed in Picasso's footsteps, including Fernand Léger (1881–1955), whose interest in developing large architectural ceramic sculpture and murals attracted him to Biot. Along with Vallauris,

also has a large collection of work by Russian-born Nicolas de Staël, who lived in Ménerbes in the Luberon before moving into a house in the Antibes ramparts before his death in 1955.

> *Matisse on Nice: 'What made me stay are the great coloured reflections of January, the luminosity of daylight.'*

Works by César, Yves Klein and Joan Miró, as well as more recent Antibes resident Hans Hartung, can also be seen.

this town became the centre of a revival of ceramic art. Shortly before Léger died in 1955 he bought a plot of land just outside Biot on which to build a studio, and his wife subsequently created the Musée National Fernand Léger here *(see page 258)*. The museum houses his personal collection, and its exterior is dominated by his massive, brilliantly coloured ceramic panels.

Matisse

Henri Matisse (1869–1954) got his first taste of the Riviera in St-Tropez, where he spent the summer of 1904. However, he is most closely associated with Nice, which he first visited in 1916, living at several addresses in the city before settling in Cimiez for the rest of his life. His move to Nice at the age of 48 precipitated a significant change in his work. 'Most people came here for the light and the picturesque quality,' he wrote. 'As for me, I come from the north. What made me stay are the great coloured reflections of January, the luminosity of daylight.' He first stayed at the Hôtel Beau-Rivage, which was at 107 quai des Etats Unis, an extenion of the promenade des Anglais. Here he had an unrivalled view of the sea, the beach and the full trajectory of the sun. At least nine paintings made from this hotel room survive.

When his hotel was requisitioned for sol-

the huge windows with decorative iron grilles, a palm tree silhouetted against the blue sea. The following year Henriette Darricarrère, a local ballet dancer and musician, became Matisse's primary model, entering into his exotic odalisque fantasy, and he painted her dozens of times in this role.

Matisse now felt ready to become a resident, and took a large flat on place Charles-Félix in the old town. It overlooked the market and had an uninterrupted view of the sea, the promenade des Anglais curving round to the west with its elegant rows of palms and the rooftops of Old Nice.

He remained in this building until 1938, posing his models against the window or using

diers, he moved his family to the Villa des Alliés in the hills that rise steeply above the old port of Nice, on the pass over to Villefranche. Here he took to painting landscapes and watching the dawn arrive.

During the winter of 1918–19 he stayed at the Hôtel Méditerranée at 25 promenade des Anglais – now demolished. He employed an 18-year-old model, Antoinette Arnoux, who was to figure in many nude and costume paintings made at the hotel, often posing in front of

LEFT: Musée National Fernand Léger in Biot. **ABOVE:** Matisse's *Blue Nude IV*, 1952. **ABOVE RIGHT:** Matisse at work in his studio in Nice.

the spacious interiors. He loved the densely patterned wallpaper and introduced it into many of his paintings. To it, he added his own collection of masks, fabric hangings and mirrors, so the studio had the lush atmosphere of an oriental bazaar. The period 1927–31 was characterised by decorative odalisques in highly stylised settings.

In 1938 he moved to the Hôtel Regina in Cimiez near the present Matisse Museum, and it was here, being too disabled by arthritis to paint, that he began to work seriously at paper cut-outs. 'Cutting straight into colour reminds me of the direct carving of the sculptor,' he wrote. He began his cut-outs at the age of 70 and was 84 when he did the last one. He made the medium his own, creating the famous 'Jazz' series, which he executed between 1943 and 1944 at the Villa Le Rêve in Vence, and his wonderful monochrome *Blue Nude* of 1952, two years before his death.

Chagall, Dufy and Cocteau

The Russian artist Marc Chagall (1887–1985) settled on the Côte d'Azur towards the end of his career, finding inspiration in the light and colour of the south. The Musée Chagall in Nice *(see page 230)* is home to the largest collection of Chagall's work; it was built to house his Old Testament series, the *Message Biblique (Bibli-*

Wunderman *(see page 270)*, which houses a vast collection of the artist's work, and work by associated artists, donated by an American collector. The Salle des Mariages in Menton's town hall, which he decorated with murals, is a seriously recherché wedding location.

Nouveaux Réalistes and beyond

In the 1950s Nice produced its own school of artists, the Nouveaux Réalistes. They are well represented at the Musée d'Art Moderne et d'Art Contemporain in Nice, and include Yves Klein (1928–62), Arman (1928–2005), Martial Raysse (*b.*1936), all from Nice, and César (1921–98), born in Marseille but settled in

cal Message). There are mosaics by Chagall in the cathedral in Vence and the Chapelle Ste-Roseline near Les Arcs.

Raoul Dufy (1877–1953) often came to the south of France, and his sensual paintings convey the delights of the region – the food, wine, palm trees and grand hotels – perhaps more than those of any other artist.

Jean Cocteau (1889–1963) was another frequent visitor, both to the grand villas of St-Jean-Cap-Ferrat and to the seedy sailors' bars of Villefranche-sur-Mer. In Villefranche, the candy-coloured Chapelle St-Pierre has an interior designed by Cocteau, and Menton has the new Musée Jean Cocteau Collection Séverin

Nice. These artists' fascination with everyday material surfaces, packaging and industrial waste is evident in Arman's transparent containers packed with rubbish and flock of birds created from pliers. There are many works by Klein, who took the inspiration of the Riviera to its limit with his startling blue paint IKB (International Klein Blue). The Fluxus artist Ben (*b.*1935), whose 1985 piece *Il y a Trop d'Art (There is Too Much Art)* is reproduced all over Nice, may have a point. ❏

LEFT: Jean Cocteau seated by one of his paintings. **ABOVE:** French artist Ben Vautier, also known simply as Ben, lives and works in Nice.

The Literary Link

It's not just artists who were attracted to Provence: some of the world's greatest writers came in search of the good life – and better health

The Riviera's climate had long been recommended as a health cure. This is what brought New Zealand writer Katherine Mansfield (1888–1923) to Menton in 1920. Here she wrote many of her best short stories, including *The Young Girl*, *The Stranger*, *Miss Bull*, *Passion* and *The Lady's Maid*.

In 1919 the American writer Edith Wharton (1862–1937) bought St-Claire-le-Château in Hyères, now part of Parc St-Claire, where she spent her winters, enjoying the company of her art historian friends.

The Jazz Age

Scott and Zelda Fitzgerald brought the Jazz Age to the Riviera and gave a name to the frivolity, hedonism and arrogance of the rich young people who had begun to arrive daily on the Blue Train (see page 29). The climate and relaxed lifestyle proved beneficial to Fitzgerald, who was able to unwind and concentrate on getting some work done on his novel *The Great Gatsby*. The following August, they returned to the Riviera, staying with Gerald Murphy and his wife Sara, rich Americans who surrounded themselves with writers and artists in their Riviera home, Villa America, just below the lighthouse on Cap d'Antibes. Fitzgerald used the summer holiday villa as the model for the Divers' house in his later novel *Tender is the Night*. In 1926 Scott and Zelda settled into the Villa Paquita in Juan-les-Pins, which they eventually passed on to Ernest and Hadley Hemingway.

Escapism

The Jazz Age bypassed much of the coast. St-Tropez, for instance, was still an unspoilt

fishing village in 1927 when Sidonie-Gabrielle Colette, better known as Colette, author of *Gigi* and by then acclaimed as France's greatest living writer, moved into a villa there to write *La Naissance du Jour*, set in the village.

The 1930s saw many intellectuals passing through the Riviera, some, like the German Thomas Mann, escaping persecution and finding unexpected inspiration in new surroundings. His neighbour in Sanary was Aldous Huxley, who wrote *Brave New World* there, and used the town as a setting for *Eyeless in Gaza*, published in 1936. Somerset Maugham was so famous by

1926 that he was able to buy a house on Cap Ferrat from King Leopold II of Belgium for $48,500. He called it the Villa Mauresque, after its Moorish architecture, and lived there for at least six months each year until his death in 1965.

Graham Greene (1904–91) moved to Antibes to 'escape the braying voices of the English middle class'. He lived quietly, each day leaving his modest flat at the Résidence des Fleurs and walking to the gates of the Old Town. There, at Bernard Patriarch's café, he would buy *Nice-Matin* and a copy of *The Times* and then make his way to Chez Félix for lunch. ❑

RIGHT: Zelda and F. Scott Fitzgerald.

PROVENÇAL WINE AND CUISINE

The secret to Provençal cooking, one of the simplest,
yet most flavoursome of French cuisines, is its total
reliance on fresh, natural ingredients and the fragrant
herbs that are so abundant in this fertile region

If there's one thing that truly distinguishes
Provençal cuisine it's the sheer wealth and
variety of local produce. To get an idea of
what's best at the moment, head to one of the
food markets that take place in almost every
town and village, where you'll find countless
varieties of tomatoes, different colours and
shapes of courgettes, bundles of purple artichokes, cherries, Cavaillon melons and figs in
summer, wild mushrooms, pumpkins and even
truffles in winter, as well as appealing displays
of cheeses, sausages, olive oil and much more.

The magic ingredients

The real essence of Provençal cuisine is based
on simplicity and quality, the respect for seasonal produce and recipes that maximise individual flavours, plus an emphasis on vegetables
and fish that are perfectly adapted to today's
demands for healthy eating.

*The region's fruits are made into all sorts
of sweet treats, from the candied fruits of
Apt and calissons of Aix to the marrons
glacés of Collobrières and stripy berlingots of Carpentras.*

Cooking here is characterised by the use of
olive oil – with none of the rich butter and cream

LEFT: vegetable stall in Aix-En-Provence. **RIGHT:** Porcini
mushrooms (*cèpes* in Provence).

sauces of northern France – and herbs. This may
be a *herbes de Provence* mix (various combinations of rosemary, thyme, marjoram, sage, savory
and bay leaves) but is often just a single herb
chosen to go with a specific ingredient: *daurade*
(sea bream) or *loup de mer* (sea bass) baked with
fennel, rabbit or lamb roasted with rosemary, a
meaty *daube* infused with thyme and bay leaves,
chicken roast with whole heads of garlic, even
crème brûlée flavoured with lavender.

Although many restaurants continue to
perpetuate age-old recipes, a new generation
of young chefs is busy revitalising southern
cuisine, dusting off old recipes, experimenting
with new techniques and foreign influences.

A cornucopia of vegetables

Tomatoes, aubergines, courgettes, onions and peppers all get into the classic Provençal ratatouille. Elsewhere one vegetable is privileged: *tomates à la provençale* are simply tomatoes halved horizontally, topped with a sprinkling of chopped garlic and breadcrumbs, and baked in a slow oven until succulent and almost caramel sweet. Red peppers are grilled and served cold marinated in olive oil. Small purple artichokes are braised *à la barigoule*, or sliced thinly and served raw dressed with olive oil and lemon. Courgettes and aubergines are baked as *tians*, gratins named after the rectangular earthenware dish in which they are cooked. A speciality

of Nice are the *petits farcis* – assorted vegetables each with their own stuffing (variants on rice, leftover meat and onion bound with egg or bread), served lukewarm as a starter, legacy of a long frugal tradition of using up leftovers.

A hearty rustic speciality found around Grasse and St-Paul-de-Vence is *lou fassum*, cabbage stuffed with a mixture of sausage meat, rice, swiss chard and onion and boiled in a *fassumier*, a sort of cotton net, to hold it together. More refined are courgette flowers, either stuffed or dipped in egg and deep fried.

A variety of *crudités* (chopped raw vegetables) might be served with an *anchoïade* (or *bagna caouda*), to be dipped in a warm

THE OLIVE

The Phocaeans are believed to have introduced the olive tree to Provence around 600 BC, and harvesting and milling methods have changed little since then. Whole olives are milled and repeatedly pressed, producing about a litre (1.75 pints) of oil per 5kg (11lbs) of fruit. Only the results of initial pressings may be called virgin oils (look for '*huile d'olive extra vièrge, première pression à froid*' on the label). The cooking qualities and health benefits of this precious golden liquid have made it one of Provence's most prized exports. Varying from pale gold to deep green in colour, some olive oils are produced from just one variety of olive, others are blends of several varieties.

The main Provençal production areas with their own *appellation contrôlée* are in the Alpilles around Les Baux-de-Provence, in the Alpes-Maritimes around Grasse, Opio and Sospel, near Aix-en-Provence and around Nîmes. With the harvest beginning at the end of September, pressing generally takes place between November and February, but many of the area's mills and co-operatives have shops open all year round. Table olives are rinsed and soaked in lye (a brine solution), then stored for up to a year prior to consumption, to be served with aperitifs, pounded into purées and *tapenades*, cooked in stews or baked in bread.

anchovy, garlic and olive oil sauce, while all sorts of vegetables accompany the *grand aioli*, the classic Friday feast of salt cod, whelks and lashings of garlic mayonnaise.

Today's chefs make the most of this vegetable bounty. For example, for a tomato tartare, Reine Sammut of La Fenière in the Luberon uses no fewer than six different varieties of tomato grown in her own vegetable garden.

Fish and shellfish

Ugly *rascasse* (scorpion fish), tiny *girelle* (wrasse), *rouget de roche* (red mullet) and silvery *congre* (conger eel) are just some of the *poissons de roche* (literally 'rock fish') that hide in the shadows of

Other species include the prized *loup de mer*, *daurade* and its cousins *pagre*, *pageot* and *sarde*, and shoals of sardines and anchovies. Shellfish include *langouste* (spiny lobster), little crabs, sea urchins collected by divers off the Côte Bleue west of Marseille and mussels cultivated in the bay of Toulon. Today the region's top restaurants often reserve the best of the artisanal catch, and overfishing of the Mediterranean means that much of the fish served in restaurants may well come from Brittany or the Channel ports.

At its best, fish may be simply chargrilled at a beach-side restaurant – the waiter will often present a basket of fresh fish for you to select

the indented Mediterranean coastline, caught at night from the little wooden boats called *pointus*. In Marseille, locals jostle for position and are prepared to pay high prices for the still flapping fresh fish at the daily fish market on the Vieux Port. In towns such as Beaulieu-sur-Mer, where the fishing fleet caters to at least a dozen restaurants, the competition is fierce; restaurant chefs position themselves on the quays to get the pick of the night's catch.

FAR LEFT: the market area of cours Saleya in Nice. Fruit, vegetables and flowers are for sale here every day except Monday. **ABOVE LEFT:** locally caught fish at Forville market in Cannes. **ABOVE:** table set for a rustic-style lunch.

BOUILLABAISSE

Bouillabaisse is *the* dish of Marseille, and you'll find it all along the Riviera coast. Several types of fish (in particular gurnard, scorpion fish, john dory and conger eel) are simmered with onion, leek, tomatoes and saffron, with mussels and potatoes added just before the end. It is traditionally served in two courses, first the broth accompanied by *rouille*, toasted baguette and grated cheese, then the pieces of fish and potatoes.

Originally a humble dish made by fishermen from the leftovers of the catch they couldn't sell, bouillabaisse is now a luxurious – and expensive – dish; be prepared to fork out at least €45 for a good one (see page 106).

Young Chefs and Baby Bistros

Provence has witnessed a surge in the popularity of low-key, more informal restaurants run by up-and-coming chefs

Ageneration of cosmopolitan young chefs has been revitalising Provençal cooking, revisiting regional recipes, rediscovering seasonal produce and rare varieties of vegetable or injecting interna-

tional influences and the foams and suspensions of molecular cuisine. While the south still has its share of very grand restaurants, many of these chefs have also been changing the style of dining out, eschewing the formality of squadrons of suited waiters and silver cutlery for a more informal (and usually more affordable) setting, where the emphasis is very much on the food. Chefs might follow the Parisian trend for opening informal bistro annexes – such as Bruno Cirino who, alongside his elegant Hostellerie Jérôme at La Turbie, also has a roaring success with the Café de la Fontaine, a village café which is now also

a superb bistro – or strike out on their own, like Alain Llorca. As well as running the luxury Hôtel-Restaurant Alain Llorca in La Colle sur Loup since 2009, he has also opened two bistros, both called Café Llorca, in Vallauris and Monaco.

Culinary Creatives

One of the most astonishing arrivals has been Argentine-born Mauro Colagreco at Mirazur in Menton. He focuses on fruit and vegetables from his own kitchen garden, combining them with his impeccable technique and original cocktails that might include such ingredients as spinach. In Nice, Keisuke Matsushima (who trained with Ferran Adria in Spain) brings influences from his native Japan to create picture-perfect Franco-Asian dishes, with a stylish, minimalist restaurant setting to match.

Pierre Reboul opened his restaurant of the same name in the old town of Aix-en-Provence in 2007, after working with Philippe Legendre and Michel Rostang in Paris. His cooking is light, creative and fun, playing with different textures and techniques. The menu, which changes every six weeks, includes such delights as 'rockfish soup revisited', 'caviar and 24-month matured parmesan gnocchi' and 'Marseille soap with honey from the Hautes Alpes'. The style of the restaurant has also adapted to today's lifestyles, with its contemporary setting and relaxed atmosphere. He is also behind the less formal bistro Le Petit Pierre, in the same building, where a three-course lunch with set you back less than €20.

Jean-Luc Rabanel has an expanding empire in Arles, where, alongside his Michelin-starred Atelier de Jean-Luc Rabanel, a restaurant he ambitiously describes as 'a gallery of culinary expression', he has also opened the less expensive Bistro A Côté, which reinterprets traditional dishes, luxury accommodation and a cookery school. In the Camargue, Armand Arnal of La Chassagnette mainly uses organic local produce. ❑

LEFT: Mauro Colagreco at work at his restaurant Mirazur in Menton.

the one you like the look of, which will then be paid for by weight. Other preparations to try include sea bream stuffed with fennel, red mullet cooked with basil, or any fish baked *à la provençale* (with white wine and tomatoes), and of course the famous bouillabaisse of Marseille *(see box, page 51)*. Inland, freshwater trout is the speciality at Fontaine-de-Vaucluse and in the fast-racing mountain torrents of the Mercantour.

Meat and game

Provence's quintessential meat dish is the *daube de boeuf*, chunks of beef marinated overnight in red wine and cooked slowly with bay leaves, thyme and a twist of orange peel until it is a deep, almost black colour; in Avignon, it is more usually made with lamb, and in Nice, the leftovers go to stuff ravioli. The rustic dish of *alouettes sans têtes* are not the headless skylarks the name might suggest but beef or veal olives – slices of meat stuffed and rolled up. In the Camargue and nearby Nîmes and Arles you'll find *viande de taureau*, the meat of the area's little black bulls. It can be grilled as steaks or on skewers or stewed with wine and

olives as *gardiane de boeuf*. The Camargue bull meat carries an AOC designation, meaning it has to come from a geographically designated area. The best lamb comes from Sisteron in the Alpes de Haute-Provence, where transhumance, the twice-yearly moving of the flocks between summer and winter grazing, is still an important ritual. The animals' tough mountain lifestyle produces lean meat with an incomparable herby flavour. Another widely used meat is rabbit, simply baked with herbs or stewed with white wine, tomatoes and herbs. In winter, the Mercantour and Maures yield plentiful game, such as *sanglier* (wild boar).

ABOVE: the transhumance, when thousands of sheep are herded through St-Rémy to summer pastures. The Fête de la Transhumance occurs in late May.

Départemental differences

Within the region, different *départements* or even different villages proudly cling on to their own specialities. The cuisine of Nice reflects its Italian past. Here you'll find gnocchi, pasta and ravioli – which the Niçois like to claim originated here – typically filled with rich, meaty *daube de boeuf*, minestrone-like *soupe au pistou* and the street snacks of *socca* and *pissaladière*. Another Niçois speciality is *estocaficada* (stockfish), made from dried cod, soaked in water for several days, then cooked with onions, leeks and tomatoes (and similar *stocafi* in Monaco). In Nîmes, *brandade* is a speciality: salt cod is soaked and then beaten up into a purée with lashings of olive oil and a little milk and served piping hot, often with croûtes. *Pieds et paquets* is a dish typical of Marseille: stuffed sheep's tripe stewed with sheep's feet.

Cheese, fruit and desserts

Provence is not a major dairy region, but you can find local cheeses mainly made from goat's or sheep's milk. Banon, produced in the mountains around Forcalquier, is easily recognisable: the creamy goat's cheese is wrapped in a chestnut leaf, which gives it a distinctive tangy flavour. Other goat's cheeses vary from moist fresh cheeses to mature, hard *crottins*; they may be rolled in herbs or marinated in olive oil.

Brousse is a soft, creamy, ricotta-like fresh cheese usually made from goat's milk, the best coming from Rove near Marseille. It makes a perfect accompaniment to the dark local figs, or is served stirred into soups or sweetened with honey and nuts for dessert.

Desserts – served after the cheese course in France – make the most of the region's wonderful fruit. St-Tropez's *Tarte Tropézienne* is a decadent brioche filled with vanilla cream and strawberries or raspberries. Menton's lemons go into lemon tart, with or without a meringue topping. In late summer fresh figs come into their own, to accompany cheese or ham, or are stewed or baked in gratins.

As for crêpes Suzette – crêpes flambéed in orange liqueur and named in honour of 19th-century actress Suzanne Reichenberg, a mistress of the Prince of Wales – they supposedly arose from a culinary mishap at the Café de Paris in Monte-Carlo: a face-saving exercise when famous chef Auguste Escoffier (or one of his kitchen boys) accidentally set a crêpe on fire.

Destination restaurants

In small villages the best place to eat may well serve as shop, newsagent and tobacconist as well as restaurant, but still be packed with diners hungry for genuine home cooking and local gossip. In recent years, there has been a trend for top chefs to open less expensive annexes. Globe-trotting chef-entrepreneur Alain Ducasse is at the head of an empire that includes the renowned Louis XV at the Hôtel de Paris in Monte-Carlo, as well as simpler (yet sophisticated) country inns, the Bastide de Moustiers, Abbaye de la Celle and Spoon Byblos in St-Tropez. Others who have opened less formal offshoots include Bruno Cirino of the Hostellerie de Jérôme in La Turbie, who transformed traditional fare in the village café.

> Great wines aren't restricted to haute-cuisine restaurants. Try Chez Serge at Carpentras for the very best from the Mont Ventoux and southern Rhône appellations.

For the best restaurants you may have to book weeks ahead; even for simpler places it's worth ringing in advance, especially in high season. It's often easier to get a table at lunch than dinner, and lunch can also be a good time to sample a top chef's style for a fraction of the dinner price, as many offer excellent-value lunch menus.

Lunch is generally served from noon to 2pm. After 2pm, you may find it difficult to get served, except in cafés and brasseries. Dinner is served from around 8pm to 9.30pm, and often later in big cities and trendy resorts. ❏

LEFT: browsing the cours Saleya market in Nice.

Regional Wines and Spirits

The sheer variety and quality of wine in Provence, also home to the famous red blend Châteauneuf-du-Pape, means you'll be spoilt for choice

Vines were introduced to Provence by the Phocaeans when they established trading posts up the Rhône valley some 2,600 years ago. The Avignon papacy gave winemaking a further boost when it established its vineyards around its summer residences at Châteauneuf-du-Pape and in the Luberon. Today, most of the wines in the Vaucluse and Bouches-du-Rhône fall within the numerous appellations of the southern Côtes du Rhône. These include the illustrious, full-bodied reds of Châteauneuf-du-Pape, grown on flat, pebble-covered terrains and made from a complex variety of grape cépages, dominated by Syrah, Mourvèdre and Cinsault. Other wines grown around Orange include Gigondas, Vacqueyras, Rasteau, Lirac and Côtes du Ventoux, while further south you'll find the Côtes du Luberon, Coteaux de Pierrevert and Costières de Nîmes. Look out also for the rarer but highly regarded white Châteauneuf-du-Pape, the rosés of Tavel and the sweet white dessert wines of Beaumes-de-Venise, made with the tiny Muscat grape.

The wines of Les Baux-de-Provence have a growing reputation. Cultivated by a dozen or so *vignerons* in tiny vineyards scattered around the white limestone Alpilles hills beneath Les Baux, most are produced according to organic or even biodynamic principles, a holistic philosophy that involves the whole ecological system and the phases of the moon and planets. The red wines have the appellation AOC Les Baux-de-Provence, but white wines come under the neighbouring Coteaux d'Aix-en-Provence label. The white

wines of Cassis, east of Marseille, are perfect for drinking with fish.

Along the coast

In the Var, by far the largest Riviera appellation is the Côtes de Provence, principally producing vast amounts of easily quaffable dry rosés, but also small quantities of white and some good-quality reds. The main vineyards are concentrated around La Londe-des-Maures, around Ramatuelle on the St-Tropez peninsula, where they grow virtually up to the sea, and inland around Les Arcs-sur-Argens and Draguignan. Further west, you'll find the Coteaux Varois

around Brignoles and the St-Baume massif. Bandol, produced in eight communes around the seaside resort of Bandol, is the *département*'s most prestigious appellation, notably for its excellent though pricey reds, made using the Mourvèdre grape. The only wine appellation in the Alpes-Maritimes *département* is the ancient but tiny Bellet appellation outside Nice, with just 60 hectares of vineyards under cultivation, producing white, red and rosé wines.

Another famous Provençal tipple is pastis, a strong aniseed-flavoured spirit created in Marseille in the 1930s. It's served with ice and a carafe of water for mixing. ❑

RIGHT: bottles of golden Beaumes-de-Venise, a fine dessert wine.

60

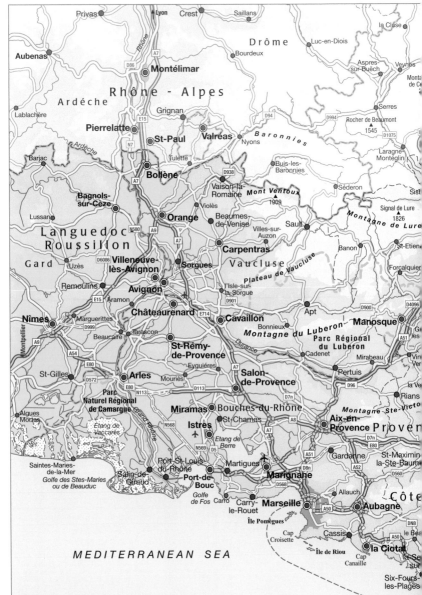

Provence and the French Riviera

| 0 | 20 km |
| 0 | 20 miles |

N

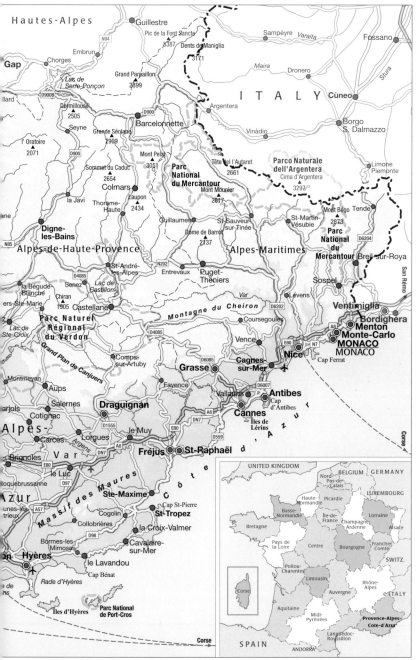

PLACES

From the wildlife of the national parks and Rhône delta to the mild climate of the coastal resorts, and from distinct cities to snow-dusted Alps, Provence and the French Riviera have much to offer visitors

The south of France stretches from the delta of the River Rhône to the Italian border and includes the Principality of Monaco. Most of this falls within the modern administrative region of Provence-Alpes-Côte d'Azur (PACA), and incorporates the *départements* of Alpes-de-Haute-Provence, Alpes-Maritimes, Bouches-du-Rhône, the Var and the Vaucluse. However, the story of Provence would be incomplete without sneaking across the Rhône into the Gard *département* in order to take in the Roman city of Nîmes and its extraordinary aqueduct.

The vigour with which Provence clings to its traditions means that each region is distinct. In the Camargue you will find bullfights to remind you of Spain; in Nice you will eat ravioli to make you think of Italy (although the Niçois claim they invented it here); in Avignon you will feel the hand of history in the papal palace; in Les Baux you will hear lute strings in the wind and imagine troubadours of medieval times; in Marseille you'll discover a dynamic multicultural city where contemporary architecture meets sparkling sea views, and, in the Parc National du Mercantour, wolves still prowl the rugged Alpine terrain.

Getting around is no problem. Motorways swoop through the region, as does the high-speed TGV, but there are also local buses and trains. You

don't need a car if you make a city the base of your visit, but a vehicle is essential for exploring the wild mountains and hill villages of the interior. At every twist and turn the landscape changes; the extraordinary light moves through ilex, oak, the silver olive and dark cypress, and the heady scrub of lavender, rock rose, thyme and rosemary intermingles with the rich ochres and glinting granites of this harmonious land. The landscape is clearly labelled: Van Gogh's Arles and St-Rémy-de-Provence, Cézanne's Aix, Picasso's Antibes, Signac's St-Tropez. The familiarity adds to the sense of well-being as you stop for roadside watermelons, to have a drink or to watch a game of *pétanque*. The routes on the enclosed touring map take in the best of the region. ❑

PRECEDING PAGES: Cannes' beach; Tourrettes-sur-Loup. **LEFT:** backstreets of Les Baux-de-Provence. **ABOVE LEFT:** sunflowers in Les Alpilles. **ABOVE RIGHT:** town square of Aigues-Mortes.

AVIGNON

Glowering within a ring of serrated city walls, Avignon preserves something of the air of the independent city state it was from its time as capital of Christendom in the Middle Ages to after the French Revolution. However, a thriving student population and the theatre festivals in July keep things lively

Strategically situated at the confluence of the Rhône, Sorgue and Durance rivers, Avignon was established by the early Gauls as a tribal capital, and it was known to the Greek traders of Marseille. During the Roman period, however, it became overshadowed by Orange and Arles. Avignon's moment of glory came when French-born Pope Clement V fled to France in 1309 to escape the papal power struggles in Rome, eventually settling in Avignon. It was the start of 70 years of the 'second Babylonian captivity of the Church', which saw the city ruling Christendom under nine successive popes *(see box page 68)*. Even after the popes returned to Rome, Avignon continued to be governed by papal legates and, although it had lost its glory, remained an important trading centre with strong links to Italy, seen in some of the fine mansions built by Italian families.

Punctuated by 39 towers and seven gates, Avignon's 4.3km (2.5-mile) ramparts still enclose its inner core: a cornucopia of historic mansions, shady cloisters, churches and palaces. French writer Rabelais called

Avignon *'la ville sonnante'* because of the number of steeples that adorned its skyline. Less poetic are the views of the modern suburbs which fan outwards. This is where the majority of the city's 92,000 inhabitants live, although pretty much everything you want to see lies within the city walls.

Orientation

It's best to explore the town centre on foot, leaving your car outside the ramparts or in one of the underground car parks by the Palais des Papes, Place

Main attractions
PLACE DE L'HORLOGE
PALAIS DES PAPES
MUSÉE DU PETIT PALAIS
PONT ST-BÉNÉZET
MUSÉE CALVET
COLLECTION LAMBERT
CHARTREUSE DU VAL DE BÉNÉDICTION, VILLENEUVE-LÈS-AVIGNON

LEFT: Le Pont St-Bénézet – the Pont d'Avignon of nursery-rhyme fame.
RIGHT: the Palais des Papes, seen from across the Rhône.

TIP

'Palais Secret' (tel: 04 90 27 50 00; www. avignon-tourisme.com; tours in English Apr– May, Sept–Oct Fri at 3pm) is a guided visit through hidden corridors and private papal apartments that are normally off limits to the public. When undertaking a regular visit, be sure to pick up an audio-video guide which shows how the rooms used to look.

Pie or cours Jean-Jaurès. If you arrive by train, the main station is at the Porte de la République, south of the centre; the TGV station outside the city has shuttle buses that depose you inside the walls.

From the station, the plane tree-lined cours Jean Jaurès, home to the tourist office at No. 41, and its continuation, the rue de la République shopping street, roughly divides the town through the middle, leading into the **place de l'Horloge**. A lively brasserie-filled square sitting on the site of the original Roman forum, this is still the epicentre of town life. On it stand the **Hôtel de Ville,** with the 14th-century clock tower that gives the square its name, and the ornate **Théâtre Municipal**. Behind the square looms the **Palais des Papes**.

The Palais des Papes

As the local saying goes, all roads lead to the **Palais des Papes** Ⓐ (Papal Palace; tel: 04 32 74 32 74; www.palais-des-papes.com; daily summer 9am–7pm, winter 9.30am–5.45pm, with exceptions; charge), the monumental symbol of papal Provence. The original city walls, built by popes Innocent VI and Urban V, were not strong enough to ward off attack by the bands of wandering knights that plagued the countryside, so the palace was designed to double as a fortress.

Step through the **Porte des Champeaux** and into the **Cour d'Honneur** and you get an instant sense of the palace as a city within a city. It's a veritable labyrinth of vaulted halls, echoing assembly rooms, small chapels and narrow staircases, illustrating the palace's multiple functions as residence, place of worship, fortress and administrative centre.

The palace is divided into two sections: the 'old' palace (**Palais Vieux**), built by Pope Benedict XII between 1334 and 1342, and the 'new' palace (**Palais Neuf**), begun under Benedict's successor, Pope Clement VI,

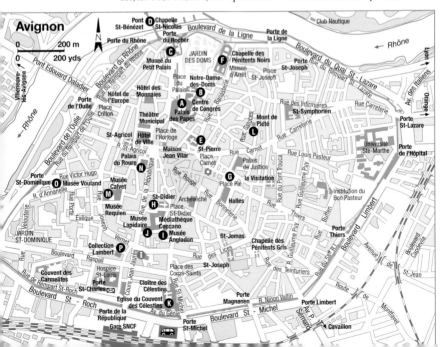

and completed in 1348. The old palace has a monastic simplicity and austerity that reflects the minimalist tastes of Benedict XII. The new palace, on the other hand, is brightly decorated with elaborate frescos and flamboyant ceilings, the hallmarks of Clement VI, patron of the arts and lover of the high life.

The first rooms, beginning with the **Grande Trésorie**, present the history of the building and some of the papal bulls and other artefacts discovered here. Frescos by the Sienese artist Simone Martini, originally from Notre-Dame-des-Doms, now hang in the **Salle du Consistoire**, where the pope held assemblies with his cardinals or received kings and ambassadors. The sheer size of the vaulted **Grande Audience** and **Grande Chapelle** is awe-inspiring. The frescos in the **Chambre du Pape** and **Chambre du Cerf** were painted by Matteo Giovanetti in 1343 and reveal the sumptuous tastes of Clement VI. These lively scenes of hunting, fishing, falconry and youths picking fruit give valuable insight into life at the papal court during the 14th century.

Around the place du Palais

In contrast to the grand Palais des Papes, Avignon's cathedral, **Notre-Dame-des-Doms ❸** (daily 8am–6pm), is a more sombre affair. This 12th-century building has undergone many structural changes over the years, but despite the 19th-century addition of a gilded Madonna to the tower, it retains its original spiritual simplicity. Rising behind the cathedral overlooking the Rhône, the **Jardin des Doms** crowns the rocky promontory that saw Avignon's Neolithic beginnings. A vineyard was planted here at the end of the 1990s, symbolising Avignon's status as capital of Côtes du Rhône wines.

Across the place du Palais, the façade of the **Hôtel des Monnaies** (the old mint) is lavishly sculpted with swags of fruit and birds; long home to the municipal music school it is being turned into a luxury shopping and leisure complex. At the north end of the square, the former bishops' palace contains the **Musée du Petit Palais ❹** (tel: 04 9086 4458; Wed–Mon 10am–1pm, 2–6pm; charge). The Gothic palace, built

Avignon's main square, the place de l'Horloge, is a hub of social activity. It is named after the 14th-century Gothic Tour de l'Horloge, the last remnant of the original town hall.

BELOW: the imposing Palais des Papes.

TIP

The Avignon Passion card allows worthwhile discounts on sights and museums in Avignon and Villeneuve, and is valid for the holder and up to four other people. After a first entrance at full tariff, subsequent sights can be visited at reduced rates. It is valid for 15 days.

around 1318 for Cardinal Bérenger Frédol the Elder, later became the bishops' palace and was given an elegant Renaissance façade. Today it houses a well-presented collection of medieval and Renaissance Italian and Provençal painting and sculpture, including a *Madonna and Child* by Botticelli.

Next to the Petit Palais you can take a footpath down to the **Pont St-Bénézet**, the celebrated Pont d'Avignon *(see box page 72)*.

Behind the Palais des Papes, a fine cardinal's palace, now the Hôtel de la Mirande, and the **Eglise St-Pierre** (Thu 2–5pm, Fri–Sat 2–6.30pm) with its pyramidal spire, Gothic façade and carved walnut doors, are further testimonies to the wealth and power of the church. The richly decorated interior of the **Chapelle des Pénitents Noirs** (Sat 2–5pm, plus Fri in summer) on rue de la Banasterie is rarely open, but worth a detour to see the façade, which has an exquisite sculpted relief of cherubs bearing the head of John the Baptist on a dish – the emblem of this charitable brotherhood which tended prisoners sentenced to death

and the mentally ill.

Southeast of place de l'Horloge, towards place Pie and place St-Didier, is a semi-pedestrianised area of ancient narrow streets, many of which contain crumbling former noble residences. **Place Pie** is home to the city's covered market (every morning except Monday), topped by an unsightly multi-storey car park – partially disguised by a 'vegetal wall' by botanist Patrick Blanc. Further east towards the Porte St-Lazare lies the **university quarter**.

On shady **place St-Didier**, the Gothic **Eglise St-Didier** (daily 8am–6.30pm), consecrated in 1359, contains an imposing pulpit in the centre of the church and an early Renaissance work by Francesco Laurana in the first chapel. Nearby discover the **Médiathèque Ceccano** (Mon–Fri 12.30–6pm, Wed, Sat 10am–6pm) on rue Laboureur, a 14th-century cardinal's palace, now the municipal library, which still has original frescos and painted wooden ceilings. Across the street, the **Musée Angladon** (5 rue Laboureur; www.angladon.com; summer Tue–Sun 1–6pm, winter

Below Right: the papal throne.

The Papal Legacy

In 1348 pope Clement VI bought Avignon from Jeanne, countess of Provence. The popes built not only the massive Palais des Papes; they also built cardinals' palaces, enlarged churches and gave the city an extensive new set of city walls. A lavish court grew up and cultural life flourished around the poet Petrarch and painters such as Matteo Giovanetti and Simone Martini. From 1378, during the Great Schism there were two popes – one in Rome, and one the 'antipope' in Avignon – the last, Benedict XIII (or Benoît XIII), was besieged in the Palais des Papes for five years before escaping one night in 1403.

Even after the popes returned to Rome, Avignon retained its independent status ruled by a papal legate – along with the nearby Comtat-Venaissin. The paper, publishing and textile industries flourished, the city's prosperity evident in fine residences put up in the 17th and 18th centuries. Avignon was reunited with France only in 1791 after the French Revolution. It remained an intellectual centre, where the Félibrige, the movement founded by Mistral and likeminded poets to preserve the Provençal language, printed its newspaper, *Aioli*.

Wed–Sun 1–6pm; charge) has a fine collection of 17th-century Dutch oils and furniture, and Post-Impressionist and modern French art. The only painting by Van Gogh in Provence, *Les Wagons du Chemin de Fer*, hangs alongside works by Modigliani, Cézanne, Picasso and Degas.

From here rue Frédéric Mistral leads back to rue de la République, where a former Jesuit chapel with sculpted Baroque facade contains the **Musée Lapidaire** ❿ (27 rue de la République; www.fondation-calvet.org; Wed–Mon 10am–1pm, 2–6pm; charge), the town's archaeological collection. Among the Egyptian, Greek, Roman and Gallic antiquities is the 1st-century Tarasque de Noves, a statue of the mysterious amphibian beast that once terrorised the region.

On place des Corps-Saints stands the unfinished **Eglise du Couvent des Célestins** ❾ – the apse and transept were completed but the nave was hurriedly truncated and shored up at the end. In summer the square is filled with café terraces. East of here, picturesque **rue des Teinturiers** was once the dyers' street supplying

local weavers, and is lined with mill wheels along a branch of the River Sorgues that flows down one side. At No. 8, the **Chapelle des Pénitents Gris** (daily 3.30–5.30pm), which still belongs to a penitent order, has paintings by Parrocel and Nicolas Mignard.

Another oddity is the **Mont de Piété** ❶ (6 rue Saluces; Mon 10am–noon, 1.30–5pm, Tue–Fri 8.30am–noon, 1.30–5pm; free), a charitable institution which functioned as the local pawnshop, offering vital credit to the city's poor. Its history is recounted in this small museum alongside an exhibition on the silk-conditioning industry.

Around rue Joseph Vernet

West of rue de la République, the circular sweep of **rue Joseph Vernet** contains Avignon's smartest shops, along with the Musée Calvet and other elegant mansions housing trendy restaurants. At the northern end of the street, towards the Rhône, is a quiet district with antiques shops and the venerable **Hôtel de l'Europe** on place de

> From afar, the admirable city... has something of the form of Athens, whose stone is golden like the august ruins of the Peloponnese, have a touch of Greek beauty. Like Athens, Avignon has its acropolis. The château of the popes is its Parthenon.
>
> VICTOR HUGO, 1839

BELOW: rue des Teinturiers.

Avignon Festival and the fringe festival 'Off'

Avignon Festival – too hybrid and highbrow or a melting pot of performances with something to appeal to everyone?

For three weeks each July, Avignon becomes the capital of French theatre – as it has ever since 1947, when Jean Vilar of the Théâtre National Populaire first put on a production in the grandiose outdoor setting of the Cour d'Honneur in the Palais des Papes. Originally just three shows and an art exhibition, it marked the birth of the Avignon Festival. In the spirit of post-war idealism, Jean Vilar's ambition was to bring first-rate adventurous theatre to the people of the provinces.

The Festival is still renowned for its adventurous theatre productions, often by leading international directors and with big-name actors, as well as some first-rate contemporary dance. Jeanne Moreau, Michel Piccoli, Isabelle Huppert, Kristen Scott Thomas and Denis Podalydès have all performed here, not just in the Cour d'Honneur but also in the Chapelle des Pénitents-Blancs or the Lycée St-Joseph.

How much it is still a festival for the people is a contentious issue. Often accused of elitism, the festival seems caught in a conflict between accessibility and the highbrow avant-garde. Many recent productions have been criticised as being too 'hybrid' – interdisciplinary mixes removed from the classic theatre of its origins. In 2003 the festival was cancelled at the eleventh hour when the *intermittents du spectacle* (the union of performing artists and backstage staff) went on strike. Since 2004, the festival has been in the hands of young directors Hortense Archambault and Vincent Baudriller, joined each year by a guest 'associated artist' – British actor, writer and director Simon McBurney in 2012; Congolese actor, writer and director Dieudonné Niangouna and French actor and director Stanislas Nordey in 2013 – intended to attract new blood.

The Avignon Fringe

However, what really makes the streets of Avignon buzz is the more spontaneous 'Off' – the offshoot and self-financed fringe festival created in 1963 by André Benedetto, which has long since outgrown its parent: in 2013 some 1,066 companies presented 1,258 shows in 125 venues. During the Off, posters are plastered on every available lamp-post and railing; the streets are full of actors, comedians and street acts handing out flyers to advertise their shows. The sheer choice of acts, mostly French but also foreign, is incredible, performed in every available small theatre, old church or café. You can easily watch five or six different shows a day, ranging from stand-up comedy to musicals to Molière, children's shows to risqué reviews or political satire. Some of the most popular acts return annually, for others Avignon is a springboard for transfers to theatres in Paris or Lyon.

For Avignon Festival details: www.festival-avignon.com; tel: 04 90 27 66 50. For Festival Le Off: www.avignonleoff.com; tel: 04 90 85 13 08. ❑

LEFT: street theatre performer at Avignon Festival, with some of the numerous flyers as a backdrop.

Crillon. The **Musée Calvet** Ⓜ (www. musee-calvet-avignon.com; Wed–Mon 10am–1pm, 2–6pm; charge) is Avignon's museum of fine art, housed in a beautiful 18th-century mansion with a stunning forecourt paved in russet-coloured pebbles from the Durance. Jacques-Louis David, Théodore Géricault, Eugène Delacroix, Camille Corot and Edouard Manet are just a few of the painters represented here. There is also a good modern section, showing work by Chaïm Soutine, Alfred Sisley, Albert Gleizes, Maurice Utrillo, Raoul Dufy and Camille Claudel. Next door is the **Musée Requien** (Tue–Sat 10am–1pm, 2–6pm), a natural history museum founded around the local botanical specimens collected by Esprit Requin.

Nearby, entered through a Gothic doorway, the **Palais du Roure** Ⓝ (3 rue Collège du Roure; tel: 04 90 80 80 88; guided visits Tue 3pm or by appointment) contains a library and research centre of Provençal culture. It is rather dry unless you are passionate about the battle to revive the Provençal language but the mansion

of the Baroncelli family is unusual and the eclectic display includes Provençal furniture and costumes, the printing press on which Mistral and Co. printed their journal *Aïoli*, and the American Indian costume donated by Buffalo Bill to would-be Camargue cowboy and Félibrige activist Falco de Baroncelli.

Keeping up the period atmosphere, the **Musée Louis Vouland** Ⓞ (17 rue Victor Hugo; www.vouland.com; Tue–Sun 2–6pm; charge) presents fine 18th-century furniture, faience from Moustiers and Marseille, and paintings by 19th-century regional artists.

Fans of contemporary art will delight in the cutting-edge **Collection Lambert** Ⓟ (Hôtel de Caumont, 5 rue Violette; www.collectionlambert.com; Tue–Sun 11am–6pm, daily 11am–7pm in July; charge). The beautifully renovated 18th-century *hôtel particulier* alternates between a revolving display from the private collection of Paris art dealer Yvan Lambert, which includes such artists as Sol LeWitt, Jenny Holzer, On Kawara, Thomas Hirschhorn and

TIP

For a vision of Avignon from the river, take a lunch cruise along the Rhône to Arles, Tarascon or Châteauneuf-du-Pape. There are also daily 45-minute trips at 3pm and 4.15pm and dinner dances. For information tel: 04 90 85 62 25, www.mireio.net

BELOW: inside the Musée Calvet.

Both the Fort St-André and the Tour Philippe le Bel offer excellent views over the papal city. On a clear evening you can watch the mesmerising colours of twilight as the sun sets on Avignon's golden stone.

BELOW RIGHT: views from the Fort St-André.

Douglas Gordon, and temporary loan exhibitions.

Take a look also at the **Cloître des Célestins** on rue du Portail Boquier. The cloister with the mossy fountain in the centre is home to the Avignon Festival offices and an exhibition space, as well as the Hôtel du Cloître St-Louis, part in former monastic buildings, part in a modern extension by Jean Nouvel.

Villeneuve-lès-Avignon

Facing Avignon across the Rhône, attractive **Villeneuve-lès-Avignon** is much smaller yet nevertheless has a rich history of its own. The French king founded the town to keep a beady eye on what was going on in Provençal and later papal territory across the river. As the papal court increased in importance, the number of adjunct cardinals rose. Finding that Avignon had no more suitable space available, many of these cardinals chose to build their magnificent estates in Villeneuve.

Towering over the town is the 14th-century **Fort St-André** (www.monuments-nationaux.fr; daily 10am–

1pm, 2– 6pm, until 5pm in winter; charge), which guarded the frontier of France when Avignon was allied to the Holy Roman Empire. Inside the crenellated ramparts are the gardens of the **Abbaye St-André** (Tue–Sun 10am–12.30pm, 2–6pm, until 5pm in winter; charge), a restored Romanesque chapel, and the ruins of the 13th-century church.

The **Chartreuse du Val de Bénédiction** (rue de la République; www.chartreuse.org; daily Aug 9am–7.30pm, July, Sept 9am–6.30pm, Apr–June 9.30am–6.30pm, Oct–Mar until 5pm; charge) was founded in the mid-14th century by Pope Innocent VI (whose tomb lies in the chapel) and has a series of beautiful cloisters. A small vaulted chapel has frescos by Matteo Giovanetti. The Chartreuse is now a centre for playwrights.

The **Musée Pierre de Luxembourg** (3 rue de la République; Tue–Sun 10am–12.30pm, 2–6pm; charge) contains some wonderful art, including a carved ivory *Virgin and Child* and the *Coronation of the Virgin* (1453), one of only two surviving works by Enguerrand Quarton. ❏

Sur le Pont d'Avignon

Immortalised in the popular children's song 'Sur le pont d'Avignon', the Pont St-Bénézet (same opening times as the Palais des Papes; charge) is one of the region's most famous landmarks. Hearing a voice from heaven, a young shepherd boy, Bénézet, left his mountains in the Ardèche and travelled to Avignon to build a bridge. At first the inhabitants mocked him, but when they saw him lift a massive rock and throw it into the river they were convinced that divine power was at work and helped to build the bridge between 1177 and 1185. The bridge was destroyed in 1226 during the Crusade waged by King Louis VIII against the heretical southern barons, but reconstructed in 1234. During the Avignon papacy, it provided a vital link between the town and the cardinals who had chosen to live across the river in less polluted Villeneuve. A chapel dedicated to St Nicholas, patron saint of sailors, was added on top of the Chapelle St-Bénézet, which stands halfway along the remaining structure. Unfortunately the Rhône's frequent floods took their toll and the bridge collapsed during the 17th century, leaving only four of its original 22 arches.

BEST RESTAURANTS, BARS AND CAFÉS

Restaurants

Prices for a three-course meal without wine. Many restaurants have a less expensive lunch menu:
€ = under €25
€€ = €25–40
€€€ = €40–60
€€€€ = over €60

Christian Etienne
10 rue de Mons
www.christian-etienne.fr
Tel: 04 90 86 16 50. Open L & D Tue–Sat (daily in July). €€€€
Avignon's top chef is renowned for his creative cuisine using different varieties of tomato or *épeautre* (wild wheat) and saffron from Mont Ventoux. Set in a splendid medieval residence.

Les Cinq Sens
18 rue Joseph Vernet
www.restaurantles5sens.com
Tel: 04 90 85 26 51. Open L & D Tue–Sat. €€€
The Five Senses is Avignon's latest gastronomic venue for Thierry Baucher's revisited classic cooking, such as his *cassoulet gastronomique* and a chocolate and black olive dessert; there's also a vegetarian menu.

C O 2
3 bis rue de la Petite Calade
Tel: 04 90 86 20 74. Open L & D Tue–Sat (daily in July). €€

The current trend in France is for *néo-bistrots*, where creative young chefs reinvent traditional dishes and the bill comes to less than €50 per head. Situated in an ancient townhouse, this is Avignon's version.

Le Diapason
1764 avenue du Moulin de Notre Dame
www.lediapason-restaurant.com
Tel: 04 90 81 00 00. Open L Wed–Sun, D Wed–Sat. €€€€
In a contemporary setting on the outskirts of Avignon, Erwan Houssin creates beautifully presented traditional dishes to which he adds his own touch. Lunch from €32.

La Fourchette
17 rue Racine
www.la-fourchette.net
Tel: 04 90 85 20 93. Open L & D Mon–Fri. Closed 3 weeks Aug. €€
This cheerful bistro is a local favourite for its good-value gastronomic take on *daube avignonnais*, *pieds et paquets* and other traditional Provençal specialities.

Ginette et Marcel
25 place des Corps Saints
Tel: 04 90 85 58 70. Open L & D Wed–Mon. €
Retro café serving *tartines* (open sandwiches), soups, salads and delicious tarts. Sit outside in the shady square in summer.

Hiély Lucullus
5 rue de la République (1st floor) www.hiely-lucullus.com
Tel: 04 90 86 17 07. Open L Fri, Sun–Tue, D Thu–Tue. €€
Opened in the early 1900s, this institution is now in the hands of chef Laurent Azoulay. The menu still has *pieds et pacquets* and *marmite de pêcheur*, alongside newer ideas.

Numéro 75
75 rue Guillaume Puy
www.numero75.com
Tel: 04 90 27 16 00. Open L & D Mon–Sat (daily in July). €€
A fine *hôtel particulier* – this one used to belong to the pastis-producing Pernod family – is now the place for modern Med-wide cooking.

Bars and Cafés

Place de l'Horloge is awash with cafés: trendy designer **Opéra Café** is ideal for both a simple lunch and night-time live music, the big brasserie **Le Forum** doubles as a theatre during Festival Off, and **Le Cid** is a popular gay haunt. On place du Palais, the **Café In et Off** has views of the Palais des Papes. Other favourites include **La Comédie** on place Crillon, while an arty intellectual crowd frequents **Utopia Bar** (4 rue Escaliers Ste-Anne). Studenty bars congregate around rue Carnot – find dance music at the **Red Zone**.

RIGHT: al fresco lunch on Place Crillon.

ORANGE AND THE MONT VENTOUX

From sunbaked plains to deep river gorges, fields of purple lavender and windswept mountains, the northern Vaucluse offers plenty to discover, from imposing Roman remains to the prestigious vineyards of the Côtes du Rhône villages

The northern Vaucluse stretches from the Rhône valley north of Avignon across the staccato peaks of the Dentelles de Montmirail to the bald summit of Mont Ventoux. There's plenty to see and do in this area, from exploring Roman remains and seeking out France's oldest synagogue to wine tasting and hill-walking.

Orange

Founded in around 35 BC by veterans of the Second Roman Legion, **Orange ❶** is famous for its two outstanding Roman monuments – the Arc de Triomphe and the Théâtre Antique (both Unesco-listed heritage sites). The second largest town in the Vaucluse, with a population of 30,000, Orange is busy all year round, and its proximity to the *autoroute* plus high-speed TGV trains direct from Paris make it a popular stopping-off point.

For centuries, Orange remained an independent principality, ruling over a domain about 12km (7.5 miles) from north to south and 25km (15.5 miles) east to west. By the 14th century, numerous religious foundations had been established, and the town had its own university. The city's name has nothing to do with the fruit but is a derivation of the

town's Roman name Arausio. It was subsequently adopted by the Dutch royal family, the House of Nassau, who inherited the city in 1559 (the King of Holland still bears the honorary title of Prince of Orange). The population of Orange was largely Protestant, making it a target during the Wars of Religion, when hundreds of Huguenots were massacred.

In the 1670s, when France was at war with Holland, ruled by William of Orange (later William III of England), Louis XIV ordered the destruction

Main attractions
THÉÂTRE ANTIQUE, ORANGE
VINEYARDS, CHÂTEAUNEUF-DU-PAPE
SYNAGOGUE, CARPENTRAS
ROMAN REMAINS, VAISON-LA-ROMAINE
MONT VENTOUX
LAVENDER FIELDS AT SAULT
GORGES DE LA NESQUE

LEFT: lavender fields, Sault.
RIGHT: walking through wine country.

St-Siffrein cathedral, Carpentras.

of the magnificent chateau built by Prince Maurice de Nassau in the 1620s on the hill behind the theatre. Its ruins in the **Colline St-Eutrope** now make pleasant grounds for a stroll. Control of Orange was finally ceded to France in 1713 by the Treaty of Utrecht.

Roman treasures

Orange's greatest Roman monument stands right in the heart of town, the **Théâtre Antique** (tel: 04 90 51 17 60; www.theatre-antique.com; daily 9am–7pm, winter 9.30am–4.30pm; charge), home to the renowned Chorégies d'Orange opera festival

evey summer. Built in the 1st century BC, it is the best-preserved theatre of the ancient world, and the only one in Europe with an intact stage wall, a massive 37-metre (121ft)-high structure that gives the theatre its distinctive acoustics. It was originally clad in marble of which just a few fragments remain. Time and the weather have taken their toll, but an ingenious high-tech glass-and-steel roof erected in 2006 protects the stage wall without weighing down the structure. Across the orchestra pit, semi-circular tiers of seating that once sat 10,000 are carved into the St-Eutrope hill.

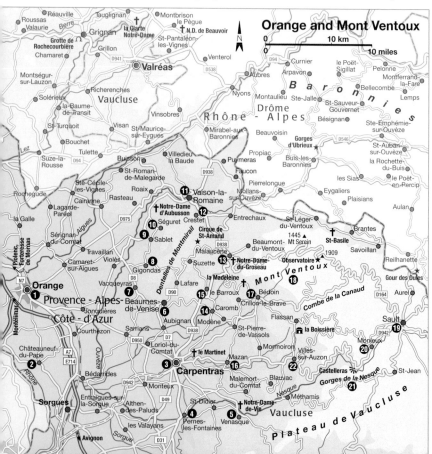

Housed in a fine 17th-century mansion opposite the theatre, the **Musée d'Art et d'Histoire** (rue Madeleine Foch; tel: 04 90 51 17 60; daily 9.15am–7pm, winter 9.45am–4.30pm; charge included with Théâtre Antique) sheds light on Roman government policy in Gaul. The collection includes fragments of a marble tablet on which land holdings were recorded in AD 77. This early form of land registry not only reveals what areas were settled but also to whom the better plots belonged, providing insight into early property ownership and social dynamics. The museum also contains a reconstructed atelier demonstrating how the famous printed indiennes fabrics were once manufactured here. The museum's art collection contains portraits of members of the Royal House of Orange.

Behind the museum the streets of the old town give way to pretty squares and fine architecture. **Place Clémenceau** (often called place de la Mairie), home to the Thursday-morning market, is graced by the handsome 17th-century Hôtel de Ville with its wrought-iron belfry and arcades and, nearby, the restored **Cathédrale Notre-Dame**.

Orange's second Roman treasure, the magnificent **Arc de Triomphe** that once straddled the Via Agrippa between Lyon and Arles, now stands at the centre of a roundabout on the N7 on the northern edge of town. Erected in 21 BC, the decorative friezes and carvings of battle scenes, enslaved Gauls and naval equipment, all visible again after cleaning and restoration in 2009, celebrate Roman supremacy on land and sea.

North of Orange up the N7, past the wine-producing village of **Piolenc**, the dramatic clifftop ruins of the **Forteresse de Mornas** (tel: 04 90 37 01 26; www.forteresse-de-mornas.com; Mar–Nov Mon–Fri times vary; charge) come into view. Built by the Count of Toulouse and later a papal stronghold, today they appear to be defending little more than the motorway but were long a strategic eyrie over the Rhône valley. Some of the guided tours are accompanied by guides in medieval costumes. Below the fortress, Mornas stretches along

KIDS

From mid-May to mid-September, the Cirque Alexis Gruss takes up summer quarters in the grounds of a chateau at Piolenc. As well as circus shows (daily 10am), there are visits to the stables, liberty horse rehearsals and elephant bathtime, and five-day circus skill courses for children and adults. N7, Piolenc, tel: 04 90 29 49 49; www.alexis-gruss.com.

BELOW: Châteauneuf-du-Pape vines are planted amid heat-absorbing stones.

Châteauneuf-du-Pape

The vineyards of Châteauneuf-du-Pape are planted with 13 different grape varieties, predominantly Grenache, followed by Mourvèdre, Syrah and Cinsault. The best wines achieve their complexity and character from skilful blends of these grapes. The end product is a supple, warm and full-bodied wine that goes well with strongly flavoured dishes such as game and red meat, as well as pungent cheese. The writer Alphonse Daudet (1840–97) praised Châteauneuf-du-Pape as 'the king of wines and the wine of kings'. This noble wine can be sampled at countless local vineyards that line the lanes around here; ask at the tourist office about times and tours.

Black Diamonds

Go on a truffle hunt, enrol on a course to learn how to cook them, savour the atmosphere of a truffle market or simply visit a restaurant with a special truffle menu

A delicacy prized by leading chefs – and in ancient times reputed to have aphrodisiac qualities – the pungent black truffle, known in Provence as the *rabasse* (also dubbed the 'black diamond' or 'black pearl of Carpentras') is the result of an unusual symbiosis between a tree, generally an oak, and the parasitic underground fungus *tuber melanosporum*, which lives on its roots. Although *tuber melanosporum* is also known as the *truffe du Périgord*, today 80 percent of French truffles come from southeast France, and of those 70 percent come from the Carpentras area.

The Foire St-Siffrein on 27 November heralds the start of the truffle season and augurs the weekly truffle auction held in Carpentras each Friday morning until March, near the Café de l'Univers on place Aristide Briand opposite Hôtel-Dieu. The auction itself is a somewhat cloak-and-dagger affair. Sellers discreetly unveil their precious black treasures from jute sacks, and bidding starts promptly at 9am. The Carpentras market serves as a reference to determine the weekly rate per kilogram for other truffle markets in the region, such as the Tuesday market at Vaison-la-Romaine.

Should you buy truffles yourself (there is also a small unregulated market for individuals), you are advised to keep them in olive oil or to store them with eggs in a closed box in the fridge, where they will help to perfume the eggs for a future *brouillard aux truffes* (scrambled egg with truffles).

Truffles were once so widespread that Parisians ate them as interval snacks at the opera, and even peasants could scoff them down as vegetables. But climate change and over-exploitation mean that truffle yields have been declining in recent years.

The first conscious attempt to cultivate truffles – as opposed to simply finding them in appropriate woods – began in the 19th century with the deliberate planting of oak trees in suitably chalky soils.

Finding truffles

Truffles often leave tell-tale rings in the ground under the trees where they might be found. But don't be tempted to go foraging for them yourself – truffle orchards are privately owned, and individuals pay high prices when truffle-collecting permits are auctioned every five years.

As to how truffle-hunting – or the art of *rabassage* – is done, both dogs and pigs have their fans. Pigs are the traditional method, as they will hunt truffles naturally, but they also adore eating them. Dogs have to be trained for the purpose, but are happier to relinquish their trophy.

The Office de Tourisme at Carpentras (97 place du 25 août; tel: 04 90 63 00 78; www.carpentras-ventoux.com) can provide information on truffle-hunting weekends, cookery courses and restaurants serving special truffle menus. ❏

Left: a truffle farmer and his truffle-sniffing pig forage for the prized *tuber melanosporum*.

the foot of the cliff, with plane tree-lined cours, remnants of old fortified gateways and an upper village, where the square-towered Romanesque Chapelle Notre-Dame du Val Romigier, the former parish church, nestles between two mountain spurs.

Châteauneuf-du-Pape

As you approach **Châteauneuf-du-Pape ❷**, rows of green vines rise out of what looks like a pebble beach on either side of the road. In fact, this land was once washed by the waters of the Rhône. The stones are said to radiate back the heat from the sun, thus 'cooking' the grapes on the vine. This curious landscape marks the beginning of a winegrowing area of 116 vineyards all classified under the Châteauneuf-du-Pape appellation (see box on page 77).

Vines have been cultivated here since the Avignon papacy (bottles bear the papal coat of arms). The town is named after the summer palace built by Pope John XXII in the 14th century. Although the **Château des Papes** looks impressive from afar when silhouetted against the sky at the top of the village, it now consists of little more than one facade and part of a tower. This is all that is left after centuries of being occupied and sacked and its near-total destruction in 1944, when German troops fought a battle against Resistance forces here. From the ruins, however, there are fine views over the tiled rooftops and across vineyards towards Avignon.

The main attractions of the village today are wine tasting and buying – almost every other house appears to be a wine producer. The **Musée du Vin Brotte** (avenue Saint-Pierre de Luxembourg; tel: 04 90 83 59 44; www.brotte.com; summer daily 9am–1pm, 2–7pm, winter 9am–noon, 2–6pm; free) is dedicated to the history and traditions of winemaking in the region.

Carpentras

Southeast of Châteauneuf-du-Pape, the market town of **Carpentras ❸** was also once part of the Comtat-Venaissin, the papal territory that roughly spanned the land between the Rhône, the Durance and Mont

When buying Châteauneuf-du-Pape wines, make sure the bottle carries either the crossed keys or the bishop's mitre design.

BELOW LEFT: the remains of Château des Papes.
BELOW RIGHT: Châteauneuf-du-Pape is renowned for its red wines.

EAT

Take a break from sightseeing with coffee or tea and a cake at Jouvaud (40 rue de l'Evêché; open daily). Try La Christine, a local speciality made with preserved fruits and almond cream and topped with pine nuts and icing sugar.

BELOW: the prayer room, Carpentras' synagogue.

Ventoux. Before the Roman conquest, the settlement was the tribal capital of the Celto-Ligurian Memini. The conquest itself is recorded in the carvings on the monumental gate in the courtyard of the **Palais de Justice**. By the 4th century, Carpentras had become a bishopric. Between 1320 and 1797 it was capital of the Comtat-Venaissin and therefore part of the Holy See.

During the Middle Ages, a thriving Jewish community, known as the *juifs du pape* (papal Jews), enjoyed freedom of worship here. Behind the Hôtel de Ville, France's oldest **synagogue** (Mon–Thu 10am–noon, 3–5pm, Fri 10am–noon, 3–4pm, closed Jewish holidays) is a testament to this enclave of religious tolerance. It was founded in 1367, but rebuilt in the 18th century when the prayer room was given its lavish fake marble interior. Sadly, the Jewish cemetery outside town was desecrated by far-right activists in 1990.

Further evidence of the Jewish presence can be seen in the 15th-century **Cathédrale St-Siffrein** in the centre of the old town. The south portal is known as the Porte

Juive, probably because it was used by Jewish converts to Christianity.

One man who was less than tolerant of the Jewish population, however, was the Bishop d'Inguimbert. In the 18th century, he decreed that the Jewish community must remain segregated within their own ghetto. Intolerance aside, the bishop played a major role in the cultural and architectural development of Carpentras. He ordered the building of the Rococo **Chapelle Notre-Dame-de-Sainte** and founded the **Hôtel-Dieu** in 1750. The well-preserved pharmacy of the former hospital is lined with faience jars and decorated with panels by court painter Duplessis. The rest of the building is being restored to house an ambitious new cultural centre (due to open in 2015), incorporating most of the town's museums.

Most notable among Carpentras's museums is the **Musée Comtadin et Duplessis** (234 boulevard A. Durand; summer Wed–Mon 10am–noon, 2–6pm, winter by appointment; charge). It covers the customs and history of the region and features

The Papal Jews

When Jews were expelled from France in the 13th century, they were allowed to remain in Avignon and the Comtat Venaissin, which were subject to papal rule rather than that of the French crown. The ancient Jewish populations of cities like Marseille and Aix took refuge in the papal territories. This tolerance has given Provence a Jewish heritage unique in France. Gradually the laws became stricter: Jews were excluded from practising many trades or owning land, and they were forced to live cramped together in the carrière or ghetto, which was locked by gates at night. By the 17th century, the Jewish communities were concentrated in four ghettos in Avignon, Carpentras, Cavaillon and L'Isle-sur-la-Sorgue. Nonetheless, the Jews enjoyed a certain prosperity, especially during the 18th century, as the rules relaxed and merchants often had the freedom to trade in neighbouring towns.

It was the French Revolution that brought an end to the official exclusion of Jews from France, allowing them full citizenship, and the ghetto disappeared. Two beautiful synagogues survive at Carpentras and Cavaillon.

works by Hyacinthe Rigaud, Joseph Vernet and local painters. Across the courtyard is the magnificent **library**, bequeathed by Bishop d'Inguimbert, which contains more than 76,000 volumes, including some rare editions of works by Petrarch.

The **Musée Sobirats** (rue du Collège; summer Wed–Mon 10am–noon, 2–6pm, winter by appointment only; charge) preserves the atmosphere and furnishings of an 18th-century mansion.

Every Friday, an excellent **market** takes over the town centre. Local specialities include strawberries and the stripy caramel sweets called *berlingots*, but Carpentras is most famous for its truffles (*see page 78*).

Pernes-les-Fontaines and Venasque

Baking on the plain 6km (4 miles) south of Carpentras, the lively little agricultural town of **Pernes-les-Fontaines ❹** preceded Carpentras as capital of the Comtat-Venaissin from 1125 until 1320. With its ramparts and fortified gateways, it's like an Avignon in miniature. The town boasts

a medieval tower, the **Tour Ferrande** (visits booked through the tourist office; tel: 04 90 61 31 04), decorated with vivid frescos depicting the victory of Charles II of Anjou over the Emperor Frederick II near Naples in 1266. But the most remarkable thing about Pernes is its multitude of sculpted fountains, mainly installed in the 18th century. Among the most beautiful of these is the 'Gigot' next to the Tour Ferrande and the cormorant by the covered market.

A few kilometres further up the Nesque River, perched on a rocky spur and bordered to the east by a dense forest, stands **Venasque ❺**, the very first capital of the Comtat-Venaissin and one of the prettiest villages in the region. From its strategic position, it offers commanding views of the Carpentras plain. At one end are the impressive remains of medieval **ramparts**. The other historic highlight is **the baptistery** (daily, but times vary; charge) within the Eglise de Notre-Dame. Founded in the 6th century and remodelled during the 11th, it is one of France's oldest religious buildings.

Poppies frame a view of Venasque.

BELOW: the Théâtre Antique, Orange.

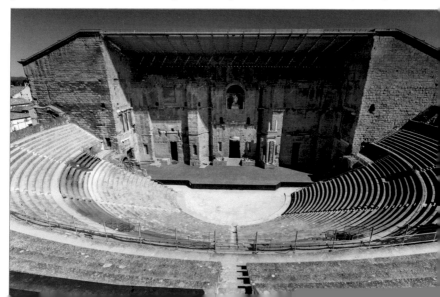

Thirteen scenic colour-coded wine routes cross the Côtes du Rhône wine region: the Azur route takes in vineyards and co-operatives around Avignon and Châteauneuf-du-Pape, the Indigo route meanders between Orange and Vaison-la-Romaine, and the Turquoise route covers Beaumes-de-Venise and the Dentelles de Montmirail (www. vins-rhone.com).

BELOW: the Dentelles de Montmirail.

Wine villages

North of Carpentras, the D7 links a string of picturesque wine-producing villages. Take a short detour along the D90 to **Beaumes-de-Venise ❻**, famed for its sweet white dessert wine made from the tiny Muscat grape, before heading to the hamlet of **Vacqueyras ❼**, home of the troubadour Raimbaut de Vaqueiras, who died while on Crusade.

The beautiful medieval village of **Gigondas ❽** has fragments of ramparts and modern sculpture dotted around the streets. The best wines here fetch high prices, but there are several lesser-known *caves de dégustation* where you can pick up a bottle or two without breaking the bank.

Continuing along the D7 will take you towards the prototypically Provençal village of **Sablet ❾**, which in turn leads into **Séguret ❿**. The latter is a charming village, with steep paved streets, an old gateway, a fountain, lavoir, belltower, Romanesque chapel and, high above the village, some castle ruins.

The sharp limestone peaks that frame the area are known as the **Dentelles de Montmirail**. The jagged forms that pierce the clear blue sky present an irresistible challenge to climbers. More accessible pathways through the hills make this an excellent area for gentle rambles through the surrounding pine and oak woods.

Vaison-la-Romaine

The Vaucluse's second great Roman town, **Vaison-la-Romaine ⓫**, grew up on the east bank of the Ouvèze River, 28km (17 miles) northeast of Orange. Vaison divides into two distinct parts: the animated modern town, which developed around the Roman remains, and the medieval Haute Ville (upper town) on the other side of the river. With the fall of the Roman Empire, the villagers no longer found it safe to live on the exposed riverbank and retreated to the more easily defensible hill.

Two archaeological sites have been excavated and although the ruins are less spectacular and less well known than those at Orange, Arles or Nîmes, the extensive traces of villas, shops and baths give a particularly good impression of everyday life under

Roman rule. The upper site, known as the **Quartier Puymin** (daily, summer 9.30am–6.30pm; winter 10am–noon, 2–5pm; charge), is a pleasant park dotted with cypress trees and the excavations of several Roman buildings, most notably the House of Laureled Apollo, where a marble head of Apollo was unearthed, the House of the Messii, a patrician villa, a colonnade known as Pompey's Portico and a nymphaeum. Reproductions of statues housed in the adjacent museum decorate the park's promenade.

The **Musée Théo Desplans** has a helpful map of the province of Gallia Narbonensis and a varied collection of mosaics, jewellery, weapons, coins and ceramics. The imposing statue of Tiberius and two larger-than-life marbles of the Emperor Hadrian and Empress Sabina speak volumes about the power and arrogance of Rome.

Built into the hillside at the top of the Puymin site, the 1st-century **Théâtre Antique** could seat 6,000 spectators and is now the main venue for the town's summer arts festival, Vaison Danses.

Southwest of the Puymin site, and separated from it by a road, the **Quartier Villasse** (daily, summer 10am–noon, 2.30–6.30pm, winter until 5pm, closed Jan; charge) contains the extensive ruins of two Roman villas, a bathing complex and the rue des Boutiques, a paved Roman street lined with shops that leads to the arch of a former basilica.

Near the exit of the Villasse site, the **Cathédrale Notre-Dame-de-Nazareth** has a fine 12th-century cloister (daily, summer 9.30am–6pm, winter until 5pm, closed Jan; charge), featuring pillars with beautifully decorated capitals.

Cross the **Pont Romain** (Roman Bridge), heavily restored following severe flood damage in 1992, to reach the picturesque Cité Médiévale or **Haute Ville** (upper town). From the fortified gate, a cobbled street climbs to a dilapidated church and ruined chateau that was once the country seat of the counts of Toulouse. Looking east from the top of the upper town will give you one of the best views over the valleys and foothills that lead to Mont Ventoux.

Each autumn the villages around Vaison-la-Romaine (www.vaison-ventoux-tourisme.com) get all souped up for the Festival des Soupes. This is when the Confrérie des Louchiers (brotherhood of ladlers) elects the best soup from a panoply of veloutés, potages *and* bouillons. *Tastings and recipes for all.*

Below: Quartier Puymin, Vaison-la-Romaine.

Hill villages

One of the simplest and best pleasures of touring Provence is persevering along a tortuously winding road, for the reward of seeing a tranquil village perched at the crest of a hill. **Crestet** ⓬, set above olive groves south of Vaison-la-Romaine, is one of many such villages tucked away in the Dentelles de Montmirail. A climb up the cobbled alleyways brings you to a 12th-century church and, after a further ascent, to the castle. The former residence of the bishops of Vaison-la-Romaine is now privately owned, but there are some stunning views across the valleys and to the peak of Mont Ventoux.

Further south the D938 will take you to the small town of **Malaucène** ⓭, a good base for hiking and biking in the nearby Mont Ventoux. The lively main street bustles with cafés and restaurants.

Heading west from here towards Mont Ventoux will take you along the very route that Petrarch followed in 1336 when he undertook to climb the mountain. First, however, you might want to make a scenic detour by the D938 and D13 south to **Caromb** ⓮, another medieval hilltop village. Long famed for its vines, its well-preserved exterior walls enclose another typical feature of the area: a church topped with a wrought-iron cage, designed to protect the bell from the fierce mistral. The interior is decorated with frescos and woodcarvings.

The base of Mont Ventoux is surrounded by many other attractive villages. Fortified **Le Barroux** ⓯, with its chateau and fine Romanesque church, **Mazan** ⓰, where the former chateau of the de Sade family is now a comfortable hotel, **Crillon-le-Brave**, **St-Pierre-de-Vassols** and **Bédoin** ⓱, a popular starting point for hikes up Mont Ventoux, all have their individual charm.

Mont Ventoux

Rejoin the D974 at Malaucène for the best route to **Mont Ventoux** ⓲, the 'Giant of Provence' that dominates the landscape. The road passes through lavender fields and meadows dotted with cedars of Lebanon. You can take a refreshment stop at

BELOW: Bédoin.

the waterfall and café beyond the **Chapelle Notre-Dame du Groseau**, before beginning the climb to the Observatory. It's possible to drive all the way to the top except when the road is blocked by snow. The temperature drops dramatically as you climb and there are often strong winds – hence the mountain's name, meaning 'windy mountain'.

Mont Ventoux is frequently included as one of the stages in the Tour de France cycle race, and it was on these steep slopes that the English rider Tommy Simpson suffered a fatal heart attack in 1967. Countless amateurs attempt to follow in the tracks of the professionals. Words of encouragement are painted in white on the road surface.

If you've time and energy it's perfectly possible to walk to the summit (detailed information on the best routes can be obtained from the tourist office in Bédoin).

Below the ski resort of Mont Serein, the lower slopes of the mountain are ferny and forested. As you approach the wind-blown summit (the peak is snowcapped for at least two-thirds of the year), the greenery gives way to harsh white limestone, where nothing grows. When the sun reflects off the bald white top, the glare is blinding. From this elevated point, at 1,909 metres (6,263ft), it is easy to appreciate why the Vaucluse has always been such an important crossroads. On a clear day – although mist and haze are more typical – you can see the Rhône, the Alps and the Mediterranean. Some people even claim to have caught sight of the Pyrenees from this spot.

Once below the tree line, the drive downhill on the D164 in the direction of Sault takes you through a nature reserve of particular interest to botanists. The Mont Ventoux has been designated a "Réserve de Biosphère" by Unesco for the rarity and diversity of its flora, ranging from Mediterranean to hardy Alpine species as the altitude mounts; panels at various stopping points indicate some of the flora and fauna found here. Pine trees give way to oak, followed by fields of aromatic wild thyme and, in the lower valleys, rolling fields of lavender.

TIP

For an unforgettable experience, take a guided night-time hike up Mont Ventoux in July or August to arrive in time for sunrise. Contact the tourist offices in Malaucène (tel: 04 90 65 22 59) or Bédoin (tel: 04 90 65 63 95) for details.

BELOW: ascending Mont Ventoux the hard way.

The Association des Routes de Lavande (www.routes-lavande. com) proposes six itineraries through the main lavender-producing areas of southeast France, with information on lavender distilleries to visit, restaurants, places to stay and traditional lavender fairs and parades.

BELOW: cycling towards the summit of Mont Ventoux.

Sault and the Gorges de la Nesque

Sault **19**, on the flanks of Mont Ventoux, is the capital of the largest area of true lavender (*lavande vraie*) production in Europe (at its colourful best in June and July). It is also at the heart of the revival of *épeautre*, a sort of hardy, primitive wild wheat that has been rediscovered by many of Provence's leading chefs and is brewed here in a *bière blanche* (white beer). The only remnants of the town's former glory as a baronial seat are the towers of a 16th-century castle. The Romanesque Eglise de St-Sauveur (also known as Notre Dame de la Tour) stands guard over the town, which acts as a marketplace for the surrounding lavender distilleries.

South of Sault between Mont Ventoux and the Plateau de Vaucluse, the drive along the D942 (towards Carpentras) to the lively hillside village of **Monieux** **20** is lush, green and lined with fields of lavender.

Monieux marks the start of the **Gorges de la Nesque** **21**, which offer breathtaking views and a sensational display of colours, with plenty of opportunities for climbing and hiking. The river itself is often dry, but the scrub-covered limestone gorges – also part of the Mont Ventoux biosphere – are impressive, a breeding ground for eagles, falcons and rare salamanders, plunging in some spots to depths of over 300 metres (1,000ft). A couple of kilometres along, the **Castelleras** belvedere looks across to the **Rocher du Cire**, a steep, wax-covered rock climbed by Frédéric Mistral in 1866 to collect honey. The belvedere is the starting point for one of several footpaths down to the medieval chapel of St-Michel de Anesca at the foot of the gorges.

The Nesque Gorges are sprinkled with attractive villages, surrounded by vineyards, olive groves and cherry trees. **Villes-sur-Auzon** **22** has had its fair share of disasters in the form of invaders, sieges and plagues; it now lives off the vineyards that surround the town. Stop at one of the town's *caves de dégustation* to sample the local Côtes du Ventoux, best drunk when young. To the south, **Méthamis** is dominated by its surprisingly large Romanesque church. ❑

RESTAURANTS AND BARS

Restaurants

Prices for a three-course meal without wine. Many restaurants have a less expensive lunch menu:

€ = under €25
€€ = €25–40
€€€ = €40–60
€€€€ = over €60

Orange

La Rom'Antique
5 place Silvain
www.la-romantique.com
Tel: 04 90 51 67 06. Open L Tue–Fri and Sun, D Tue–Sun. Closed Sun eve Oct–May. **€€**
Chef Cédric Bremond worked at the best addresses in Avignon before opening his own place near the Théâtre Antique. Decent selection of local wines.

La Table du Verger
Chemin des Aigras, off N7
www.masdesaigras.com
Tel: 04 90 34 81 01. Open L & D, days and times vary.
€€–€€€€
Located 4km (2 miles) north of the town centre, this hotel-restaurant has an attractive countryside setting. The chef only uses seasonal, (mainly) organic and local ingredients. Specialities include sea bass with flax seeds and rose macaroons. As well as good-value set menus, there are vegetarian options.

Carpentras

Chez Serge
90 rue Cottier
www.chez-serge.com
Tel: 04 90 63 21 24. Open L & D daily **€€**
Serge Ghoukassian is a local personality and his restaurant near the cathedral is a fashionable venue for both the cooking and wines, the latter coming mainly from the Rhône. Local truffles are a speciality, with the prized *tuber melanosporum* in winter and the nutty-flavoured *tuber aestivum* in summer appearing in dishes such as asparagus soup with summer truffles, and foie gras and duck tart.

Le Saule Pleureur
145 chemin de Beauregard, Monteux
www.le-saule-pleureur.com
Tel: 04 90 62 01 35. Open L & D Wed–Sun. **€€€**
Provençal native Laurent Azoulay has worked for many of the top chefs in France and shows off his talent with dishes like a *barigoule* of langoustines, sea bream with artichokes and anchovies, rabbit prepared in four different ways, or a dessert combining raspberries and red peppers. A good-value weekday lunch menu introduces you to his style.

Séguret

Le Mesclun
rue des Poternes
www.lemesclun.com
Tel: 04 90 46 93 43. Closed Sun eve, Tue eve and Wed except July and Aug.
€€–€€€€
Sit on the shady terrace with a view over the vineyards or in one of the dining rooms of this attractive 16th-century house. Young chef Christophe Bonzi's artistic creations draw on both Mediterranean and local traditions. Irresistible desserts.

Vaison-la-Romaine

Le Brin d'Olivier
4 rue du Ventoux
www.restaurant-lebrindolivier.com
Tel: 04 90 28 74 79. Open L Sun, Tue, Thu, Fri, D Thu–Tue. **€€–€€€**
Friendly restaurant serving traditional Provençal food in the vaulted dining room or outside on the shady terrace.

Le Moulin à Huile
quai Maréchal Foch, route de Malaucène
www.moulin-huile.com
Tel: 04 90 36 20 67. Open L Tue–Sun & D Tue–Sat.
€€€€
Gourmet restaurant set in an old watermill on the banks of the Ouvèze river. Traditional products such as lamb and lobster are given an international twist with the likes of banana chips or soya *jus*. The wine list is excellent.

THE LUBERON AND PLATEAU DE VAUCLUSE

With its sensuous landscape of wooded limestone hills, rolling vineyards and orchards, peppered with picturesque hill villages, historic châteaux and country farmhouses, the Luberon has become one of the most fashionable areas of the Vaucluse

The Luberon is the quintessential rural Provence of most people's imaginings. An area protected as a regional nature park since the 1970s, an authenticity mixes with the good life and a certain cosmopolitan chic. It's hardly surprising that this area is a favourite with France's champagne socialists, American actors and international tourists in search of the idyllic corner of France evoked by the English expat Peter Mayle's best-selling book, *A Year in Provence*. But the area's wealthy second-homers remain a more discreet breed than those on the show-off Riviera. A dedicated local population ensures that it remains a lived-in area, with an economy based on agriculture – notably fruit-growing and respectable wines – as well as tourism.

This area of the Vaucluse has gone through several waves of fortune. It was decimated by the Black Death and ravaged by the Wars of Religion, but later prospered as a centre for silkworm farming and the paper, glass, ochre and faience industries. Severely depopulated after World War I, it was rediscovered by writers and artists (among them Camus, De Staël and Vasarely), who helped restore and repopulate its historic villages.

Orientation

The regional park stretches between Cavaillon in the west and Manosque in the east, taking in villages such as Gordes and Roussillon on the Plateau de Vaucluse, as well as the main mountain ridge.

Two main roads run either side of the Montagne du Luberon: the D900 to the north and the D973 along the Durance valley to the south. The D943 runs from Cadenet and Lourmarin along the Aigue Brun River through the Combe de Lourmarin

Main attractions

CATHEDRAL AND SYNAGOGUE, CAVAILLON
PERCHED VILLAGES OF MÉNERBES AND BONNIEUX
SATURDAY MARKET AT APT
ANTIQUES MARKETS, L'ISLE-SUR-LA-SORGUE
LA SOURCE, FONTAINE-DE-VAUCLUSE
VILLAGE DES BORIES, GORDES
COLORADO DE RUSTREL

LEFT: hillside Lacoste. **RIGHT:** shady viewpoint at Bonnieux, a typical Provençal hill village.

Created in 1171, the Canal St-Julien, which runs alongside the River Durance, is the oldest irrigation canal in Provence and centre of a complex network of channels and sluices that ensure the water table is high even in summer. Originally the canal was used both for irrigation and as a source of energy for watermills. Cavaillon tourist office (tel: 04 90 71 32 01; www.cavaillon-luberon.com) organises guided visits around the canal, a 15th-century aqueduct and a pumping station.

gorge. It is the only road that crosses the massif, dividing it into the Petit Luberon to the west and the Grand Luberon to the east, and forks to Apt (D943) and Bonnieux (D194).

The Luberon offers plenty of opportunities for walking, cycling, riding and rock-climbing, and is crossed by numerous footpaths, including stretches of the GR4, GR6 and GR9 long-distance footpaths.

Cavaillon

Cavaillon ❶, the main town on the western edge of the Luberon, is known as the melon capital of France. Melon-growing here dates back to the days of the Avignon papacy, when cantaloupe melons were introduced from Italy and flourished thanks to irrigation from the medieval Canal St-Julien *(see left)*.

Although the modern town sits on the heat-baked plain, its history began on the hill up above – the **Colline St-Jacques**. A footpath ascends the hill from behind a Roman triumphal arch on place du Clos (Cavaillon was an important Roman settlement), past traces of ramparts to the hilltop, where there is an ancient hermit's chapel and a fine view over the plain.

On Monday morning a lively **market** fills the town centre, but the more serious business goes on at the edge of town, where the daily wholesale fruit-and-vegetable market (not open to the public except on guided tours by the tourist office) is one of the most important in France.

The melon is not the only thing that is legendary in this town. Popular mythology suggests the area around Cavaillon was once flattened by a monster called the 'Coulobie'. Basically an oversized lizard, he was chased away by St Véran, a hermit from nearby Fontaine-de-Vaucluse and later bishop of Cavaillon. The Coulobie is the subject of a painting that hangs in the 13th-century **Cathédrale Notre-Dame-et-St-Véran**

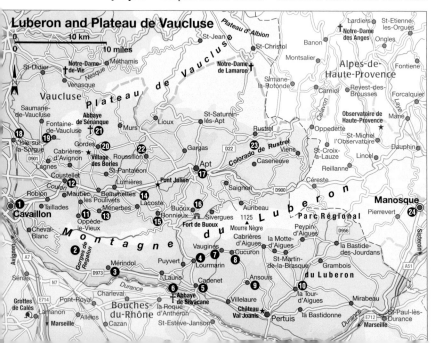

Luberon and Plateau de Vaucluse

on place Joseph d'Arrard, worth visiting for its altarpieces and the lovely Romanesque cloister. Go round the side of the cathedral to see its unusual octagonal tower and carved sundial, and the fine old houses on shady **square Philippe de Cabassole**. From here a covered passage leads to the elegant 18th-century **Hôtel de Ville** (town hall).

The **Musée Archéologique de l'Hôtel-Dieu** (Porte d'Avignon; Mon, Wed–Sat 2–6pm; charge), a collection of local archaeological finds, is housed in the chapel of the former hospital.

As part of the papal Comtat Venaissin, Cavaillon, like Carpentras, 'tolerated' a significant Jewish community when Jews were being expelled from the rest of France *(see box on page 80)*. The present **synagogue** was built in 1772, a time of prosperity and increasing freedom for the Jews. It has a splendid interior in pastel pink and blue with fine Rococo carving and a beautiful wrought-iron gallery. Below the prayer room, the former bakery houses the small **Musée Juif-Comtadin** (rue Hebraïque; Wed–Mon 10am–noon, 2–6pm; guided tours every hour from 10.30am; charge), containing Jewish prayer books, tombstones and Torahs, as well as the original bread oven. Outside, an archway across the street marks the former gate into the ghetto, which was locked at night.

Gorges de Regalon and the Mérindol memorial

About 13km (8 miles) east of Cavaillon on the D973, a lane leads to the **Gorges de Regalon ❷**. The high walls of the limestone gorge make this a refreshing walk in summer. Note that it is closed after heavy rain.

Modern **Mérindol ❸** has little of interest, but the town remains the symbol of the horror of the religious massacres of 1545 *(see box on page 92)*. A memorial footpath climbs amid olive trees, rosemary and evergreen oak through the still partly ruined old village to the top of the hill, where a simple memorial plaque on the battered castle ruins remains extraordinarily evocative. From here there is good access to several footpaths over the Petit Luberon, and an orientation

TIP

In summer, classical music festivals abound in the Luberon, often providing an opportunity to see inside its churches and chateaux.

BELOW LEFT: Cavaillon melons. **BELOW:** inside the synagogue.

Busy markets are held on different mornings around the Luberon: Monday in Cadenet and Cavaillon, Tuesday in Cucuron, Gordes, Lacoste and La Tour d'Aigues, Thursday in Roussillon, Friday in Bonnieux, Lourmarin and Pertuis, Saturday in Apt and Manosque. Expect printed Provençal fabrics and pottery, fruit and veg, goats' cheeses, dried sausages, olives and tapenade.

BELOW RIGHT: Château de Lourmarin.

table points out the views stretching to the Alpilles, the Montagne Ste-Victoire and the Sainte-Baume.

Lourmarin

Chic but not showy, **Lourmarin ❹** is a pleasant place to stop off, with a choice of good restaurants, lively cafés and an unusual semi-buried pathway ringing the village centre. Existentialist author Albert Camus (1913–60) bought a house here in 1958 and is buried in the cemetery outside the village.

At the opposite edge of the village, the **Château de Lourmarin** (www.chateau-de-lourmarin.com; daily, summer 10–11.30am, 2.30–5.30pm, July–Aug 10am–6pm; winter 10–11.30am, 2.30–4pm, Jan Sat and Sun afternoons only; charge) bridges the period between medieval fortification in the 15th-century 'old' wing and the new, more comfortable lifestyle of the 16th-century Renaissance wing – seen in the large mullioned windows, Italianate loggia and cantilevered staircase. Note the unusual fireplace with carved Corinthian columns below and column figures

of Native American Indians above, inspired by the recent discovery of the Americas.

The chateau was rescued from dilapidation in the 1920s and turned into an arts foundation with residences for writers and musicians in summer, when it is also used for classical concerts.

Nearby **Cadenet ❺** is a more workaday village, with a good market on Mondays. It was once a centre of *vannerie* (basket-making), using willows from the nearby river bank.

South from Cadenet, across the Durance River, is the austerely elegant **Abbaye de Silvacane ❻** (June–Sept daily 10am–6pm, Oct–May closed Mon; charge). Completed in 1144, it is considered the finest of three Cistercian abbeys in Provence (the others are Sénanque and Le Thoronet), although the least visited, and is one of the venues for the prestigious Roque d'Antheron international piano festival.

East of Lourmarin, a web of lanes runs through vineyards and olive groves under the eastern flank of the Montagne du Luberon. At tiny

The Massacre of Mérindol

The Vaudois or Waldensian sect was founded in Lyon in 1180 by Pierre Valdes, who preached the virtues of poverty. The Vaudois took refuge in the Alps of Savoie and northern Italy, then spread to the Luberon, encouraged by local landlords looking to repopulate the area after the Black Death. Then came the Reformation and its subsequent condemnation by the Catholic Church. Being associated with Protestantism, the Vaudois suffered a brutal repression that was particularly violent in the Luberon. The Wars of Religion split the region in two: some villages, such as Mérindol, Lourmarin and La Motte d'Aigues, had large Vaudois populations; others, such as Cucuron, Bonnieux and Oppède, remained staunchly Catholic. On 16 April 1545, Jean de Meynier, Baron of Oppède, sent in his troops to implement the Decree of Mérindol, which condemned the Vaudois as heretics. Within six days 22 villages were pillaged and burnt and an estimated 2,500 people were killed. Mérindol was razed to the ground. The route des Vaudois climbs up through the still partly ruined village to the top of the hill, where the bleak ruins of the citadel, now bearing a memorial plaque, are a potent reminder of the bloodshed.

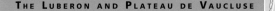

Vaugines ⓺ many of the houses are built into the rock. Several footpaths lead up from here to Mourre Nègre, the Luberon's highest point at 1,125 metres (3,690ft).

There's much more to explore at **Cucuron ⓼**. At the foot of the pretty village you'll find the **Moulin à Huile Dauphin** (tel: 04 90 77 26 17), whose AOC olive oil is used by many of the area's top chefs, and the Etang, a rectangular pool of water around which the weekly market is held on Tuesday mornings. Above, still contained within fragments of ramparts and fortified gateways, the old village is scattered with fine doorways, fountains and traces of medieval and Renaissance windows, and even remnants of a Roman kiln in one of the shops. The large Eglise Notre-Dame de Beaulieu, a bastion of Catholicism when much of the area was Protestant, has a fine Baroque altarpiece.

Further east beneath the ridge, small, sleepy villages like **Cabrières d'Aigues** and **La Motte d'Aigues**, with tall houses, painted shutters and narrow alleyways, seem to be have

been bypassed by the fashionable revival of much of the Luberon.

Ansouis and the Tour d'Aigues

The D56 south of Cucuron heads to the village of **Ansouis ⓽**, which spirals up around a small hill to the impressive **Château d'Ansouis**. It has an elegant 16th-century classical façade overlooking terraced gardens with topiaried hedges. The interior likewise reflects different periods, including the panelled dining room, the chapel and the big old-fashioned kitchens. After belonging to the Sabran-Pontevès family for 800 years, the château changed hands in 2008 and is gradually being refurnished (tel: 04 90 77 23 36; guided tours Apr–Oct Thu–Mon 3pm and 4.30pm; charge).

In one old village house, the **Musée Extraordinaire de Georges Mazoyer** (rue du Vieux Moulin; daily 2–7pm, winter until 6pm; charge) is a somewhat eccentric one-man show created by a painter with a passion for marine life and now run by his widow. It includes a recreated underwater cave in the cellars.

The Luberon à Velo is a 235km (146-mile) cycle route taking in many of the area's prettiest villages. It runs between Cavaillon and Forcalquier, via Oppède-le-Vieux, Lacoste and Apt on the north side of the Montagne du Luberon, and Manosque, Lourmarin and Lauris by the southern route. See www.veloloisirluberon.com for details

BELOW: the chapel, Château d'Ansouis.

TIP

The award-winning jams produced by Confiturerie La Roumanière in Robion are made out of every conceivable fruit. The factory is a rehabilitation project employing disabled adults, who also run the shop and offer guided tours. Find them at place de l'Eglise, Robion; www. laroumaniere.com.

The third of the great chateaux of the southern Luberon at **La Tour d'Aigues** ❿ (daily, July–Sept 10am–1pm, 3–6pm, Oct–June 10am–12.30pm, 2–5pm, Sun–Mon afternoons only year round; charge) is only a shadow of its former self. The pedimented entrance with its crisply carved friezes and the remains of the central pavilion and two towers only hint at what must have once been the finest Renaissance château in the Luberon if not all Provence, until it was pillaged by the revolutionary mob in 1792. There are regular events, concerts and exhibitions and a pottery museum.

Towards Pertuis, the **Château Val Joanis** (tel: 04 90 79 20 77; www.val-joanis.com; gardens open July–Aug daily 10am–7pm; rest of year times vary; charge) is known both for its wines and its imaginative modern formal gardens.

From La Tour d'Aigues, the D956 continues northeast across the eastern flank of the Luberon towards Manosque and Forcalquier, through unspoilt villages such as **Grambois** and the **Bastide-des-Jourdans**.

The northern villages

A string of old villages runs along the northern side of the Petit Luberon. At the western end, the quiet villages of **Taillades** and **Robion** were once important for stone-quarrying. Taillades' castle and houses are strangely perched on rectangular blocks of rock; an imposing 18th-century watermill stands at the foot of the village.

Further east, **Oppède-le-Vieux** ⓫ is a symbol of the Luberon revival. Largely deserted in the 19th century when the population moved to a new village on the plain, Oppède has since been resettled, often by writers, craftsmen and artists, who have restored some of its ancient houses and the village church. A footpath climbs up a cobbled street to the **Collégiale Notre-Dame d'Alidon** (July–Aug daily 10am–7pm, Easter–June, Sept–Oct Sat–Sun 10am–7pm, closed Nov–Easter), a fine Romanesque church where gargoyles leer from a hexagonal belltower. Above it is the ruined château of mercenary Baron Meynier d'Oppède, who ordered the massacres of the Vaudois in 1545 *(see box on page 92)*.

Starting from the car park below the village, a footpath has been created through the vineyards, with panels explaining the soils and different grape varieties cultivated here.

Back down on the plain, **Coustellet** ⓬ is known for its farmers' market held in the main square beside the D900 on Sunday mornings (Easter–Dec) and Wednesday evenings (May–Sept). The **Musée de la Lavande** (route de Gordes; tel: 04 90 76 91 23; www.museedelalavande.com; daily, May–Sept 9am–7pm, Oct–Apr 9am–12.15pm, 2–6pm, closed Jan; charge) nearby has a collection of lavender stills, archive photos and a film explaining the distillation processes. Nearby, Beaumettes is a curiosity for its troglodyte homes carved into the rock.

BELOW: lavender field near Coustellet.

Ménerbes

Today the village of **Ménerbes** ⑬ is particularly associated with Peter Mayle as the central focus of his best-seller *A Year in Provence*, but it was long renowned for its impregnable fortress. During the Wars of Religion, Protestants captured the stronghold in a surprise attack in 1573, holding out until 1578 when it fell back into Catholic hands after an 18-month-long siege.

Walk along the main street following signs for the Mairie, past the fine 18th-century house that belonged to Picasso muse and companion Dora Maar from 1944 to 1997, and is now used for residencies by American writers and artists. At the top of the hill is a small square where you'll find the elegant town hall, the church and clocktower with wrought-iron campanile and the 17th-century Hôtel d'Astier de Montfaucon, recently restored as the **Maison de la Truffe et du Vin** (tel: 04 90 72 38 37; daily, Apr–Oct 10am–12.30pm, 2.30–6.30pm, Nov–Mar times vary). Here you can join a truffle and wine-tasting workshop or visit the Oenothèque, which has an excellent selection of the three wine appellations found in the Luberon (Côtes du Luberon, Côtes du Ventoux and Coteaux de Pierrevert) arranged by village. The truffle museum is fairly limited, with a collection of old prints, photos and documents about truffles and truffle hunting, but the house itself has vaulted ceilings and an impressive grand staircase, and is also used for painting exhibitions. There's a café on the terrace, serving truffle-rich snacks and salads.

Just outside the village, the **Domaine de la Citadelle**, which produces some of the Luberon's best wines, is home to the surprisingly interesting **Musée du Tire-Bouchon** (tel: 04 90 72 41 58; Apr–Oct daily 10am–noon, 2–7pm, Nov–Mar Mon–Sat 9am–noon, 2–5pm; charge), a vast collection of corkscrews ranging from historic items to novelty pieces.

Lacoste and Bonnieux

Lacoste ⑭ sits beneath the imposing ruins of the castle that once belonged

The cross in front of Ménerbes' church.

Below: tranquil street scene in Ménerbes.

Apt is known for two distinctive styles of faience: the historic creamy yellow monochrome wares, and the more modern Aptware, characterised by the swirling multicoloured patterns that result from mixing white, red, ochre and green clays. If you're interested in buying some faience visit Atelier Savalli, 20 rue Eugène Brunel.

to the notorious Marquis de Sade, who lived here from 1771 until his arrest in 1778 for sodomy and other nefarious deeds. The castle now belongs to veteran fashion designer Pierre Cardin, who has established a summer opera festival here.

The village itself is an intimate place, with a ruined gateway leading to some tastefully restored houses and an overgrown tangle of old arches and stairways. Despite the increased glamour quotient some semblance of ordinary village life continues, where the inevitably named Café de Sade is still the sort of place where you can stop by for a *plat du jour* and eavesdrop on local gossip.

Zigzagging up a hillside further east, **Bonnieux** ⑮ is an archetypal Provençal hill village. It was once a property of the Knights Templar and later part of the papal enclave and home to a powerful clergy. Several elegant carved doorways and two churches hint at a village that was rather grander than it is today. The village was well known for its bread, and you can find out about its history at the **Musée de la Boulangerie**

(12 rue de la République; Apr–Oct Wed–Mon 10am–12.30pm, 2–6pm; charge), housed in a former bakery.

From Bonnieux you can head south towards the Combe de Lourmarin, or north towards the D900 via **Pont Julien**, a well-preserved Roman bridge from the 1st century BC, or northeast towards Apt.

One detour worth making is to **Buoux** ⑯. Its crags are popular with rock-climbers, and at the valley entrance are the scattered ruins of the **Fort de Buoux**, a Protestant stronghold until dismantled under the orders of Cardinal Richelieu. The main attraction, however, is the quiet valley of L'Aigrebrun, where there is a simple hotel with friendly buvette bar. This is a good starting point for several walks up towards the Mourre-Nègre or across to the isolated hamlet of **Sivergues**.

Apt

Apt ⑰, the Roman city of Apta Julia and an ancient bishopric, is the main town of the northern Luberon, and headquarters of the regional park. Apt comes to life on Saturday morn-

BELOW: bird's-eye view of Bonnieux.

ings, when its food market, one of the best in Provence, fills the old town from place de la Bouquerie up to the **Ancienne Cathédrale Ste-Anne** (Mon–Fri 9am–noon, 2.30–6pm, Sun 2.30–6pm). For centuries, this curious Baroque and Gothic structure was a place of pilgrimage due to the relics of St Anne, mother of the Virgin Mary, supposedly buried in the crypt. There are, in fact, two crypts, one dating from the 4th century where you can see the niches left by ancient tombs, and a later 11th-century one with medieval tombs. In 1660 the Baroque Royal Chapel was added when Anne of Austria, wife of Louis XIII, came here to give thanks for the birth of her son Louis XIV.

Apt's past prosperity came from the three industries of faience, ochre production and crystallised fruit (*fruits confits*). Its history is traced in the interesting **Musée de l'Aventure Industrielle** (June–Sept Mon–Sat 10am–noon, 2–6.30pm, Oct–May Tue–Sat 10am–noon, 2–5.30pm; charge), housed in a converted crystallised fruit factory just behind the cathedral. Nearby, an 18th-century

hôtel particulier contains the **Maison du Parc** (place Jean Jaurès; Mon–Fri 8.30am–noon, 1.30–6pm; free) which focuses on the Luberon's fauna, flora and geology.

Four km (2.5 miles) southwest of Apt, **Saignon** sits on a magnificent escarpment, with a cluster of fine houses under some impressive crags, a Romanesque church and a rocky belvedere with the ruins of a castle that blend into the rock.

L'Isle-sur-la-Sorgue

Watery **L'Isle-sur-la-Sorgue** ⓲, 12km (7 miles) north of Cavaillon, was once a marshy island in the middle of the Sorgue River. The old town was built on piles in the 12th century, and the river's numerous branches were channelled to surround it in a double – in places triple – ring of canals. Countless waterwheels remain from the mills that supplied silks, wools and paper to the Avignon court.

Today L'Isle-sur-la-Sorgue is famous for the biggest antiques and flea market (Sat–Mon 10am–6pm) outside Paris (*see box on page 98*), but

The Sorgue River is a popular spot for kayaking.

BELOW: watery L'Isle-sur-la-Sorgue.

TIP

The D25 between L'Isle-sur-la-Sorgue and Fontaine-de-Vaucluse gets extremely busy in summer. There's much less traffic if you arrive at Fontaine-de-Vaucluse by the D100a from the east via Lagnes or Cabrières-d'Avignon.

the old centre, sprinkled with Renaissance doorways and old town houses, is worth exploring. On a square in the centre stands the church of **Notre-Dame des Anges**. Its stern Romanesque exterior is in marked contrast to the exuberant Baroque interior, awash with cheerful angels.

Fontaine-de-Vaucluse

Seven km (4 miles) up the Sorgue River, **Fontaine-de-Vaucluse** ⑲ is named after the mysterious spring that surges out of the bedrock into an incredibly deep pool a few minutes' walk from the village in the Vallis Clausa (closed valley) that has given its name to the Vaucluse *département*. Despite diving trips and exploratory robots, no one has yet discovered the base of the pool, which is fed by rainwater that drains through the Vaucluse Plateau. In winter and spring the flow rate can be so great that water does indeed bubble out like a fountain.

Although full of souvenir shops and tourist restaurants, the village is worth visiting for its spectacular situation, beneath the ruins of a castle surrounded by rocky cliffs, and its

BELOW RIGHT: antiques for sale in Isle-sur-la-Sorgue.

spring, a pleasant 10-minute walk from the centre. Along the footpath, the **Monde Souterrain de Norbert Casteret** (daily, Feb–Nov 10am–12.30pm, 2–7pm, winter until 6pm; charge), dedicated to a famous potholer, has displays of potholing and cave systems, and attempts to explain the Fontaine-de-Vaucluse phenomenon. Further along, curiously situated at the end of a shopping mall, you can watch fine handmade rag paper still being made at the village's last waterpowered paper factory, **Vallis Clausa Moulin à Papier** (daily, July–Aug 9am–7.30pm, May, June, Sept 10am–12.30pm, 2–7pm, times vary rest of the year; free). On the other side of the footpath, the **Musée d'Histoire Jean Garcin 1939–1945 l'Appel de la Liberté** (tel: 04 90 20 24 00; June–Sept Wed–Mon 10am–6pm, days and times vary rest of year; charge) traces life in the Vaucluse during World War II and the maquisards of the Resistance movement.

Near the village entrance, the Romanesque **Eglise de St-Véran** is dedicated to the 6th-century bishop of Cavaillon, who is said to have

The Antiques Trail

Ever since a *brocante* was first held in L'Isle-sur-la-Sorgue in 1966, antiques dealers, bric-a-brac-ers and cosmopolitan collectors have been arriving to give the town the largest concentration of antiques dealers in France outside Paris. There are four main arcades open Monday to Saturday. Le Quai de la Gare (4 avenue Julien Guigue), by the station, and Hôtel Dongier (9 place Gambetta), an 18th-century coaching inn, are rather upmarket. Many items reflect the south – carved Beaucaire mirrors, faience from Apt and Moustiers, marriage wardrobes and elaborate openwork bread cupboards. The Village des Antiquaires de la Gare (2bis avenue de l'Egalité), in a ramshackle old carpet factory, and the Isle-aux-Brocantes (7 avenue des Quatre Otages), reached across its own canal, are more bohemian in mood. The goods tend more towards 20th-century items and collectables, such as Art Deco furniture, vintage toys, garden furniture and old bar and hotel fittings. Every Sunday, the permanent shops and arcades are joined by a flea market that sprawls along avenue des Quatre Otages. For the big Easter and 15 August fairs, stalls take over the local park and meadows as well.

freed the area of the Coloubie monster *(see page 90)*, and who is buried in the crypt. It has an unusual 11th-century open altar table made from an antique tombstone.

Fontaine-de-Vaucluse is also associated with Italian poet and scholar Petrarch, who lived here from 1337 to 1353, where he composed his famous sonnets to the love of his life, Laura. He is commemorated by the tall column near the bridge on place de la Colonne, and in the **Musée Bibliothèque Pétrarque** (quai du Château Vieux; Apr–Oct Wed–Mon 10am–noon, 2–6pm, closed Nov–Mar; charge). A narrow road runs out of Fontaine-de-Vaucluse over a bleak mountainside to Cabrières d'Avignon. One curiosity here is the fragments of the **Mur de la Peste**, a dry stone wall built in 1721 in an attempt to keep out the plague.

Gordes and the Plateau de Vaucluse

With its pristine dry stone walls and renovated houses, smart hotels and interior-decoration shops, **Gordes ⓴** epitomises the Luberon's social rise.

During the summer, the town is one of the most popular tourist spots in the Vaucluse. It's dominated by its **Château** (tel: 04 90 72 02 75; daily 10am–noon, 2–6pm; charge), a medieval castle transformed during the Renaissance, which houses the tourist office and an exhibition of paintings by Belgian artist Pol Mara.

The majority of tourists, however, come here to see the **Village des Bories** (tel: 04 9072 0348; daily 9am–sunset; charge), a cluster of 20 restored beehive-shaped *bories* (dry stone huts) that lies below the town. The wind-resistant dwellings are believed to date from the 16th to 19th centuries, but may have replaced much earlier structures. Similar dry stone huts are found throughout the area, some used as sheep pens, others as holiday homes.

The winding D177 Vénasque road leads from Gordes across the plateau to the **Abbaye de Sénanque ㉑** (tel: 04 90 72 05 72; www.senanque.fr; Feb–Dec, guided visits in French only, but leaflet in English available, hours vary, reservation advised; charge). One of the three great

One of the drystone huts in Village des Bories.

BELOW: Abbaye de Sénanque.

Map on page 90

TIP

Visits to the l'Occitane factory to see the production of traditionally made perfumes, soaps and cosmetics using natural ingredients can be arranged through L'Occitane, ZI St-Maurice, Manosque, tel: 04 92 70 19 00, www.loccitane.com.

12th-century Cistercian abbeys of Provence (along with Thoronet and Silvacane), it is a typically austere structure, sitting in calm isolation amid lavender fields.

Ochre country

With its colourful ochre-washed houses, the hill village of **Roussillon** ㉒ is the most visible reminder of the ochre industry that once thrived here, thanks to a 50km (30-mile) seam of ochre-bearing rock that runs through the area. The only industrial-scale mine still in operation is in Gargas. Roussillon's economy is now driven by tourism, and it can get suffocatingly overrun in summer. On the edge of the village is the **Sentier des Ochres** (tel: 04 90 05 60 25; mid-Feb–Dec, times vary; charge), a waymarked trail through the reddish landscape.

Even more spectacular than Roussillon, though more difficult to find (look for signs from the D22), is the **Colorado de Rustrel** ㉓, situated south of the village of Rustrel to the northeast of Apt. From the car park, footpaths lead through a surreal landscape of orangey-red rocks sculpted into chimneys, turrets, bowls and narrow valleys, by a combination of ochre-quarrying and natural erosion.

Manosque

At the eastern edge of the Luberon, just into the *département* of Alpes-de-Haute-Provence, is the town of **Manosque** ㉔. This once sleepy town has become a thriving economic axis. Agriculture in the Durance valley (Manosque is known for its peaches) is blossoming, the proximity of the Cadarache nuclear research centre has drawn scientists to settle here, and the global success of skincare group Occitane means it is now the town's largest employer.

The central core of Manosque, ringed by the busy boulevards that replaced the ancient ramparts, has changed little from the 'tortoiseshell in the grass' described by the town's own Jean Giono *(see box below)*. Two imposing gateways – **Porte Saunerie** and **Porte Soubeyran** – stand guard at the south and north ends of the **Vieille Ville** respectively. ❏

BELOW RIGHT: the library in Jean Giono's house, Lou Parais.

Jean Giono

Writer Jean Giono (1895–1970) was a lifelong resident of Manosque. An ecologist and pacifist, he was imprisoned by the Nazis for his beliefs at the start of the Occupation, and by the French at the end of the war because his philosophical love of nature had been twisted to support Nazi propaganda. He made his name with a series of novels on village life in the Alpes-de-Haute-Provence, including the swashbuckling *Hussard sur le Toit*. Giono's Provence has little in common with the sunny region of Pagnol or even Daudet. His main themes were the abandonment of the mountain villages, the destruction of the traditional patterns of rural life and the rough sensuality of man's communion with nature. A plaque marks the writer's birthplace at 14 Grande Rue, above his parents' shoe shop. Outside the old town, the **Centre Jean Giono** (tel: 04 92 70 54 54; times vary; charge), in a yellow 18th-century house, puts on temporary exhibitions and has a permanent display about the writer's life and work. Giono's house, **Lou Parais** (Montée des Vrais Richesses; tel: 04 92 87 73 03), north of the Old Town, is open for guided visits by appointment.

RESTAURANTS AND BARS

Restaurants

Prices for a three-course meal without wine. Many restaurants have a less expensive lunch menu:

€ = under €25
€€ = €25–40
€€€ = €40–60
€€€€ = over €60

Cavaillon
Carte sur Table
35 rue Gustave Flaubert.
Tel: 04 90 78 15 27. Open L & D Tue–Sat. €€
Seasonal market cuisine in a chic dining room or on a shady terrace. Melon in season.

Lourmarin
Auberge La Fenière
route de Cadenet
www.reinesammut.com
Tel: 04 90 68 11 79. Open L & D Wed–Sun. Closed mid-Nov–Mar. €€€€
Chef Reine Sammut produces stylish food at this modern *mas* between Cadenet and Lourmarin. Nearby, La Cour de la Ferme serves a less expensive *menu du jour* and spit-roast meats.

Cucuron
La Petite Maison
place de l'Etang
Tel: 04 90 68 21 99. Open L & D Wed–Sun. €€€€
Chef Eric Sapet puts his gourmet touch on fresh

market produce at this pretty bistro.

Ansouis
La Closerie
boulevard des Platanes
www.laclolserieansouis.com
Tel: 04 90 09 90 54. Open L Fri–Tue D Mon, Tue, Fri, Sat.
€€–€€€€
Gourmet Provençal cuisine by chef Olivier Alemany. Reservations advised.

Coustellet
Maison Gouin
44 route d'Apt. Tel: 04 90 76 90 18. Open L & D Mon, Tue, Thu–Sat. €€
Small bistro within an upmarket butcher and deli. More elaborate menu by night.

Ménerbes
Café Véranda
avenue Marcellin Poncet
Tel: 04 90 72 33 33. Open L & D Tue–Sun. €€–€€€€
The trio behind this excellent bistro previously had a restaurant in the Dordogne, explaining are southwestern touches on the menu, which might include delicate salmon ravioli.

Bonnieux
Le Fournil
5 place Carnot.
www.lefournil-bonnieux.com
Tel: 04 90 75 83 62. Open L

& D Tue–Fri and Sun, D only Sat. Closed Dec–Jan. €€€
This troglodyte restaurant draws a fashionable set with its updated Provençal food.

L'Isle-sur-la-Sorgue
Le Jardin du Quai
91 avenue Julien Guigue
www.danielhebet.com
Tel: 04 90 20 14 98. Open L & D Thu–Mon. €€
Chef Daniel Hebet serves simple bistro fare at lunch and more complicated gastronomic cuisine at night.

Fontaine-de-Vaucluse
Philip
chemin de la Fontaine
Tel: 04 90 20 31 81. Open L Apr–June & Sept, L & D

mid-June–Aug. Closed Oct–Mar. €€–€€€€
Last stop on the footpath towards the spring, with a terrace overlooking the rushing torrent, Philip serves traditional Provençal cuisine at lunch, including the local speciality of river trout, and ice creams and sandwiches in the afternoon.

Gordes
Ferme de la Huppe
off the D156 route de Gault
www.lafermedelahuppe.com
Tel: 04 90 72 12 25. Open L & D daily. Closed Nov–mid-Mar. €€–€€€€
Upmarket Provençal cuisine in a lovely 18th-century farm near Gordes. Sit on the terrace in summer.

RIGHT: tables set at La Petite Maison.

WILD PROVENCE

If you wish to escape the crowded cities and coast, the countryside isn't far away. Here, among mountains and rivers, you can seem miles from civilisation

This swallowtail butterfly is a common visitor to Provence and is just one small component in the colourful landscape which runs from the salt marshes and brackish lagoons of the Camargue in the Rhône delta, pink with flamingos and home to countless waterfowl and waders, to the Alpine summits along the Italian border. It includes four national parks and six regional parks. The *maquis* scrub of rock rose and lavender, myrtle and thyme is the enduring attraction of the region, typified by the Luberon, with its evergreen oak, abundance of wild flowers and herbs, and beavers busy in the Durance and Calavon rivers. Eagles and vultures gaze down on the spectacular limestone Gorges de Verdon. The Valensole plateau, also in the Parc Naturel Régional du Verdon, is the place to head in June and July to see and smell the lavender fields and buy honey. Mushroom- and boar-hunting take place in autumn, which also sees chestnut-gatherers roam the Maures Massif. Wildest of all is the Mercantour National Park, with its glaciated landscape of mountains and lakes.

LEFT: Swallowtail butterfly.

ABOVE: cornflowers and poppies, which flower between March and June, in an Alpine meadow.

LEFT: glimpse chamois in Mercantour National Park, on steep slopes in forested areas and Alpine pastures.

LEFT: this prehistoric ammonite fossil comes from near Dignes.

GET OUT AND GET ACTIVE

Provence's wonderful landscape provides endless opportunities to enjoy the outdoors. For the sedate and leisurely, it's great walking country, while for the more energetic there are well-marked long-distance routes *(grandes randonnées)*, or strenuous challenges such as the Sentier Martel in the Gorges de Verdon or the Vallée des Merveilles in the Mercantour. Cycling can also be leisurely or demanding. The Luberon is a popular place for bikers, while Mont Ventoux is one of the arduous climbs on the Tour de France. The local rivers run swiftly, particularly the Verdon *(above)*, making canoeing, kayaking and white-water rafting a possibility, and because its gorge is so deep you can go bungee jumping from bridges. The rivers also offer a chance for trout-fishing. Mountains and escarpments present opportunities for climbing at every level, and of course there are the ski resorts of the Alps. There are few more evocative places to go horse-riding than the Camargue, where the local horses are perfect for a day's hack in the marshes. Equestrian centres *(centres équestres)* can be found throughout the region.

ABOVE: the famed white horses live wild in the marshy delta of the Rhône. Each year they are rounded up and the foals are branded.

ABOVE: diving at Freighter le Donateur off the coast of Ile de Porquerolles, one of the islands off the coast of Hyères.

ABOVE: the bee eater, relative of the kingfisher, is often seen around vineyards and meadows. Look out for roller birds and, near woodlands, hoopoes.

BELOW: heathland and stone pine woodland in the Ribeirotte Valley, in the Var.

MARSEILLE AND THE CALANQUES

France's oldest and second-largest city is a gloriously gutsy multicultural port, where tower blocks jostle with historic monuments. A city in evolution, it is redeveloping its docklands and basking in its recent status as European Capital of Culture

rance's oldest city and leading port, **Marseille**  is a magnificent mix of urban and marine, the grandiose and the intimate. With 2,600 years of history, the town abounds in historic monuments, fine churches, old fortresses, interesting museums and some icons of modern architecture. It is a city of 860,000 inhabitants, where ancient tenements, fishermen's cottages, Haussmannian boulevards, Belle Epoque villas and modern tower blocks alternate with docks, beaches and tiny coves. In one district you'll find luxury fashion boutiques, in another North African grocers and backstreet mosques. Some 40km (25 miles) of seaboard stretch from the fishing port and industrial suburb of L'Estaque in the north, past the docks, ferry terminal, fishing inlets and the long expanse of the Prado beach to tiny Les Goudes. Even the remote, fjord-like Calanques which stretch east between Marseille and Cassis largely fall within the urban limits of Marseille.

Birth of a city

It was 2,600 years ago that Greek sailors from the Ionian city of Phocaea first sailed into the harbour at Marseille, establishing a prosperous trad-

ing post called Massilia. The new settlement set up a string of outposts including Hyères, Antibes and Nice, and was also a thriving intellectual centre, home to one of the principal universities of the Greek Empire. Later a major Roman port, Marseille was an early centre of Christian monasticism around the important abbey of St-Victor. The city briefly set itself up as an independent republic in 1214, until it was taken by Charles d'Anjou in 1256. Along with the rest of Provence, the city became part

Main attractions
VIEUX PORT
MuCEM
LE PANIER
NOTRE-DAME-DE-LA-GARDE
MUSÉE CANTINI
CITÉ RADIEUSE
LES CALANQUES

LEFT: Marseille's Notre-Dame-de-la-Garde.
RIGHT: the tranquil beauty of the Calanques.

TIP

Bouillabaisse is the quintessential Marseille dish, originally made out of the unsold leftovers of the day's catch. Its name is supposed to come from 'quand ça bouille... abaisse' – 'when it bubbles lower the heat' – in an instruction on how to cook it without the fish disintegrating. To find a truly memorable bouillabaisse in Marseille, avoid the tourist traps around place Thiers behind the Vieux-Port and choose one of the restaurants that adheres to the bouillabaisse charter.

BELOW: The Vieux Port Pavilion, by Foster + Partners, part of the newly renovated waterfront.

of France in 1481. As a vital part of Louis XIV's maritime strategy, he built the star-shaped Fort St-Nicolas and enlarged Fort St-Jean, on either side of the Vieux-Port, as much to control the unruly citizens as to protect the port.

In 1720, an outbreak of the plague – the worst of several epidemics that hit the city – wiped out half the population, and despite efforts to isolate the city, spread to the rest of Provence.

Unsurprisingly, the Marseillais were active in the Revolution. In 1792, 600 Marseillais *fédéralistes* marched towards Paris to defend the revolutionary government, singing the rallying song that has since become France's national anthem, known as la Marseillaise *(see box on page 115)*. In the 19th century Marseille became the most powerful port on the Mediterranean, serving the expanding French Empire, its wealth reflected in the construction of grand hotels, the Docks de la Joliette, the new cathedral and Palais du Pharo.

Today the city is still a major port, and adminstrative capital of the Bouches-du-Rhône *département* and

the Provence-Côte d'Azur region. This is one of the most invigorating cities in France: a place where most of the city's residents proudly consider themselves Marseillais before being Provençal, with a take it or leave it attitude to tourists – although it now receives more than 4 million visitors annually.

The arrival of the TGV high-speed train in 2001, bringing Marseille within three hours of Paris, and massive investment in urban regeneration have tranformed the city's image; facades have been cleaned and the city has gained a sleek new tramway. The refurbishment of the 19th-century Joliette docks, flagship of the larger Euroméditerranée redevelopment project, illustrates the transformation of the local economy, as design and advertising agencies and service companies replace shipping ones and the dockworkers of old. In 2013, the city's status as European Capital of Culture rejuvenated its artistic and cultural life. Marseille has long been an entry point for immigrants – Italians, Greeks, Spanish and, more recently,

North and West Africans have all contributed to a melting pot where France's often uneasy racial mix for once largely seems to work.

The Vieux-Port

Any visit to Marseille should begin at the **Vieux-Port Ⓐ** (old port), the heart of the city, with its yachts, fishing boats and café-lined quays framed by forts at either end. There's a lively fish market each morning along the quai des Belges; this is also where boats leave for trips to the Calanques, the Château d'If and the Iles du Frioul *(see page 113)*. A tiny passenger ferry runs across the Vieux-Port between the quai du Port and quai de Rive Neuve.

The Quai du Port was heavily bombed by the Germans during World War II, but was sensitively rebuilt in the 1950s by architect Fernand Pouillon. His tinted reinforced concrete housing frames one of the rare buildings to survive, the ornate 17th-century **Hôtel de Ville Ⓑ** (town hall). From here various stairways lead up to Le Panier district. Just beside the Hôtel de Ville, terraced gardens climb up to the **Hôtel-Dieu**, the city's old hospital, designed in the 18th century by Jules Hardouin-Mansart (who was responsible for some of the greatest buildings in Paris including the redevelopment of Versailles), and which opened in 2013 as a luxury hotel *(see page 292)*. On the other side of the town hall stands the **Maison Diamantée Ⓒ**, built in the 16th century and one of the oldest surviving houses in Marseille, so called because of the unusual diamond-faceted façade.

A little further along the quai, look in on the **Musée des Docks Romains Ⓓ** (10 place du Vivaux; www.marseille. fr; Tue–Sun 10am–6pm; charge), which shelters relics of Roman docks on the site of their excavation. At the end of the quay, Fort St-Jean forms the centrepiece of the **MuCEM Ⓔ** (Musée National des Civilisations de

TIP

The City Pass, available for one or two days, gives free access to 12 museums in Marseille, free travel on the bus, metro and tram network and the tourist train, and discounts on selected shops, shows and city tours. Information from the Office de Tourisme: 4 rue de la Canebière; tel: 91 13 89 00; www. marseille-tourisme.com. Note that all municipal museums are free on Sunday and that all have the same opening times.

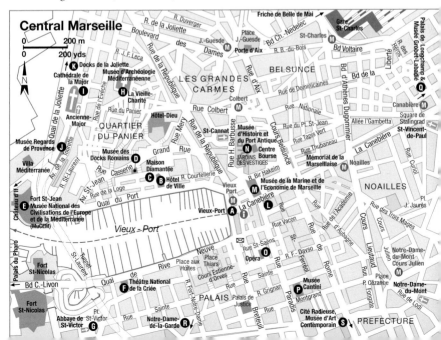

First created in 1781 in Le Four des Navettes, navettes are biscuits flavoured with orange-flower water. They are blessed during the Fête de la Chandeleur on 2 February.

l'Europe et de la Méditerranée; tel: 04 84 35 13 13; www.mucem.org; summer Wed–Mon 11am–7pm, winter until 6pm in winter, Fri until 10pm; charge). Opened in 2013, this ethnographic and folk art museum focusing on the Mediterranean cultures was designed by Bandol-based Rudy Ricciotti, who was also responsible for the Musée Jean Cocteau-Collection Séverin Wunderman in Menton (*see page 270*) and the new Department of Islamic Art at the Louvre in Paris. Themes covered include arts and industry, domestic life, belief and religion, theatre arts and agriculture. The highlight of any visit is a meal on the roof terrace in Le Môle, one of four restaurants here overseen by Michelin-starred chef Gérald Passédat – and far more accessible than his renowned restaurant Le Petit Nice (*see page 119*).

On the dockside to the west of the museum is the **Villa Méditerranée** (J4 esplanade; tel: 04 95 09 42 52; www.villa-mediterranee.org; Tue–Thu noon–7pm, Fri noon–10pm, Sat–Sun 10am–7pm; free, charge for temporary exhibitions), a stunning modern building designed by Stefano Boeri with an overhanging roof – a technical feat unique in Europe – which hosts permanent and temporary exhibitions on the people and history of the Mediterranean as well as music, dance and theatre performances.

On the opposite side of the Vieux-Port, the quai de Rive Neuve has lively bars and cafés amid ships' chandlers. The former fish market at No. 33 is now Marseille's highly renowned **Théâtre National de la Criée F**.

The quai leads towards the star-shaped Fort St-Nicolas (now occupied by the French Foreign Legion) and the **Jardins** and **Palais de Pharo** , the palace built for Napoléon III. The gardens, much loved by Marseillais, offer great views of boats coming in and out of the port and are the perfect spot for a picnic.

Behind the quai, **place Thiars**, place aux Huiles and cours d'Estienne d'Orves are busy with restaurants, fashion boutiques and galleries, many of them in converted warehouses and arsenal buildings. Parallel to the quai, long rue Sainte has an enclave of Marseillais tradition, the Four des Navettes bakery at No. 136, which has been baking *navettes* – biscuits flavoured with orange-flower water cooked in the shape of the boat that is said to have brought Mary Magdalene to the shores of Provence 2,000 years ago – since 1781.

Rue Sainte ends at Marseille's oldest church, the **Abbaye de St-Victor G** (daily 9am–7pm; charge for crypt), an ancient basilica that looks as much like a fortress as a church. It was built on the site of an age-old burial ground in the 5th century and is named after local martyr St Victor, patron saint of sailors, millers (Victor was ground to death between two millstones) and Marseille. Throughout the Middle Ages, the abbey's power was felt across the Mediterranean as it set up daughter houses from northern Spain to Italy. What

BELOW: sunset over the port.

remains is the extraordinary two-storey fortified church – the original 5th-century church in the crypt and the lofty 11th- to 13th-century church above. In the crypt, ancient sarcophagi, some hidden in candlelit alcoves, line the walls; in the centre stands the sombre tomb of two slain martyrs over which the basilica was built. In a rocky alcove is the 3rd-century tomb of St Victor.

Nearby is the studio Santons Marcel Carbonel (49 rue Neuve Sainte-Catherine; www.santonsmarcelcarbonel.com; Tue–Sat 10am–12.30pm, 2–6pm; free). Marcel Carbonel is one of the finest makers of these little Provençal figures which are traditionally displayed by families, crèche-style, at Christmas. There is a small museum at the back of the shop.

Le Panier

Climbing up the hill behind the quai du Port, bordered to the east by the 19th-century apartment buildings of rue de la République, is the picturesque **Quartier du Panier**. Characterised by leaning colour-washed houses, narrow streets, flights of steps

and little squares, it holds a small morning market in place Lenche, the site of the original Greek agora. Traditionally the immigrant quarter, it has recently been colonised by artists, craftsmen and Parisians in search of a southern pied-à-terre. However, not much remains of the original Panier, as 1,500 of its houses and buildings were blown up by the Germans in World War II. The Hôtel de Cabre, which dates from 1535, survived and is now the oldest house in Marseille; it is situated on the corner of rue de la Bonneterie and de la Grande.

At the heart of Le Panier is **La Vieille-Charité ❶** (2 rue de la Charité; Tue–Sun, June–Sept 11am–6pm, Oct–May 10am–5pm; charge). Erected as a charity hospital in the 17th century, it is the masterpiece of Marseille-born architect and sculptor Pierre Puget (1620–94), who also created several sculptures for Louis XIV at Versailles. The three storeys of galleried arcades are amazingly serene and beautiful for a building originally destined to round up beggars, fallen women and other social rejects. The restored buildings now

TIP

A fun way to explore Marseille is with a greeter (www.marseille provencegreeters.com; daily 9am–7pm; free). These are local people who are passionate about their city and want to share it with visitors. Themes include street art, architecture, football, and food. Book at least a week in advance via the form on the website.

BELOW: streets in the Quartier du Panier, Marseille's oldest quarter.

TIP

Marseille has an extensive public transport network, with two metro lines, two tramlines and numerous bus routes run by RTM (www.rtm.fr). If you're planning several journeys, buy a Carte 10 Voyages (for 10 journeys) or a one-day Pass 24H. Le Vélo is a municipal bike hire scheme (www.levelo-mpm.fr).

contain the **Musée d'Archéologie Méditerranéenne** (www.marseille.fr), which features local archaeology and a small but well-presented Egyptian collection, and the **Musée d'Arts Africains, Océaniens et Amerindiens** (www.marseille.fr), particularly strong on American Indian art and artefacts. At the centre of the courtyard, the **Chapelle**, which has an unusual oval dome, makes a striking setting for temporary exhibitions.

Looming over the coast is the stripy neo-Byzantine **Cathédrale de la Major** ❶ (Tue–Sun 10am–7pm, until 6pm in winter). Built between 1852 and 1893, its interior is a riot of coloured marble and porphyry. Adjacent to la Major is the 12th-century Romanesque Ancienne-Major, the earlier cathedral, which was undermined by the construction of the new cathedral and the flyover below it, and is closed for restoration. Almost next door, to the south, is the new **Musée Regards de Provence** ❶ (rue Vaudoyer; tel: 04 96 17 40 40; daily 10am–6pm, Thu until 9pm; charge), housed in a 1940s immigration building given

a 21st-century makeover, which not only showcases modern art associated with 'the south' but the region's history too.

Euroméditerranée

Stretching north along the seaboard from Fort St-Jean and inland as far as the Gare St-Charles train station is Marseille's ambitious 480-hectare (1,186-acre) Euroméditerranée urban regeneration district. This is the largest state-funded regeneration project after La Défense in Paris. The beautiful 19th-century brick warehouses of the **Docks de la Joliette** ❸ have been restored as offices and restaurants. On the waterfront the **FRAC** (Fonds Régional d'Art Contemporain; 20 boulevard de Dunkerque; tel: 04 91 91 27 55; Wed–Sat 10am–6pm, Sun 2–6pm; charge) contemporary art gallery, in a white glass building designed by Kengo Kuma, has joined the MuCEM and Le Silo, a vast 1920s concrete grain silo rehabilitated as a music and dance venue. Also in this area is Zaha Hadid's 33-storey skyscraper, which is the HQ of shipping company CMA CGM. Due to open

BELOW: along cours Belsunce.

in 2015 is the Euromed Center, a complex of offices, shops, a hotel, a park and a 15-screen multiplex cinema conceived by Luc Besson, who directed the movies *Subway*, *Nikita* and *The Fifth Element*.

Inland, the rundown Belle de Mai district is centred on the arty **Friche de Belle de Mai** (41 rue Jobin; tel: 04 95 04 95 04; Mon–Sat 9am–midnight), a former tobacco factory converted into artists' studios, a local radio station and dance and theatre companies; there is even a local produce market here every Monday evening. The Gare St-Charles station has also been renovated, with a bright glass shopping mall extension and paved esplanade leading to Marseille's main university district.

Around La Canebière

Running inland from the Vieux-Port is **La Canebière ❶**, Marseille's equivalent of the Champs-Elysées. It was laid out in 1666 as part of Louis XIV's expansion of the city, but its heyday came in the 19th century when its smart hotels, banks, cafés and department stores were a symbol

of Marseille's booming port economy at the height of the French Empire. The avenue gets its name from *canèbe* (hemp), after the rope-makers who were based in the area.

Near the port, at No. 4 is the tourist office. Almost directly opposite, the Palais de la Bourse – the ornate 19th-century maritime stock exchange (note the ship carvings on the façade) – contains the **Musée de la Marine et de l'Economie de Marseille ❶** (9 La Canebière; tel: 04 91 39 33 33; daily 10am–6pm; charge), which documents Marseille's maritime history.

Between here and the Vieux-Port, excavations during the construction of the Centre Bourse shopping centre in the 1960s unearthed Greek and Roman fortifications, wharfs, wells and a road, dating from between the 3rd century BC and the 4th century AD. These now lie exposed in the **Jardins des Vestiges**. The adjoining **Musée d'Histoire et du Port Antique ❶** (2 rue Henri Barbusse; www.marseille.fr; Tue–Sun 10am–6pm; charge, free Sun morning), reopened in 2013 after a complete renova-

The brasserie La Samaritaine on the Vieux-Port is a Marseille institution. It celebrated its centenary in 2010.

BELOW: Notre-Dame-de-la-Garde interior.

Cafés and Bars

Naturally the Vieux-Port is first port of call if you're pausing for a drink or a snack. Elegant **La Samaritaine** (2 quai du Port), with its corner vantage point, is a favourite meeting place; while the **OM Café** (3 quai des Belges) is the rallying point for supporters of Olympique de Marseille football team. **La Caravelle** (34 quai du Port), on the first floor of the Hôtel Bellevue, is a cocktail hotspot. Across the harbour, the **Bar de la Marine** (15 quai de Rive Neuve) is a local classic. Up the hill east of the Canebière, place Jean Jaurès and the bars and music venues around cours Julien draw a younger, bohemian set: try **Au Petit Nice** (place Jean Jaurès) or **E-Wine** (94 cours Julien).

The massive 9.7-metre (32ft) -high statue of the Virgin that crowns Notre-Dame-de-la-Garde was a technical feat. It was sculpted by Lequesne and cast in bronze at the Christofle workshop near Paris, then covered in gold leaf and installed on the church in 1870.

tion, presents some of the finds and the city's subsequent history. It was recently discovered that this was the site of the original Greek port and the 10 shipwrecks found here are regarded as some of the most important maritime finds from the ancient world. When the museum reopens, it will also have a replica of the Grotte Cosquier *(see page 116)*.

Behind here, running north of La Canebière, is the **cours Belsunce**, a broad promenade laid out in the 17th century. It has a souk-like atmosphere with its stalls, street traders and oriental patisseries. The striking municipal library at No. 58 is housed in an old theatre, L'Alcazar, where Yves Montand made his singing debut in 1939. The street continues into rue d'Aix, leading up to a busy road junction crowned by the Porte d'Aix triumphal arch.

Rue Beauvau leads to Marseille's **Opéra** , reconstructed in Art Deco style behind an 18th-century classical

facade after the original caught fire in 1919. It is used for both opera and ballet. Near here, amid Marseille's smartest shops on rue Paradis, rue St-Ferréol, rue Francis Davso and rue Grignan, is the **Musée Cantini** (19 rue Grignan; www.marseille.fr; Tue–Sun 10am–6pm, Thu until 10pm; charge), named after art-lover Jules Cantini, who donated the building and his artworks to the city in 1916. This notable collection has Fauve, Surrealist, early abstraction and post-war art, including paintings and sculptures by Derain, Signac, Léger, Kandinsky, Ernst, Arp, Brauner and Bacon. At the end of pedestrianised rue St-Ferréol is the grandiose Préfecture. Behind here rue Edmond Rostand is the focus of a small antiques district. On the other side of rue de Rome, rue d'Aubagne is lined with North African grocers, with sacks of couscous, spices, nuts and dates. Steps climb up the hill to Notre-Dame-du-Mont and the colourful **cours Julien**, the coolest

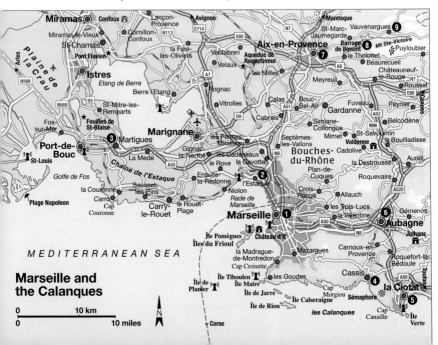

Marseille and the Calanques

MEDITERRANEAN SEA

part of town, with its fountain, cosmopolitan bars and restaurants, food market (Mon–Sat), shops including the hip Oogie Lifestore at No. 55 and live music venues such as Espace Julien at No. 9.

Palais de Longchamp

Crowning the top of boulevard de Longchamp, the **Palais de Longchamp**  is a glorious confection of fountains and waterfalls, with a winged colonnade around a central fountain. It is in fact a grandiose water tower that celebrated the arrival of a much-needed drinking-water supply to the city in 1869. The pavilions on either side house two newly renovated museums: the **Musée des Beaux-Arts** (tel: 04 91 14 59 18; Fri–Wed 9am–7pm, Thu noon–11pm; charge) has old master paintings and an excellent collection of 17th- to 19th-century Provençal art, while the **Muséum d'Histoire Naturelle** (Tue–Sun 10am–6pm; charge, free on Sun) features a variety of zoological and geological exhibits.

A little way down the street is the **Musée Grobet-Labadié** (140 boulevard de Longchamp; www.marseille.fr; Tue–Sun 10am–6pm; charge), the restored private mansion of a couple of avid 19th-century collectors, filled with the treasures they amassed: Northern and Italian Renaissance paintings, French 18th-century paintings, Provençal furniture and faience and a unique array of Flemish, Beauvais and Gobelins textiles.

The Good Mother

Perhaps the best-loved site in all Marseille is the church of **Notre-Dame-de-la-Garde**  (www.notredamedelagarde.com; daily, Apr–Sept 7am–7pm, Oct–Mar 7am–6pm), dubbed 'la Bonne Mère' (the Good Mother) by the Marseillais. Erected on a bluff of 162 metres (530ft), no matter where you go in Marseille, you can't miss the extravagant 19th-century basilica with its stripy marble walls and massive gilded statue of the Virgin atop the campanile. Inside, the two-storey church glitters with neo-Byzantine mosaics and white marble ex-votos offering thanks for recovery for everything from shipwrecks to armed holdups. The terrace in front offers the best

A gilded statue of the Virgin crowns Notre-Dame-de-la-Garde.

BELOW LEFT: Château d'If.

Château d'If and the Iles du Frioul

The Iles du Frioul, a rocky archipelago off the shore of Marseille, are just minutes from the frenetic Vieux-Port activity, yet miles away in mood. Regular boat trips leave from the quai des Belges out to the tiny Ile d'If, site of the Château d'If (summer daily 9.30am–6.30pm, winter Tue–Sun 9.30am–5.30pm; charge), France's version of Alcatraz. It was built by François I in the 1520s to keep an eye on the unruly Marseillais, and later used for the internment of Protestants and political prisoners. Its most famous inmate was fictional – Edmond Dantès, hero of Alexandre Dumas's novel *The Count of Monte-Cristo*. As well as visiting the fortress, you can enjoy a great view of the city, and even take a swim off the rocky shores.

You can combine the trip with a visit to the Iles de Frioul, two rocky, sparsely vegetated islands linked by a causeway. There are a few cafés and apartments near the quay, and some little creeks for swimming. Climb the hill to see the ruins of the Hôpital Caroline, an 18th-century quarantine hospital, today used for the MIMI music festival in July.

The statue of David on Le Prado.

view over the city. Supposedly a look-out post since prehistoric times and later a fort, it also became a place of worship for seafarers.

Along the corniche

The Château du Pharo and the tiny plage des Catalans, a small sandy beach and little harbour of the Anse des Catalans, mark the start of the **corniche Président-J.-F.-Kennedy**, the 5km (3-mile) stretch of road that follows the coastline east of the Vieux-Port. Take a short detour up the picturesque **Vallon des Auffes**, with its colourful *pointu* fishing boats, old fishermen's *cabanons* and renowned bouillabaisse restaurants.

The road eventually leads to the **Plages du Prado**, a large area of lawns, sports facilities and mainly pebble beaches on artificial land created with landfill from the construction of the Marseille metro system. The beach here has been split into two parts, the first half being pebble and the second sand, and the water is quite clean. Like most places on the French Riviera, Marseille has its own selection of private beaches including family-friendly Patabeach (tel: 06 15 71 27 12), which has a crêperie, and Baie des Singes (tel: 04 91 73 68 87), at the far end of Cap Croisette, which is the perfect place to get away from it all and enjoy a waterside meal before snoozing on a comfortable sunbed.

On the avenue du Prado, **Parc Borély** is Marseille's largest park, with its landscaped *jardins à l'anglaise*, French formal gardens, botanical garden with tropical greenhouse and racetrack, laid around the Château Borély, most elegant of all the *bastides*. A huge 18th-century neoclassical country house put up by the Borély family in 1766, it is now the **Musée des Arts Décoratifs, de la Faïence et de la Mode** (Museum of Decorative Arts, Earthenware and Fashion; 134 avenue Clôt Bey; tel: 04 91 72 43 47; Tue–Sun 10am–6pm; charge). As well as viewing thousands of objects relating to these art forms, visitors will also be able to see what life was like for a well-to-do 18th-century family.

The coast road continues past the **Plage de la Pointe Rouge**, a sandy beach that is known for its restaurants and watersports facilities, notably windsurfing and water-skiing, past La Madrague de Mondredon to finish at Les Goudes and tiny Callelongue. You're still technically in Marseille, but with the bare white rock, glittering blue sea and whirling seagulls you could well be on a Greek island.

Modern monuments

Heading inland up avenue du Prado from the beaches, past the giant replica of Michelangelo's *David* on boulevard Michelet, are two modern shrines. At No. 3, the **Stade Vélodrome** (tel: 08 26 10 40 44; www.arema-velodrome.com; guided tours; charge) is the stadium of Marseille's much-loved football team, which is being expanded, with work due to be completed in 2014. At No. 280, a must-see for modern architecture

BELOW: Château Borély.

enthusiasts is the **Cité Radieuse ❺** by the Modernist architect Le Corbusier. Built in 1947–52, the block illustrated Le Corbusier's principles of mass housing with its reinforced concrete structure built on *pilotis*, clever duplex apartments with balconies and built-in furniture, use of colour, and sculptural roof. As well as 337 apartments, it contains a supermarket, a gym, an infant school and a new contemporary rooftop art space called MOMA (Marseille Modular) designed by Ora-Ïto. The building is open for guided tours run by the tourist office (tel: 04 91 13 89 00), but you can also stay in the hotel or eat in the restaurant (tel: 04 91 16 78 00; www.hotellecorbusier.com); the restaurant/hotel staff can put you in contact with residents who will let you visit their apartments (charge).

Nearby is the **Musée d'Art Contemporain (MAC;** 69 avenue d'Haïfa; www.marseille.fr; Tue–Sun 10am–6pm; charge), Marseille's hangar-like contemporary art museum, which has an impressive international collection from the 1960s up to the present day. Artworks by Robert Rauschenberg,

Marseille-born César, Andy Warhol, Dieter Roth, Martial Raysse and Nan Goldin are shown in rotation along with temporary exhibitions. A huge bronze cast of César's sculpture *La Pouce (The Thumb)* stands incongruously in the centre of the roundabout down the street.

L'Estaque

For all its air of unassuming fishing village, **L'Estaque ❷**, on the northwestern tip of Marseille, is one of those places that changed art history. When he came here in the 1870s, Cézanne painted its red-roofed houses, the chimneys of its tile factories and the view across the bay to Marseille. In 1906–8, André Derain, Raoul Dufy, Othon Friesz and Georges Braque (whose Cubism was highly influenced by Cézanne) painted the coast here, appreciating its authenticity and the variety of subject matter. Dubbed the Fauves – or wild animals – by the critic Vauxcelles for their savage use of colour, they used colours that no longer sought to capture the changing times of day or weather like the Impressionists; instead they used

Although locals nicknamed it the Maison du Fada (madman's house), Le Corbusier's Cité Radieuse is much loved by its residents.

Below: *L'Estaque*, by Cézanne.

La Marseillaise

France's national anthem is one of the world's most recognisable and a new attraction, Le Mémorial de la Marseillaise (22–25 rue Thubaneau; tel: 04 91 91 91 97; mid-June–mid-Sept daily 10am–6pm, mid-Sept–mid-June Tue–Sun 2–6pm, closed Jan; charge), tells the story of this rousing song. The 'museum' is housed in the building, a former real tennis court, which was the base of the 18th-century revolutionaries whose 'Song for the Rhine Army' was later adopted as the country's national anthem. Learn about Marseille's role in the French Revolution and its main activists, hear different versions of the song and browse the shop – there are even some books in English.

Les Calanques

Explore the fjord-like Calanques on foot or by boat and find unspoilt nature in an area that appeals to divers, birdwatchers, rock-climbers and walkers

Stretching for 20km (12 miles) south-east of Marseille, between Cap Croisette and Cassis, lies a stunning landscape of rocky inlets, sheer white cliffs, sparse *garrigue* vegetation and tiny beaches, offering superb opportunities for walking, rock-climbing, birdwatching and swimming. Although most of the area is within the city limits of Marseille, it remains a haven of unspoilt nature, largely because most of it is accessible only by foot or boat – and in 2012 gained further protection as a Parc National. Often compared to the Norwegian fjords, the Calanques are technically *rias* – valleys flooded by the rising sea level at the end of the Ice Age some 10,000 years ago. Over 700 species of plant, including 14 types of orchid, grow here; birdlife includes the rare Bonelli's eagle, the peregrine falcon and huge colonies of seagulls.

You can reach the Calanques by taking boats from the Vieux-Port in Marseille and the harbour in Cassis, or by walking along the GR98 footpath between Marseille and Cassis. Certain roads offer access out of season and at night for those with restaurant reservations. From July to mid-September access is severely restricted due to fire risk. Most footpaths are closed; only the GR98 remains open. The rest of the year, the Marseille tourist office organises walks in the Calanques on Friday afternoons and Saturday mornings (reserve on 04 91 13 89 00). If walking alone, be sure to take a good map, sun cream and water.

Along the GR98

The Marseille coast road ends just beyond Les Goudes at Calanque de Callelongue, a starting point for the GR98 path, which follows the coast to the Calanque de Cortiou and the series of little Calanques of the Massif de Marseilleveyre. The broad Calanque de Sormiou, with its small beach, and Morgiou, with its fishing harbour, are two of the most picturesque, still lined with some old *cabanons* – simple rickety shacks built by fishermen or as weekend homes by the ordinary workers of Marseille. Further east, Sugiton, accessible by foot from Luminy in the northeast of Marseille, sits under a sheer cliff face favoured by rock-climbers, while its flat, waterside rocks attract nude bathers.

From Cassis the first inlet, the only one reachable by car, is Port-Miou; this is dedicated to harbouring yachts. The second is Port-Pin, so named for the shrubby pines that decorate its rocky walls, with a small sandy beach. The breathtaking Calanque d'En-Vau, about an hour's walk further on, has a difficult descent at the end, where white cliffs fall into water of the deepest blue-green imaginable. A sandy white beach adorns one end.

The Grotte Cosquier, an underwater cave covered with prehistoric paintings, is closed to the public, but diving expeditions can be organised from Marseille and Cassis to other underwater caves and shipwrecks. ❑

LEFT: Port-Miou, first inlet on the route from Cassis.

colour for its expressive value. Visitors can follow a trail around town where painted panels depict the artists' works (details from the tourist office: 90 plage de l'Estaque; www.estaque.com). In 2010, a new museum, the Fondation Monticelli (Fortin de Corbières, Route du Rouve; tel: 04 91 03 49 46; Wed–Sun 10am–5pm; charge) opened in a renovated fort high above the bay, paying homage to Marseille-born Adolphe Monticelli, whose work influenced Cézanne and was admired by Van Gogh.

One of the main summer events in town is *la joute marine* (water jousting), where men battle it out on passing boats rather than horses; the Provençal water jousting championships take place here on the last Sunday in July.

Along the Côte Bleue to Martigues

West of l'Estaque, the attractive Côte Bleue is a popular weekend jaunt for the populations of Aix and Marseille, less known yet more accessible than Cassis and the Calanques *(see page 116)* to the east. Set against the backdrop of the red hills of the Chaîne de l'Estaque, villas hide up on the hillsides, and a succession of tiny harbours and small resorts includes **Niolon**, which is a renowned centre for diving, **Carry-le-Rouet**, famed for its *oursinades* (sea urchin feasts in February), **Sausset-les-Pins** and **Carro**, a small fishing port and beach popular with windsurfers. A good way to explore this part of the coast is by the train TER Côte Bleue, which runs from Marseille to Miramas; an all-day ticket called a 'Zou! Pass' costs €15.

North of Carro, bridging the mouth of the heavily industrialised and polluted Etang de Berre lake, **Martigues ❸** is a surprisingly picturesque place consisting of three ancient fishing villages linked by a network of canals and bridges. There's a striking contrast between

the modern Théâtre des Salins and the pretty fishermen's cottages along quai Brun and quai Baron. The main sight is the ornate Baroque **Chapelle de l'Annonciade** (rue du Dr Sérieux, Jonquières), with its *trompe l'oeil* walls and gilded altarpiece.

Nineteenth-century marine and orientalist painter Félix Ziem was so seduced by the light of the little port that he set up his studio here. His works form the centrepiece of the **Musée Ziem** (boulevard du 14 Juillet, Ferrières; tel: 04 4241 3960; July–Aug Wed–Mon 10am–noon, 2.30–6.30pm, Sept–June Wed–Sun 2.30–6.30pm; charge), installed in the old customs house. It includes paintings by Dufy, Picabia, Manguin and contemporary artists, and a statue of St Pierre (St Peter), patron saint of fishermen, which comes out for a procession down to the harbour every June.

Cassis

In the opposite direction, 20km (14 miles) east from Marseille over the bleak Col de la Gineste is **Cassis ❹**. The first of the Riviera resorts, Cas-

The vineyards of Cassis produce some very quaffable wines.

BELOW: Cassis harbour.

Provençal writer Marcel Pagnol was born in Aubagne in 1895. Pagnol captured the spirit of the region in works such as Manon des Sources *and* Jean de Florette*, both turned into successful films. Drive through Cugeles-Pins and up to Riboux, where the pastoral scenes were shot. The tourist office in Aubagne (8 cours Barthélémy) can give details of the Circuit Pagnol, which covers many of the sites mentioned in his works.*

sis possesses none of the glamour or urbanity of St-Tropez or Cannes, and therein lies its special charm. Numerous modern painters spent many summers in this delicate port, with its pretty old town and a lively harbour front lined with shops, restaurants and diving stores. The town has three beaches, the best being the **Plage de la Grande Mer**, and you can take boat trips from the harbour to the Calanques *(see page 116)*. Dominating the village is the 13th-century Château de Cassis (www.chateaudecassis.com), which has been turned into a luxury B&B.

The wine from Cassis is highly regarded – Frédéric Mistral described the white as 'shining like a clear diamond, smelling of rosemary, heather and myrtle' – and is made by just 12 vineyards surrounding the town. It was one of the first wines in France to receive the AOC status. Of the 1 million bottles produced each year, around 80 percent is white wine. The tourist office organises visits (tel: 08 92 39 01 03; Apr–Oct daily; charge) to some of the winegrowers but you can try a glass or buy a bottle at vint-

ner-cum-winebar Le Chai Cassidain (6 rue Séverin Icard).

La Ciotat and Aubagne

Looming over Cassis to the east is **Cap Canaille**, which at 416 metres (1,400ft) is the highest cliff in continental Europe. For a panoramic thrill, take a drive along the **Route des Crêtes**, which climbs up, over and down to the neighbouring city of **La Ciotat ❺**. From summer homes to clinging vineyards to rubble, the road seems to disappear up into the sky. The giddy view is fabulous.

La Ciotat has a very different character. A genteel Belle Epoque resort and long an important shipbuilding centre, it now rather resembles a resort in Florida, with a long flat beachfront lined with souvenir shops, and a harbour where you can take boat trips to the tiny Ile Verte out in the bay. Among summer residents were the Lumière brothers, who shot the world's first moving picture here, showing a train pulling into La Ciotat station. It was projected at the Eden cinema on boulevard Georges Clémenceau in 1895. At the time, the spectators fled in horror, afraid they would be crushed by the oncoming train. The cinema was renovated in 2013.

Travelling inland along the A50, north of La Ciotat and east of Marseille, will bring you to **Aubagne ❻**, home town of writer and film director Marcel Pagnol *(see margin)*. The house where he was born, **Maison Natale de Marcel Pagnol** (16 cours Barthélémy; Apr–Oct daily 10am– 1pm, 2–6pm, Nov–Mar Tue–Sun 2–5.30pm; charge) is now open to the public. Long a centre for everyday pottery, Aubagne still has several workshops turning out high-quality garden and plant pots, such as the family-run Poterie Ravel (8 avenue des Goumes; www.poterie-ravel.com); look out for the pottery markets in July, August and December. ❏

Below: a view of Cassis Bay from Cap Canaille.

RESTAURANTS

Restaurants

Prices for a three-course meal without wine. Many restaurants have a less expensive lunch menu:
€ = under €25
€€ = €25–40
€€€ = €40–60
€€€€ = over €60

Marseille

Les Arcenaulx
25 cours d'Estienne d'Orves
www.les-arcenaulx.com
Tel: 04 9159 8030. Open L
& D Mon–Sat. **€€€**
This stylish restaurant-cum-tearoom-cum-bookshop and deli is located within the renovated arsenal buildings behind the Vieux-Port. Draws a dressy crowd for upmarket Provençal fare.

Le Café des Epices
4 rue Lacydon
Tel: 04 91 91 22 69. Open L
Tue–Sat & D Tue–Fri.
€€–€€€€
The well-travelled young chef turns out exquisite dishes based on local cuisine imbued with an international touch. The best place to sit in summer is on the olive-lined terrace.

La Cantinetta
24 cours Julien
Tel: 04 91 48 10 48. Open L
& D Tue–Sat. Closed Sept.
€–€€
Buzzy Italian restaurant in Marseille's hippest

area. The wine list is small but perfectly formed and includes organic local and Italian wines. A good place to start a night on the tiles. Reservations advised.

Chez Fonfon
140 vallon des Auffes
www.chez-fonfon.com
Tel: 04 91 52 14 38. Open L
Tue–Sat & D Mon–Sat.
Closed Mon eve Nov–May.
€€€–€€€€
A good fish restaurant and classic address for bouillabaisse, in a picturesque little harbour just off the Corniche.

Le Péron
56 corniche J.-F.-Kennedy
www.restaurant-peron.com
Tel: 04 91 52 15 22. Open
L & D daily. **€€€€**
Stylish contemporary restaurant with stunning sea views. Cooking is accomplished and inventive. A Marseille hotspot.

Le Petit Nice Passédat
Anse de Maldormé,
corniche J.-F.-Kennedy
www.passedat.fr
Tel: 04 91 59 25 92. Open L
& D Tue–Sat. Closed Nov,
Jan and Feb. **€€€€**
Gérald Passédat, the third generation of Passédats to run this elegant seaside hotel restaurant, is considered by some the best fish chef in southern France, revisiting bouillabaisse and little-known fish.

Pizzeria Etienne
43 rue de Lorette
No telephone. **€**
This ever-busy Le Panier restaurant is renowned for the best pizza in town.

Une Table au Sud
2 quai du Port.
www.unetableausud.com
Tel: 04 91 90 63 53. Open L
Tue–Sun & D Tue–Sat.
€€€–€€€€
Young chef Ludovic Turac makes inventive use of southern produce in a room overlooking the Vieux-Port. Try the 3-, 5- or 7-course tasting menu; the 'deconstructed' strawberry dessert is delicious.

For bars and cafés in Marseille, see page 111.

Carry-le-Rouet

Le Madrigal
4 avenue Docteur Gérard-Montus
www.restaurant-lemadrigal.com
Tel: 04 42 44 58 63. Open L
Tue–Sun & D Tue–Sat.
€€–€€€€
Stylish restaurant in a pink-painted villa with a terrace overlooking the sea. Try the salt-crusted sea bass followed by a *café gourmand* (coffee accompanied by a selection of small desserts).

Cassis

Poissonnerie Laurent
5 quai Barthélémy
Tel: 04 42 01 71 56. Open L
& D Tue–Sun. **€€–€€€€**
A former fishmongers turned into a quietly chic portside restaurant.

RIGHT: the harbour in front of Chez Fonfon.

AIX-EN-PROVENCE

Elegant, aristocratic Aix-en-Provence is the former capital of Provence. Seat of a prestigious university, the home town of Emile Zola and Paul Cézanne is still a delightful place to visit, with its handsome town houses, bubbling fountains, smart shops and lively café society

R oman spa and garrison town, former capital of the counts of Provence and historic university city, **Aix-en-Provence** ❼ is still the epitome of civilised aristocratic Provence. The Romans first founded Aquae Sextiae – so named for its hot springs – in 122 BC, after conquering the nearby Ligurian settlement of Entremont. It was overshadowed, however, by Marseille and Arles until the 15th century when 'Good' King René, Count of Provence and Anjou, made it his city of preference, and a cultural as well as political capital. René's death brought Provence under the rule of the French crown, and Aix was made the seat of a parliament designed to keep the region under Gallic control.

Much of Aix's renowned architecture dates from this period of prosperity, as the parliamentarians and wealthy burghers built themselves fine town houses and lavish country *bastides*. During the Industrial Revolution, Aix fell back under Marseille's shadow. In the 20th century, however, new industries managed to find a niche here: the city remains the European capital for prepared almonds, but it also has a growing high-tech industry and the region's main law courts. Whole new university, business and residential districts have grown up around the historic centre. Today, Aix is particularly renowned as a university town (of its 150,000 inhabitants around 40,000 are students) and attracts many American exchange students, one of the best known being the American actor Bradley Cooper.

Cours Mirabeau

The best place to begin exploring the city is the **cours Mirabeau ➊**, which

Main attractions
COURS MIRABEAU
MORNING MARKET ON PLACE RICHELME
RUE GASTON DE SAPORTA
CATHÉDRALE ST-SAUVEUR
MUSÉE GRANET
ATELIER PAUL CÉZANNE
BALLET PRELJOCAJ – PAVILLON NOIR

LEFT: strolling through Aix.
RIGHT: the fountain on place d'Albertas.

EAT

Aix's culinary speciality is the white diamond-shaped *calisson d'Aix*, made out of a mixture of sugar, almonds and preserved melon. Those by Léonard Parli (35 avenue Victor Hugo) are regarded as the best.

marks the dividing line between Vieil Aix (Old Aix), the commercial heart of the city, and the aristocratic Quartier Mazarin. Laid out in the 17th century as a carriageway on the trace of the old ramparts, the plane tree-lined avenue is flanked by café terraces and punctuated by fountains: the Fontaine du Roi René with a 19th-century sculpture of the king by David d'Angers (note that he's holding a bunch of Muscat grapes, which he introduced to Provence), the Fontaine des Neuf Canons, the Fontaine d'Eau Chaude, which burbles out water at a constant 34°C (93°F), and at the western entrance to the avenue, the ornate **Fontaine de la Rotonde ❸**, on place du Général de Gaulle, which is recognisable by its majestic lions. West of La Rotonde, beyond the new Allées Provençales pedestrian shopping street, where the tourist office is situated, a modern arts district has been developing *(see box on page 126)*.

About two-thirds of the way up the cours, the **Café des Deux Garçons**, affectionately dubbed 'les Deux Gs', is an Aix institution, an intellectual hub since 1792; the café's terrace is still the ideal place for people-watching – you might even be lucky enough to spot George Clooney, Hugh Grant or Sophie Marceau, who have all been here – while the inside is all gilt mirrors and period light fittings. Just a couple of doors up at No. 55 once stood the *chapellerie* – hat shop – of Cézanne's father Louis Auguste, where Paul Cézanne lived when he was a child. On the opposite side of the cours at No. 12 is Béchard, arguably the finest cake shop in town and correspondingly crowded; look out for the *tarte aixoise* (sponge cake with a layer of cream in the middle). A little further along at No. 38 is the Hôtel Maurel-de-Pontevès, which has two magnificent telamons (carved male figures) either side of the doorway supporting the balcony above.

BELOW: handsome architecture on cours Mirabeau.

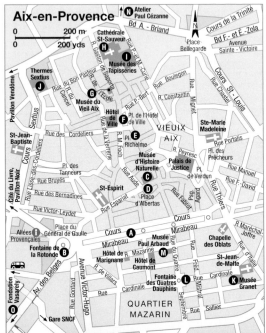

Vieil Aix

North of cours Mirabeau the largely medieval narrow streets of **Vieil Aix** are the beating heart of the city: a tangle of small squares and ancient buildings, many with carved heads looming over doorways, and busy with fashion shops and snack stalls.

On rue Espariat you can see the Baroque church of St-Esprit and the belfry of a former Augustinian monastery. At No. 6, the **Musée d'Histoire Naturelle** (www.museum-aix-en-provence.org; daily 10am–noon, 1–5pm; charge) is located inside a 17th-century *hôtel particulier*, built according to the Parisian fashion with the main building at the rear of a fine entrance courtyard. The collection's star attraction is the thousands of dinosaur eggs found on Montagne Ste-Victoire.

Almost opposite is the delightful semicircular **place d'Albertas**. When the parliamentarian Albertas built his home in the 1720s, he also bought all the land in front of it – to 'protect his view'. The four contiguous buildings that now enclose the square were not constructed until 1740. Nearby, **rue Aude** and **rue Fabrot** are home to many of Aix's most fashionable stores. Rue Aude runs into **place Richelme**, with an excellent morning fruit-and-vegetable market, which adjoins the more genteel **place de l'Hôtel de Ville**, a good place to stop and have a drink or a bite to eat.

On the western side of this square is Aix's **Hôtel de Ville** (town hall), built 1655–78, originally the regional assembly of the Etats de Provence. If you go into the town hall, glance up at the beautiful wrought-iron gateway, which fans out in a representation of the sun. Inside, an elegant staircase leads up to the Salle des Etats de Provence, where regional taxes were voted, hung with portraits and mythological paintings.

On the south side of the square is **la Poste** (post office), built in the 18th century as the splendid corn exchange. Note the cavorting figures, intended to represent the Rhône and Durance rivers, that drape themselves around the pediment.

East of the town hall, small streets lead towards the place de la

Every Tuesday, Thursday and Saturday morning the Marché d'Aix takes over the centre of town, joining the daily fruit and vegetable stalls of place Richelme. The food and produce heart is on place de la Madeleine. Stalls of household goods, textiles and second-hand goods take over streets and squares towards the Palais de Justice and flower stands are by the Hôtel de Ville.

BELOW: the ornate Fontaine de la Rotonde.

Cézanne

Paul Cézanne, born in Aix-en-Provence in 1839, was a post-Impressionist painter whose work laid the foundations for Cubism and modern art

Cézanne's work is inextricably linked with the landscape of his native Provence, and above all the countryside around Aix-en-Provence. While still at school, the young Paul had drawing lessons, which helped him decide upon a career as an artist. In the 1860s and 70s he moved between Paris, L'Estaque and Aix, meeting Pissarro, Monet and Renoir and forming part of the circle of Impressionists, with whom he exhibited in 1874 and 1877. Initially his work was rejected by the prestigious Paris Salon – he exhibited instead at the Salon des Refusés, which displayed paintings rejected by the Salon – but his *Portrait of Louis-Auguste Cézanne, Father of the Artist, reading l'Evénement* was finally accepted in 1882.

Although he is known for painting portraits, still lifes of fruit and female nude bathers, Cézanne's favourite *motif* was the Montagne Ste-Victoire. A tireless walker, he spent many hours on the mountain, and depicts it in over 80 works, searching for the key to its structure: 'To paint a landscape well, I must first discover its geological characteristics,' he wrote. In the mountain, Cézanne found the geometrical ordering of nature – 'Nature must be treated by the cylinder, the sphere, the cone...' – that would lead him towards a new concept of perspective. Moving away from the Impressionists' moulding through light and colour, he developed a relationship with landscape that approaches abstraction and prefigures the Cubism of Braque and Picasso. The latter referred to him as 'the father of us all' and bought a house in the shadow of Mont Ste-Victoire at Vauvenargues *(see page 128)* to be closer to his idol, although it is said that the pair never met.

The Cézanne Trail

A Cézanne trail around Aix picks out numerous spots associated with the artist. Pick up a leaflet from the tourist office (300 avenue Giuseppe Verde; tel: 04 42 16 11 61; www.aixenprovencetourism.com) or follow the brass medallions inserted in the pavement. You'll see the building where he was born on rue de l'Opéra, the site of his father's hat shop on 55 cours Mirabeau where he lived as a small child, the Café des Deux Garçons at No. 53, where he would often stop for an aperitif, the Collège Mignet (then Collège Bourbon) where he went to school, and the Hôtel de Ville where he got married in 1886.

The Jas de Bouffan, the family estate, is also open to the public *(see page 127)*, and although now surrounded by modern housing you can still see the chestnut trees painted by the artist. The Carrières de Bibémus, atmospheric disused quarries where the shapes of the rocks might have influenced his 'Cubism', can also be visited (reserve at tourist office) with a route taking you past views depicted by Cézanne, and the simple dry stone cottage he rented to store his materials. He died of pneumonia in 1906 and is buried in St-Pierre cemetery (avenue des Déportés de la Résistance). ❑

LEFT: *Jas de Bouffan*, 1876.

Madeleine, with its central gigantic obelisk, and the large Baroque church of **Ste-Marie Madeleine**, containing an *Annunciation* attributed to 15th-century Flemish painter Barthélemy Van Eyck.

On the north side of the Hôtel de Ville is the whimsical **Tour de l'Horloge**, dating from 1510. This clocktower houses four statues, each of which marks a season: in the summer, you'll see a woman holding wheat; autumn shows the wine harvest; winter has a wood-bearer, and spring appears as a woman carrying fruit and a young salmon. Originally part of the city wall, the tower marked the division between the count's city and that of the clergy around the cathedral to the north. Continue up rue Gaston de Saporta with its string of 17th-century *hôtels particuliers*. Several of them are linked to the university or theatres, so you can often wander in on weekdays to see the magnificent entrance stairways. At No. 23 is the Hôtel Maynier-d'Oppède, now the Institut d'Etudes Françaises pour Etudiants Etrangers (Institute of French Studies for For-

eign Students) whose courtyard is used for concerts in summer, and at No. 19 is the Hôtel de Châteaurenard, which played host to Louis XVI when he visited Provence in 1660.

At No. 17, the Hôtel Estienne de St-Jean contains the **Musée du Vieil Aix** ⓖ (Wed–Mon, Apr–Oct 10am–12.30pm, 1.30–6pm, Nov–Mar 1.30–5pm; charge), the town's local history museum. The collection focuses on local folk art, including an array of mechanised puppets. But it's worth going in just to have a look at the building as it's one of the finest houses on the street.

The **Cathédrale St-Sauveur** ⓗ (place des Martyrs de la Résistance; Mon 3.45–5pm, Thu 4–6pm, Sat 10am–noon, 4–6pm but check with the tourist office as times can vary) is an eclectic structure. Its façade combines the 12th century with the 16th, the belfry belongs to the 15th, and there are three naves in Romanesque, Gothic and Baroque styles. The highlight inside is Nicolas Froment's 15th-century triptych, *Le Buisson Ardent (The Burning Bush).* Off the right-hand nave is the 5th-century

TIP

Aix's prestigious international opera festival (Festival d'Art Lyrique; tel: 08 20 92 29 23; www.festival-aix. com) each July features top-rate performers and directors, and a repertoire that varies from Mozart to new commissions. The main venue is the courtyard of the Palais de l'Evêché.

BELOW AND LEFT:
Cathédrale St-Sauveur.

Painting the Fontaine des Quatre-Dauphins.

BELOW: in the courtyard of the Atelier Paul Cézanne.

baptistery, one of the rare surviving Merovingian baptisteries in Provence (others being in Fréjus and Riez). The cloister is particularly attractive.

The Baroque **Palais de l' Ancien Archevêché** (Archbishop's palace) contains the **Musée des Tapisseries** (Tapestry Museum; Wed–Mon mid-Apr–mid-Oct 10am–12.30pm, 1.30–6pm, mid-Oct–mid-Apr 1.30–5pm; charge), which includes a rare series depicting the adventures of Don Quixote, from 1735. There's a section dedicated to performance arts, and the opera festival in particular. The courtyard is used for the most prestigious opera productions in Aix's Festival d'Art Lyrique *(see margin page 125)*.

Rue du Bon Pasteur leads towards the **Thermes Sextius** , now a luxury glass-and-marble spa but originally a series of 1st-century BC Roman baths (the remains of which can be seen to the right of the present entrance), fed by the water from the *Source Impériatrice*. The baths were expanded in the 18th century, and a fountain from this period is still on view to visitors.

The Quartier Mazarin

Back across the cours Mirabeau, the Quartier Mazarin was a speculative property venture laid out in the 17th century on a geometric grid plan. It still has a calmer, more discreet residential atmosphere than Vieil Aix, with its 17th- and 18th-century *hôtels particuliers*, now often housing antique shops, as well as Aix's most important museum. The **Musée Granet** (place St-Jean-de-Malte; www.museegranet-aix-enprovence.fr; mid-June–mid-Oct daily 9am–7pm, mid-Oct–mid-June Tue–Sun noon–6pm; charge), in the former monastery of the Knights of Malta; recently reopened after restoration; it has one of the best fine art collections in Provence. Archaeological finds from the Oppidum at Entremont and from Roman Aix, 18th-century statues and portrait busts are on display, along with French paintings from the 16th to the 20th centuries, and Dutch, Flemish and Italian art, including Ingres' extraordinary and disturbing *Jupiter and Thetis*. Although the original curator spurned Cézanne, the collection now includes 10 paintings by the artist, as well as a recent Philippe

Artistic Aix

New districts are transforming the area south of the station and Vieil Aix, where university buildings, a landscaped esplanade and several important arts buildings are giving new all-year facilities to a city long dominated by its summer festival. Marked by a sculpture of a giant open book, the **Cité du Livre** is a vast complex of library, cinema, performance and exhibition spaces, housed in a converted match factory. Next door stands the striking modernist black concrete and glass skeletal structure of the **Ballet Preljocaj – Pavillon Noir** (www.preljocaj.org) dance venue and the tiered structure of the **Grand Théâtre de Provence** concert hall.

Meyer donation of modern art, which includes superb works by Bonnard, Mondrian, Picasso and Giacometti.

Next door is the 13th-century **St-Jean-de-Malte**. The long single-naved building was one of the first Gothic structures in Provence; note the Maltese cross carved over the door. Further down the street at No. 41 is the Collège Mignet (then Collège Bourbon), where Cézanne went to school and became friends with the future writer Emile Zola, who spent his childhood in the town.

West down the rue Cardinale lies the **Fontaine des Quatre-Dauphins** ⓛ. Dating from 1667, it was the first fountain in Aix to be placed in the middle of a street rather than against a wall, giving it an unprecedented decorative purpose. Kids are usually charmed by the four baby-faced dolphins with their tails upturned.

The **Musée Paul Arbaud** Ⓜ (2 rue du Quatre-Septembre; Tue–Sat 2–5pm; charge) has a fine collection of Provençal faience (pottery) from Moustiers, Marseille and Apt. There is also a fine collection of rare books, mainly notable for their bindings.

Beyond the Thermes Sextius, past a medieval turret, is another architectural gem, the **Pavillon Vendôme** (Wed–Mon summer 10am–6pm, winter 1.30–5pm; charge). Louis de Mercœur, duke of Vendôme and governor of Provence, built this home in 1665 so he could meet his lover here in secret.

Cézanne and Vasarely

Up chemin des Lauves, north of Vieil Aix, is the **Atelier Paul Cézanne** Ⓝ (9 avenue Paul-Cézanne; tel: 04 42 21 06 53; www.atelier-cezanne.com; daily, July–Aug 10am–6pm, Apr–June and Sept 10am–noon, 2–6pm, Oct–Mar until 5pm; guided tours in English at 5pm, winter at 4pm; charge), built by the artist in 1902; it was here that he painted his last works. The scrupulously preserved studio is an atmospheric place, still cluttered with easels, palettes and objects familiar from Cézanne's still lifes. A steepish 15-minute walk further up the hill brings you to the plateau where Cézanne painted many of his views of the distant Montagne Ste-Victoire – or 'the motif' as he called it.

The manor house at **Jas de Bouffan** (www.aixenprovencetourism.com;

TIP

A terrible episode of Provençal history can be traced at the **Mémorial des Milles** (40 chemin de la Badesse; www.campdesmilles.org; Tue–Sun 10am–7pm; charge), a former tile factory to the south of the city which was used as an internment camp during World War II. The refectory is painted with moving murals made by the prisoners showing the daily atrocities of internment.

BELOW: Fondation Vasarely gallery.

Fondation Vasarely.

visit by guided tour only; reserve at tourist office) gives a sense of the country residence it was when bought by Cézanne's father in 1859. Cézanne had a studio in the attic and painted many works directly on the walls, all since dispersed to museums around the world. Here you have to make do with a multimedia presentation in their place, but outside you can still recognise the long avenue of chestnut trees from his paintings.

Another artist who left his mark on Aix was Hungarian-born Victor Vasarely. The **Fondation Vasarely** (1 avenue Marcel-Pagnol; www.fondatio-nasarely.fr; tel: 04 42 20 01 09; Tue–Sun 10am–1pm, 2–6pm; charge; take bus No. 2 from la Rotonde), on the Jas de Bouffan hill, is unmistakable, with its bold black-and-white Op Art architecture that is itself a piece of kinetic art.

The Montagne Ste-Victoire

East of Aix is the Montagne Ste-Victoire, ringed by the D10 road to the north and D17 to the south, which makes a pleasant excursion from Aix. Along the D10, you come to the **Barrage de Bimont** dam ❽, with its dra-

matic waterworks and nature reserve. Several footpaths lead to the Barrage Zola, designed by Emile Zola's father in 1854. Further along the D10 is the pretty village of **Vauvenargues** ❾, famous for its Renaissance chateau, bought by Picasso in 1958, where he died aged 91 in 1973; he and his wife Jacqueline are buried in the garden. The house opened to the public for the first time for a few months in the summer of 2009 so check with the Aix tourist office about any future openings. A path leads up onto the mountain, more accessible from this side than the vertiginous southern crags.

Opposite Vauvenargues around the other side of the mountain in St-Antonin-sur-Bayon is the Maison de Ste-Victoire (tel: 04 13 31 94 70); here you'll find information about the site and a nature trail. On the D17 back towards Aix is Le Tholonet, where Cézanne rented a room to paint at the Château Noir; he used to eat at the restaurant which is now called Relais Cézanne. Also of note in the town are the remains of the Roman aqueduct that supplied water to Aix from St-Antonin. ❑

BELOW: the much-painted Montagne Ste-Victoire.

BEST RESTAURANTS, BARS AND CAFÉS

Restaurants

Prices for a three-course meal without wine. Many restaurants have a less expensive lunch menu:
€ = under €25
€€ = €25–40
€€€ = €40–60
€€€€ = over €60

Brasserie Léopold
2 avenue Victor Hugo
Tel: 04 42 26 01 24. Open L & D daily. €€
A classic brasserie near la Rotonde with excellent old-fashioned service. Vintage photos reveal that the Art Deco interior was once a garage.

La Cerise sur Le Gâteau
7 place Ramus
Tel: 04 42 27 46 46. Open Thu–Tue 9am–5pm. €
Vegetarians will be delighted to find this lovely little organic restaurant, although there's plenty for carnivores too. Come for brunch in the morning or tea and cake in the afternoon.

Côté Cour
19 cours Mirabeau
www.restaurantcotecour.com
Tel: 04 42 93 12 51. Open L & D Mon–Sat. €€€€
With its conservatory-style setting in a courtyard, this long-standing local favourite is now run by celebrity chef Ronan Kerven.

Les Deux Frères
4 avenue de la Reine Astrid
www.les2freres.com
Tel: 04 42 27 90 32. Open L & D daily. €€–€€€
The success story of the Benchérif brothers, this restaurant has a pared-back contemporary design, spacious terrace and a screen on which images of the excellent modern Mediterreanean food are projected.

Le Formal
32 rue Espariat
www.restaurant-leformal.com
Tel: 04 42 27 08 31. Open L Tue–Fri & D Tue–Sat. €€€
Hidden in a cool cellar in Vieil Aix, haute cuisine-trained chef Jean-Luc Le Formal modernises classic ingredients with real flair.

Le Petit Verdot
7 rue d'Entrecasteaux
Tel: 04 42 27 30 12. Open L Sat & D Mon–Sat. €€
Atmospheric wine bar with wooden tables and a traditional menu – try lamb with thyme followed by calisson-flavoured crème brulée. Good local wines.

Pierre Reboul
11 petite rue St-Jean
www.restaurant-pierre-reboul.com
Tel: 04 42 20 58 26. Open L Wed–Sat & D Tue–Sat. €€€–€€€€
Michelin-star cuisine in an old house with stunning contemporary décor. The chef likes to 'reinvent' dishes and play with flavours – try the char with hot lemon mayonnaise.

Ze Bistro
31 bis rue Manuel
www.zebistro.com
Tel: 04 42 39 81 88. Open L & D Tue–Fri. €€–€€€
Traditional dishes with a nod to the Mediterranean and the occasional touch of the Far East. Try the soufflé with Chartreuse for dessert. Contemporary dining room and professional service.

Bars and Cafés

All the great and good from Cézanne to Colette to Churchill have frequented **Les Deux Garçons** (53 cours Mirabeau), or 'les Deux Gs'. This intellectual hub, founded in 1792, has a perfect people-watching terrace and a Consular-period interior. Almost as venerable is **Café Grillon** at No. 49, with another fine terrace and an elegant dining room. The laidback **Le Verdun** on place de Verdun near the Palais de Justice is very popular with the town's student population, as are the small bars on rue de la Verrerie in Vieux Aix. **La Rotonde** is a branché cocktail haunt with a cosmopolitan menu, overlooking the Rotonde fountain.

ST-RÉMY AND LES ALPILLES

Les Alpilles may not reach Alpine heights, but the jagged crags and ravines of these miniature mountains are nonetheless impressive. It was here, amid the dazzling limestone, pine woods and olive groves, that Van Gogh was inspired to paint some of his best-known works

The limestone Alpilles form the backdrop for elegant St-Rémy-de-Provence, the dramatic ruins of Les Baux-de-Provence and a cluster of chic villages, while along the Rhône, impressive castle remains serve as a reminder that this was once the frontier between France and Provence.

St-Rémy-de-Provence

The mini-capital of the Alpilles, **St-Rémy-de-Provence** ❶, makes a good base for exploring the area, with its combination of archaeological remains, fine architecture and a thriving café society that gives the town a distinctly Parisian air. As in many Provençal towns, the dense network of narrow streets that makes up the old city is ringed by broad, plane tree-shaded boulevards which trace the line of the former ramparts.

On boulevard Marceau, the cavernous **Collégiale St-Martin** was rebuilt in neoclassical style in 1821 after the previous church collapsed. An enormous organ dominates the interior and there are recitals every weekend from July to September.

Behind here lies the old town, full of cafés, art galleries, smart interior-design shops, and some remarkable Renaissance houses. The 16th-century Hôtel Mistral de Mondragon, on the corner of the main thoroughfare, rue Carnot, is home to the **Musée des Alpilles** (place Favier; www.musees-mediterranee.org; May–Sept Tue–Sun 10am–6pm, Apr–Oct Tue–Sat 1–5.30pm; charge). The superb Renaissance mansion has an ornate façade decorated with Ionic pilasters, carved friezes and a tower with rams' and lions' heads. An arcaded courtyard is graced by a bust of Van Gogh by Zadkine. The museum focuses on local history and folk art, with dis-

Main attractions
MUSÉE DES ALPILLES, ST-RÉMY-DE-PROVENCE
MONASTÈRE ST-PAUL-DE-MAUSOLE, ST-RÉMY-DE-PROVENCE
LES BAUX-DE-PROVENCE
JARDIN DE L'ALCHIMISTE, EYGALIÈRES
CHÂTEAU DU ROI RÉNÉ, TARASCON
ZOO DE LA BARBEN

LEFT: Les Baux-de-Provence.
RIGHT: café-life in St-Rémy.

Although he spent most of his adult life in Salon-de-Provence, Nostradamus was born Michel de Nostradame in St-Rémy on 14 December 1503. You can see (but not visit) his birthplace in rue Hoche. There is a fountain topped with a bust of the seer in rue Carnot.

plays on everything from quarrying in the Alpilles, agriculture, dinosaurs and cicadas (a symbol of Provence) to folk costumes, pottery and tile-making, and collections of *santons* (traditional terracotta nativity figures).

The elaborate Renaissance facade of the **Hôtel de Sade** across the square and the **Mairie** (town hall), housed in a former convent, are also worth a look. On Tuesday evenings in July and August, a craft market is held beneath the arcades fronting the square. An 18th-century residence, formerly the Centre de Présence Van Gogh, now contains the **Musée Estrine** (rue Estrine; due to reopen in Oct 2013). It focuses on 20th-century art, including several paintings by Cubist artist Albert Gleizes, who lived in St-Rémy from 1939 to 1953, and works by Alechinsky, Leroy and Rebeyrolle, although there is still an annually changing audiovisual and documentary presentation about Van Gogh.

The Van Gogh trail

Many people come to St-Rémy on the trail of Vincent Van Gogh, who checked himself into the local asylum on 8 May 1889, after an argument with Gauguin in Arles during which he famously sliced off part of his ear. The Dutch artist spent a year here, painting some 150 canvases. These included many of his most famous works, including *Irises* and *Starry Night*. Follow the avenue Vincent Van Gogh south of the centre to the **Monastère St-Paul-de-Mausole** (daily, Apr–Sept 9.30am–6.45pm, Oct–Mar 10.15am–5.15pm, closed Jan–Feb; charge), the medieval monastery that houses the clinic where he stayed, which is still a working psychiatric home. The pretty cloisters and the Romanesque chapel can be visited, as can a reconstruction of Van Gogh's room. There is also a trail through the adjoining field where visitors can see reproductions of the works he painted there – the

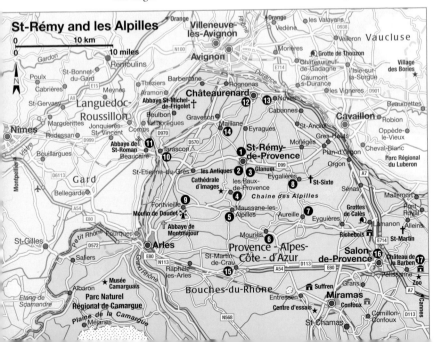

artist was not entirely confined to the clinic but allowed to take supervised walks through the immediate surroundings.

Glanum

Ancient **Glanum** lies just south of St-Paul-de-Mausole en route to Les Baux. Marking the entrance are two particularly well-preserved monuments, an arch and a mausoleum, known collectively as **Les Antiques** ❷. The **triumphal arch** straddles what was once the Via Domitia, the Roman road connecting Spain to Italy. It was built during the reign of Augustus to mark the entrance to the city of Glanum, and decorated with reliefs illustrating Caesar's conquest of Gaul. The **Mausolée de Jules**, dated 30–20 BC, is a three-tiered funereal monument built by members of a powerful Roman family in honour of their ancestors.

Slightly further up the road is the archaeological site of **Glanum** ❸ (www.monuments-nationaux.fr; Apr–Aug daily 10am–6.30pm, Sept closed Mon, Oct–Mar Tue–Sun 10am–5pm; charge). A Celto-Ligurian sanctuary city built beside a sacred spring was succeeded during the Gallo-Greek era by a flourishing Phocaean trading post that served as a commercial and religious centre. This role continued under the Romans, until the city was virtually destroyed by invaders in the 3rd century.

The remains of baths and villas around a paved main street have been unearthed, as has a separate district of temples, where a couple of facsimile columns provide a sense of scale. Even if it is not easy to work out what the different remains represent, the setting – a hollow in the mountains – is remarkably beautiful.

Les Baux-de-Provence

For a change of scenery, take the D5 south from St-Rémy and then the D27A, climbing up through wooded hills and the award-winning vineyards of the Mas de la Dame towards spectacularly situated **Les Baux-de-Provence** ❹. The name Baux comes from *baou*, Provençal for rocky spur, and gave its name to bauxite, the reddish ore, which was discovered near here by geologist Pierre Berthier in 1821.

Although Les Baux has been inhabited for 5,000 years, its fame derives from the period between the 11th and 14th centuries, when the arrogant lords of Baux made their presence felt throughout the region. Today, more than 1.5 million tourists a year come to see where the lords raged and troubadours once roamed. In July and August Les Baux resembles a theme park, its streets thronged with coachloads of tourists, and souvenir shops and ice-cream parlours spill out of old buildings. Visit in early spring, autumn or on a crisp winter's day, and you can appreciate this extraordinary place in relative calm.

The site divides into two parts: the 'Château', which contains the ruins of the feudal court, and the partially ruined 'Village' below it, an attractive

TIP

St-Rémy is a good place to come if you are interested in herbalism and aromatherapy. There are many charming shops selling essential oils, soaps and more. The boutique Florame (34 boulevard Mirabeau; www.florame. com) also has a small museum, the Musée des Arômes, a collection of perfume bottles and alembics. Find it at 34 boulevard Mirabeau; tel: 04 3260 0518; www. florame.com

BELOW: the Mausolée de Jules, Glanum.

The feudal life of Les Baux presents a fascinating paradox. Here, amidst these 'impregnable fortresses, inhabited by men whose roughness was only matched by that of their suits of armour, the "Respect of the Lady" and ritual adoration of her beauty was born.' The patronage of the troubadours by these lords gave rise to the chivalric code, and a tradition of romantic poetry emerged from the bloody citadel.

mixture of shops and galleries set in medieval and Renaissance houses. One well-restored house contains the **Musée Yves Brayer** (Hôtel Porcelet, rue de l'Eglise; www.yvesbrayer. com; Apr–Sept daily 10am–12.30pm, 2–6.30pm, Oct–Mar Wed–Mon 11am–12.30pm, 2–5pm, closed Jan–Feb; charge) with paintings of the region by the popular landscape artist (1907–90).

Best-preserved of all the monuments in the old city is the **Eglise St-Vincent**, which has a central nave dating back to the 12th century and stained glass that is a striking *mélange* of ancient and modern. Across the road is the lovely 17th-century **Chapelle des Pénitents Blancs**, painted with Nativity scenes by Brayer in 1974.

The castle and its ramparts

The 'Cité Morte' or **Château des Baux** (www.chateau-baux-provence.com; daily, July–Aug 9am–8.15pm, Apr–May and June–Sept until 7.15pm, Mar and Oct 9.30am–6.30pm, Nov–Feb 10am–5pm; charge), stronghold of the lords of Baux, is entered through

the rectangular Tour de Brau, dating from the late 14th century. Beside it lies a small modern cemetery filled with lavender, and the 12th-century **Chapelle de St-Blaise**. Press on to the highest point of the ruins, where a round tower stands. The view from here is incredible: on one side, the crags of the Alpilles, on the other, a sheer drop to the rolling vineyards and olive groves. Much of the Château is a big open space, dotted with reproductions of a giant catapault and other siege warfare machines, which are put into action four times a day between April and September. By the northern ramparts, investigate what is left of the 15th-century castle, the 10th-century keep and the Paravelle tower, as well as some troglodyte dwellings.

For more breathtaking views head northwards out of Les Baux on the D27, which winds along a perilous precipice overlooking the **Val d'Enfer** (valley of hell), said to have inspired Dante's *Hell*. Just outside Les Baux, stop off at the **Cathédrale d'Images** (route de Maillane; www.carrieres-lum ieres.com; daily, Mar–Sept 9.30am–7pm, Oct–Jan 10am–6pm, closed Feb;

Below: view from the ramparts at Les Baux-de-Provence.

charge), a vast former quarry where a sophisticated *son et lumière* show, which changes annually, is projected onto the rocky walls.

Olive country

Head south of Les Baux and you're in vine and olive country. Gentrified **Maussane-les-Alpilles** ❺ and more workaday **Mouriès** ❻ vie for the title of the village with the most olive trees in France, and both have reputable olive mills. Others swear by the olives of **Aureille** ❼, a half-forgotten town a little further east, with a friendly central bar and the ruins of an 11th-century castle rising above it on a hill that is only accessible on foot.

North of here, **Eygalières** ❽ provides some of the prettiest perspectives in the Alpilles with its cluster of old houses climbing up a small hill and, 1 km (0.5 miles) outside the village, the quaint Romanesque Chapelle St-Sixte, ringed by cypresses. The main attraction here is the **Jardin de l'Alchimiste** (Mas de la Brune; www.jardin-alchimiste.com; May–mid-June daily 10am–6pm, mid-June–Sept Sat–Sun 10am–6pm; charge), a herb garden laid out in medieval style.

Daudet's Windmill

Towards Arles and west of Maussane-les-Alpilles, the picturesque town of **Fontvieille** ❾ is notable for its series of modest oratories, erected in 1721 in thanksgiving for an end to the plague. The town's primary attraction is the **Moulin de Daudet**, immortalised in Alphonse Daudet's (1840–97) *Letters from My Windmill*. The fact that the windmill actually belonged to Daudet's friends and witnessed little penmanship has done little to deter the hordes of tourists that come to see it. The mill does enjoy a picturesque location and contains some interesting features, such as a circular ceiling inscribed compass-fashion with the names of the winds that sweep the hill.

However, it is currently closed to the public and is in poor repair.

Tarascon

Bordering the Rhône, 14km (6 miles) west of St-Rémy, the historic town of **Tarascon** ❿ became the stuff of Provençal legend in AD 48 when its resident monster, the Tarasque, was tamed by St Martha *(see page 136)*. By the Middle Ages the town had become an important place of pilgrimage thanks to the saint's relics, which are held in the crypt of the **Collégiale Ste-Marthe**. The church also contains some of the countless paintings of Martha and the Tarasque that exist, while a marble Tarasque de Noves sculpture sits in the archaeological museum in Avignon.

The feudal **Château du Roi René** (daily, June–Sept 9.30am–6.30pm, Oct–Jan until 5pm, Feb–May until 5.30pm; charge) on the banks of the Rhône is a grandiose affair. The castle was begun in 1400 by Louis II d'Anjou and completed by his son Good King René, who turned it into a sumptuous Renaissance palace. The building proudly rivals the Château

TIP

Olive oil AOC Les Baux-de-Provence is made from a blend of oils. Two mills making high-quality oil according to traditional methods are the 17th-century Moulin Jean-Marie Cornille (rue Charloun-Rien, Maussane-les-Alpilles; www.moulin-cornille. com; open daily), and the Moulin de Calanquet (vieux chemin d'Arles, St-Rémy-de-Provence; open daily).

BELOW: olive grove, Vallée des Baux.

According to legend a scaly amphibious monster had for years terrorised the people of Tarascon, drinking the Rhône dry and devouring villagers. In the 1st century, Martha, member of the saintly boat from Bethany crew (see page 23) tamed the beast, then converted the grateful and hitherto pagan Tarasconnais to Christianity. Tarascon celebrates the legend with the annual Fête de la Tarasque.

de Beaucaire on the opposite bank, built from the same white limestone. The interior of the Château du Roi René is mostly empty, apart from six magnificent 17th-century Flemish tapestries and the reconstructed interior of an old pharmacy.

Architectural highlights in the old town itself include the three fortified gateways, the Renaissance cloisters of the former Couvent des Cordeliers and the arcaded rue des Halles. On rue Proudhon, the Hôtel d'Aiminy contains the **Musée Soleïado** (Mon–Sat, Apr–Oct 10am–7pm, Nov–Mar 10am–12.30pm, 2.30–7pm; charge), with a collection of woodblocks, printed *indiennes*, costumes, pottery and objects belonging to the Tarascon textile house *(see box below)*.

Beaucaire

Across the Rhône, Tarascon's twin and historic rival **Beaucaire** ⓫ grew up as a stop on the Via Domitia. The town is dominated by the ruined stronghold of the medieval counts of Toulouse – and later of the French king from where he could keep an eye on Provence. The mas-

sive **castle ruins** (Wed–Mon 10am–12.30pm, 2–6pm; free) house a small archaeology museum. The castle was destroyed on the orders of Richelieu in 1632 when it was a Huguenot stronghold but the town continued to prosper in the 17th and 18th centuries when wealthy merchants built themselves fine houses, thanks to its river port and 10-day-long annual fair, the Foire de la Madeleine. Beaucaire's importance as a port was confirmed with the construction of the Canal du Rhône à Sète in the 19th century, and the town still has a lively port at its heart, with numerous quayside cafés, moored barges and companies offering boat trips on the Rhône to the Camargue or along the canal to Sète.

On a hill just north of Beaucaire, the **Abbaye de St-Roman** (July–Aug daily 10am–1pm, 2–7pm, Apr–June and Sept–Oct Tue–Sun 10am–1pm, 2–6.30pm, Nov–Feb Sat–Sun 2–5.30pm, Tue–Sun during school hols; charge) is a fascinating troglodyte abbey. Allow a 15-minute climb from the car park to explore the remains of individual cells and

Provençal Textiles

Today no Provençal hotel or restaurant seems to be without its colourful Provençal print curtains and tablecloths, still called *indiennes* after the woodblock-printed textiles first imported from India in the 17th century. The prints soon became a craze adopted by the latest fashions and copied by local manufacturers in kaleidoscopic floral and geometric patterns. Although Louis XIV's minister Colbert banned their production in France in 1686 to protect the Compagnie des Indes, and local manufacturers moved to Orange within the Comtat Venaissin, production in Provence flourished again when the law was repealed in 1759. The original Indian designs were gradually replaced by the classic Provençal motifs of lavender, olives, sunflowers, cicadas, mimosas and lemons.

Two companies continue to produce quality traditional *indiennes*, although even they are no longer printed by hand: Les Olivades, at St-Etienne-des-Grès in the Alpilles, produces fabrics from both modern designs and those based on 17th- and 18th-century fabrics, and Soleïado, which uses motifs from its huge archive of old woodblocks and is based in Tarascon *(see above)*.

chapel carved out of the rock between the 5th and 14th centuries by hermits and Benedictine monks.

The Petite Crau

Between Avignon and St-Rémy, **Châteaurenard** ⓬ is a quiet Provençal town – except during its colourful horse-drawn wagon parades (see page 154) – set amid a network of 17th-century canals that turned the Petite Crau plain into a major centre for market gardening.

You may want to make a quick sweep through **Noves** ⓭, to the east. The town today has little to attract tourists (all that remains of its château are segments of the 14th-century ramparts), but it was here that Petrarch first laid eyes on his beloved Laura, about whom he would later write some of the world's most famous love poems.

Another town of literary significance crops up on the D5 between St-Rémy-de-Provence and Graveson. **Maillane** ⓮ was both the birth and burial place of Frédéric Mistral (see page 29). The house where the poet lived from 1876 until his death in 1914 has been turned into a museum. The **Musée Frédéric Mistral** (11 avenue Lamartine; Tue–Sun Apr–Sept 9.30–11.30am, 1–6pm, times vary in winter; charge), contains his desk and gloves just as he left them, while the Maison du Lézard, where he lived earlier with his mother, now contains the tourist office and public library.

Salon-de-Provence

South of the Alpilles, the landscape changes radically as you cross the Grande Crau plain, an area of sheep pasture and hay cultivation centred around the market town of **St-Martin-de-Crau** ⓯. Here, a small **Ecomusée** (Mon–Sat 9am–5pm; free) in an old sheepfold explains the local habitat and agriculture.

Situated on the eastern edge of the Crau, the sprawling, dusty traffic-filled **Salon-de-Provence** ⓰ has been dubbed the 'crossroads of Provence' for its central location. Its role in the olive oil trade, aided by the arrival of the railway in the late 19th century, turned it into the heart of the soap industry. A few of the elaborate villas built by the soap barons survive,

Transhumance is the moving of sheep flocks between their winter grazing on the Crau plain and summer grazing up in the Alps. The practice is celebrated each year with a festival in St-Rémy at Pentecost (Whit Monday).

BELOW: horse-drawn wagon parade in Châteaurenard.

Salon-de-Provence is well known for its fountains, the most famous being the fontaine moussue *(mossy fountain) in place Crousillat, which looks like a giant mushroom.*

BELOW: Château de la Barben.

mostly on and around rue de la République, though only two companies still make soap. **Marius Fabre** (148 avenue Paul Bourret) has been in operation here since 1900. You can see how the soap is made on tours of the factory (10.30am July–Aug Mon–Thu, Sept–June Tue and Thu). There is also a small **museum** (www.marius-fabre.fr; Sat 9.30am–noon all year, Mon–Fri July–Aug 9.30am–12.30pm, 2–6.30pm, Sept–June 9.30am–noon, 2–5.30pm).

The town is dominated by the forbidding turrets of the **Château de l'Emperi**, built between the 10th and 16th centuries as a residence of the bishops of Arles. Inside, the **Musée de l'Emperi** (Tue–Sun, Apr–Sept 9.30am–noon, 2–6pm, Oct–Apr 1.30–6pm; charge) showcases one of France's largest collections of militaria, 1700–1918. Several rooms are dedicated to the Napoleonic era, with the diminutive general's short blue bed among the treasures.

The hub of the town is the cours Gimon, where you'll find the 17th-century Hôtel de Ville and tourist hotspot, the **Maison de Nostrada-mus** (13 rue Nostradamus; Mon–Fri 9am–noon, 2–6pm, Sat–Sun 2–6pm; charge), where the renowned physician-turned-astrologer wrote his famous book of predictions. It has been turned into a waxworks experience, with ten scenes recounting episodes from his life.

Also in the old town is the beautiful early Gothic Eglise St-Michel, dating from 1220 to 1239. Lying outside the old town walls is the grander Eglise St-Laurent, built in characteristically sombre Provençal Gothic style. In the Lady Chapel is the tomb of Nostradamus, who died in Salon in 1566, marked with a plaque which reads: 'Here lie the bones of Michel de Nostradame, alone at the judgement of humans worthy of knowing the stars of the future. He lived 62 years, 6 months and 17 days.'

A second famous inhabitant of Salon, Adam de Craponne, the 16th-century engineer who transformed the dry Crau plain by constructing an irrigation canal from the Durance River, is commemorated by a statue in front of the Hôtel de Ville.

Château de la Barben

Six km (4 miles) east of Salon-de-Provence on the D572/D22, the impressive **Château de la Barben** (www.chateaudelabarben.com; guided visits daily, times vary; charge) is yet another of Good King René's castles; five of the rooms are rented out for B&B. Its formal gardens were allegedly laid out by the landscape gardener of Versailles, André Le Nôtre. In the centre is a fountain in which Napoleon's sister, Pauline Bonaparte, liked to bathe *au naturel*.

Outside the château, the **Zoo de la Barben** (www.zoolabarben.com; daily, July–Aug 9.30am–7pm, Sept–Nov and Feb–June 10am–6pm, Dec–Jan 10am–5.30pm; charge) is the largest zoo in the region, where some 120 species of animal, including bears and elephants live in roomy open-air enclosures. ❑

RESTAURANTS

Restaurants

Prices for a three-course meal without wine. Many restaurants have a less expensive lunch menu:
€ = under €25
€€ = €25–40
€€€ = €40–60
€€€€ = over €60

St-Rémy-de-Provence

Bistrot Découverte
19 boulevard Victor Hugo
www.bistrotdecouverte.com
Tel: 04 90 92 34 49. Open L & D daily. Closed Nov–Mar.
€€
Wine sommelier Claude and wife Dana opened this attractive little bistro in 2005. The menu might include an accomplished risotto with *girolles*, the fish of the day or roast veal with seasonal vegetables, accompanied by well-chosen wines. The cellar contains a wine shop and holds tastings.

La Maison Jaune
15 rue Carnot
Tel: 04 90 92 56 14. Open L Wed–Sat, D Tue–Sat. Closed Nov–Mar. €€–€€€€
Michelin-star Provençal cuisine from François Perraud in an elegant 18th-century townhouse. In summer, try the cherry 'soup' for dessert. Lunch from €32. Booking advised.

Les Baux-de-Provence

Hostellerie de la Reine Jeanne
Grande Rue
www.la-reinejeanne.com
Tel: 04 90 54 32 06. Open L & D daily. €€
Les Baux's chic eateries hide out in the hills, but if you want to eat in the village itself, then this place offers reliable traditional Provençal cooking and lovely views. Garlicky lamb from the Alpilles is a speciality.

L'Oustou de Baumanière
Val d'Enfer
www.oustoudebaumaniere.com
Tel: 04 90 54 33 07. Open L & D daily. Closed Jan–Feb.
€€€€
The luxurious *bastide* of Jean-André Charial is the place for a gastronomic splurge and draws a jet-set clientele from heads of state to film stars, for cuisine based on home-grown vegetables and a magnificent wine list. Talented chef Sylvestre Wahid, previously chez Ducasse, produces dishes like gently spiced spider crab.

Paradou

Le Bistro du Paradou
57 avenue de la Vallée-de-Baux.
Tel: 04 90 54 32 70. Open L & D Tue–Sat. €€€

This Provence institution occupies a pretty beamed stone farmhouse in a village near Maussane-les-Alpilles. Simple home-cooked dishes like garlicky lamb, Camargue bull stew, Ventoux pork and sea bream in *beurre blanc* sauce make the most of local produce. It's popular, so reserve in advance.

Fontvieille

Villa Regalido
rue Frédéric Mistral
www.laregalido.com
Tel: 04 90 54 60 22. Open L Tue, Wed, Fri–Sun, D Tue–Sat. €€–€€€
Grand classic Provençal cuisine is served in the vaulted dining room or on the shady terrace of a restored olive-oil mill. Dishes such as partridge cooked in Les Baux wine sauce are a culinary and aesthetic treat.

Tarascon

Méo
1 place du Colonel-Berrurier
www.meo-tarascon.fr
Tel: 04 90 91 47 74. Open L Wed–Sun & D Wed–Sat
€€–€€€
Excellent-value Michelin-star cuisine in stylish surroundings near the station. Chef Johan creates starters and mains using the finest local ingredients while wife Emily looks after the desserts. There is also a wine bar and an outside terrace.

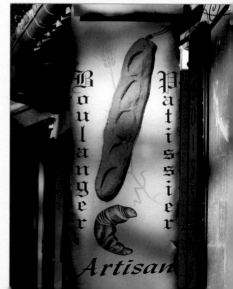

RIGHT: an artisan bakery.

ARLES AND THE CAMARGUE

The Rhône delta city of Arles is a delightful maze of
Roman remains, Romanesque churches, noble town
houses and sun-dappled cafés. Arles is also gateway
to the Camargue, an area of desolate beauty,
famed for its white horses, pink flamingos,
black bulls and cowboys

D espite its grand past and impressive architectural heritage,
Arles ❶ still has an intimate,
villagey atmosphere that makes it easily accessible to the visitor. While the
Arlesiens are fiercely proud of their
past and dedicated to upholding Provençal and, especially, Camarguais traditions, the town also has an active
cultural scene. Home to a world
music festival and one of France's
most respected publishing houses,
Actes Sud, it also hosts the annual
Rencontres de la Photographie.

Arles in its heyday

Founded by the Massilians as a trading post in the 6th century BC, Arles'
position at the crossroads of the
Rhône and the Via Aurelia made it
a natural choice for development by
the Romans. The town grew slowly
for several hundred years, cementing
its position as a river and maritime
port. Then, during the struggle for
power between Caesar and Pompey,
Arles got its lucky break. Marseille
made the fatal error of showing
friendship towards Pompey, and
Caesar turned to Arles, known for its
skilled boatbuilders, with the request
that 12 war vessels be built for him
within 30 days. The city complied,

and Arles' good fortune was sealed.
Caesar designated Arles the first city
of Provence, leading to the construction of temples, baths, the theatre,
amphitheatre and circus.

The city continued to prosper, and
was briefly capital of the 10th-century
kingdom of Bourgogne-Provence.
Although its predominance waned
over the following centuries, Arles
enjoyed a new period of prosperity in
the 16th and 17th centuries, reflected
in the fine Renaissance and classical
town houses of local landowners. It

Main attractions
SATURDAY MARKET ON
   BOULEVARD DES LICES, ARLES
CLOÎTRE ST-TROPHIME, ARLES
PLACE DU FORUM, ARLES
ARÈNES, ARLES
HORSE RIDING, CAMARGUE
MARAIS DU VIGUEIRAT,
   CAMARGUE
AIGUES-MORTES

LEFT: riding is an excellent way to experience
the Camargue. **RIGHT:** Théâtre Antique, Arles.

TIP

If you're planning to do a lot of sightseeing, invest in the Passe Liberté (€9) which allows entry to one museum and four monuments of your choice or the Passe Avantage (€13.50) which allows entry to all sites. Get it from the tourist office on place des Lices.

BELOW: portal sculptures, St-Trophime.

remained a key maritime and river port right until the advent of the steam engine. With the construction of the Marseille-Avignon railway (later the Paris-Lyon-Marseille line) in the 1840s, Arles' economy took a new direction. It became a centre for the construction and repair of locomotives that employed generations of workers until the SNCF ateliers closed in 1984.

The Vieille Ville

At the heart of Arles is the **Vieille Ville** (old town), an attractive maze of narrow stone streets where crumbling Roman edifices mingle with sturdy medieval stonework and elegant classical town houses. The old town is bordered to the south by the wide boulevard des Lices, to the east by the remnants of ancient ramparts and to the north and west by the grand sweep of the River Rhône.

Most visitors will arrive in Arles via the boulevard des Lices. If you

have a car, it's a good idea to leave it in the car park on the street's south side. Almost all of the main sights are within easy walking distance. Although often traffic-clogged, the boulevard des Lices is a lively spot with numerous cafés and the tourist office. Its high points come during the huge produce market on Saturday morning and the flea market on the first Wednesday of the month.

Eglise St-Trophime

The cobbled rue Jean Jaurès will bring you to the spacious **place de la République** Ⓐ, with an ancient obelisk in the middle and the 17th-century **Hôtel de Ville** (town hall) at one end, which was built following designs by Jules Hardouin-Mansart, the architect of Versailles. One of the town's hidden treasures can be accessed here: **Les Cryptoportiques** (May–Sept daily 9am–7pm, Mar–Apr and Oct until 6pm, Nov–Feb until 5pm; charge), or, to give them

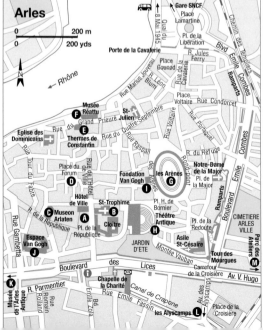

their Latin name, 'cryptoporticus', the three arched underground tunnels, which date from 1BC, supported the forum above. The most impressive building in the square, however, is the **Eglise St-Trophime** Ⓑ (daily 9am–noon, 2–7pm), named after the saint credited with bringing Christianity to Provence. The richly carved doorway is a glorious example of the Provençal Romanesque style. Built between 1152 and 1180, its intricate tympanum shows the Last Judgement overseen by a barefoot and crowned Jesus, while dozens of winged angels soar over the archway. The barrel-vaulted nave is, at over 20 metres (60ft), the highest in Provence. To the left of the entrance, a 4th-century sarcophagus serves as a baptismal font. Further in, the life of the Virgin is depicted on a huge 17th-century Aubusson tapestry.

St-Trophime's 12th- to 14th-century **cloisters** (daily, summer 9am–7pm, winter 10am–5pm; charge), Romanesque on two sides, Gothic on the other two, are a feast of intricately carved capitals, crowded with stylised figures, some depicting biblical scenes, others the life of St Trophime. The rooms above are the setting of the annual Salon des Santonniers (mid-Nov–mid-Jan), a display of traditional and contemporary nativity-scene figurines (*santons*) typical to Provence. Take a look too at the courtyard of the adjacent **Palais de l'Evêché** (bishop's palace), now part of the university, which is used for exhibitions during the Rencontres event.

Museon Arlaten

A couple of blocks down rue de la République, the **Museon Arlaten** Ⓒ (closed for renovation until 2016; www.museonarlaten.fr) occupies an imposing Renaissance mansion built over Roman remains, some of which jut up in the courtyard. Regional poet Frédéric Mistral founded this ethnographic museum and funded it with the money he was awarded when he won the Nobel Prize for literature in 1904, with the proviso that it be dedicated to all things Provençal.

The *museon* is not the only mark left on the city by the poet. A formidable **bust of Mistral** looks down over the **place du Forum** Ⓓ, once the

Traditional Arlésienne dress is still worn for local festivals and for the féria, when Arlésiennes parade around the arena prior to the bullfighting. There is even a Fête du Costume on the first Sunday in July.

BELOW: old town, Arles.

Bullfights of various types are still held in the Arènes, as are concerts and other shows. The first of May welcomes the Fête des Gardians, when cowboys from the Camargue gather for an extravaganza. More annual bullfights take place during the Féria de Pâques at Easter and the Prémices du Riz in September.

commercial heart of the Roman city. A couple of columns from an ancient temple can be spotted in the façade of the Grand Hôtel Nord-Pinus. Much of Arles' nightlife is concentrated on this lively square. Several cafés, including the Café de la Nuit, done up in homage to Van Gogh's painting, make it a great place to enjoy a drink or a laid-back meal. Bullfighting aficionados frequent Le Tambourin, whose walls are lined with autographed photos of local champions.

Towards the river

If you continue towards the river, you will come to the **Thermes de Constantin** ❸ (rue Dominique Maisto; daily, times vary; charge). These 4th-century baths were once the largest in Provence, but not much remains. The **Musée Réattu** ❺ (10 rue du Grand Prieuré; www.museereattu.arles.fr; May–Oct Tue–Sun 11am–7pm; charge) across the street is far more interesting. Many of the rooms are devoted to historical paintings by Jacques Réattu (a local artist who bought the former priory in 1790) and his collection of 17th-century paintings. Much more

worthwhile, however, are the collections of modern sculpture – including works by Zadkine, Richier and Toni Grand – photography, and the Picasso Donation, a collection of 57 Picasso sketches and two paintings.

The Arènes and Roman Arles

At the very heart of the old city, the **Arènes** ❼ (rond-point des Arènes; daily, May–Sept 9am–7pm, Mar–Apr and Oct until 6pm, Nov–Feb until 5pm; charge) is another place to chase Roman ghosts. It is now used for bullfights and concerts, though on summer afternoons they also put on gladiator shows. This vast amphitheatre measures an impressive 136 by 107 metres (440 by 345ft) and holds more than 20,000 spectators. Built in the 1st century AD, it is larger and older than its counterpart in Nîmes. A climb up one of the remaining medieval towers offers a view over the red-roofed expanse of the old city, its modern environs, the Rhône and the Alpilles hills beyond.

Follow the Arènes round and you'll come across another trace of ancient Arles, the neighbouring **Théâtre Antique** ❽ (rue de la Calade; same times as Arènes; charge). By day, this 1st-century BC theatre equates to little more than a few piles of rubble, worn stone seating and two half-standing columns, but it makes a romantic setting for summer evening concerts.

Van Gogh in Arles

Visitors who come to Arles with the intention of making a pilgrimage to Van Gogh's old haunts may be disappointed. The Maison Jaune, where he and Gauguin lived, worked and argued no longer stands, and the Café de la Nuit on place du Forum is a reconstruction. However, you can visit the **Fondation Van Gogh** ❾ (35 rue du Docteur Fanton; www.fondation-vincentvangogh-arles.org; closed for

BELOW: bullfighters waiting to enter the arena.

renovation until 2014), which has a collection of works by contemporary artists in tribute to Van Gogh.

The **Espace Van Gogh** ● (place du Docteur Félix Rey) is the courtyard of the 16th-century hospital building where Van Gogh was treated by Docteur Félix Rey, and which featured in several of his paintings. It incorporates a bookshop, café, library and temporary exhibition space.

Museum of Roman Arles

Once you've seen the monuments, you can learn about the former splendour of Roman Arles at the **Musée départemental Arles antique** ● (avenue de la Première Division Française Libre; www.arles-antique.cg13.fr; Wed–Mon 10am–6pm; charge), outside the old town. Inside the striking blue triangular building, designed by Henri Ciriani, models of Roman Arles complement ancient statues, jewellery and richly carved marble sarcophagi. Among highlights are a bust of Julius Caesar and statue of Neptune discovered in the bed of the Rhône. Outside is the partially excavated **Circus**, used by

the Romans for chariot-racing; the site has now been transformed into an attractive public garden.

Also outside the centre, **Les Alyscamps** ● (avenue des Alyscamps; daily, May–Sept 9am–7pm, winter times vary; charge), an atmospheric ancient necropolis, still looks very much as it did when Van Gogh painted it in October 1888. The cemetery was begun by the Romans, but by the 4th century had been taken over by Gallic Christians. As you walk down the lane, lined with stone sarcophagi, look for the plaque that reads: 'Van Gogh. Here, struck by the beauty of the site, he came to set up his easel.' There is a solemn tranquillity under the poplars that makes it a favourite place for afternoon walks.

Just north of here, or an easy walk from the town centre along avenue Victor Hugo, is the **Parc des Ateliers** ●. The huge complex of abandoned SNCF railway repair sheds, some still with trade union graffiti on the wall and rails running across the floor, is now one of the main venues of the Rencontres d'Arles *(see below)* and an interesting testimony to the city's

Four separate colour-coded walks around Arles allow you to discover different aspects of the town's heritage: blue for ancient Arles, green for medieval Arles, red for Renaissance and classical Arles, and yellow for Van Gogh. Pick up a brochure at the tourist office.

BELOW: the Espace Van Gogh.

The Rencontres d'Arles festival was founded by Arles-based photographer Lucien Clergue. Although these days he is best known for his nudes, Clergue made his name by photographing Pablo Picasso, whom he met at a bullfight. He documented their relationship in a book, Picasso, mon ami *(Editions Plume, 1993.)*

industrial past. In future the site will also contain the Fondation Luna, designed by Frank Gehry, housing studios, gallery and research facilities intended to turn the town into a year-round centre for photography.

The annual summer **Rencontres d'Arles – Photographie** (www.rencontres-arles.com) brings together photographers from around the world for a panorama of exhibitions. Many take place in the historic monuments, chapels, deconsecrated churches and museums of old Arles. While the sixty or so exhibitions last until mid-September, the opening week in early July lives up to the festival's name (encounters) with a packed programme of debates, lectures, workshops and presentations, and parties with DJs and VJs. Most of the event is devoted to art and documentary photography but the 'Nuit de l'Année' (Night of the Year) pays tribute to photo-journalism.

Abbaye de Montmajour

Just 5km (3 miles) northeast of Arles, the **Abbaye de Montmajour ②** (route de Fontvieille; www.monuments-

nationaux.fr; Apr–June daily 9am–6pm, July–Sept daily 10am–6.30pm, Oct–Mar Tue–Sun 10am–5pm; charge) was founded in the 10th century by Benedictine monks who turned the island refuge, surrounded by marshland, into an oasis, by draining the swamp and building an abbey. By the Middle Ages it became rich with the thousands of pilgrims who flocked here to buy pardons. However, the abbey fell on hard times in the 18th century, when the head abbot, Cardinal de Rohan, became embroiled in a scandal involving Marie Antoinette. In the 1790s, the property was bought and stripped by antique dealers. Restoration didn't begin until 1872. The enormous 12th-century **Eglise de Notre-Dame** is a Romanesque masterpiece. The central crypt forms a perfect circle, and the restored cloister has some remarkable capitals carved with beasts, plants and little figures. For stunning views, climb to the top of the 14th-century tower.

The Camargue

Arles is the gateway to the Camargue, a mysterious, flat wild area of lagoons

BELOW: the flat plains of the Camargue.

and marshes, rice fields and salt flats, cowboys riding white horses, herds of black bulls and thousands of flamingos that turn the waters pink in summer. Bordered to the west by the Petit-Rhône, which flows to the sea past Stes-Maries-de-la-Mer, and to the east by the Grand-Rhône, which runs down from Arles to Port St-Louis, the marshlands of the Rhône delta form an unusual natural environment that has helped shape the Camargue's unique history. The setting for one of France's greatest wildlife reserves also provides a spiritual home for the country's gypsies, stages a national windsurfing championship, and offers a range of historic towns and churches to visit as well as the joys of riding across beaches and salt plains.

The celebrated horizons that inspired the poet Frédéric Mistral and the light that fascinated Van Gogh have also encouraged an onslaught of tourism resulting in pseudo-rustic hotels, brash campsites, and piles of debris generated by holidaymakers. In places you'll have to get around by boat, in a 4WD, on horseback or by bicycle. Some areas are best discovered on foot. Even if you spend only a few days in the region, visits to two or three well-chosen spots can reveal an amazingly rich variety of wildlife.

The white horses of the Camargue, like white horses everywhere, are not born white. They are born dark brown or black and change colour as they become older.

Getting to know the area

For a good introduction to the area, take the D570 southwest from Arles to the **Musée de la Camargue** ❸ (Mas du Pont de Rousty; tel: 04 90 97 10 82; Wed–Mon, Apr–Sept 9am–12.30pm, 1–6pm, Oct–Mar until 5pm; charge). This sheep farm-cum-regional museum contains an exhibition illustrating the history, agriculture and traditional way of life of the Camargue and its different natural habitats.

A signposted footpath to the rear leads to the beginning of the marshes. The walk will take you about an hour and give you a feel for these strange flatlands and the chance to see a wide variety of birds: the black-winged stilts with their long pink legs, herons, and all sorts of wading birds. Spring is the ideal season for bird-watching, as this is when the migrat-

BELOW: *gardian* rounding up bulls.

Cowboy Country

The Camargue cowboys *(gardians)* cling passionately to their traditional way of life, herding the small black bulls destined for the arenas of Nîmes or Arles, and riding their beautiful white horses in costume – black hat, moleskin trousers, high leather boots and shirts in Provençal fabric. Many still live on *manades* (bull-breeding ranches) in the Camargue, in traditional white cabins with reed-thatched roofs and rounded north ends as protection against the blasts of the mistral wind. If you enquire about the *manades* that offer horse-riding or demonstrations, you will be able to see *gardians* at work. They can also be seen before the bullfights and *féria* in Arles and Nîmes.

TIP

Because of the lay of the land, exploration of the Camargue inevitably entails a certain amount of zigzagging, so it's worth considering basing yourself at its edge, in or near Arles, and making a series of day trips. Bear in mind it is not always possible to wander off the main track without a permit. If you hate crowds, avoid July and August, when the mosquitoes are also out in force.

ing birds visit the Camargue on their journey back north.

Once you've left Mas du Pont de Rousty, continue along the D570 through paddy and wheat fields, towards the Camargue's main town, Les Stes-Maries-de-la-Mer. En route, you'll pass numerous advertisements for roadside ranches which run half- or full-day pony-trekking and trips into the marshes. Just before Stes-Maries, the information centre at **Ginès ❹** has an exhibition about the indigenous flora and fauna. Next door is the **Parc Ornithologique de Pont de Gau** (tel: 04 90 97 82 62; daily, Apr–Sept 9am–7pm, Oct–Mar 10am–5pm; charge), where you can see regional bird species in aviaries and follow birdwatching trails.

Stes-Maries-de-la-Mer

Situated at the southern tip of the Camargue, **Stes-Maries-de-la-Mer ❺** resembles a mirage after the flat landscape. The flourishing resort owes its name to a group of travellers that landed on this shore. According to legend, these early Christians had set out to sea from Palestine around AD 40 in a small boat without sails. They were miraculously washed ashore, safe and sound, at this spot. Among the saintly company were Mary Jacoby (sister of the Virgin Mary), Mary Magdalene, Mary Salome (mother of Apostles John and James), Martha and the miraculously resurrected Lazarus, along with their Egyptian servant Sarah. After their deaths, the two Marys who had stayed in the Camargue gained a cult following among newly Christianised gypsies and nomads. The town has been a place of pilgrimage ever since.

In the 9th century, the **Eglise de Notre-Dame-de-la-Mer** replaced the simple chapel that existed on the site and was fortified against invading Saracens. Excavations beneath this structure, begun in 1448 at the behest of Good King René, led to the

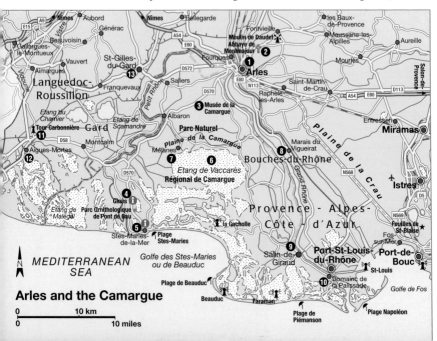

Arles and the Camargue

0   10 km
0   10 miles

discovery of a well and a spring filled with 'the fragrances of sweet-scented bodies'. The remains of the saints were uncovered in this same spot and their tomb was placed in the church's Chapelle de St-Michel. The stones on which the bodies had rested are kept below in the crypt and have become 'miracle' stones, said to have the power to cure infertility and heal sore eyes. Climb to the roof of the church for stunning panoramic views across the sand dunes to the sea.

Stes-Maries-de-la-Mer is a thriving summer resort, with numerous inexpensive hotels and campsites, and places where you can rent horses and boats, swim or play tennis. The little **Musée Baroncelli** (currently closed to the public) contains material on bullfighting and Camargue traditions donated by Marquis Folco de Baroncelli-Javon, aristocratic champion of the *gardians*.

The beaches close to town can get very busy. Frédéric Mistral, who set the tragic end of his famous work *Mireille* (*Mireio* in Provençal) on these sandy shores, would no longer be able to write of it 'no trees, no shade and not a soul'. There are some quieter beaches west of Les Stes-Maries-de-la-Mer if you brave the weathered tracks off the main road to reach them. Or you can escape the bustle with a boat trip along the Petit-Rhône. Excursions leave at regular intervals from the port and offer the opportunity to get close to Camargue wildlife.

Marshes and lagoons

If you turn off the D570 at Albaron, eastwards onto the D37 and then the D36, you skirt around the **Etang de Vaccarès ❻**, a huge brackish lagoon, and head into the regional park. Travelling in this direction offers excellent sightings of flamingos and other waterfowl, even from a car. On foot, a sharp eye should be able to spot beavers, turtles or lime-green tree frogs. Remember that the lagoon is a protected area. Hunting, fishing and the picking of plants and flowers are prohibited.

The black bulls of the Camargue also roam here, and sometimes you will see a *gardian* astride his white horse. Twilight is particularly lovely here, when the setting sun casts its colours over the lagoon. To get a closer

In May, gypsies flock to Stes-Maries-de-la-Mer to celebrate the cult of Sarah (see page 148), on 24th and 25th, and on the last Sunday of October, the feast day for Mary Salome is commemorated by colourful processions around the church (above).

BELOW: flamingos on the marshland bordering Stes-Marie-de-la-Mer.

KIDS

The Marais de Vigueirat is particularly geared to kids, with a footpath on duckboards (pushchair-accessible) through the marsh via a series of log cabins with interactive displays.

look at the famous white horses of the Camargue, you may want to check in at one of the Camargue's 'ranches', where the *gardians* take you out on horseback for a tour of the marshes. The *mas* belonging to Paul Ricard (of pastis fame) at **Méjanes** ❼, (tel: 04 90 97 10 10) is particularly popular. Around the fortified medieval buildings of a Templar *commanderie*, you will find an efficient pony-trekking centre, and some particularly knowledgeable *gardians* willing to show off their skills, such as calf-branding. The estate can also be explored on foot, by bike and aboard a little train.

Two further areas of protected marshland, managed by the Conservatoire du Littoral (the French coastal conservation trust) are open to the public, with footpaths and observation posts. The **Marais du Vigueirat** ❽ (www.marais-vigueirat. reserves-naturelles.org; tel: 04 90 98 70 91; office and shop open daily, Apr–Sept 9.30am–5.30pm, Oct–Mar 10am–5pm, footpaths accessible sunrise–sunset) at Mas Thibert sits at the junction of two remarkable eco-

systems: the marshy Rhône delta and the Crau plain; it receives numerous bird species, including storks, egrets and nine types of heron. Access is free, but ring ahead if you want to join one of the guided walks, visit in a horse-drawn cart or fish for crayfish. Located on the eastern bank of the Grand-Rhône, it is most easily reached by the D35 from Arles, although you can cross the river by the Bac de Barcarin *(see tip, page 151)* at Salin-de-Giraud.

Around Salin-de-Giraud

Southeast of the Etang de Vaccarès along the D36, the landscape changes to one of powdery white hills and salt pans. This corner of the Camargue, around **Salin-de-Giraud** ❾, a town of red-brick workers' housing, is the French capital for salt production. Over half of the country's supply comes from here, providing both table salt and road salt in winter. From March to October you can visit the salt flats by tourist train, the last stop being the **Ecomusée du Sel** (tel: 04 42 86 70 20; daily, July–Aug 9.30am–12.30pm, 2–7pm, Mar–June and Sept–Oct

BELOW: Aigues-Mortes.

10.15am–12.15pm, 2–6pm; museum free, charge for tours by train).

On the edge of the salt flats, southeast of Salin-de-Giraud along the D36D, the **Domaine de la Palissade** ⑩, (tel: 04 42 86 81 28; daily 9am–5pm) is rare in that it subsists in its quasi-natural state. Continually affected by the tides, it has never been controlled by the dykes that separate the Rhône from the sea nor cultivated for agriculture. Again, several footpaths and bridleways have been created, and the reed beds and remains of dunes that trace the former coastline provide a habitat for rare plants, eels, herons and egrets.

This area is also the gateway to the Camargue's dune-backed beaches: the **Plage de Piémanson** is a well-known 'clothing optional' beach, drawing an anarchic community of tents, caravans and cabanons each summer, and the even wilder, remote white sands of the **Plage de Beauduc**.

The western Camargue and Aigues-Mortes

West of the Petit-Rhône, the D58 takes you across the plain of Aigues-Mortes, a part of the Camargue that has hardly changed in decades. Every so often an authentic *cabane de gardian* comes into view – a single-storey whitewashed cabin with a thatched, mistral-defying roof. At the end of the D58, the **Tour Carbonnière** ⑪ offers a splendid view to the foothills of the Cévennes in the northwest, the Petite Camargue in the east and across the salt flats of Aigues-Mortes to the south. Built as a watchtower for the garrison of Aigues-Mortes during the Crusades, the tower was long a tollhouse guarding what was the only route in and out of town.

Aigues-Mortes ⑫ itself was built in the middle of the marsh in 1241 by King Louis IX (St Louis), who wanted a port on the Mediterranean from which to launch the Seventh Crusade in 1248. Laid out on a square grid plan, the new town was named for its location (Aigues-Mortes means 'dead waters') as it contrasted with the town of Aigues-Vives ('living waters') in the hills about 20km (12 miles) further north. Aigues-Mortes flourished under its royal patronage, but the incorporation of Marseille

TIP

All year round, a system of *bacs* (miniature ferries) carries both vehicles and horses across the Rhône. The Bac de Barcarin crosses the Grand Rhône between Salin-de-Giraud and Port St-Louis-du-Rhône; the Bac du Sauvage crosses the Petit-Rhône near Stes-Maries-de-la-Mer.

BELOW: practising for the *course camarguaise*.

Course Camarguaise

The *course camarguaise*, in which the bull is chased but not killed, is the style of bullfighting practised in towns and villages all over the Camargue and the nearby Crau and Alpilles. It is more light-hearted than Spanish-style bullfighting (although you will also find the latter at the big *férias* in Arles and Nîmes). The *course* began as a game with lions, dogs, bears and men chasing bulls. Now the real competition is between the *manades* (bull-breeders), who raise the bulls, and the *raseteurs*, who take the animals on. In Arles, the fighting season starts with the April *féria*, when the Queen of Arles is crowned. It ends at the beginning of July with the awarding of the *Cocarde d'Or*.

Plage d'Arles, one of the Camargue's beaches, leads into Plage de Piémanson, the nudist beach along the same stretch of coast.

and Provence into the French kingdom and the recession of the sea meant it didn't last long as a major port – although it is still connected to the sea by a canal that leads to the fishing village and beach resort of le Grau-du-Roi.

Today Aigues-Mortes is still contained within its remarkably intact city wall, punctuated by 20 defensive towers. Once you've passed through the gateway, narrow streets crisscross the town. They lead to place St-Louis, the main square, lined with cafés and restaurants – although you will get a better meal by wandering down the more secluded side streets in search of little restaurants serving local specialities, such as *gardiane de taureau* (a delicious bull-meat stew with olives) or seafood.

Dominating the town is the circular **Tour de Constance** (www.monuments-nationaux.fr; daily, May–Aug 10am–7pm, Sept–Apr 10am–5.30pm; charge). The defensive keep, built by Louis IX, served as both watchtower and lighthouse. It looks over the Renaissance Logis du Gouverneur, which replaced the royal palace

BELOW:
course camarguaise in Aigues-Mortes.

burnt down in the 15th century. Later, the tower became an infamous prison where Protestant women were held during the 16th-century Wars of Religion. Visiting the tower also gives you access to the walk along the ramparts.

Aigues-Mortes is still a centre for salt production, vine-growing and the cultivation of asparagus and carrots. In summer, the **Salins du Midi** (route du Grau du Roi; www.salins.com; daily July–Aug 10am–6.15pm, mid-Apr–June and Sept 10.30am–5.30pm, Mar–mid-Apr and Oct tours at 10.30am, 2pm and 4pm; charge) organises tours in a little train around the crystallisation tables and evaporation basins, as well as longer expeditions in 4WD vehicles through the salt marsh.

Back inland towards Arles, **St-Gilles-du-Gard ⓮**, a busy little agricultural town hemmed in by canals, is also worth visiting, chiefly for the carvings on the western front of the town's 12th-century abbey church – a masterpiece of Provençal Romanesque architecture with a fine stone spiral staircase. ❏

RESTAURANTS

Restaurants

Prices for a three-course meal without wine:
€ = under €25
€€ = €25–40
€€€ = €40–60
€€€€ = over €60

Arles

L'Atelier de Jean-Luc Rabanel

7 rue des Carmes
www.rabanel.com
Tel: 04 90 91 07 69. Open L & D Wed–Sun. **€€€€**
Innovative chef Jean-Luc Rabanel's elegant restaurant serves the most inventive food in town, designed like artworks in what Rabanel calls his 'gallery of culinary expression'. He has also opened the simpler Bistro A Côté, which reinterprets traditional dishes, and a cookery school.

La Caravelle

1 place Constantin
www.la-caravelle.net
Tel: 04 90 96 39 09. Open L & D Wed–Mon. **€– €€**
Expect cosmopolitan dishes and a trendy young crowd at this restaurant and cocktail bar opposite the Thermes de Constantin. The produce, dishes and wine are mainly local.

L'Entrevue

23 quai Max Dormoy
Tel: 04 90 93 37 28. Open L & D daily. **€**
More than decent Moroccan restaurant near the Rhône with a shady outside terrace. Feast on lamb or chicken tagine, then finish the meal with a fresh mint tea and exotic pastry.

Stes-Maries-de-la-Mer

Casa Romana

6 rue Joseph Roumanille
Tel: 04 90 97 83 33. Open L Wed–Sun & D Tue–Sun. **€–€€**
Well-prepared Camargue cuisine in a renovated village house; the tender bull steak is always a winner. There's a street-side terrace for eating out on warm days. Booking advised, particularly during peak holiday times.

Hostellerie du Pont de Gau

route d'Arles
www.pontdegau.camargue.fr
Tel: 04 90 97 81 53. Open L and D daily (closed Wed in winter). Closed Jan–mid-Feb. **€€–€€€**
Right next to the bird reserve is this serious restaurant, serving expertly prepared classic and regional dishes. Expect the menu to feature foie gras, eel stew, local bull's meat and hare, plus wild boar and other seasonal game.

Etang de Vaccarès

La Chassagnette

route du Sambuc
www.chassagnette.fr
Tel: 04 90 97 26 96. Open L & D Thur–Mon (daily in July & Aug). **€€€€**
This spacious, stylishly converted barn southeast of Arles on the D36 to Salin-de-Giraud serves creative cuisine from Ducasse-trained young chef Armand Arnal. The dishes are inspired by the organic produce from the restaurant's own kitchen garden, along with local fish and meat from the Camargue.

Le Mazet du Vaccarès

Domaine de Méjanes
Tel: 04 90 97 10 79.
Open L Fri–Sun & D Fri–Sat. **€€**
Fresh seafood is the speciality in this rustic restaurant in a wonderful location next to the Etang de Vaccarès. Try *tellines* (the local shellfish) in lemon cream; they're fished by the owner's son. Booking advised.

Aigues-Mortes

Restaurant Marie-Rose

13 rue Pasteur
Tel: 04 66 53 79 84. Open D daily. **€€**
A lively restaurant in an old presbytery, with dishes such as rabbit with *tapenade* or little fillets of sole with *pistou*, to be accompanied by local *gris de gris* wine.

RIGHT: cafés line the place du Forum in Arles.

FESTIVALS

Merrymaking activities take place across Provence all year round. Everything is celebrated, from saints and cowboys to lavender and lemons

Though religious observance has declined, the Christian history of Provence still influences the *fêtes* that are part of the cultural life of every village. Christian tradition is particularly obvious in the *fêtes* on Christmas Eve, when the Nativity is enacted by members of the village (one of the best-

known of these is in the village of Séguret in the Vaucluse) or in the Christmas feast which ends in 13 symbolic desserts. In many cases, though, the Christian foundations of a festival have been forgotten or overlayed with new meaning, and the *fête* has become a popular celebration. The rowdy Bravades of 16 May in St-Tropez, originally to commemorate its martyred patron saint, is one example; another is the gypsy *fête et pèlerinage* to Stes-Maries-de-la-Mer. The 700-year-old pilgrimage to the town where the Boat of Bethany (carrying Mary Magdalene) landed is now famous for its energetic two-day festival *(see right).*

Summer arts festivals abound: Avignon is known for its theatre festival, Aix-en-Provence for its prestigious opera festivals and La Roque d'Antheron and Menton for classical music. Jazz festivals are held in Nice, Ramatuelle and Juan-les-Pins, dance at Vaison-la-Romaine, and world music in Vence.

ABOVE LEFT: people on floats throw flowers into the crowds, Nice carnival. **ABOVE RIGHT:** Tarascon's dragoness La Tarasque, c.1910.

ABOVE: Châteaurenard's Fête des Charrettes Ramées in July is a horse-and-cart parade, part of the festival of St Eloi, patron saint of farriers.

LEFT: Maceo Parker performs during Jazz à Juan in Juan-les-Pins.

ABOVE: Roma in the Saint Sarah (patron saint of the gypsies) pilgrimage to Stes-Maries-de-la-Mer, where a two-day festival is held.

ABOVE: Transhumance festival.

RIGHT: Menton's three-week Fête du Citron in February celebrates the area's main crop with lemon-decorated floats.

FOOD AND WINE

Countless festivals across the region celebrate the richness and variety of Provençal produce: truffles, rice, mushrooms, olives, chestnuts, cherries and lemons, not to mention the many Provençal wines. All are fêted with parades, bands, fairs, fireworks and, of course, plenty of eating and drinking. Most of these festivals take place around harvest time. Some of the best:

● *Mid-September: Prémices du Riz, Arles.* Annual rice festival.
● *October: Fête de la Châtaigne, Collobrières.* Celebration of the chestnut harvest. Takes place on the last three Sundays of the month.

● *End October: Rencontres Gourmandes, Vaison-la-Romaine.* Three-day festival of feasting on regional specialities.
● *Mid-November: Fête du Côtes du Rhône Primeur, Avignon.* Celebration of the first wines of the year, with lots of opportunities for tasting.
● *February : Les Oursinades, Carry-le-Rouet.* Tastings of sea urchins and other shellfish that thrive in the shallow waters of la Côte Bleue.
● *December: Fête du Millésime, Bandol.* Lively wine festival. First Sunday of the month.

TOP: L'Isle-sur-la-Sorgue's floating market takes place every August.
ABOVE RIGHT: Truffle Mass Sunday in Richerenches, Vaucluse.

NÎMES AND THE PONT DU GARD

Nîmes•
Nice•
Marseille•

Nîmes is a far-sighted city which combines the ancient with the avant-garde. Alongside the 2,000-year-old amphitheatre stands Norman Foster's Carré d'Art, a steel-and-glass tribute to Roman architectural flair. The nearby Pont du Gard aqueduct is another unmissable marvel on the Roman trail

Main attractions

LES ARÈNES
LA MAISON CARRÉE
LE CARRÉ D'ART
LES HALLES
MUSÉE DU VIEUX NÎMES
JARDIN DE LA FONTAINE
PONT DU GARD

BELOW: the Pont du Gard.

Nîmes may rival Arles as the ancient Rome of France, but far from being a museum city, here ancient monuments – some of the best-preserved in Europe – co-exist with Renaissance lodgings, high-tech architecture and contemporary works of art typical of a modern multicultural city. Its lively streetlife mingles Provençal traditions with a Spanish-tinged love of bullfighting. During *féria* time the whole town resounds with flamenco music and outdoor *bodegas* set up on the boulevards. High unemployment and some dodgy housing estates have given the outskirts a slightly rough reputation, but new biotechnology companies are bringing employment opportunities and sensitive rehabilitation, while ongoing renovation programmes are keeping the old centre alive.

Nîmes' three principal Roman monuments, the Arènes, the Maison Carrée and the Tour Magne, can all be visited using one combined ticket. Visit www.arenes-nimes.com for details.

The Arènes

Originally, Nimes was a Celtic settlement that grew up around the spring Nemausus. It then became a staging post on the road to Spain, and was the first French city to be colonised by the Romans. Almost the first thing you'll see if you arrive by train is the vast elliptical amphitheatre, the **Arènes**  (boulevard des Arènes; daily, July–Aug 9am–8pm, June until 7pm, Apr–May and Sept until 6.30pm, Mar and Oct until 6pm, Nov–Feb 9.30am–5pm, hours vary during *féria* and concerts; charge). It was built between AD 90 and 120, roughly at the same time as the Colosseum in Rome, for gladiatorial combat *(see box on page 160)*. Today the amphitheatre has been restored to something approaching its former glory, and a clever glass-and-steel roof, removable in summer, allows the arena to be used for a variety of activities all year round. Most famous are the bullfights, both the traditional Spanish *corrida* (in which they do kill the bull) and the more light-hearted, Provençal-style *course camarguaise* (in which they don't).

The **Musée des Cultures Taurines**  (6 rue Alexandre Ducros; Tue–Sun 10am–6pm; charge) displays information on all the different kinds of bullfight, and has an eclectic array of posters, costumes and miscellaneous *tauromachie* – bullfighting memorabilia.

The Maison Carrée

Behind the amphitheatre, the heart of old Nîmes lies within the shield-shaped ring, known as the escutcheon, formed by the boulevards Victor Hugo, Gambetta and Amiral Courbet. Nîmes' second-most important Roman sight is the **Maison Carrée**  (daily, July–Aug 10am–8pm, June until 7pm, Apr–May and Sept until 6.30pm, Mar and Oct until 6pm, Nov–Feb 10am–1pm, 2–4.30pm; charge), further up boulevard Victor Hugo on the western side of the old town, just inside the escutcheon.

Known as the 'square house' despite being twice as long as it is wide, the 1st-century BC structure is generally considered to be the best-preserved Roman temple in existence. It is entered up a flight of

The most important of Nîmes' férias is the Féria de la Pentecôte, held on Pentecost weekend in May or June, when bodegas fill the streets, the sangria flows and the whole town is in high festive spirits.

BELOW: the Arènes, in the very heart of Nîmes.

Norman Foster's Carré d'Art complements the form of the Roman temple opposite.

tall steps and surrounded by a set of fluted columns with carved Corinthian capitals.

Its original dedication has long been debated – some say it was dedicated to Juno, others cite Jupiter or Minerva. Like the amphitheatre, it underwent several incarnations, serving as a stable, the town hall and a monastery church temple. Inside, a 3D film presents daily life in ancient Nîmes, medieval Nîmes and during the *féria*.

Statues, mosaics, frescos, tombs and other Roman and Iron Age archaeological finds can be seen at the **Musée d'Archéologie** ❶ (13 boulevard Amiral Courbet; Tue–Sun 10am– 6pm; free), housed in an old Jesuit college.

A superb Roman mosaic, uncovered here in 1883, holds centre stage amid the eclectic painting collection of the **Musée des Beaux-Arts** ❶ (20–22 rue de la Cité Foulc; Tue–Sun 10am–6pm; charge).

The Carré d'Art

Facing the temple is the **Carré d'Art** (place de la Maison Carrée; Tue–Sat 10am–6pm; permanent collection free, charge for exhibitions), a contemporary art museum and public library in a glass-and-steel building designed by the British architect Sir Norman Foster, which brilliantly echoes the form of the ancient temple. The collection focuses on European art since 1960, with particular emphasis on movements such as Arte Povera and New Realism, and work by French and Mediterranean artists. Artists well represented include Martial Raysse, Christian Boltanski and Arman.

This mix of the ancient and the modern is typical of Nîmes. There are commissioned artworks all over the city, notably a Philippe Starck bus stop (Abribus on avenue Carnot) and crocodile fountain by Martial Raysse in the place du Marché.

The origins of denim

From the Maison Carrée, rue du Général Perrier leads to Les Halles, Nîmes' excellent covered market (mornings daily) and La Coupole shopping centre. At the far end of the market, rue Nationale follows the traces of the Via Domitia to **Porte Augustus** on boulevard Gambetta, which was one of the city's original Roman gates. It has two large arches that provided a dual carriageway for chariots, while the two smaller arches took pedestrian traffic. South of the market, explore the old town with its 18th-century facades, Renaissance courtyards and medieval vaults.

On the place aux Herbes, the elegant 17th-century former bishops' palace now houses the **Musée du Vieux Nîmes** (Tue–Sun 10am–6pm; free), which has rooms furnished with regional furniture, pottery and paintings. It also features an interesting display on the famous hard-wearing, blue cotton serge 'de Nîmes' that has since conquered the world under the name of… denim.

The neighbouring **Cathédrale** was severely damaged during the Wars of Religion, particularly violent in this town which was a major centre of Protestantism in the 16th century. The town's Protestant heritage can

EAT

The culinary speciality of Nîmes is *brandade de morue* – dried salt cod soaked in milk and then whipped into a purée with olive oil, served piping hot. The tourist office can supply a list of restaurants where it's served or you can buy a jar to take home: Raymond Geoffroy is the brand to look out for in Les Halles or local supermarkets.

BELOW: the 1st-century BC Maison Carrée.

KIDS

About 20 minutes' drive west of the Pont-du-Gard is the Musée du Bonbon Haribo (Pont des Charettes, Uzès; Aug daily 10am–8pm, July daily 10am–7pm, Sept–June Tue–Sun 10am–1pm, 2–6pm; charge), an interactive museum where kids can learn about sweet making and, of course, taste them.

still be seen in the imposing Grand Temple and Petit Temple in the **Ilot Littré**, the former dyers' district situated near the tourist office.

Jardin de la Fontaine

Just west of the old town, the quai de la Fontaine leads along a canal lined with patrician houses to the lovely **Jardin de la Fontaine** (open daily). The park was laid out in the 18th century with gravel paths, canals, terraces and sculptures and is still a favourite place for the Nîmois to promenade. On one side is the so-called Temple de Diane, the ruins of a mysterious Roman sanctuary. At the top of Mont Cavalier, the **Tour Magne** watchtower (daily, July–Aug 9am–8pm, June until 7pm, Apr–May and Sept until 6.30pm, Mar and Oct 9.30am–1pm, 2–6pm, Nov–Feb until 4.30pm; charge) was built by the Celtic Volques tribe and later enlarged and incorporated within the Roman ramparts.

The Pont du Gard

BELOW RIGHT: walking on the Pont du Gard.

The extraordinary three-storey **Pont du Gard** dates from around AD 50 and stands 27km (17 miles) northeast of Nîmes. A testament to the Romans' engineering prowess, it remains in excellent condition and stood firm against devastating floods in 1988 and 2002, when several nearby bridges collapsed. The structure spans the Gardon valley and was part of an aqueduct built – mostly underground – to bring water along a 50km (31-mile) -long channel to Nîmes when the growing city's water requirements were no longer met by the Nemausus spring. At 360 metres (1,200ft) long and 48 metres (157ft) high, it was the tallest bridge that the Romans ever built. It was declared a Unesco World Heritage Site in 1985.

The aqueduct is at its most stunning early in the morning or at dusk. Car parks (daily 7am–1am; charge) are on both banks. A visitor centre (tel: 04 66 37 50 99; www.pontdugard. fr; daily, July–Aug 9am–8pm, June and Sept until 7pm, Mar–May and Oct until 6pm, Nov–Feb until 5pm; charge), complete with museum, cinema, café and Ludo, an activity centre for 5- to 12-year-olds, is located on the left bank. ❏

The Arena – 2,000 Years of History

Slightly smaller than its counterpart in Arles, the two-tier arcaded oval amphitheatre could originally seat nearly 24,000 spectators, with a complex system of stairways providing access to the tiers of seats and *vomitoria* (exit tunnels). The structure was used for gladiatorial combat, wild-animal shows and the public executions of Christian martyrs, condemned slaves and foreigners, who would be thrown into the arena with wild beasts. It could also be flooded for aquatic events. The seating plan respected the social hierarchy: the lower tiers were reserved for notables, with citizens in the middle and the populace and slaves far up at the top.

Over the centuries, the amphitheatre was subjected to a variety of indignities. Visigoths substantially altered its form for use as a fortress, and it suffered further changes to accommodate a village for 2,000 poor people, with many houses and a chapel added. In the 19th century, when attempts were finally begun to unearth the original structure, it was by then concealed under 8 metres (25ft) of rubble. Now it once again echoes with the sound of thundering hooves when summer bullfights are held.

RESTAURANTS, BARS AND CAFÉS

Restaurants

Prices for a three-course meal without wine. Many restaurants have a less expensive lunch menu:

€ = under €25
€€ = €25–40
€€€ = €40–60
€€€€ = over €60

Aux Plaisirs des Halles
4 rue Littré
Tel: 04 66 36 01 02. L & D Mon, L & D Tue–Sat. **€€–€€€**
An upmarket establishment where chef Sébastien Granier turns out excellent modern Mediterranean fare, with dishes such as scorpion fish with black olives, and meats and fish grilled *a la plancha*.

La Bodéguita
3 boulevard Alphonse Daudete www.royalhotel-nimes.com
Tel: 04 66 58 28 29. Open L & D daily. **€€**
The trendy restaurant of the arty Royal Hôtel serves up grilled fish and Spanish specialities in its restaurant and tasty tapas in the bar by night, accompanied by both Nîmois and Spanish wines. A *féria* hotspot.

Le Chapon Fin
3 rue du Château Fadaise
www.chaponfin-restaurant-nimes.com
Tel: 04 66 67 34 73. Open L & D Mon–Sat. **€€**
This popular, convivial bistro, plastered with Bardot posters, is a Nîmes stalwart. The traditional food includes *brandade de morue*, regional dishes and a smattering of south-western classics, such as *cassoulet*.

Le Ciel de Nîmes
3rd floor, Carré d'Art, 16 place de la Maison Carrée
www.lecieldenimes.fr
Tel: 04 66 36 71 70. Open L Tue–Sun, plus late May–Sept D Fri & Sat. **€–€€**
The café at the top of the Carré d'Art is a stylish relaxed place and has the benefit of an outdoor terrace with a superb view of the Maison Carré. Light dishes are served for lunch, with cakes and desserts all afternoon. In summer it's also open for dinner, with a DJ adding to the loungey atmosphere.

L'Imprévu
6 place d'Assas
Tel: 04 66 38 99 59. Open L & D Thu–Mon. **€–€€**
Formerly of Paul Bocuse in Lyon, 'maître-restaurateur' Laurent Brémond now turns out seasonal, market cuisine in stylish surroundings – there's an interior patio – on the other side of the square from La Bodeguita. The decent wine list includes plenty of labels from the region.

Le Jardin d'Hadrien
11 rue de l'Enclos Rey
www.lejardindhadrien.fr
Tel: 04 66 21 86 65. Open L Fri–Sat, D Mon–Sat. **€€**
This well-reputed restaurant presents a modern take on French cuisine, with dishes like pork tenderloin with caramel sauce served in the spacious beamed dining room. In summer, you can dine outside in the lovely courtyard garden.

Tendances Lisita
2 boulevard des Arènes
www.lelisita.com
Tel: 04 66 67 29 15. Open L & D Tue–Sat (daily in July & Aug) **€€€**
Nîmes' gastronomic destination of choice is a collaboration between young chef Olivier Douet and sommelier Stéphane Debaille. Douet's stylishly presented modern French dishes are colourful works of art based on fresh market produce. Tapas are served in the wine bar on Friday and Saturday evenings.

Bars and Cafés

Place aux Herbes, place du Marché and the western side of place de la Maison Carrée buzz with café life, while the Arènes is ringed by classic brasseries.

RIGHT: café beside the Maison Carrée.

THE GORGES DU VERDON

France's very own Grand Canyon – the deepest gorges in Europe – provides spectacular views of dramatic cliffs and sheer drops to the blue-grey River Verdon below. This is a favourite area for hiking, white-water sports, paragliding and birdwatching

C utting through the limestone, the River Verdon leaves a breathtaking, sweeping gorge in its wake. It flows from its source near the Col d'Allos at 2,200 metres (7,220ft) into the Durance River, 175km (108 miles) further west near Gréoux-les-Bains, marking the boundary between the *départements* of Alpes-de-Haute-Provence to the north and the Var to the south. Despite the rise in tourism, many of the villages here retain a rustic authenticity, and there are opportunities aplenty for walking, rock-climbing and white-water sports.

Grand Canyon du Verdon

The most spectacular section of the gorge is the **Grand Canyon du Verdon ❶**, the area roughly between Aiguines and Rougon. Statistics only hint at the Grand Canyon's magnificence. Around 21km (12.5 miles) in length and up to 700 metres (2,300ft) deep, the vertiginous limestone cliffs were gouged out by the Verdon River when the Mediterranean receded some five million years ago. Cave dwellings, ruined castles and abandoned farms show that the gorges have been inhabited for thousands of years but by the early 20th cen-

tury the canyon was largely deserted. In the late 1940s the construction of the Corniche Sublime provided easy access. Tourism has now moved in wholesale, and the area is best avoided in August, when the roads become clogged with tour buses. Out of season, most of the restaurants and hotels will be closed, but you'll have the views and wildlife pretty much to yourself. Autumn puts on a particularly breathtaking display, when the ochres and russets of nearby trees contrast dramatically

Main attractions

GRAND CANYON DU VERDON
MOUSTIERS-STE-MARIE
CASTELLANE
MUSÉE DE LA PRÉHISTOIRE, QUINSON
GRÉOUX-LES-BAINS

LEFT: Grand Canyon du Verdon.
RIGHT: white-water rafting.

With a wingspan of 2.5–2.8 metres (8–9ft), the griffon vulture is an impressive sight as it glides on the air currents high above the Gorges du Verdon. Easily recognisable by its white ruff and buff plumage with darker wing tips, the bird was once widespread in the mountains of southern France, but had died out. It has now been successfully reintroduced, with the 90 birds released in the Verdon Regional Park between 1999 and 2004 having formed a breeding colony.

with the turquoise waters. Whenever you travel it's worth checking with the tourist board which route they recommend, as the roads on either side of the Canyon are regularly closed for maintenance.

Moustiers-Ste-Marie

First stop on the Canyon trail is **Moustiers-Ste-Marie ❷**, where an astonishing backdrop of craggy cliffs offers a taste of what's to come. Moustiers is an attractive small town perched above a narrow torrent on the sides of a ravine. High up behind the town, the two sides of the ravine seem held together by a massive chain 225 metres (740ft) long from which a man-sized gilded star is suspended. The story goes that it was placed there by a knight fulfilling a religious vow on his return from the Crusades. The star has been replaced on a number of occasions after being blown down during storms, most recently in 1957.

During the 16th century, tanneries, paper mills and potteries flourished here. Moustiers' major claim to fame, however, is its faience *(see box, page 165)*. Established in the late 17th century by Antoine Clérissy, the recipe for the white tin glaze was believed to have come via an Italian monk from Faenza. The village streets are crammed to bursting with shops and studios producing this decorative glazed pottery, though quality is highly variable. The **Musée de la Faïence** (July–Aug daily 10am–12.30pm, 2–7pm, Apr–Oct Wed–Mon until 6pm, Nov–Mar Sat–Sun and school hols 2–5pm, closed Jan; charge), on the ground floor of the Mairie (town hall), has a good collection of historic wares by the Clérissy and Olerys families, on whom Moustiers built its reputation.

It's an energetic walk to the chapel of **Notre-Dame de Beauvoir** high above the village. The approach is from the eastern side of the stream,

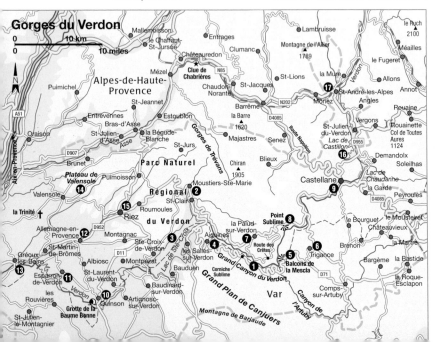

up 365 steps punctuated by a couple of ancient oratories and the 12 Stations of the Cross.

On the other side of the river, crossed by a small bridge, the village church on the main square has a three-storey Romanesque belfry and fine carved choir stalls.

Less than 3km (2 miles) south of Moustiers, a fork in the road offers a choice of two routes along the Grand Canyon du Verdon. Both have their virtues and require at least a half-day trip – the distance may not be long but the roads are narrow and winding.

The Corniche Sublime

Along the southern route, the D957 first skirts the man-made **Lac de Ste-Croix ❸**, an 11km (7-mile) stretch of azure water created in the 1970s by the installation of a hydroelectric dam. It is now a popular spot for hiring pedalos and canoeing and sailing, and has several beaches where you can bathe in summer. The small village of **Les Salles-sur-Verdon** was submerged by the creation of the lake and reconstructed on its eastern edge.

The D19 then dog-legs east via the village of Aiguines, continuing along the D71 to follow the southern ridge of the canyon, known as the **Corniche Sublime**. The village of **Aiguines ❹** itself is a tranquil spot, where houses and narrow *ruelles* cluster around an attractive turreted chateau. There are many opportunities nearby for climbing and rafting.

The Corniche Sublime offers consistently spectacular views, most notably those at the **Balcons de la Mescla ❺**, where the Verdon converges with the smaller canyon formed by the Artuby River. The single-span, concrete **Pont de l'Artuby** (Artuby Bridge) is a favourite spot for bungee jumpers.

East of here you can opt either to quit the Verdon and go south towards Draguignan, or head back towards the Verdon via the village of **Trigance ❻**, which sits under a vast 11th-century fortress, now a romantic hotel.

La Palud-sur-Verdon

Alternatively, the northern route along the Grand Canyon snakes along the old road to Castellane

TIP

If you want to try canyoning, caving, rafting, climbing or kayaking, Des guides pour l'aventure (tel: 0685 944661; www.guidesaventures.com), based in Moustiers-Ste-Marie, offer outings for all levels.

BELOW LEFT: Moustiers-Ste-Marie.

Faïence

Moustiers-Ste-Marie has been a centre of faïence (or tin-glazed earthenware) since the 16th century, when the technique was introduced by an Italian ceramicist. The industry prospered for the next 200 years, counting Madame de Pompadour among its clients. Competition from porcelain and English bone china brought about its decline in the 19th century, and the art was not revived until the mid-1920s.

The finest indigenous clays are formed in moulds or turned on a wheel, biscuit-fired, then covered with a white tin glaze and given a second firing, resulting in a hard opaque finish, before the decoration is painted on using pigments made from various metal oxides. The most characteristic motif of the 'Moustiers style' is inspired by the engravings of Jean Berain, which represent fantastic monsters, donkey musicians, monkeys and plumed birds.

The best-known of all the hiking trails is the Sentier Martel, which descends to the bed of the Grand Canyon between the Chalet de la Maline and the Point Sublime. The 15km (10-mile) trail takes around seven hours and is for experienced walkers only. Invest in a detailed map and check weather conditions before you set off.

BELOW: pedalos on Lac de Ste-Croix.

(the D952). On the plain between the gorges and the Montdenier and Mourre de Chanier ridges, 19km (11 miles) from Moustiers, the village of **La Palud-sur-Verdon** ❼ is a popular stop-off for hikers. It offers a few cafés and a sturdy chateau housing the **Maison des Gorges du Verdon** (tel: 04 92 77 32 02; Wed–Mon, July–Aug 10am–1pm, 4–7pm, mid-Mar–June and Sept–mid-Nov 10am–noon, 4–6pm; charge), which focuses on the natural history, early inhabitants and village life of the region, as well as providing information on walks and nature trails *(see margin, page 167)*.

For the best views of the canyon, continue east out of La Palud on the D952, then turn right on the D23, the scenic **Route des Crêtes**, which brings you back in a clockwise zig-zagging loop, past a series of belvederes, to La Palud. Here you can park your car to admire the views of the gorges below and perhaps spot the impressive griffon vultures that were reintroduced here at the end of the 1990s *(see margin, page 164)*.

Just before you get back to La Palud, the **Chalet de la Maline** (where there's a popular restaurant), marks one of the main routes for serious hikers down to the canyon floor, starting point for the Sentier Martel *(see left)*. Back on the road to Castellane, a footpath off the D23a side road leads to the aptly named **Point Sublime** ❽, a dizzying belvedere 180 metres (600ft) above the river.

Castellane

Visitors to the gorges and traffic taking the north–south route along the Route Napoléon converge at **Castellane** ❾. Another spectacularly situated small town, Castellane, like Moustiers, has its own miracle-rendering Virgin to whom the chapel of **Notre-Dame-du-Roc**, perched on a cliff above the town, is consecrated. Count on a 30-minute walk up to the chapel, past fragments of the old ramparts. The current chapel, filled with ex-votos, dates from the 18th century, but the shrine has been a place of pilgrimage for centuries.

Back down the hill, a fortified gateway-cum-clocktower leads into the attractive pedestrianised old quarter, where the place de l'Eglise is the

scene of the annual *Fête des Fêtardiers*. Held on 31 January, it commemorates the lifting of a Huguenot siege in 1586. Look out for the plaque on 34 rue Nationale which commemorates Napoléon's stop here in 1815 on his return from exile on Elba.

On the main street below the old quarter, arcaded place Marcel-Sauvaire is home to a lively market on Wednesday and Saturday mornings, as well as the **Maison Nature et Patrimoines** (tel: 04 92 83 19 23; www.maison-nature-patrimoines. com; July–Aug daily 10am–1pm, 3–6.30pm, Apr–June and Sept Wed, Sat–Sun same times; charge for museums) which houses the Musée du Moyen Verdon, a small museum of local crafts and traditions, and the curious Musée des Sirènes et Fossiles. Run by the Geological Reserve of Haute-Provence, it is devoted to Sirenians, a group of herbivorous aquatic vertebrates, linked in mythology to mermaids. Ancestors of the sea cow and manatee that lived 40 million years ago in the nearby Vallée des Sirènes, (8km/5 miles northwest of Castellane on the Route Napoléon,

now D4085), some of their fossils can still be seen in situ on a waymarked footpath from the Col de Lèques. Also in the Maison is the Relais du Parc, an information centre; you can find out here about all the different activities on offer.

Quinson and the Basses-Gorges

Southwest of Moustiers the gorges are less dramatic; here you cross a sparsely inhabited landscape where little seems to have changed for centuries. One recent arrival, however, is the brilliantly presented **Musée de la Préhistoire des Gorges du Verdon** (tel 04 92 74 09 59; July–Aug daily 10am–8pm, Apr–June and Sept Wed–Mon until 7pm, Feb–Mar and Oct-mid–Dec Wed–Mon until 6pm; closed mid-Dec–Jan; charge) at **Quinson ⑩**, a spectacular, half-buried elliptical building designed by Sir Norman Foster. A ramp leads you back one million years as you work your way through time, past arrowheads, bones, pottery and other archaeological finds from some 60 sites in the region. About 500 metres

TIP

If the Sentier Martel is too daunting or you are with children, the Maison des Gorges du Verdon at Le Palud-sur-Verdon sells a booklet of short waymarked walks that are easily accessible, such as the Sentiers de la Découverte du Lézard, indicated by a lizard symbol. It also organises guided walks that explore different aspects of the area. www.lapaludsur verdon.com

BELOW: rock-climbing in the gorge.

Next to the village of Esparron-de-Verdon, the small man-made Lac d'Esparron is used for sailing and canoeing.

(550yds) outside the museum, a village has been constructed based on archaeological evidence, with a range of dwellings from different epochs of prehistory.

You might well ask why such an ambitious museum has been created in such a tiny hamlet. The answer lies a little further down the River Verdon, where the cave known as the **Grotte de la Baume Bonne** (guided visits as part of a 3.5-hour walk on Wed and Sat mornings, reserve at the museum) was discovered in 1946. First inhabited 500,000 years ago, bones of bouquetin, horses, bison, marmots and even rhinoceros and lions have been excavated here.

From Quinson a choice of roads crosses the plateau, either rejoining the Verdon at **Esparron-de-Verdon** ⑪, a small village built around a château and next to the pretty **Lac d'Esparron**, or heading north on the D15 to **Allemagne-en-Provence** ⑫. The L-shaped **Château** (tel: 04 92 77 46 78; guided visits July–mid-Sept Tue–Sun, 4pm, 5pm, Easter–June, mid-Sept–Oct Sat–Sun 4pm,

BELOW: view of Valensole across lavender fields.

5pm; charge) reveals both a medieval fortified aspect with its crenellations, and another, Renaissance one. The interior is noted for its fanciful moulded stucco chimneypieces.

Gréoux-les-Bains

Twelve km (8 miles) west of here, **Gréoux-les-Bains** ⑬ has been a spa town since Roman times, later a Templar stronghold. The castle courtyard is used for theatre, concerts and outdoor film screenings in summer, while exhibitions are held in the former guardroom. In the new quarter on the road towards Riez are the baths themselves. The 42°C (108°F) sulphate- and magnesium-rich water still draws plenty of elderly devotees, though a modern establishment built in the 1970s has replaced the baths frequented by Pauline Bonaparte and the king of Spain in the early 1800s. Children might enjoy **Le Petit Monde d'Emilie** (16 avenue des Alpes; mid-Apr–Oct Mon, Wed and Fri 4–7pm; charge), a small museum of period dolls and toys arranged in scenes around the rooms of an old house.

Plateau de Valensole

Sweeping northeast of Gréoux, the flat **Plateau de Valensole** ⑭ is France's leading centre for the production of lavender, but this has not always been the case. The cultivation of lavender is only a 19th-century phenomenon, important to both the fragrance and honey industries (in fact the almond trees that blossom here so spectacularly in early spring are a much more ancient mainstay of the economy). Summer is the time to see the Valensole in all its purple magnificence. On the cusp of July and into August, the dusky violet rows stretch away to the horizon and their intoxicating scent fills the air.

The few villages that huddle on the plain, surviving the winter lashings of wind and hailstorms, are

for the most part unremarkable. The exception is **Riez** ⑮, 15km (10 miles) west of Moustiers on the D952, where four Corinthian columns – remains of a Roman temple of Apollo – standing alone in a field on the edge of town recall its foundation by the Emperor Augustus in the 1st century BC. Gaining enough importance in later years to become a bishopric, Riez's other 'sight' is the **Merovingian baptistery** (enquire at the tourist office about guided visits: tel: 04 92 77 99 09), built in the 5th century reusing masonry from a Roman baths complex. The town has an appealingly scruffy old quarter, reached through two fortified gateways. Several fine houses on Grande Rue, notably the Renaissance Hôtel de Mazan, bear witness to its more illustrious past.

East of Castellane

The Verdon River keeps its luminous colour in the northern reaches. In the Vallée du Haut Verdon (Upper Verdon Valley), the **Lac de Castillon** ⑯ is edged by odd, vertically grooved

rock formations that alternate with white sand spits, providing pleasant spots for swimming in summer.

The D955 follows the lake round to the east. At **St-Julien-du-Verdon**, you can branch off towards **Annot** (*see page 177*), passing through the dramatic Col de Toutes Aures (Pass of All Winds) which lies in the shadow of the 1,878m (6,160ft) -high Pic de Chamatte. This richly forested landscape contrasts sharply with the bleak beauty of the canyon region. Here, shaly, precipitous slopes are cloaked with sweeps of dark evergreens. Minuscule villages, such as **Vergons** and **Rouaine**, consist of little more than a handful of drystone houses.

In a valley of orchards and lavender fields, at the head of the lake, sits **St-André-les-Alpes** ⑰, a haven for windsurfers, hang-gliders and anglers, and a stop on the Train des Pignes line (*see page 286*).

North of St-André, the Verdon valley becomes progressively more Alpine as it ascends towards Colmars and its source in the Sestrière. ❏

Hidden on a garrigue-covered hill southeast of Gréoux-les-Bains, the tiny chapel dedicated to Notre-Dame-des-Oeufs (Our Lady of the Eggs) was long believed to have the power of curing infertility. Women would climb to the church on Easter Monday with an egg in each hand, eating one egg and burying the other. If the buried egg was still intact on a second pilgrimage on 8 September, the woman would be able to have children.

RESTAURANTS

Moustiers-Ste-Marie
La Bastide de Moustiers
chemin de Quinson
www.bastide-moustiers.com
Tel: 04 92 70 47 47. Open L & D Apr–Oct daily, Mar, Nov–Dec Thu–Mon. Closed Jan–Feb. €€€€
The restaurant at Alain Ducasse's lovely country inn serves up refined regional cuisine, chef Christophe Martin drawing inspiration from the Bastide's kitchen garden as well as local lamb and pigeon.

La Palud-sur-Verdon
Bar-Restaurant de la Place
Tel: 04 92 79 91 45. Open L & D daily. €
Bar at the front, simple restaurant at the rear. Expect hearty dishes such as *haricot de mouton* (lamb with beans) or *boudin noir* with mashed potato. Popular with the rock-climbing fraternity.

Castellane
La Main à la Pâte
2 rue de la Fontaine. Tel: 04 92 83 61 16. Open L & D

daily. Closed mid-Dec–mid-Feb. €
Copious salads and pizzas are the speciality at this establishment, which has two cheerful beamed dining rooms and an outdoor terrace.

La Treille Muscate
place de l'Eglise
Tel: 04 92 74 64 31. Open L Fri–Wed D Fri–Tue (July–Aug daily). Closed Dec–Jan. €–€€€
This rustic-chic bistro by the church puts a light touch on Provençal cuisine in tasty dishes such as organic snail stew followed by local goats' cheese.

Quinson
Relais Notre-Dame
Tel: 04 92 74 40 01. Open L & D daily, D only mid-Nov–Mar. Closed mid-Dec–mid-Feb. €–€€€
Duck breast with Valensole lavender honey or roast local lamb are two good reasons to visit this attractive restaurant with a lovely outside terrace.

Prices for a three-course meal without wine. Many restaurants have a less expensive lunch menu:
€ = under €25
€€ = €25–40
€€€ = €40–60

DIGNE AND THE SOUTHERN ALPS

A zone of transition between the Mediterranean and the Alps, north of the Alps, this region shows the wild, rugged face of Provence, where forbidding citadels sit on top of clifftops, and the landscape switches from rolling fields of lavender to rocky Alpine terrain

At the border between Provence and the Alps, north of the Verdon gorges, the Alpes-de-Haute-Provence is a land of beautiful lakes, bizarre rock formations and inaccessible mountainous terrain. Stark citadels crown many towns, and villages are built to give maximum protection against the elements. Like its architecture, the region's cultural heritage is characterised by its simplicity and austerity. In common with the rest of inland Provence, many villages became depopulated over the 20th century as locals moved south to work along the coast. The Route Napoléon N85, supplemented by the A51 motorway between Aix-en-Provence and Gap, makes this area a through-route for summer holiday traffic attempting to avoid the Rhône corridor, bringing additional visitors in the process.

Digne-les-Bains

Digne-les-Bains ❶, last stop on the Train des Pignes *(see page 286)*, is a genteel spa town and administrative centre in the sparsely populated Pré-Alpes de Digne. It was here that Victor Hugo set the first chapters of *Les Misérables*. However, Digne is not simply a town of fictional unfortunates,

rheumatics and departmental officials. The shady boulevard Gassendi tempts with several pleasant cafés, and in August the town hosts the Corso de la Lavande, four days of revelry where flower-decked floats parade through the town.

Architecturally, Digne's greatest attraction is the **Cathédrale de Notre-Dame-du-Bourg** (June–Sept Wed–Mon 3–6pm), north of boulevard Gassendi on the outskirts of town. Built in the Lombardy Romanesque style that continued

Main attractions
MUSÉE GASSENDI, DIGNE-LES-BAINS
CITADELLE, SISTERON
LES ROCHERS DES MÉES
MUSÉE DÉPARTEMENTAL ETHNOLOGIQUE DE HAUTE-PROVENCE, FORCALQUIER
ENTREVAUX
MEXICAN VILLAS, BARCELONNETTE

LEFT: spa-town Digne-les-Bains.
RIGHT: Gorge de Dalius.

Digne and the Southern Alps

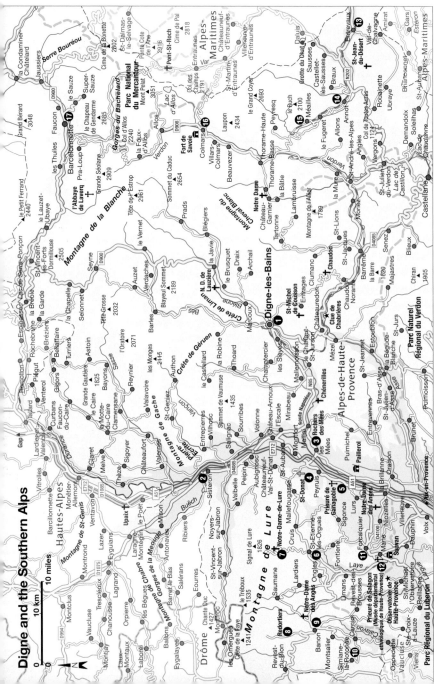

to be employed in Provence long after northern France was well into the Gothic, it has a characteristic 13th-century portal in striking blue-and-white limestone guarded by two stone lions, and remnants of frescos inside. Traces of an earlier 6th-century church were revealed in recent excavations, now visible in an archaeological crypt underneath the church (May–Sept Wed–Mon 10am–noon, 3–6pm; charge). In the later Middle Ages, a second church, **Cathédrale St-Jérôme**, was built in the Gothic style.

Housed in a 16th-century hospice, the **Musée Gassendi** (64 boulevard Gassendi; Wed–Mon, Apr–Sept 11am–7pm, Oct–Mar 1.30–5.30pm; charge) combines fine art and science and, since 2003, has reunited the two in an adventurous contemporary art project with the Réserve Géologique de Haute-Provence. Old master and regional paintings, natural history collections and the scientific instruments of 16th-century Digne-born astronomer, Pierre Gassendi, are displayed alongside works by contemporary artists including

Andy Goldsworthy (*see margin tip, right*), Herman de Vries, Bertrand Plossu and Mark Dion.

Across the River Bléone, by the Pont des Arches, is the **Musée-Promenade** (July–Aug Mon–Fri 9am–1pm, 2–7pm, Sat–Sun 10am–12.30, 1.30–7.30pm, Apr–May and Oct–Nov Mon–Fri 9am–noon, 2–5.30pm, until 4.30pm Fri, June daily and Sept Sun–Fri same times as Apr–May, closed Dec–Mar; charge), part of the **Réserve Géologique de Haute-Provence**. Two footpaths lead from the car park through the Parc St-Benoît, past a waterfall and several outdoor works of art, and on to the museum at the top of the tufa knoll, where aquariums and a collection of fossils and prehistoric skeletons await you. Back near the car park, the **Cairn** is a centre for contemporary art exhibitions.

A particularly astonishing array of fossils can be seen at the **Dalle d'ammonites**, 4km (2.5 miles) north of town on the D900A towards Barles, where over 1,500 giant ammonites protrude out of what was the seabed 200 million years ago.

TIP

Refuges d'Art is a 10-day walking itinerary created by British land artist Andy Goldsworthy, starting at the *River of Earth*, a clay wall inside the Musée Gassendi, and following footpaths in the Réserve Géologique de Haute-Provence surrounding Digne. Goldsworthy has built cairn-like stone sentinels and restored abandoned farm buildings and an old chapel as 'refuges d'art', in some of which walkers can stop for the night. Information and reservations at Musée Gassendi.

BELOW: bright façades in Digne.

Buddhist Retreat

On the outskirts of Digne is the Alexandra David-Néel Foundation (27 avenue Maréchal Juin; www.alexandra-david-neel.org; guided visits daily 10am, 2pm, 3.30pm, closed Mon Oct–June; free). This cultural centre-cum-museum is named after a Parisian adventurer who spent much of her life travelling in remote parts of Asia. Seduced by the beauty of the Alpes-de-Haute-Provence, which she called a 'Himalayas for Lilliputians', she bought a house in Digne in 1927 and named it Samten Dzong (the fortress of meditation). When she died in 1969, aged 101, David-Néel left the house and its contents to the city. The Foundation continues to attract visitors and Buddhist pilgrims.

Sisteron's citadel provides an atmospheric setting for Les Nuits de la Citadelle (www. nuitsdelacitadelle.fr), one of Provence's oldest arts festivals, founded in 1928. Each year from late July to early August it features top names in contemporary dance, theatre and classical music who perform outdoors.

BELOW: Sisteron's fortress rock.

Sisteron

About 40 km (25 miles) further up the Route Napoléon, **Sisteron** ❷ occupies an impressive site on the Durance River, towered over by its imposing stronghold. **La Citadelle** (daily, July–Aug 9am–7.30pm, June and Sept until 7pm, May until 6.30pm, Apr until 6pm, Oct until 5.30pm, Nov 10am–5pm, closed mid-Nov–Mar; charge) was begun in the 13th century, then redesigned by Henri IV's military engineer Jean Erard during the 16th to double as a fortress and prison. Keeps and dungeons, watchtowers, a small chapel and crenellated battlements crowning mighty buttresses rise up on the massive rock that overshadows the town. It's a steep, sticky climb up to the fortress, so take the tourist train that runs from place de l'Eglise.

In 1944 the citadel was bombed by the Allies in an attempt to speed up the retreat of the German occupying army that had taken refuge there. More than 100 people died and the town was badly damaged. Fortunately, a good deal still remains of the **Vieille Ville** (old town), huddled at the foot of the fortress rock, including the large Romanesque Cathédrale Notre-Dame des Pommiers and some fortified medieval towers. Most of the action takes place along rue Saunerie – where Napoleon stopped for lunch at the Auberge du Bras d'Or on 5 March 1815 on his triumphal return from exile in Elba – today busy with bistros and tourist shops. The numerous little streets and stairways running off to the side down to the Durance are known here as *andrónes* – from the Latin for 'alleyway' or the Greek for 'between two houses', depending on whom you ask. At the end of the street place de l'Horloge is home to a busy food market on Wednesday and Saturday mornings; the lamb from this area is protected by an *appellation*.

The Rochers de Mées

As the Durance snakes its way south and meets the Bléone flowing from the east, a sprawling collection of light industrial plants appears. Across the apex of the confluence, south of Château-Arnoux, the village of Les Mées itself does not tempt much, but the staggering '**Pénitents**', or **Roch-**

ers des Mées ❸ do. The curious row of limestone pinnacles, some as high as 100 metres (330ft), rise out of a stunted forest – some alone, some clustered in groups – until they close ranks to form a single mini-massif, standing eerily over miles of fruit orchards and flat maize fields.

On the opposite bank of the Durance, the ruins of the early Romanesque **Eglise de St-Donat** ❹, reached by the narrow D101, sit isolated in oak woods. The retreat of St Donatus, a 6th-century monk, has eight mighty pillars supporting its ancient vaulting. A faded white apse, decorated with pale, terracotta-coloured stars, hints at its former glory.

More obviously impressive is the nearby medieval **Prieuré de Ganagobie** ❺ (Tue–Sun 3–5pm; free), famed for its lively 12th-century mosaics, in red, black and white, depicting knights, dragons and other mythical birds and beasts.

Montagne de Lure

The vast, forbidding **Montagne de Lure** is a continuation of lavender-covered Mont Ventoux to the west,

and is bordered by the Luberon to the south. Its highest point, the **Signal de Lure** (1,826 metres/5,990ft) offers sweeping views as far as the Cévennes and Mont Ventoux. It can be reached from the north by the D946 that winds out of Sisteron, or from the south via the pretty village of **St-Etienne-les-Orgues** ❻. The village's prosperity was traditionally based on its medicinal remedies concocted from mountain herbs.

A road lined with lavender fields leads out of the village. Before long, the lavender gives way to the dense oak-and-fir forest of the mountain. Though seemingly deserted, this route becomes animated in August and September, as locals continue the centuries-old tradition of pilgrimage to the isolated **Chapelle de Notre-Dame-de-Lure** ❼, halfway to the summit. Also founded by the reclusive St Donatus, the chapel has none of the architectural distinction of the Eglise de St-Donat, but its setting is compensation enough.

The wild isolation of the Lure was the inspiration for many of Jean Giono's novels *(see page 100)*. It is

A sad legend is connected to the strange rock formations known as the 'Pénitents'. The story goes that during the Arab invasions in the Middle Ages, a group of monks from the Montagne de Lure were bewitched by the beauty of some Moorish girls, who they were unable to resist. As the cowled, disgraced figures were banished from the village, St Donatus turned them to stone as punishment for their impropriety.

BELOW LEFT: a welcoming mountain bistro.

Bistrots de Pays

Travel anywhere in France and you'll soon discover how vital a role the café plays as a focus of local life, not just as a place to eat and drink but also as a hub of gossip and social life. The Bistrot de Pays movement aims to help keep open or recreate the village café in small rural communities, where many of the shops and bars have closed, both to serve locals and to act as an ambassador for their area to tourists. The cafés and bistros sign a quality charter promising to provide snacks using local produce (many go much further, with full meals and regional specialities), to stay open all year, where possible to provide basic services not found elsewhere in the village, such as selling newspapers, cigarettes, vital groceries, or serving as a bread depot, to provide tourist information and to organise at least three cultural events a year, such as literary dinners, storytelling or musical evenings. First created in the sparsely populated area around Forcalquier and the Montagne de Lure, the concept has spread to remote rural districts in many corners of France, including the Haut-Var and Verdon (www.bistrotdepays.com).

Made from the milk of goats raised on the Montagne de Lure and the Plateau d'Albion, the small, round banon cheese, an ancient cheese dating back to at least the Middle Ages, is instantly recognisable, wrapped as it is in a dry chestnut leaf tied with raffia.

BELOW: Simiane-la-Rotonde.

widely believed that his fictional Aubignane is based on the ruined village of **Redortiers** , just north of **Banon** , worth a visit to sample its renowned goat's cheese, wrapped in chestnut leaves, which is celebrated in the Fête du Fromage each May. The remote village of **Simiane-la-Rotonde** is dominated by a strange 12th-century rotunda, actually the old castle keep. There are some fine period doorways and an old covered market here. Outside the summer months, however, its closed shutters and deserted streets make it a desolate place.

The Pays de Forcalquier

Rather livelier is **Forcalquier** , especially on Monday market day, when countless stalls groaning with local produce crowd the spacious **place du Bourguet** and the streets around it. The counts of Forcalquier once rivalled those of Provence, before the two dynasties were united when the Countess Gersande married Count Alphonse of Provence in 1195.

Forcalquier's main sight is the austere **Ancienne Cathédrale de Notre-Dame**, which has a wide triple nave and impressive organ loft. A wander through the narrow streets of the old town reveals fine stone doorways and arches decorated with chiselled plaques, scrolls and intricate reliefs, and there's a fine Gothic fountain on place St-Michel. Climb rue St-Mary to the grassy castle mound, now topped by a neo-Gothic **chapel** ringed by amusing sculptures of angels playing musical instruments.

South of Forcalquier on the D4100, just past the pretty village of Mane, is the **Musée départemental ethnologique de Haute-Provence** (June–Aug daily 10am–8pm, Feb–Apr daily 10am–6pm, May and Sept daily until 7pm, Oct–Dec and Feb–Mar Wed–Mon until 6pm; closed Jan; charge) housed in the beautiful medieval **Prieuré de Salagon**. The former priory buildings contain an ethnographic collection, including a blacksmith's forge, a tonnelier, a display about beekeeping and photographic archives of rural life in the Luberon; the simple chapel has modern windows by Aurélie Nemours. The most interesting aspect, though, is the series of themed gardens: a garden of medicinal plants used in local remedies, a perfume garden, and a medieval garden based on plants found in medieval manuscripts. This includes a kitchen garden, where the pulses and root vegetables that formed the staple diet in medieval times, before the arrival of tomatoes or aubergines, are a far cry from the typical Provençal cuisine of today. About 10 minutes' drive southwest is pretty St-Michel-l'Observatoire, home of the **Observatoire de Haute Provence** (tel: 04 92 70 65 40; July–Aug Tue–Thu 1.30–5pm, Apr–June and Sept–Oct Wed 2–6pm; charge) astronomical observatory.

Entrevaux

On the eastern fringes of the *département*, the citadels fortified by Louis

XIV's brilliant military architect, Sébastien Le Prestre de Vauban, give an indication of the strategic importance of this region – for a long time this was the border between Provence and what was then the Comté de Nice. The area is most easily reached by car (D6202 and D4202) from Nice or by the Train des Pignes.

The fairy-tale town of **Entrevaux**  is still surrounded by 17th-century ramparts, turrets, drawbridges and a deep moat formed by the Var River. Cars are firmly relegated to the busy Nice road on the opposite bank.

Like the ramparts, the majority of Entrevaux's tall stone houses date from the 17th century, as does the former **cathedral**. Its severe facade conceals a Baroque interior with a richly decorated high altar. The tiny main square, **place St-Martin**, has a pleasant café, a clutch of chestnut trees and a butcher who dispenses the local speciality, *secca de boeuf*, a type of dried salt beef best eaten with olive oil and lemon juice. The **citadel** (open daily 24 hours; take coins for the entrance token or buy tickets at the *bureau d'accueil* by the

drawbridge) bears testimony to the town's key strategic position.

Annot

West of Entrevaux in the Vaire valley – and another stop on the Train des Pignes line – **Annot** ⑭ is typical of this area's dual aspect: the wrought-iron balconies and stone *lavoirs* are typically Provençal, but the majesty of the Alps comes through in the purity of the air and the steely grey streams that tumble through the town. In winter, the town sleeps under a thick blanket of snow. East of the main square, with its fine esplanade of ancient plane trees, the narrow streets of the picturesque old town climb steeply in medieval formation. Vaulted archways and carved stone lintels decorate the tall houses of the Grande Rue. At the top of the old town, the streets converge on a pretty square with the parish church and surrounding houses painted in a rainbow of pastel hues.

Just outside the town to the south, a group of mammoth rocks known as the **Grès d'Annot** dots the hillside as if scattered there by giants. Locals have

Entrevaux's citadel is reached by an ascending path of nine zigzag ramps, a remarkable feat of engineering that took 50 years to complete.

Below: Entrevaux.

*The ski resorts of Pra-
Loup and Super-
Sauze are looking to
the future. As well as
81 ski runs, Pra-Loup
has opened the 'Rider
Space' for snow-
boarding and freestyle
activities, and
provides floodlit night
skiing and the chance
to snowscoot (a type
of snow cycling).
Super-Sauze has 37
ski runs and the
modern 'Snow Park'
aimed at daring
snowboarders with a
love of acrobatics.
www.ubaye.com*

BELOW: Villa Morélia,
Jausiers, a hotel and
prestigious restaurant.

built houses directly beside them,
often using their sheer faces as an
outside wall. To this day, they are the
subject of local legends which tell of
troglodytes and primitive religions.

Those with stamina and sturdy
boots can follow the spectacular hiking trails into the high-altitude **Val
du Coulomp** nearby. Alternatively,
continuing north up the Vaire valley
on the D908 towards Colmars will
bring you to the mountain village
of **Méailles** , before rejoining the
upper Verdon valley.

Colmars-les-Alpes

If Entrevaux seems uniquely
untouched by its proximity to the
Alps, **Colmars-les-Alpes** ⑯, 50km
(31 miles) to the north, could hardly
be more Alpine. Colmars is crowned
by two massive fortresses, and, like
Entrevaux, is a former border post
between Provence and Savoy. Inside
the town ramparts, houses have been
constructed with tidy wooden balconies known as *solerets* (sun traps) and
shop windows display amber bottles
of *génépi* liqueur, made from Alpine
flowers. Of the two castles, only the

17th-century **Fort de Savoie** (tel: 04
92 83 41 92; July–Aug daily 2.30–
7pm, Sept–June visits by appointment; charge) is open to the public.
About 30 minutes' drive northeast
on the D908 then D226 is the Lac
d'Allos, the highest Alpine lake in
Europe; it's then a 30-minute walk
from the car park.

Barcelonnette and the Ubaye Valley

In the northwest corner of the
Alpes-de-Haute-Provence, just north
of the Parc National du Mercantour
(*see page 228*), **Barcelonnette** ⑰
squeezes into the glacial valley of
the Ubaye, surrounded by towering peaks that draw skiers to the
modern resorts of Super-Sauze and
Pra-Loup (*see margin, left*). It owes its
unlikely name to its 12th-century
rulers, the counts of Barcelona. The
Hispanic connection does not end
there. Early in the 19th century, a
period of emigration to Mexico
began, prompted by the success of
three local brothers who opened a
textile shop there. Many followed,
founding textile factories, department stores and banks. Having
made their fortune, some of them
returned to Barcelonnette to build
the incongruous, so-called 'Mexican'
villas for which the town is famous.
Set in large gardens around the edge
of the old town, as well as in the
nearby village of **Jausiers**, they were
shaped by Italian craftsmen or took
the forms of the new Art Nouveau
style from Nancy. At 10 avenue de
la Libération, the handsome 1870s
Villa La Sapinière now contains the
Musée de la Vallée (mid-July–Aug
daily 10am–noon, 2.30–6.30pm, rest
of year Wed–Sat 2.30–6pm; charge),
which traces the history of this emigration in documents and artefacts.

The 'Mexican connection' continues
today with the annual August Fêtes
Latino-Méxicaines, cultural exchanges
and a Mexican restaurant. ❏

RESTAURANTS AND BARS

Restaurants

Prices for a three-course meal without wine. Many restaurants have a less expensive lunch menu:

€ = under €25
€€ = €25–40
€€€ = €40–60
€€€€ = over €60

Digne-les-Bains
Le Grand Paris
19 boulevard Thiers.
www.hotel-grand-paris.com
Tel: 04 92 31 11 15. Open L Fri–Sun, D daily. Closed Dec–Mar. €€–€€€€
Noémie Ricaud has taken over from her father at this long-established restaurant housed in a former monastery. Expect lavish cooking in the classic mould with some modern touches.

Sisteron
Grand Hôtel du Cours
place de l'Eglise.
www.hotel-lecours.com
Tel: 04 92 61 00 50. Open L & D daily. Closed Dec–Feb. €€–€€€
A Sisteron institution for three generations. A lively atmosphere prevails, especially outdoors on the terrace in summer. Herby Sisteron lamb, raised on the pastures of the upper Durance valley, is a speciality, and is served in large portions.

Château-Arnoux
La Bonne Etape
chemin du Lac.
www.bonneetape.com
Tel: 04 92 64 00 09. Open L & D daily (Nov–Apr Wed–Sun). Closed Jan–mid-Feb. €€€€
At this family-run hotel, in a town along the Route Napoléon south of Sisteron, part of the luxury Relais et Châteaux group, chef Jany Gleize combines local lavender and honey with luxury ingredients such as pigeon and lobster. A second, bistro-style restaurant, Au Goût du Jour (14 avenue Général de Gaulle; open daily, €€), serves up more rustic dishes, including *aioli*, pumpkin soup and *pieds et paquets* (sheep's feet and tripe).

Montagne de Lure
Café-Restaurant de la Lavande
place de la Lavande, Lardiers
Tel: 04 92 73 31 52. Open L & D Tue–Sun. Closed for 2 weeks in Nov and 2 weeks in Feb. €€
Prime example of a Bistrot de Pays (see page 175), with its bar, newspapers, literary evenings and menu based on local produce, such as truffles, figs, banon cheese and *petits farcis*

(stuffed vegetables). It also has an excellent wine list, rare for these parts. Book ahead.
Les Vins au Vert
rue Pasteur, Banon
TTel: 04 92 75 23 84. Open L Wed–Sun D Thu–Sat. €
Well-stocked vintner-cum-winebar which offers plates of delicious charcuterie and cheese. They often have theme nights and tastings. Book in advance.

Forcalquier
Le 9
9 avenue Jean-Giono.
Tel: 04 92 75 03 29. Open L & D Thu–Mon. €–€€
Seasonal market cuisine in a restaurant with great views over the citadel; there's an outside ter-race. Choose from a good selection of Provençal meat and fish dishes, and try the goats' cheese with honey for dessert. Book ahead.

Barcelonnette
Villa Morélia
Jausiers.
www.villa-morelia.com
Tel: 04 92 84 67 78. Open D Wed–Sat (daily in July–Aug). Closed Nov–Dec and Apr. €€€
Beautifully presented fresh market cuisine is what's on offer at this upmarket restaurant and hotel, located in one of the famous 'Mexican' villas, with lovely gardens overlooking the Ubaye valley. The menu changes daily.

RIGHT: Mexican flavours come to the Alps.

TOULON AND THE WESTERN VAR

Standing on a superb natural harbour, the vibrant, historic city of Toulon merits a visit. It offers good museums and a great daily market, and ongoing restoration projects are giving run-down quarters a new lease of life

The history of **Toulon ❶** has been determined by its natural deep-water harbour, sitting in the huge bay known as the Rade de Toulon. When Provence became part of France in 1481, Toulon inevitably took on a key role in French naval strategy. It was fortified by Henri IV, Richelieu and Louis XIV's military engineer Vauban, and home to the naval arsenal and convict galleys, but was then virtually destroyed in World War II. The city is still home to France's leading naval base today – a massive town within the town, covering 268 hectares (662 acres) and employing 12,000 people – and home of the aircraft carrier *Charles de Gaulle*, flagship of the French Navy.

Many tourists bypass the city. Its gritty reputation, busy through-roads, seedy alleyways, some disastrous post-war reconstruction and a reputation marred in the 1990s by extreme-right politics offer little obvious entice-ment to the casual visitor. However, along with all the low-life trappings of a major seaport, Toulon has its own share of grand buildings, chic boutiques, lively markets, an all-year cultural scene that ranges from the Belle Epoque opera house to modern Oméga-Zénith concert venue, and a cosmopolitan energy that is matched in Provence only by Marseille.

Much of the town centre has been renovated, as have several once seedy hotels. Part of the motorway has been funnelled underground and a new coast path has been created. Even the naval base is no longer completely off limits to the public: as well as an idea of its scale and glimpses of docked naval vessels from boat trips around the Rade, the small tourist train which leaves from the port now takes visitors inside the base (tel: 06

Main attractions
MARCHÉ PROVENÇAL, COURS
    LAFAYETTE, TOULON
BOAT TRIP ON THE RADE DE
    TOULON
BEACHES AT LE PRADET
MONT FARON, TOULON
TAMARIS
HARBOUR, BANDOL
BASILICA, ST-MAXIMIN-LA-
    SAINTE-BAUME

LEFT: Sanary-sur-Mer's harbour.
RIGHT: along Bandol's waterfront.

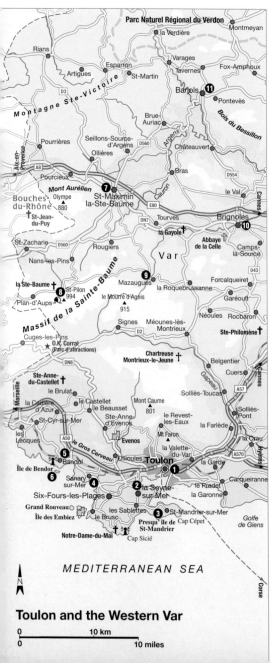

Toulon and the Western Var

0   10 km

0   10 miles

20 77 44 43; June–Sept, bring ID, no photography allowed).

Central Toulon divides broadly into two districts: the Haute Ville, laid out in the late 19th century with expansive Hausmannian squares and avenues, and the Basse Ville, leading towards the port, which incorporates the medieval alleys of the old town.

Haute Ville

Centrepiece of the Haute Ville is the **boulevard de Strasbourg**, which bisects the grid of tall apartment blocks, department stores and imposing administrative buildings that make up 19th-century Toulon. Admire the elaborate **Opéra de Toulon** on place Victor Hugo, with its sculpted façade and splendid gold-and-red interior, still used to stage dance, theatre and opera productions, and spacious **place de la Liberté**, with its palm trees, café terraces, ornate fountain and the sweeping façade of the former **Grand Hôtel**.

The neo-Renaissance **Musée d'Art** (113 boulevard du Maréchal Leclerc; Tue–Sun noon–6pm; free) has paintings by the Provençal school and a collection of contemporary art. Further down the road (at No. 236) a fine 19th-century villa houses the **Hôtel des Arts** (Tue–Sun 10am–6pm, closed between exhibitions; free), which puts on contemporary art exhibitions, often with a Mediterranean emphasis.

Basse Ville

South of the Opéra lies the warren of narrow streets of the Basse Ville (Lower Town). Long insalubrious, it has been going through a major clean up, bringing back attention to its ancient buildings and numerous small squares with fountains. The attractive place Puget, with its pavement cafés, plane trees and a picturesquely overgrown fountain, draws elegant locals. Stalls laden with superb fish, vegetables and flowers under colourful umbrellas characterise the **Marché Provençal** (Tue–Sun mornings) in the cours Lafayette. Here you'll also find the **Musée du Vieux Toulon** (69 cours Lafayette; Mon–Sat 2–5.45pm; free), which evokes Toulon's history. On a nearby side street is Toulon's **Cathédrale Ste-Marie des Seds** (place de la Cathédrale), begun in the 11th century, of which Romanesque sections remain, and expanded in the 17th, when it gained its Baroque facade and the altar sculpted by Pierre Puget's nephew and pupil Christophe Veyrier. At the end of cours Lafeyette nearest the port is the pink Baroque facade of the Eglise St-François-de-Paule, with the tourist office opposite it.

The port

Much of the Basse Ville's bad press comes from the avenue de la République, a grubby roadway lined by a long concrete post-war housing block. Go through one of the archways to quai Cronstadt or quai de la Sinse, however, and the vision changes totally as you find yourself beside Toulon's lively marina and its

quayside cafés and brasseries, such as the ever-fashionable **Grand Café de la Rade**, which are popular with locals for lunch or an early evening aperitif. Spot the doorway from the old town hall bombed in 1944 incorporated into the new town hall annexe, with its two muscular atlantes, sculpted in 1657 by Marseille sculptor Pierre Puget.

Boats leave from here for trips around the port and across the bay to La Seyne-sur-Mer, Tamaris and Les Sablettes, and to the Iles d'Hyères (in high season).

The original gateway to the arsenal, a rare relic of the old port, now forms the entrance to the **Musée de la Marine** (Place Monsenergue; www.musee-marine.fr; July–Aug daily 10am–6pm, Sept–June Wed–Mon same times; charge), housing historic ships' figureheads, model ships and marine paintings.

East of the port, the **Plages de Mourrillon** have a distinctly urban feel, drawing a local city population rather than tourists to their long stretch of sand, restaurants, lawns and playgrounds in the shelter of the

Grand Hôtel on Toulon's spacious place de la Liberté.

BELOW: bird's-eye view of Toulon.

KIDS

A trip to Mont Faron makes a good break from the beaches if you have children, thanks to its ride up in the Téléphrique, zoo and picnic spots at the top.

circular Fort St-Louis, constructed in 1696 at the entrance to the bay to warn of enemy ships. The corniche continues through Toulon's more upmarket suburbs to **Cap Brun**, where a coastal path leads to a series of little creeks, and the tranquil Anse de Méjean with its fishermen's shacks. Further east, Le Pradet has several pretty sandy coves, such as the Plage de la Garonne and Plage des Bonnettes.

Mont Faron

For a terrific bird's-eye view of Toulon, take a ride up to Mont Faron, the white limestone mountain that frames the city. You can reach it by car via a long and winding road, but the best way up is on the **Téléphrique** (tel: 04 94 92 68 25; daily, July–Aug 10am–7-.45pm, May–June and Sept until 7pm, times vary rest of year, closed Dec–Jan; charge), which leaves from the Gare Inférieure on boulevard Amiral-Vence. Views from the cable car as you climb are stunning. At the top, amid a rocky landscape of parasol pines, evergreen oaks and maquis scrub, lie miles of footpaths, picnic areas, children's

BELOW RIGHT: Plages de Mourrillon.

play areas, restaurants and the **Zoo du Mont Faron** (tel: 04 94 88 07 89; daily, July–Aug 10am–7.15pm, May–June and Sept until 6.30pm, Oct–Apr until 5.30pm; charge), which specialises in breeding tigers, panthers, snow leopards and other wild cats.

Not far from the Téléphrique station is the Tour Beaumont, a 19th-century surveillance tower housing the **Mémorial du Débarquement** (tel: 04 94 88 08 09; summer daily 10am–noon, 2–5.30pm, closed Mon in winter; charge), a museum dedicated to the Liberation of Provence in August 1944.

La Seyne-sur-Mer

Rounding the bay west of Toulon, the first impression of **La Seyne-sur-Mer** ❷ is one of industrial dereliction, but this once important shipbuilding town hides some unusual gems. On the seashore, the 17th-century **Fort Balaguier** (924 corniche Bonaparte; Tue–Sun, July–Aug 10am–noon, 3–7pm, Sept–June 10am– noon, 2–6pm; charge) now contains a museum which commemorates Napoleon's capture of Toulon and

The Naval Port

Though the city was a base for the royal navy as early as 1487, Toulon's era of major expansion occured in the 17th century. During the reign of Louis XIV, Toulon became the lynchpin of royal naval strategy against the Anglo-Spanish alliance (Marseille was favoured for commerce). The arsenal was expanded and the city's fortifications enlarged by the king's brilliant military engineer Vauban, who added the *darse neuve* (new dock), new forts and a set of star-shaped ramparts. The port was protected by over 20 new forts and towers, constructed both on the coast and on the surrounding hills.

A century later, the city took the side of the English against the Revolutionary government and was promptly brought to heel by a young Napoleon Bonaparte. The English fleet was defeated in 1793, ensuring that the general's name would never be forgotten. During World War II the French sabotaged their own fleet in 1942 to blockade the harbour and try to prevent the Nazis from taking the city, but in 1944 much of the town was razed by retreating Germans and advancing Allied troops.

also has a display about the notorious penal colony La Bagne.

Up on the Caire hill, the **Fort Napoléon** (Chemin Marc Sangnier; Tue–Sat 2–6pm; free), built by Napoleon after his victory over the English in 1793, is today used for a summer jazz festival and other cultural events. But most fascinating of all here are the remains of **Tamaris**, an early seaside resort built in the 1890s by wealthy sailor and marine adventurer Michel Pacha, who made his fortune as director of lighthouses of the Ottoman Empire. Extravagant villas, hotels and a casino were built, most of them in a neo-Moresque style, as was his own vast château. Tamaris never quite made it big, and by the 1920s it had gone out of fashion. But it was bypassed rather than destroyed, and a number of buildings remain intact, including the classical-style **Villa Tamaris** (avenue de la Grande Maison; Tue–Sun 2–6.30pm; free), now used for contemporary art shows, and the palatial Ottoman-style Institut Michel Pacha, a marine research institute on the sea front.

The **Baie de Lazaret** is used for mussel production, and is filled with mussel beds and picturesque mussel farmers' cabins on stilts (long known as *moules de Toulon*, you'll now find mussels on many menus referred to as *moules de Tamaris*). Sea bream and sea bass are also farmed in the bay.

From Tamaris you can cross a little isthmus to **Presqu'île de St-Mandrier ❸**, which has an attractive fishing port with numerous restaurants, or continue around the Six Fours peninsula to the sandy beaches of **Les Sablettes**, **Mar Vivo** and **Fabregas**.

At Cap Sicié, the southern point of the peninsula, the **Chapelle de Notre-Dame-du-Mai** sits on a high clifftop. The Fôret de Six-Fours is a protected natural habitat with a wide variety of pines, oaks, eucalyptus and aromatic plants. Its beauty is in sharp contrast to the downmarket hotels of sprawling Six-Fours-les-Plages down on the coast, whose beaches are popular with windsurfers.

Sanary and Bandol

Continuing westwards along the coast, the pretty pink-and-white

TIP

A fun way to explore the towns around Toulon – La-Seyne-sur-Mer, Sablettes and St-Mandrier – is to take one of the regular commuter ferries from the port (€2 per journey or €3.90 for a day's unlimited travel).

BELOW: Sanary-sur-Mer.

The vaulted nave in the Eglise Ste-Marie-Madeleine, St-Maximin-la-Ste-Baume.

BELOW: St Maximin-la-Ste-Baume basilica.

resort of **Sanary-sur-Mer** ❹ benefits from a sheltered position supplied by a rocky outcrop known as the Gros Cerveau (big brain). Family-oriented and low key, with its pastel façades, palm trees along the promenade and a handful of wooden fishing boats in the harbour, Sanary has a timeless charm often lacking in more fashionable resorts.

Artists and writers began to flock to Sanary in the early 1930s, inspired by the presence of Aldous Huxley (1894–1963), who wrote *Brave New World* at his villa on Cap de la Gorguette in 1931. They were soon joined by a group of German intellectuals, headed by Nobel Prize-winning writer Thomas Mann (1875– 1955) and his novelist brother Heinrich (1871–1950), who fled here after Hitler's rise to power in 1933.

Screened from the ravages of the mistral by an arc of wooded hills, **Bandol** ❺ has attracted numerous visitors to its sandy coves and pleasant promenades since the arrival of the railway at the beginning of the 20th century. Among its more famous

visitors were the New Zealand author Katherine Mansfield (1888–1923), who wrote *Prelude* in the quayside Villa Pauline in 1916.

Most modern-day visitors come for the town's sandy beaches and lively harbour. Another plus is Bandol's vineyards, spread over 1,000 hectares (2,500 acres) between the Ste-Baume Massif and the coast, around pretty medieval villages such as **La Cadière d'Azur** and fortified **Le Castellet**, which produce wines (particularly reds) that are rated among the best in Provence.

About 2km (1 mile) off the coast of Bandol lies the tiny island of **Bendor** ❻, which was enterprisingly transformed into a holiday village in the 1950s by the pastis magnate Paul Ricard. On the island is a hotel, a clutch of rather expensive cafés, and a re-creation of a Provençal fishing village. Though the island has an air of artificiality, its shady paths, lined with mimosa and eucalyptus, and tiny sandy beach are reason enough for a visit. Boats leave regularly from Bandol harbour for the seven-minute crossing (information from

Bandol tourist office, Allées Vivien, tel: 04 94 29 41 35).

St-Maximin

On the western edge of the Var lies **St-Maximin-la-Ste-Baume ❼**. Pilgrims have poured into this town since the 5th century to view one of the greatest Christian relics – the presumed bones of Mary Magdalene, which were discovered here in an ancient crypt. After the Boat of Bethany *(see page 148)* landed at Stes-Maries-de-la-Mer in the Camargue, its saintly crew dispersed to preach the word of God throughout Provence. Mary Magdalene is said to have made her way to the Massif de la Ste-Baume, where she lived in a cave for more than 30 years. She died in St-Maximin, where her remains were jealously guarded by the Cassianites.

In 1295 work began on the **Eglise Ste-Marie-Madeleine** (Place des Prêcheurs; tel: 04 94 59 84 59), founded by Charles II, king of Sicily and count of Provence, as a suitably magnificent receptacle for the relics. The result is the finest Gothic church in Provence, with its tall vaulted nave, Baroque high altar and elaborately carved walnut choirstalls. The well-preserved abbey buildings adjoining the church have been converted into a charming hotel, with a restaurant in the chapter house and cloister.

The Ste-Baume Massif

To the south of St-Maximin, in the heavily forested limestone mountain range of Ste-Baume, is the evocative, dank cave where Mary Magdalene is said to have spent her last years. From the village of **Nans-les-Pins**, the GR9 long-distance footpath follows the chemin des Rois, the pilgrimage path taken by popes and sovereigns for centuries. Reaching the cave's entrance involves a strenuous climb through towering beech trees and lush undergrowth (around 40 minutes from the Hôtellerie de la Baume,

above the village of **Le Plan d'Aups-Ste-Baume**). Some 150 stone steps lead up to the cliffside cave. Inside, the dark, dripping recess is filled with altars and saintly effigies. A final effort will bring you to **St-Pilon ❽**, which is almost the highest point of the massif. Mary Magdalene was said to have been lifted up to this peak by angels seven times a day during her years of cave-dwelling.

The massif was used for sheep rearing, as well as a number of small industries including charcoal, slake lime and ice production. The main centre of ice production was the village of **Mazaugues ❾** on the eastern side of the massif, which for centuries produced ice for Marseille and Toulon through a complex system of underground freezing reservoirs and ice stores. There's a small museum (Hameau du Château; tel: 04 94 86 39 24; June–Sept Tue–Sun 9am–noon, 2–6pm; charge).

Brignoles and La Provence Verte

East of St-Maximin, **Brignoles ❿**, once a mining centre for bauxite, has

The old quarter of Barjols (see page 188).

BELOW: the Ste-Baume massif.

Held on the weekend nearest to 16 January, Barjols' Fête de St Marcel marks the town's victory over nearby Aups in securing the relics of St Marcel for its chapel. The day the relics arrived, in 1349, coincided with the pagan practice of sacrificing an ox for a village feast. Every four years (next in 2014) an ox, decorated with garlands, is roasted on the place de la Roquière and shared among the revellers.

BELOW: one of Barjols' 28 fountains.

an attractive medieval quarter, containing the former residence of the counts of Provence, now home to the small **Musée du Pays Brignolais** (Apr–Sept Wed–Sat 9am–noon, 2.30–6pm, Sun 9am–noon, 3–6pm, Oct–Mar Wed–Sat 10am–noon, 2.30–5pm, Sun 10am–noon, 3–5pm; charge). It's devoted to local history, with an eclectic collection of paintings, fossils and an early Christian sarcophagus.

Brignoles sits at the heart of what is known as La Provence Verte (Green Provence), because of its verdant landscape watered by several rivers and underground springs. It is a popular area for walking, cycling and canoeing. The green tag has also taken on a double meaning because of the significant amount of organic produce grown in the area.

Twenty km (12 miles) north of Brignoles along the D554 is **Barjols** ⓫, dubbed the 'Tivoli of Provence' – a small industrious town filled with streams, fountains and plane trees. What is reputedly the largest plane tree in France, measuring an impressive 12 metres (40ft) in circumfer-

ence, casts its shadow over the most celebrated of Barjols' 25 fountains, the vast moss-covered 'Champignon' (mushroom) fountain, next to the Hôtel de Ville in the tiny place Capitaine Vincens.

Though the Tivoli tag attracts a good number of summer visitors, Barjols is more a workaday town than a tourist trap. Its prosperity was originally based on its tanneries, the last of which closed in 1986, and the industrial buildings were largely taken over by craftspeople. Barjols is still known for the manufacture of the traditional Provençal instruments, the *galoubet* (a three-holed flute) and *tambourin* (a narrow drum), which are played simultaneously by a single musician.

Barjols' old quarter, known as '**Réal**', is being extensively renovated. Low medieval archways stand in the dusty alleyways around the church of **Notre-Dame-de-l'Assomption**. An undistinguished square close to the church conceals one of Barjols's best treasures, the magnificent entrance to the Renaissance **Maison des Postevès**. ❑

RESTAURANTS

Restaurants

Prices for a three-course meal without wine. Many restaurants have a less expensive lunch menu:

€ = under €25
€€ = €25–40
€€€ = €40–60
€€€€ = over €60

Toulon

Au Sourd
10 rue Molière
Tel: 04 94 92 28 52. Open L & D Tue–Sat. **€€**
Toulon's oldest restaurant was opened in 1862 by a soldier who had returned deaf (sourd) from the Crimean war. Today it serves high-quality fish straight from the local catch, whether grilled with herb butter, as calamari or in bouillabaisse.

Sanary-sur-Mer

Hôtel-Restaurant de la Tour
24 quai Général de Gaulle
www.sanary-hoteldelatour.com
Tel: 04 94 74 10 10. Open L & D Thu–Mon (plus Tue July–Aug). **€€–€€€**
Sanary's most pleasant hotel also has an excellent restaurant with a terrace overlooking the port. The speciality is fresh fish and shellfish, perhaps baked in a salt crust or simmered in a bouillabaisse.

Bandol

Le Clocher
1 rue de la Paroissel
Tel: 04 94 32 47 65. Open L & D Thu–Sun. **€€**
Revised Provençal specialities are served in an attractive setting on a pedestrianised street near the church.

Les Oliviers
Hôtel L'Ile Rousse, 25 boulevard Louis Lumièrel
www.ile-rousse.com
Tel: 04 94 29 33 00. Open L & D daily (D only in July–Aug). **€€€€**
Find elegant Mediterranean dining in this gastronomic restaurant situated within a five-star hotel and spa. There are also two private beaches, one with a restaurant.

La Table du Vigneron
Domaine de Terrebrune, 724 chemin de la Tourelle, Ollioules
Tel: 04 94 88 36 19. Open L & D Thu–Mon. **€€€**
Inland, half way between Toulon and Sanary, this pretty restaurant is situated in one of the Bandol vineyards. Try beef cooked in the estate's own red wine followed by local strawberries and don't forget to buy some of the vino to take home. They have a smarter restaurant in Ollioules village, L'Atelier du Vigneron (348 avenue de la Résistance; tel: 04 94 62 42 34).

St-Maximin-la-Ste-Baume

Le Couvent Royal
place Jean Salusse
www.hotels-historiques.fr
Tel: 04 94 86 55 66. Open L & D daily. **€€€**
Expect attractively presented classic French cuisine and regional wines. You can dine either in the lovely Gothic chapterhouse or out under the arcades of the cloister of this beautiful royal abbey.

Brignoles

Hostellerie de l'Abbaye de la Celle
place du Général de Gaulle, La Celle
www.abbaye-celle.com
Tel: 04 98 05 14 14. Open L & D daily (Thu–Mon in winter). **€€€–€€€€**
Foodies make a beeline for Alain Ducasse's elegant country inn and restaurant, 4 km (2.5 miles) southwest of Brignoles. The 18th-century auberge adjoining a medieval abbey has a sophisticated restaurant run in partnership with truffle king Bruno Clément. Ducasse disciple Benoît Witz puts a refined spin on regional dishes, most of them incorporating produce from the kitchen garden. From mid-July to mid-Aug the abbey hosts weekly classical music concerts.

RIGHT: mussels are a menu staple in this coastal region.

INLAND VAR HILL VILLAGES

Picturesque hill villages and remote abbeys dot the interior of the Var, but much of this area still has a rural feel with densely forested hills and vine-covered valleys that make it good territory for walking and wine tasting

North of the A8 *autoroute*, the landscape of the inland Var progresses upwards in a series of tiers. Vineyards on the plain and lower valleys give rise to olive groves, then to densely forested hills – prowled by game-hunters, truffle-seekers and walkers – which open onto the sparse expanses of the Grand Plan de Canjuers. Most of this high mountain plateau belongs to the French army.

Le Cannet and Le Luc

On the central Var plain, squeezed between the *autoroute* and the Maures, the wine-producing commune of **Le Cannet-des-Maures** has two distinct halves. Clustered around an 11th-century church, **Le Vieux-Cannet** ❶ is a pretty hill village, while down on the plain the modern town developed with the arrival of the railway in the 1860s. Remnants of the Roman settlement of Forum Voconi, a halt on the Via Aurelia, have recently been excavated here. The nearby small market town of **Le Luc** ❷ has as its centrepiece a 27-metre (90ft) -high hexagonal tower, built in the 16th century. Although rather overladen by traffic, Le Luc has a rich history as a Roman

spa town and Protestant refuge, which can be traced in the **Musée Historique du Centre Var** (tel: 04 9460 7451; 15 June–15 Oct Mon–Sat 3–6pm, rest of year by appointment; charge). It is located in the Château des Comtes de Vintimille along with the tourist office.

Abbaye du Thoronet

The main reason to pass through Le Cannet, however, is to access the Maures massif to the south (*see page 203*) or to visit the magnificent

Main attractions
ABBAYE DU THORONET
CHAPELLE STE-ROSELINE, LES ARCS
TOURTOUR
COTIGNAC
CHÂTEAU D'ENTRECASTEAUX
COLLECTION MAX ERNST
DONATION DOROTHEA TANNING, SEILLANS

LEFT: the plane tree-shaded main square, Cotignac. **RIGHT:** Abbaye du Thoronet.

Two summer music festivals are held in the lovely setting of the Abbaye du Thoronet. The first, in mid-July, focuses on medieval music. The Musique et Esprit festival in August features classical and choral music. Obtain information from the Office de Tourisme, tel: 04 94 60 10 94.

Abbaye du Thoronet ❸ (tel: 04 94 60 43 90; www.thoronet.monuments-nationaux.fr; Apr–Sept Mon–Sat 10am–6.30pm, Sun 10am–noon, 2–6.30pm, Oct–Mar Mon–Sat 10am–1pm, 2–5pm, Sun 10am–noon, 2–5pm; charge). Thoronet is the oldest of the Provençal trio of 'Cistercian sisters', which includes the abbeys of Sénanque (*see page 99*) and Silvacane (*see page 92*). Built in the 12th century to the ascetic precepts of the Cistercian Order, it is striking in its unadorned simplicity and masterful proportions. The abbey church is renowned for its fine acoustic, and you can also visit the cloister, dormitory, and olive press and cellars where monks made olive oil and wine.

Les Arcs-sur-Argens

Les Arcs-sur-Argens ❹, east of Le Cannet, is a focus for the Var's wine industry, and its **Maison des Vins** on the DN7 (tel: 04 94 99 50 20; www.maison-des-vins.fr) is a useful place to embark on a wine trail. It runs tasting courses, provides information on touring the vineyards, and has cellars containing over 800 Côtes de Provence wines. The town has an attractive old quarter, known as Le Parage, and the remains of a feudal castle destroyed after the Revolution.

Just east of Les Arcs, the **Château Ste-Roseline** (tel: 04 94 99 50 30; www.sainte-roseline.com; daily), a former Carthusian nunnery, is now one of Provence's best-known vineyards but for centuries was the focus of an ancient pilgrimage cult around local saint Roseline. You can visit the Romanesque **Chapelle Ste-Roseline** (Tue–Sun 2.30–6pm), where an ornate reliquary contains the 'living' eyes of Roseline, who was born in 1263 in the castle at Les Arcs. According to legend, she was caught by her father in the act of giving away the rich family's possessions to the needy poor; when she opened up her apron, the items were miraculously trans-

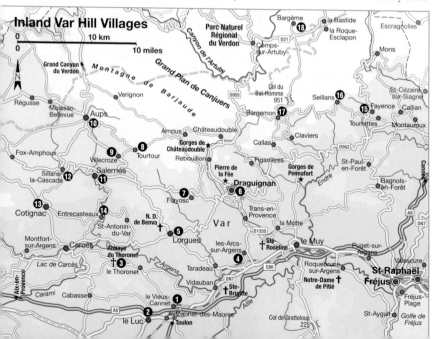

formed into roses. After her death, her body miraculously failed to decompose, and is now preserved in a glass sarcophagus. The chapel also has a mosaic by Chagall, stained glass by Ubac and Bazaine and church furnishings by Diego Giacometti (brother of Alberto).

Northwest of here, **Lorgues ❺**, a busy town with some fine 18th-century buildings and tiny medieval alleyways draws foodies to the restaurant of truffle king Clément Bruno.

Draguignan

Draguignan ❻, the main town in inland Var and home to two military academies, is ringed by an unfortunate rash of supermarkets, some of which were badly damaged when the Nartuby River flooded in 2010.

After the Revolution, Draguignan became administrative capital of the Var from 1795 to 1974 (to punish Toulon, which had supported the monarchy) gaining a set of broad boulevards laid out by Baron Haussmann, who was Préfet of the Var in the 1840s.

Within the boulevards is a compact but appealing old town and a superb market on place du Marché every Wednesday and Saturday morning. Housed in an old monastery, the **Musée des Arts et Traditions Populaires** (15 rue Joseph Roumanille; Tue–Sat 9am–noon, 2–6pm, plus Sun Apr–Sept 2–6pm; charge) relays the social and cultural history of the community through reconstructed scenes. The venerable art museum, **Musée Municipal d'Art et d'Histoire** (rue de la République; Mon–Sat 9am–noon, 2–6pm; free), holds French and Flemish paintings, faience and furniture, in the former summer palace of the bishops of Fréjus.

At the top of the hill stands the Tour de l'Horloge, an impressive fortified clocktower built in 1663. Nearby, on rue de la Juiverie, you can see remains of a synagogue façade, a relic of the sizeable Jewish community that thrived here in the Middle Ages.

An American military cemetery on the town's eastern edge is the legacy of a bloody battle fought here in August 1944. Five km (3 miles) west of Draguignan, pretty **Flayosc ❼** huddles around an 11th-century

The town of Draguignan is named after a dragon which was said to have terrorised the town in the 5th century, until vanquished by Hermentaire, bishop of Antibes. This mythical creature can be seen in stone crests on many of the old town's medieval gateways and houses.

BELOW: picturesque Trans-en-Provence, near Draguignan.

TIP

If you plan on touring the Var *département*, ask for a free 'Pass-Sites Var' when you pay full price for entry at one of the 30 member sites. Then when you visit the other sites in the scheme you will get a reduced entry fee on presentation of the card. See www.visitvar.fr for details.

church. It is known for its excellent olive oil; there's a working oil mill (Moulin du Flayosquet; tel: 04 94 70 41 45) just north of here in the hamlet of Flayosquet,

North of Draguignan on the D955 is the mysterious dolmen known as the Pierre de la Fée (Fairy Stone), a vast slab of rock on three stone legs, dating from 2500 to 2000 BC. Shortly after, you'll reach the **Gorges de Châteaudouble**, cut through by the River Nartuby. Perched dramatically above the gorges is the village of **Châteaudouble** and, upstream, **Ampus**, another picturesque village.

Tourtour and Villecroze

More gentrified but more spectacular is **Tourtour** ❽, 'the village in the sky', with its medieval vaulted passageways that open onto breathtaking views. People congregate on the café terraces of place des Ormeaux, the main square. Sadly, the *ormeaux* – two elms planted to commemorate Louis XIV's birth – fell prey to disease and were replaced by olive trees.

Tourtour has two castles: the ruined old castle, and the square,

four-towered Château Communal, now home to the tourist office and post office. The village is a magnet for artists and there are many galleries.

At neighbouring **Villecroze** ❾, mullioned Renaissance windows peer out of the red cliff face from troglodyte dwellings carved into the soft tufa rock. Below, the unusual Jardin de la Cascade was laid out in the 19th century, with pools and basins fed by water that cascades down the cliff.

Aups

Aups ❿ is an access point for the Grand Canyon du Verdon (*see page 163*) and a busy market town, famed for its truffle market on Thursday mornings in winter. The town is crowned by a fine 16th-century clocktower adorned with a sundial. Aups has a strong tradition of republican resistance, and was the scene of several popular uprisings during the mid-19th century.

Housed in an old Ursuline chapel, the **Musée Municipal Simon Segal** (Wed–Sun, June–Aug 10am–noon, 4–7pm, Sept until 6pm; free) has a collection of works by the Russian-

BELOW: Aups.

born painter and other artists associated with the Ecole de Paris in the 1920s. Outside town, the **Musée de Faykod** (www.musee-de-faykod.com; tel: 04 94 70 03 94; July–Aug Wed–Mon 10am–noon, 3–7pm, Sept–June Wed–Mon 2–6pm, Oct–Apr Wed, Sat–Sun 2–6pm; charge) is a sculpture garden of romantic white Carrara marble sculptures by Maria de Faykod, a Hungarian-born sculptor who carried out numerous commissions for public sculptures and religious works in France.

Salernes ⑪ is larger and more sprawling than Aups, with one of the best markets in the area, held on Wednesday and Sunday mornings on the central square. Above all, Salernes is known as the tile-making capital of Provence. Tiles have been made here for centuries, thanks to the combination of local clay, spring water and abundant forests for fuelling the kilns. Today it still has over a dozen tile workshops. The tiles range from the most traditional hand-moulded hexagonal unglazed floor tiles, known as *tommettes*, to hand-painted wall tiles and the contemporary glazed tiles and extravagant creations of Alain Vagh.

A few kilometres west of Salernes, **Sillans-la-Cascade ⑫** has several remnants of its fortified town wall and an impressive waterfall, now sadly closed to the public after a landslide. Minuscule **Fox-Amphoux** crouches on a hill to the west, its pretty streets clustered round a Romanesque church.

The animated village of **Cotignac ⑬** is set against the dramatic backdrop of a red cliff crowned with the remains of two fortified towers. It is popular with tourists, as the antique and gift shops testify, but it retains a workaday charm. South of town, the **Chapelle Notre-Dame-de-Grâce**, built after an apparition by the Virgin in 1519, was one of the three churches where the devout Queen Anne of Austria, wife of Louis XIII, made a vow, after a Parisian monk dreamt that the only way she could have a child was to carry out three novenas. The result was the birth of Louis XIV in 1638.

The D50 snakes east to **Entrecasteaux ⑭**, a delightful village

TIP

Lac de St-Cassien, a large man-made lake surrounded by wooded hills south of Montauroux, is a popular spot for swimming, birdwatching and carp fishing. Watersports fans can hire pedalos, rowing boats or kayaks.

BELOW: Draguignan's belltower.

Campaniles

Originally housing the bell that served as a warning in times of danger, located either on the town hall or the church, campaniles soon became far more than mere functional structures. With their fancy curlicues and finials, the elaborate wrought-ironwork became a way of proclaiming the village's identity and showing off the craftsman's skill, especially in the 18th century, when they were often added to much earlier structures. Countless campaniles can be found throughout Provence, but there are some particularly fine examples in the Var hill villages, including the clock-tower gateway at Aups, the village churches at Flayosc and Le Vieux Cannet and the town belfry at Lorgues.

The ruins of a medieval fortress in the village of Bargème.

overlooking the River Bresque, dominated by an imposing 16th- to 18th-century classical **château** (tel: 04 94 04 43 95; www.chateau-entrecasteaux.com; guided visit Easter–15 June Sun at 4pm, 15 June–Sept Sun–Fri at 4pm, plus 11.30am in Aug; charge). In 1974, the chateau was bought by Scottish painter, soldier and adventurer Ian McGarvie-Munn, who set about its restoration. The formal gardens (open daily) were designed by André Le Nôtre, creator of Louis XIV's gardens at Versailles.

Fayence and Seillans

Fayence ⓯, the largest town in the eastern Var and a big hang-gliding centre, has little overt charm, but is surrounded by a series of pretty satellite villages, such as Montauroux and Mons. On the edge of town, the **Ecomusée de Fayence** (Tue–Sun May–Sept 2–6.30pm, Oct–Apr until 6pm; free) displays vine- and olive-growing equipment, wine presses and other traditional agricultural implements.

BELOW: Seillans.

The Surrealist painter Max Ernst (1891–1976) spent the last 11 years of his life in **Seillans** ⓰, a pink-and-ochre village west of Fayence. A bronze cast of his *Génie de la République* stands on place de la République. The **Collection Max Ernst Donation Dorothea Tanning** (place du Valat; Mon–Sat, mid-June–mid-Sept 2.30–6.30pm, mid-Sept–mid-June until 5.30pm; charge), containing lithographs and etchings he made while living in the village, and prints by his wife Dorothea Tanning, can be seen in a gallery above the Office de Tourisme. The countryside around Seillans is known for its igloo-shaped dry stone *bories*.

Bargemon and Bargème

Bargemon ⓱, west of Seillans, with fragments of ramparts dating back to the 11th century, has medieval streets to wander and a good Thursday market. From here you can head south to **Callas** and the stunning landscapes of the **Gorges de Pennafort** or head 17km (10 miles) north, climbing in steep hairpin bends over the Col du Bel Homme pass, to tiny **Bargème** ⓲, the highest village in the Var. ❑

RESTAURANTS

Restaurants

Prices for a three-course meal without wine. Many restaurants have a less expensive lunch menu:

€ = under €25
€€ = €25–40
€€€ = €40–60
€€€€ = over €60

Les Arcs-sur-Argens
Le Relais des Moines
route Ste-Roseline
www.lerelaisdesmoines.com
Tel: 04 94 47 40 93. Open L & D July–Aug Tue–Sun, rest of year Wed–Sun. €€–€€€€
In an historic stone farmhouse, *cuisine de terroir* is revisited with finesse by young chef Sébastien Sanjou. There's an excellent wine list, too.

Lorgues
Chez Bruno
route de Vidauban
www.restaurantbruno.com
Tel: 04 94 85 93 93. Open L & D daily (winter closed Sun D & Mon). €€€€
Expect extremely rich menus based around truffles and foie gras at this beautifully situated country *mas*, where truffle king Clément Bruno, draws the sort of clientele arrive by helicopter.

Flayosc
L'Oustaou
5 place Brémond. Tel: 04 94 70 42 69. Open L Thu–Sun,

D Thu–Sat (daily July–Aug). €–€€€
A well-regarded restaurant on the village square, where specialities include *daube* and local goat's cheese. Watch the world go by from the terrace.

Tourtour
La Bastide de Tourtour
Montée St-Denis
www.bastidedetourtour.com
Tel: 04 98 10 54 20. Open July–Aug L & D daily, rest of year D Mon–Fri, L & D Sat–Sun. €€
Modern French cuisine served in the elegant dining room of this upmarket hotel, or on the terrace with stunning views of the Haut Var.

Salernes
Chez Gilles
20 avenue Victor Hugo
www.chez-gilles.com
Tel: 04 94 70 72 80. Open L & D Tue–Sun. €
A tiny, animated bistro, where chef Gilles makes the most of the Var's organic produce. Live music some evenings.

Cotignac
Le Clos des Vignes
route de Montfort
Tel: 04 94 04 72 19. Open L & D daily (closed Sun eve and Mon in winter). €€–€€€
In a rural setting outside

town with a view over vineyards. Offers French classics (foie gras, game, *daubes*) and an interesting selection of wines.

La Table de la Fontaine
27 cours Gambetta
Tel: 04 94 04 79 13. Open L & D Tue–Sun. Closed Dec–Feb. €
This good-value little bistro with a terrace on Cotignac's main street is a popular place for lunch after the Tuesday market or dinner in summer.

Montauroux
Auberge Eric Maio
Quartier Narbonne
www.eric-maio.com Tel: 04 9447 7165. Open L & D Thu–Mon. Closed Jan. €€–€€€€

A rising name on the French culinary scene, MIchelin-starred owner-chef Eric Maio is another fan of the truffle, which even appears in the ice cream.

Seillans
Hôtel des Deux Rocs
1 place Font d'Amont
www.hoteldeuxrocs.com
Tel: 04 94 76 87 32. Open L & D Tue–Sun. Closed Jan–mid-Feb. €€€
This village house is a lovely characterful hotel with an adventurous restaurant, where you can sample the personalised seasonal cuisine of chef David Carré, previously No. 2 at the grand Lameloise restaurant in Burgundy.

RIGHT: La Bastide de Tourtour.

ST-TROPEZ, THE MAURES AND THE ESTÉREL

Glitzy St-Tropez, the star of the Var coast, is as fashionable as ever, but just beyond its boundaries is the surprisingly wild hinterland of the Massif des Maures and the Massif de l'Estérel. Sun-worshippers and nature-lovers are both well catered for here

From Hyères to the Estérel, the Var coast provides some of the most spectacular colours in the south, with glorious sandy beaches set against mountain backdrops, where red rocks contrast with the azure seas and magnificent chestnut trees. The glamour of St-Tropez and busy resorts like Le Lavandou and St-Raphaël contrast starkly with the forested expanses of the Massif des Maures and the Estérel. Vineyards, fruit production and the steep terrain means that this area has been spared the worst of the concrete developments of the Alpes-Maritimes further east.

Hyères-les-Palmiers

Grandmother of the Riviera towns, **Hyères ❶** was the first resort to be established on the Côte d'Azur, setting a trend that spread rapidly east from the late 18th century onwards. The list of famous consumptives and pleasure-seekers drawn to its balmy winter climate reads like an international Who's Who: Queen Victoria, Tolstoy, Pauline Bonaparte, Aubrey Beardsley, Edith Wharton. Robert Louis Stevenson, though very ill during his stay, wrote: 'I was only happy once – that was at Hyères.'

By the 1920s, however, medical opinion had switched its allegiance to the curative properties of mountain rather than sea air. This and the arrival of the summer season soon relegated Hyères, sitting above the coast rather than down by the shore, to a distinctly unfashionable position.

In many ways, the town's air of faded gentility is now its most attractive quality. Its thriving agricultural economy centres around market gardening, cut flowers and palm trees, and the restoration of the Villa

Main attractions

VILLA NOAILLES, HYÈRES
BORMES-LES-MIMOSAS OLD
  VILLAGE
DOMAINE DU RAYOL GARDENS
VIEUX-PORT, ST-TROPEZ
PLAGE DE PAMPELONNE,
  ST-TROPEZ
CATHÉDRALE ST-LÉONCE, FRÉJUS
CORNICHE D'OR COAST ROAD

LEFT: classic boat moored at the Vieux-Port of St-Tropez.
RIGHT: the coast at Le Lavandou.

Villa Noailles, a 1920s Cubist house visited regularly by members of the Dada and Surrealist movements.

Noailles has given it a cultural boost. Toulon-Hyères airport, located next to Hyères racetrack, also makes it a jumping off point for the Ile de Porquerolles and St-Tropez.

Amid the modern sprawl and a complicated one-way system lies the compact medieval **Vieille Ville** (old town). It is best entered through the Porte Mabillon, a fragment of the old city fortifications. From here rue Mabillon leads to the lively, café-filled place Mabillon, where the square **Tour des Templiers** (Wed–Mon 10am–noon, 2–7pm, Wed–Sun until 5pm in winter), the remains of a

Templar *commanderie*, is now used for exhibitions. Steps next to the tower lead up to the **Collégiale St-Paul**, a large, mainly Gothic church most notable for the array of naive ex-voto paintings on the walls.

Hyères' most interesting sight is the **Villa Noailles** (tel: 04 98 08 01 98; www.villanoailles-hyeres.com; July–Sept Wed–Mon 2–7pm, Fri 4–10pm, Oct–June Wed–Sun 1–6pm, Fri 3–8pm; free), further up the hill below the castle ruins. In its heyday, this masterpiece of Modernist Cubist architecture, built in the 1920s by Robert Mallet-Stevens for aristocratic

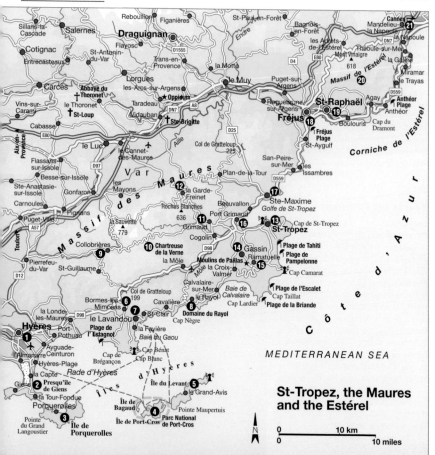

St-Tropez, the Maures and the Estérel

art patrons Charles and Marie-Laure de Noailles, was the ultimate expression of modern living and aesthetics, complete with indoor pool, gymnasium, guest rooms and garages. Buñuel, Giacometti, Stravinsky, Man Ray and other arty guests lounged on its sun terraces. Restored in the 1990s, the villa is now used for temporary exhibitions, with a fashion photography festival each spring and design festival in summer.

Above the villa, the road continues to the ruins of a 12th-century castle and the 19th-century Castel Ste-Claire, home from 1927 to 1937 of American novelist Edith Wharton, who planted the surrounding **Parc Ste-Claire** with numerous species from South America and Australia. The house previously belonged to Olivier Voutier, a naval officer, who discovered the Venus de Milo on the Greek Island of Milos in 1820; he is buried in the garden.

The modern town retains some of its 19th-century elegance in the stucco villas of avenue Joseph Clotis and the renovated Casino des Palmiers on avenue Amboise Thomas.

Around the exotic **Jardins Olbius Riquier**, notable for its palm trees, are some notable examples of neo-Moorish architecture dating from the late 19th century, including La Villa Mauresque (2 avenue Jean Natte) and La Villa Tunisienne (1 avenue David de Beauregard), both of which are privately owned.

Lower down, towards Le Capte, lies the **Site Archéologique d'Olbia** (quartier de l'Almanarre; tel: 04 94 65 51 49; Wed–Sat and Mon, July–Aug 9.30am–noon, 3.30–7pm, Apr–June and Sept–Oct 9.30am–noon, 2–5.30pm, closed Nov–Mar; charge), the remains of the maritime trading post of Olbia founded by the Greeks in the 4th century BC.

Jutting out into the sea south of Hyères-Plage is the **Presqu'île de Giens ❷**; on the sheltered eastern side of the isthmus, the beach road of La Capte is lined with cheap hotels and campsites. The road along the western side runs between the abandoned salt marshes of Les Pesquiers, now a nature reserve and home to flamingos, and the long windswept Plage de l'Almanarre, a favourite with

Ile de Porquerolles, one of the unspoilt Iles d'Hyères off the Var coast. Boats to the islands are frequent in July and August, but limited the rest of the year.

Below: Hyères rooftops.

TIP

TLV (tel: 04 94 58 21 81; www.tlv-tvm.com) operates ferries from Hyères to Port-Cros (1 hour) and Ile de Levant (1.5 hours), and from La Tour-Fondue on the Presqu'île de Giens to Porquerolles (30 mins). **Vedettes Iles d'Or** (tel: 04 94 71 01 02; www. vedettesilesdor.fr) runs ferries from Le Lavandou to the Ile de Levant (35 mins; 1 hour via Port-Cros), and to Porquerolles in summer, as well as boats from Cavalaire.

BELOW: beach life on Porquerolles.

windsurfers. The Presqu'île itself is rather built up but is encircled by a lovely coast path which gives access to pretty creeks.

The Iles d'Hyères

Most people come to Giens to catch a boat from **La Tour-Fondue** – the remains of a fortress built by Richelieu – to **Porquerolles** ❸, the largest of the Iles d'Hyères, also known as the Iles d'Or (Golden Islands), because of the mica or 'fool's gold' that sparkles in the sand and rocks. Luxuriant Porquerolles was the inspiration for Robert Louis Stevenson's *Treasure Island*. Its village was established as a small military base in the 19th century, and is more colonial than Provençal in character, with a large parade ground-like square surrounded by eucalyptus trees and several cafés. Above the village, ancient **Fort Ste-Agathe** (May–Oct 10am–12-.30pm, 1.30–5pm; free) offers good views over the bay of Hyères and is next to a windmill, which can also be visited. Numerous footpaths and cycle tracks traverse the island – bicycles can be hired near the harbour

– but note that some parts may be out of bounds due to fire risk in summer. Major beauty spots include the lighthouse at Cap d'Arme, a small botanical garden, and the Plage d'Argent, with its white sand and Caribbean-clear water, a short walk through pinewoods on either side of the village.

Rugged, mountainous **Port-Cros** ❹, reached by boat from Port d'Hyères, Le Lavandou and Cavalaire, is a national park – France's smallest – and strict rules against smoking and fires must be observed. A small tourist centre, open in summer, provides maps and advice. Perhaps the most rewarding walk (around two hours for the round trip) takes you along the Vallon de la Solitude, which cuts across the southern end of the island. Divers can follow an underwater 'path' to see the marine flora and fauna.

The third island, **Levant** ❺, is inhabited by the French military and mostly out of bounds, except for the dramatic western tip which is occupied by Héliopolis, a nudist colony founded in the 1930s.

Bormes-les-Mimosas and the Corniche des Maures

West of Hyères, **Bormes-les-Mimosas** ❻ is a chocolate-box pretty medieval hill village perched above the coast, its streets overflowing with bougainvillea, mimosa and other exotic plants. Place Gambetta is the hub of Bormes life, with its restaurants and frequent live entertainment in summer; from here rue Carnot winds through the old village with stepped streets and covered alleyways leading off to either side, lined with arts and crafts studios. Look out for the painted sundial on the Eglise St-Trophime and the small **Musée d'Art et d'Histoire** (103 rue Carnot; Tue–Sun except Wed am and Sun pm, June–Sept 10am–noon, 3–6.30pm, Oct–May 10am–noon, 2–5.30pm; free), which contains some terracottas by Rodin and neo-Impressionist paintings. Above the town, a road leads up to the remains of the Château des Seigneurs de Fos (private), offering magnificent views from the terrace.

South of Bormes, linked to the exclusive promontory of Cap Bénat by a dyke, the sturdy medieval Fort de Brégançon, one of the official residences of the French president, sits proudly on its own peninsula. The fort cannot be visited, but **Cap de Brégançon**, planted with vineyards and pine woods, has some lovely unspoilt beaches, such as the Plage de Cabasson (parking fee), the Plage de l'Estagnol (open Easter–Oct; parking fee) and the Plage de Pellégrin (open Easter–Oct; parking fee).

Bormes' own modern beach suburb of La Favière, north of Cap Bénat, has a sandy beach, a marina, watersports facilities and numerous restaurants. Almost adjoining it is the popular resort of **Le Lavandou** ❼. Glitzy bars and discos make this a lively place by night, although there are also a few relics of the old fishing town behind the port, and a huge general market behind the prom-

enade on Thursday morning. (This is also the best place for boats to Port-Cros and the Ile de Levant.)

Lavandou marks the start of the **Corniche des Maures** (D559), which winds around the coast past the Plage de St-Clair, the prettiest of Le Lavandou's beaches, the small Aiguebelle cove, the beach restaurants of Cavalière, and exclusive Cap Nègre. It then climbs up towards Le Rayol-Canadel and the wonderful gardens of the **Domaine du Rayol** ❽ (www.domainedurayol.org; tel: 04 98 04 44 00; daily. July–Aug 9.30am–7.30pm, Apr–June and Sept–Oct until 6.30pm, Nov–Mar until 5.30pm; charge), laid out according to different tropical and desert habitats around the globe; there is a very nice café here too. After the big brash resort of Cavalaire-sur-Mer, a side road leads to **Gigaro**, one of the landing beaches for the Liberation of Provence in August 1944.

The Massif des Maures

Only a couple of miles from jet-set St-Tropez, you'll find yourself in the steep, densely forested mountains of the Maures – the name comes from

TIP

A relaxing way to explore the Massif de Maures is on the back of a horse. There are several trekking stables in the area, including the Relais de la Mène (tel: 04 94 43 35 96) in Grimaud and Les Ecuries de l'Eau Blanche (tel: 06 73 41 12 86) in Cavalaire-sur-Mer.

Below: beach volleyball, Le Lavandou.

EAT

Delicious chestnut-based ice cream sundaes are served in summer at the Confiserie Azuréenne (boulevard Général Koenig; tel: 04 94 48 07 20) in Collobrières. A small museum explains the process of making *marrons glacés*: chestnuts are harvested in autumn, peeled and cooked then soaked in syrup for seven days, coated in icing sugar, dried in the oven and individually wrapped.

old Provençal *mauro*, meaning dark – an ancient massif made up of deep grey schist shot through with glittering mica and serpentine. It is wonderful walking country, traversed by numerous footpaths, including the long-distance GR51, GR9 and GR90, indicated by red-and-white striped markings, offering sea views and relative cool and solitude. Sadly, the area has often been ravaged by forest fires, sparked either by human carelessness or arsonists, so many of the footpaths may be closed in high summer, especially on windy days (check at a local tourist office).

The D98 main road follows the vineyard-filled valley via La Môle in the middle of the Maures, the most direct route between Hyères and St-Tropez. To reach the heart of the mountains, however, it's better to take the narrow, sometimes hair-raisingly twisty D41 from Bormes-les-Mimosas, which climbs over the Col de Gratteloup and Col de Babaou passes (a good place to join the GR51 footpath), descending through magnificent chestnut woods towards Collobrières.

Collobrières ❾ is a refreshingly workaday place, dedicated to the timber trade and the cultivation and transformation of chestnuts – *marrons glacés* and *crème de marrons* are local specialities *(see margin, left)* – with a pleasant low-key old town stretching along the Real Collobrier river. The chestnut harvest is celebrated with the Fête de la Chataigne on the last three Sundays in October.

Further east along the D14 towards Grimaud, turn off to the **Chartreuse de la Verne ❿** (June–Aug daily 11am–6pm, Sept–Oct Wed–Mon until 5pm; charge), an imposing fortress-like monastery hidden at the end of a remote valley. Built out of local schist edged with green serpentine, the Carthusian monastery was founded in 1170. Abandoned after the Revolution, it is now home to a community of nuns, and you can visit the granary, church and one of the monk's cottages.

Grimaud ⓫ itself is a picturesque hilltop village with a maze of streets draped in bougainvillea and oleander. Wander along the rue des Templiers for its medieval arcades, then head up to the ruined castle. You can catch a train from here down to Port Grimaud *(see page 208)*.

Detour inland up the winding D558 amid cork oaks, chestnut trees and pines to **La Garde-Freinet ⓬**, an ancient Arab stronghold and, much later, a centre of cork production. By 1846, the town produced more than 75 percent of France's wine corks. Since the early 1980s, the industry has diversified into other uses of cork, and neatly stripped trunks of cork oaks line the massif's winding roads. In the town, the only obvious evidence of cork production are the cork bowls and ornaments on sale to tourists in the pricey shops of the rue St-Jacques, although the village still has some down-to-earth local cafés and stores, especially on place Vieille. North of the village, a climb to the

BELOW: red rooftops of La Garde-Freinet.

ruins of **Fort Freinet** is rewarded with great views, although excavations have revealed more evidence of a medieval village here rather than the supposed Arab fortress.

Cogolin, 3km (1.5 miles) south of Grimaud, is a small but lively town known for the manufacture of briar pipes and carpets. It was the headquarters of General de Lattre de Tassigny during the 1944 battle to liberate Provence.

St-Tropez

Once on the peninsula, you won't be able to resist the pull of **St-Tropez** ⑬, enduringly connected with the French sex symbol Brigitte Bardot. What had been a simple fishing village 'discovered' by Guy de Maupassant and Paul Signac in the 19th century, and by the writer Colette in the early 20th century, was confirmed as the playground of the rich and famous when Bardot starred in Roger Vadim's film *And God Created Woman* here in 1956. Although besieged by traffic jams in summer, 'St-Trop' still has the allure of a Provençal fishing village (it even has a daily morning fish market on place aux Herbes behind the tourist office) combined with legendary nightlife, café society and designer shopping. It could all be ridiculous except that St-Trop gets away with it, and the rest of the year reverts to relatively normal small town status.

Whether you leave your car by the Nouveau Port or arrive by boat, the first essential port of call is the **Vieux-Port**, lined with tall rust-coloured houses and legendary café terraces, including Senequier, the Bar du Port and Café de Paris, from which to celebrity-spot and ogle the swanky yachts lined up along the quay. On the west side the **Musée de l'Annonciade** (place Grammont; tel: 04 94 17 84 10; July–Aug daily 10am–1pm, 3–7pm, Sept–June Wed–Mon 10am–1pm, 2–6pm; charge) is a superb collection of modern art displayed in a deconsecrated chapel, featuring many of the artists who visited St-Tropez at the beginning of the 20th century, including Signac (whose idea it was to create such a collection), Bonnard, Marquet, Maillol, Matisse, Braque and Dufy.

It was the film And God Created Woman, made in 1956 by Brigitte Bardot's then husband, Roger Vadim, that rocketed the overtly sexy actress to stardom, and put St-Tropez, where it was filmed, on the map.

Below: the Vieux-Port, St-Tropez.

Brigitte Bardot

From a pouting young starlet to a controversial animal rights campaigner, BB remains one of France's most famous exports

When the film *And God Created Woman* appeared in 1956, it made Brigitte Bardot a world star and a sexual icon. It also put St-Tropez on the map and sun-worship on every budding starlet's agenda. Today the film seems tame, but in 1956 its nudity and love scenes caused a furore, particularly in the US.

In 1957, it earned over $8 million, more than France's biggest export, the Renault Dauphine. It was Bardot's 17th film, and hers was by no means a rags-to-riches story. Her parents were well-to-do: her father was an industrialist and her mother ran a clothes boutique in Paris. At 14, Brigitte, having done some modelling, was recruited as a cover girl for *Elle*. Her parents insisted she could only be identified by her initials, BB.

Film-director Marc Allegret was developing a film-script written by a 19-year-old White Russian, Roger Vladimir Plemiannikov

(known as Vadim). He asked Vadim to investigate the new *Elle* cover girl. While they made a formal visit to Brigitte's parents, the 15-year-old Brigitte and Vadim sneaked out to the balcony together. Although the screen test was a flop, the pair soon became lovers, though Vadim had to wait until she was 18 before they could marry.

The breakthrough

Enthusiastically promoted by Vadim, Brigitte was given a number of small parts in a series of mediocre films. Her fifth film, Anatole Litvak's *Act of Love*, starring Kirk Douglas, was promoted at the 1953 Cannes Film Festival. It was the opportunity Vadim had been waiting for. A US aircraft carrier was in Cannes entertaining the best-known film stars on deck: Gary Cooper, Lana Turner, Olivia de Havilland and Leslie Caron all posed for the cameras. But the cameramen spotted a slender girl in a raincoat who had not been invited on board. Brigitte let slip her coat to reveal a tiny little-girl outfit, tossed her ponytail and smiled. The next day she was splashed across the front pages of newspapers around the world.

Young girls everywhere copied her ponytail and her famous pout. Her movies became more daring, peaking with *And God Created Woman*. It was after this that Brigitte bought La Madrague, a large villa near St-Tropez, where she still spends part of the year. The presence of such an icon attracted other celebrities and jet-setters, and the tiny fishing port was transformed.

At the age of 38, after three marriages and numerous love affairs, Bardot declared that she preferred animals to men and devoted herself to animal causes. In recent years she has been surrounded by controversy: she has been fined more than once for expressing racist and homophobic views, and in 2012 she publicly supported Marine Le Pen, leader of the Front National, in the French Presidential elections. However her influence on popular culture is undeniable and she still features in *Empire* magazine's 100 Sexiest Filmstars list. ❑

LEFT: Brigitte Bardot on the beach at St Tropez.

Behind the port, **Château Suffren** is a remnant of the fortress built by Guillaume, first count of Provence, in 980. From here rue Portalet leads to the little cove of the Glaye, starting point of a coast path that winds its way round waterside houses, tiny coves and the old Port des Pêcheurs. Above the old town the 16th-century **Citadelle** (Montée de la Citadelle; tel: 04 94 97 59 43; daily Apr–Sept 10am–6.30pm, Oct–Mar 10am–12.30pm, 1.30–5.30pm; charge) boasts an impressive set of ramparts and bastions. The dungeon houses the **Musée moderne et vivant de l'histoire maritime tropézienne** (same times as Citadelle), opened in 2013, which traces the village's maritime history.

One of the best places to see the real St-Tropez is on the **place des Lices**, where there is a colourful market on Tuesday and Saturday mornings. At other times, the square serves as a terrain for boules (*pétanque*), where white linen-suited millionaires, who've just jetted in that morning to the airstrip at La Môle, play at being Provençal villagers before retiring to one of its fashionable brasseries; you can even hire a set of boules from the famous Le Café. Across the square, the **Lavoir Vasserot** (rue Joseph Quaranta; times vary), an old wash house, is now used for art exhibitions. Narrow shopping streets run between the square and the Vieux-Port, and a small house contains the **Maison des Papillons** (9 rue Etienne Berny; tel: 04 94 97 63 45; Apr–Oct and Christmas hols Tue–Sat times vary by day; charge), a display of over 35,000 French and exotic butterflies, including rare and now extinct species. collected by painter Dany Lartigue. Dany was son of the famous 1920s society photographer Jacques Henri Lartigue.

Apart from people-watching, the main attraction of St-Tropez, however, is its glorious beaches, fringed with restaurants, and packed with sun-bronzed bodies all summer long. Those nearest to town are the Plage de la Bouillabaisse on the road in from Ste-Maxime and the Plage des Graniers and Plage des Salins to the east of town, but it is the fashionable **Plage de Pampelonne**, with its

TIP

Designer fashion labels and jewellers to rival any world capital are concentrated in St-Tropez on rue Allard, rue Sibille and place de la Garonne. Between the quay and the square are narrow streets lined with small boutiques, including Atelier Rondini and K Jacques, famed for their strappy (and pricey) leather gladiator sandals.

BELOW: Pampelonne bay.

Plage de Pampelonne

The Plage de Pampelonne is a 5km (3-mile) stretch of sand between Cap Pinet and Cap Camarat, bordered by bamboos, pines and vineyards. Much of the bay is taken up by 'private' beach clubs, ranging from the boho bamboo shack with its beach restaurant and sun loungers to designer haunts offering cosmopolitan menus, cocktail bars, DJs and spas. Trendy spots include Tahiti, Club 55, Nikki Beach, Key West, and Nioulargo, while Neptune, Pirata and Plage des Jumeaux are more relaxed affairs; Chez Camille is a fashionable fish restaurant. But there are also free public stretches where you can park your parasol – and the shorefront is accessible to anyone.

TIP

Les Bâteaux Verts (tel: 04 9449 2939, www. bateeauxverts.com) runs frequent ferries between Ste-Maxime and St-Tropez, an excellent way of beating the traffic jams. The company also runs sightseeing trips around the headlands and past celebrity villas on the St-Tropez peninsula.

exclusive private beaches, that is the main upholder of St-Tropez's sun, sea and sex image (*see box, page 207*).

Gassin and Ramatuelle

Many of St-Tropez's more glamorous residents hide out in discreet villas hidden among the vineyards of the St-Tropez peninsula. Perched up above are two gorgeous hill villages, **Gassin** ⓮, where Mick Jagger married Bianca de Macias in 1971, and **Ramatuelle** ⓯, both offering chic restaurants and gorgeous views. Ramatuelle is well known for its summer jazz and theatre festivals. On a hill between the two villages are a group of ancient windmills, the Moulins de Paillas.

Port Grimaud and Ste-Maxime

Heading around the Golfe de St-Tropez towards Ste-Maxime, **Port Grimaud** ⓰ is a modern resort designed in the 1960s by the architect François Spoerry around a network of canals to resemble a miniature Venice, with space for boats to moor outside the houses. Le Petit Train de Grimaud (June–Sept 10.05am–5.35pm, Apr–

May until 4.25pm, mid-Mar–mid-Oct 11.05am–4.25pm; charge) takes passengers on a 50-minute tour up to the medieval hill village of Grimaud, (*see page 204*) and back again. This being Côtes de Provence country, the wine co-operative **Les Maîtres Vignerons de St-Tropez** (tel: 04 94 56 40 17; www.vignerons-saint-tropez.com) at La Foux junction is the best place to taste the local vintage and pick up other regional products.

Low-key **Ste-Maxime** ⓱ offers an old-fashioned taste of the Côte with its palm trees, promenade and golden beaches. Facing the port, from where a ferry takes passengers to St-Tropez, the stone **Tour Carrée** (place de l'Eglise; Wed–Sun 10am–noon, 3–6pm; charge) built in 1520 as a refuge against pirates, is now a small folk museum, after having served as barn, town hall and prison. A covered market (daily in summer, every morning except Monday in winter) is held a few streets back on rue Fernand Bessy. Jean de Brunhoff, the creator of Babar the Elephant, had a house in the town and there is a beach called Plage des Eléphants in his honour.

BELOW: Port Grimaud.

Fréjus and St-Raphaël

Squeezed between the massifs of the Maures and Estérel, the next main resort heading east is **Fréjus** ⑱, which is scattered with Roman remains. Located on the Via Aurelia, it was founded as a port in 49 BC by Julius Caesar. It was developed into a naval base by Emperor Augustus – an alternative to unruly Marseille. The **Lanterne d'Auguste**, one of two towers that originally guarded the harbour, still survives. The Roman harbour has long since silted up. In its place there's a modern marina and apartment complex known as **Port-Fréjus**.

Fréjus' most impressive Roman remain is the 2nd-century **Arènes** (rue Henri Vardon; tel: 04 94 51 34 31; Tue–Sun 9.30am–12.30pm, 2–6pm, Oct–Mar Tue, Thu–Sat until 4.30pm) on the western edge of town, which could once accommodate 10,000 spectators. Although substantially damaged, the amphitheatre is still used for rock concerts.

In the centre of town overlooking place Formigé stands the medieval **Cathédrale St-Léonce** (Cité Episcopale; tel: 04 94 51 26 30; June–Sept daily 9am–6.30pm, Oct–May Tue–Sun 9am–noon, 2–5pm; charge). Begun in the 10th century, it is bordered by a 12th-century cloister that features a fantastical wooden ceiling decorated with animals and mythical beasts. You must take one of the frequent guided tours to see the cathedral's elaborately carved Renaissance wooden doors and the 5th-century baptistery, an octagonal structure with granite columns and carved marble capitals pilfered from Roman remains.

Nearby on place Calvini, the **Musée Archéologique** (tel: 04 94 32 15 98; Apr–Sept Tue–Sun 9.30am–12.30pm, 2–6pm, Oct–Mar Tue, Thu–Sat until 4.30pm) has a good collection of Roman and early Ligurian tiles, mosaics and sculptures, including the two-faced bust of Hermes that has become the symbol of the town.

In addition to Fréjus's Roman and medieval attractions, there are a couple of very un-Gallic curiosities. A **Buddhist pagoda** sitting in an oriental garden, just off the DN7 to Cannes, commemorates the death of 5,000 Vietnamese soldiers in World War I, while a replica of the Missir **Mosque** in Mali lies unprepossessingly in the middle of an army camp off the D4 to Bagnols.

Merging into Fréjus to the east, lively **St-Raphaël** ⑲ started life as a holiday resort for the Roman legionaries of Fréjus. In the 19th century, Napoleon landed in St-Raphaël on his return from Egypt, and this was also his departing point 14 years later when he was banished to Elba. St-Raphaël's status as a fashionable resort is largely down to Alphonse Karr, a former editor of *Le Figaro*, who discovered St-Raphaël in 1865 and encouraged his friends, Alexandre Dumas and Guy de Maupassant amongst them, to follow him. Now, though less trendy and marred by

Vineyard near St-Tropez, one of many producers of the Côtes de Provence wines made in the warm coastal hinterland.

BELOW: ochre-hued Fréjus.

Gaspard de Bresse, the Robin Hood of the Estérel, was the most notorious of the brigands operating in the Estérel in the 18th century. He targeted tax officers and wealthy voyagers, always giving a portion of his proceeds to the poor. A gentleman thief who robbed without bloodshed, a prankster and a dandy, he won over several of his female victims. He was arrested for good at an inn in La Valette du Var and executed in 1781.

Below: St-Raphaël's busy harbour.

some huge apartment blocks, St-Raphaël has no lack of visitors, even if they're just here to lose a few euros at the rather hideous casino on the palm-lined seafront.

More fun is the daily fish market in the old port, where you can take boats in summer to St-Tropez, Port Grimaud and the Ile de Port-Cros. Behind here is the small, rather unkempt old town, with a good covered market on place Victor-Hugo. The **Musée Archéologique** (rue des Templiers; Tue–Sat 9am–noon, 2–6pm; charge), in the presbytery of the 12th-century Romanesque church of St-Pierre-des-Templiers, contains Roman amphorae and a display of underwater equipment.

The Massif de l'Estérel

The red porphyry rock of the Estérel tumbles down to the sea in a dramatic sweep of hills and ravines. Highwaymen and sundry criminal types ruled the impenetrable reaches of the **Massif de l'Estérel 20** for many centuries, the most notorious of them Gaspard de Bresse *(see left)*, who hung out at the village of Les

Adrets de l'Estérel. These days it's popular with hikers and mountain bikers. Forested with pines, cork oak, juniper, rosemary and arbousiers (strawberry trees), in winter the hills turn yellow with mimosa, like many parts of this coast.

The **Corniche d'Or** coast road (D559) makes a scenic alternative to the autoroute to Cannes, though the familiar pattern of private villas, hotels and apartments 'de grand standing' blocking views and access to the sea can be very frustrating even here. East of St-Raphaël, the forested **Cap du Dramont** has some lovely stretches of coast path. The Plage du Dramont was one of the main landing beaches for Allied forces in the liberation of Provence: 20,000 America GIs, commemorated in a marble monument, landed here in less than 10 hours on 15 August 1944. Opposite the beach is the Ile d'Or (private), with its medieval-style tower, which it is said to have inspired Hergé's Tintin adventure *L'Ile Noire*.

Nearby **Agay** has a sheltered bay with three sandy beaches that are

wonderful for swimming. Next to the beach is a house once owned by the sister of Antoine de Saint-Exupéry, creator of *Le Petit Prince*, where the writer holidayed many times. East of here, between Anthéor and Trayas, is the most picturesque stretch of road winding between rocky outcrops and deep sea inlets, with plenty of places to stop and admire the view. Inland, those with an eye for a panorama should head for **Mont Vinaigre** (at 618 metres/2,027ft, the highest point of the massif) or the Pic de l'Ours.

Further east, the tiny port and sandy beach of **La Figueirette**, just before Théoule-sur-Mer, is the starting point for several footpaths into the Estérel. Follow the signs to **Notre-Dame d'Afrique**. Placed here in 2002, the 12-metre (39ft) -high statue facing across the Mediterranean is a copy of the black statue of the Virgin at Notre-Dame d'Afrique in Algiers. It is a place of pilgrimage for the French *pieds noirs* returned from Algeria, with a blessing ceremony each May.

Another curiosity to look out for

high above the corniche is the **Palais Bulles** built in 1968 by experimental Finnish architect Antti Lovag for the couturier Pierre Cardin. Lovag rejected straight lines and angles: everything here is globular curves. The outside amphitheatre is the setting for a summer music festival.

Sitting on the seafront at **Mandelieu-la Napoule** ㉑, just west of Cannes, is the fantastical **Château de la Napoule** (www.chateau-lana-poule.com; mid-Feb–mid-Nov daily 10am–6pm, mid-Nov–mid-Feb Sat–Sun and school hols 10am–5pm, Mon–Fri 2–5pm; charge). Originally a fortress belonging to the powerful Villeneuve family, later a glass factory, it was acquired by eccentric American artist Henry Clews in 1918. He and his wife gave the place a complete medieval makeover with turrets, crenellations and gargoyles, adding Clews' own weird sculptures and topiaried gardens, which are one of France's *jardins remarquables*. Today the castle is an arts foundation offering residences to writers and artists, and a treasure hunt for children. ❏

Nougat for sale in St-Raphaël.

Below: Côte de l'Estérel.

RESTAURANTS

Restaurants

Prices for a three-course meal without wine. Many restaurants have a less expensive lunch menu:
€ = under €25
€€ = €25–40
€€€ = €40–60
€€€€ = over €60

Hyères
Le Baraza
2 avenue Ambroise Thomas
Tel: 04 94 35 21 01. Open L & D Tue–Sat. €€€
Fashionable wine bar-cum-bistro where the food is typically French but often with a touch of the Far East, such as tuna with a peanut crust accompanied by noodles. The *plat du jour* is €12 and there are also platters of charcuterie and cheese.

Bormes-les-Mimosas
La Rastègue
48 boulevard du Levant, Le Pin des Bormes
Tel: 04 94 15 19 41. Open L Sun & D Tue–Sun. Closed Jan. €€€–€€€€
Creative Provençal cooking has earned young chef Jérôme Masson a Michelin star. Try roast pigeon breast in cocoa sauce washed down with a regional wine. The dining room is classy but the views from the terrace are stunning.
Restaurant de l'Estagnol
Parc de l'Estagnol
Tel: 04 94 64 71 11. Open L & D in summer. €€

Alfresco eating under the pines, set just back from the beach at l'Estagnol. The speciality is fresh fish and langoustines grilled on an open wood fire, although you can also opt for a bouillabaisse.

Le Lavandou
Les Tamaris 'Chez Raymond'
Plage de St-Clair
Tel: 04 94 71 02 70. Open L Wed–Mon (winter only) & D daily (June–Sept only), Closed Nov–Feb. €€€
The most upmarket of the fish restaurants along the Plage de St-Clair is especially renowned for its *bourride* (garlicky fish stew) and the excellent daily catch.

Rayol-Canadel
Maurin des Maures
boulevard du TCF
www.maurin-des-maures.com
Tel: 04 94 05 60 11. Open L & D daily. €€
This noisy, animated institution has lots of atmosphere, combining a popular restaurant where you are packed elbow to elbow down long tables, and a local bar with pinball and table football. Come for fish dishes and Provençal classics like *daube de boeuf* and rabbit. Book ahead.

Collobrières
Hôtel-Restaurant des Maures
19 boulevard Lazare Carnot
Tel: 04 94 48 07 10. Open July–Aug L & D daily, Sept–June L daily. €
A popular, unpretentious restaurant-bar with a terrace spanning the Real Collobrier River. Sustaining rustic fare includes roast pork with figs.

Grimaud
Le Coteau Fleuri
place des Pénitents
Tel: 04 94 43 20 17. Open L Wed–Thu Sat–Sun (D only July–Aug), D Wed–Mon. Closed Nov–Dec. €€–€€€€
In an 18th-century house, quietly situated in the old village. Re-

LEFT: style and colour.

nowned locally for its gastronomic take on regional cuisine by Jean-Claude Paillard.

Cogolin
Grain de Sel
6 rue du 11 novembre
Tel: 04 9454 4686. Open D Tue–Sun. €€
Fresh seasonal bistro cooking, such as stuffed vegetables, roast lamb and fruit tarts, prepared by a haute cuisine-trained chef.

St-Tropez
Brasserie des Arts
5 place des Lices
www.brasseriedesarts.com
Tel: 04 94 40 27 37. Open L & D daily. €€–€€€
The 'BA' was reborn in 2008 as a sleek cream and teak affair for people-watching from the terrace. The menu ranges from carpaccios, risottos and crumbles to classic steak tartare, fish with olives and herby lamb, as well as brunch on Sunday. Dress up to look as cool as the staff. Service until 2am and weekly DJ sets in peak season.

Le Girelier
quai Jean Jaurès
www.legirelier.fr
Tel: 04 94 97 03 87. Open Apr–Oct L & D daily. €€–€€€€
This harbourside fish and shellfish restaurant has gained a chic fisherman's shack-inspired decor from designer Kristian Gavoille following a change of ownership. Fish *a la plancha*

is a speciality along with Le Girelier's own take on bouillabaisse. Serves all day noon–midnight.

Senequier
quai Jean Jaurès
www.senequier.com
Tel: 04 94 97 20 20. Open daily. Closed mid-Jan–mid-Feb. €€
This St-Tropez institution, which opened as a patisserie specialising in nougat in 1887 (still available at 4 place aux Herbes), has had a makeover by hot young designer Noé Duchaufour Laurence but happily kept the rows of red directors' chairs for surveying the portside scene. Not cheap but a must at apéritif time.

La Tarte Tropézienne
place des Lices
Tel: 04 94 97 04 69. Open B & L daily. €
As well as savoury snacks, this *boulangerie-pâtisserie-salon de thé* serves its famous sgnature *Tarte Tropézienne* – sponge cake filled with custard – which apparently got its name from Brigitte Bardot. A great place for breakfast but be prepared to queue on market day and in peak season.

La Vague d'Or
Hôtel Résidence de la Pinède, plage de la Bouillabaisse
www.residencepinede.com
Tel: 04 94 55 91 00. Open Apr–Oct D daily. €€€€
In 2013, this gourmet restaurant won its third Michelin star, making it only the third restaurant

in the Provence region to have this accolade. Expect to pay upwards of €120 to sample Arnaud Donckele's inspired Provençal cuisine such as turbot in a Camargue salt crust flavoured with lemon grass and seaweed.

La Voûte by BB
24 rue du Portail Neuf
Tel: 04 94 54 32 76 Open L & D daily. Closed Nov–Mar. €€
A small restaurant with an 80s vibe which is a haven for carnivores in a fish-heavy region. On the menu you'll find cuts of the best beef: Kobe, Angus, Salers and Charolais, but there's tapas too.

Gassin
La Verdoyante
866 chemin vicinal Coste-Brigade
www.la-verdoyante.fr
Tel: 04 94 56 16 23. Open L Tue, Thu–Sun & D Thu–Mon. Closed Nov–Jan. €€–€€€
Inspired by the vegetables and herbs of Provence, Laurent Mouret's traditional cuisine is served in the idyllic surroundings of his family's farmhouse. You can see the Bay of St-Tropez from the terrace.

Ramatuelle
Chez Camille
route de la Bonne Terrasse
Tel: 04 98 12 68 98. Open L & D Wed–Sun. Closed Oct–Mar. €€€–€€€€
Right at the Cap Camarat end of the Plage

de Pampelonne, this ancient fisherman's shack draws *le tout St-Trop* for its bouillabaisse and fish.

Fréjus
L'Amandier
19 rue Marc-Antoine Desaugiers. Tel: 04 94 53 48 77. Open L Tue, Thu–Sat & D Mon–Sat. €€
The surroundings are contemporary, albeit in an ancient vaulted dining room, but the food is traditionally Provençal with a modern touch. Try rabbit with asparagus risotto followed by strawberry sorbet.

St-Raphaël
La Brasserie Tradition et Gourmandise
6 avenue de Valescure
www.labrasserietg.fr
Tel: 04 94 95 25 00. Open L & D Mon–Sat. €–€€
Using seasonal produce, this cosy Provençal restaurant is the latest offering from Philippe Troncy. The magnolia-shaded terrace is perfect in warm weather.

Mandelieu
Le Bistrot L'Etage
rue J-H Carle
www.oasis-raimbault.com
Tel: 04 93 49 95 52. Open L & D Tue–Sat. €€–€€€
The more affordable offering from the Raimbault brothers, whose gourmet restaurant, L'Oasis (€€€€), is downstairs. Traditional Provençal food.

TROPICAL GARDENS

The Riviera's mild climate and abundant sunlight have made it a paradise for a remarkable range of flora

All sorts of tropical and subtropical plants have been naturalised in the Riviera region – not just cultivated in gardens and public parks, but growing wild, like the mimosa trees that thrive in the Estérel hills, and the eucalyptus in the Maures forests. The Belle Epoque was the golden age of Riviera gardens. Most of these exotic edens were created between the 1890s and the 1920s, many of them by the foreigners who came to winter in the region. Almost as varied as the plants they contained were the people who created them: English aristocrats and colonels, American writers, Russian princesses, landscape designers, architects and artists, explorers, botanists and other scientists. Some gardens were created for scientific purposes, others as luxuriant backdrops to go with their exuberant *palazzi* and avant-garde villas.

These green-fingered eccentrics introduced countless new species to the native Mediterranean flora of herbs, parasol pines, olive trees and cork oaks, ranging from the agaves and date palms of desert regions to the dank ferns, banana trees and purple bougainvillea of the tropics. Against the formal restraint of traditional French gardens, with their gravel paths and neatly trimmed hedges, these places were often flamboyantly exotic creations bursting with colour.

ABOVE: Jardins d'Ephrussi Rothschild, St-Jean-Cap Ferrat. The seven themed gardens, created by Béatrice Ephrussi, are arranged around a central formal French garden with a pool and musical gardens.

LEFT: cactus fruit at the Jardin Exotique, Monaco.

ABOVE: Monaco's Jardin Exotique. This collection, begun at the turn of the 20th century, has over 1,000 species of cacti and other succulent plants, as well as a cave with stalactites and stalagmites.

GARDEN TRAILS

1. The Route des Parcs et Jardins du Var (www.visitvar.fr) follows a 325km (200-mile) loop between Saint-Zacharie in the Ste-Baume Massif to Hyères, taking in tiny hill village, herb and scent gardens, historic château gardens and the arty gardens of Hyères, as well as addresses of some of the *département*'s best nurseries.

2. The Route des Jardins de la Riviera follows the Alpes-Maritimes coast between Mandelieu-la Napoule and Menton, visiting gardens, villas and grand hotels of the Belle Epoque, including the famous Villa Ephrussi, the gardens of Menton, Villa Eilen Roc in Antibes and the garden of actor-playwright Sacha Guitry at Cap d'Ail.

3. The Route du Mimosa (www.bormeslesmimosas.com).

4. Menton, famed for its lemons *(above picture)* is the undisputed garden capital of the coast. Some of its gardens can be visited through the Service du Patrimoine de Menton (tel: 04 92 10 97 10, www.jardins-menton.fr).

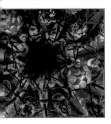
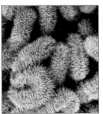

ABOVE LEFT AND RIGHT: cacti in the exotic garden at Jardin d'Ephrussi Rothschild.
BELOW: Jardin Botanique Exotique Val Rahmeh, Menton. Over 700 species grow in profusion on a hilly site around a 1920s villa.

ABOVE AND RIGHT: Menton's Serre de la Madone garden, full of rare species, classical statuary and fountains.

ST-PAUL, VENCE AND THE GORGES DU LOUP

The hilly interior of the western Alpes-Maritimes is home to two shrines of modern art: the Fondation Maeght at St-Paul-de-Vence and Matisse's Chapelle du Rosaire at Vence. Around the Gorges du Loup are some classic *villages perchés*, and fragrant Grasse is the centre of perfume production

West of the River Var, the ancient city of Vence and historic hill towns such as St-Paul-de-Vence and Tourrettes-sur-Loup rest against a mountain backdrop. This part of the Alpes-Maritimes remained part of Provence, and later France, even when the Comté de Nice to the east was under Piedmontese-Sardinian sovereignty – hence some impressive fortifications put up by the French monarchy anxious to control the border. Less crowded and built-up than the coastal strip, the hinterland has an artistic and architectural heritage spanning medieval chateaux and modern masterpieces, while the gentle climate favourable for flower cultivation has made Grasse a world centre for the perfume industry.

St-Paul-de-Vence

Sitting within ramparts on top of a hill, **St-Paul-de-Vence ❶** epitomises all that is best and worst about Provence: while undeniably picturesque, the village is easily overrun with tourists and any semblance of everyday life has long been glossed over by arts-and-crafts galleries and souvenir shops. Thankfully, far more illustrious than the art touted in the

old village are the works on show at the **Fondation Maeght** *(see box, page 219)*, outside the village. One of the finest collections of modern art in the world, it is a wonderful example of the integration of art with architecture and nature.

The village gained its reputation as an artistic centre in the 1920s. The **Auberge de la Colombe d'Or** became a meeting place for a bevy of artists – including Picasso, Bonnard, Chagall, Modigliani and Soutine – who, as the tale goes, left their

Main attractions
FONDATION MAEGHT, ST-PAUL-DE-VENCE
CHAPELLE DU ROSAIRE, VENCE
OLD TOWN, VENCE
LE SAUT DU LOUP, GORGES DU LOUP
MUSÉE INTERNATIONAL DE LA PARFUMERIE, GRASSE
JARDINS DU MIP, MOUANS-SARTOUX

LEFT: Vence facade.
RIGHT: the Colombe d'Or.

For centuries, St-Paul served as a fortress guarding the border between France and the Comté de Nice. When King François I built the ramparts of the village in the 16th century, he uprooted all the inhabitants and packed them off to live in nearby La Colle-sur-Loup. Over 100 years later, new residents arrived: the monks of the Ordre des Pénitents Blancs.

BELOW: a splash of colour in St-Paul-de-Vence.

canvases behind, sometimes to settle long-running accounts. Whatever the truth, the Colombe d'Or has now assembled its own priceless collection of paintings and sculptures, which includes a Calder mobile and a Braque mosaic dove by the swimming pool. You must dine or stay here, however, a delightful if pricey experience, in order to see the collection. Lesser mortals can at least take a seat opposite the Colombe d'Or at the **Café de la Place**.

The ring of sturdy ramparts, built in 1536 by François I, remains unbroken. A walk around them gives a good view of the surrounding countryside studded with dark cypresses and azure swimming pools. Glimpses of bougainvillea-filled gardens hint at the luxurious life beyond the stout wooden doors that are visible from the street.

Within the town walls, rue Grande forms a spine through the town, lined with art galleries and

craft shops between the 14th-century Porte Nord (or Porte Royale) to the Porte Sud (or Porte de Nice). Many of the 16th- and 17th-century houses bear coats of arms and are now artists' ateliers. Some of the medieval shops survive, usually as private homes; look out for a wide arch, beneath which is a doorway and an adjoining window. The window has a large marble sill which used to be the shop counter - it is a direct descendant of the Roman shop. At No. 3 rue Grande is the **Musée de St-Paul** (June–Sept Mon–Fri 10am–7pm, Sat–Sun 10am–1pm, 2–7pm, Oct–May Mon–Fri 10am–6pm, Sat–Sun 10am–1pm, 2–6pm; free), the municipal museum which also hosts temporary exhibitions by artists associated with the village including Marc Chagall, who lived in St-Paul from 1966 to 1985. About halfway along, at the place de la Grande Fontaine, a street climbs to a small square at the top of the village. Here you'll

St-Paul, Vence and the Gorges du Loup

find the **Eglise Collégiale**, in which is a painting attributed to Tintoretto, the **Chapelle des Pénitents Blancs**, the Mairie (town hall) housed within the remains of the castle keep, and the small **Musée de l'Histoire Local** (daily, Apr–Sept 11am–1pm, 3–6pm, Oct and Dec–Mar 2–5pm; closed Nov; charge) where costumed figures illustrate key moments in St-Paul's history; its most interesting attraction is the exhibition of photographs taken of celebrities taken in St-Paul: Greta Garbo, Sophia Loren, Yul Brynner, Burt Lancaster, Jean-Paul Sartre and many others enjoyed holidays here.

Outside the south gate is the cemetery in which the painter Marc Chagall is buried. You can also follow the path along the western ramparts, which provide good views over vineyards and palatial villas down to the coast.

Vence

Modern-art pilgrims should also make for **Vence ❷**, just 4km (2.5 miles) further north, and its **Chapelle du Rosaire** (466 avenue

Henri Matisse; tel: 04 93 58 03 26; Mon, Wed, Sat 2–5.30pm, Tue, Thu 10–11.30am, 2–5.30pm, closed mid-Nov–mid-Dec; charge), on the edge of town on the route de Ste-Jeannet. It was designed between 1948 and 1951 by the elderly Henri Matisse (1869–1954), who had moved to the Villa le Rêve in Vence during World War II, encouraged by the Dominican nun Sister Jacques-Marie (*see margin, right*).

The chapel is strikingly pure and bright: the roof in glazed blue-and-white pantiles, and the only colour in its white interior contributed by the stained-glass windows and the reflections they create. The figurative tiles on three of the walls capture Matisse's fluid mastery of line in the single stroke of his drawings. On the simple stone altar lies a tiny bronze crucifix. In an adjacent room you can see Matisse's preparatory sketches.

A spiritual testament by the aged artist, Matisse called the chapel his most satisfying work. He was not the only artist attracted to Vence: Chagall also lived here. The writer D.H. Lawrence came here after having

TIP

The Villa le Rêve in Vence, where Matisse lived from 1943 to 1949, is now used for painting courses and artists' residences. Half- or one-day visits can be arranged by appointment: 261 avenue Henri Matisse, tel: 04 93 58 82 68.

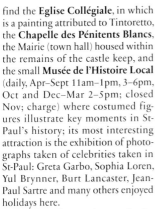

Below: Giacometti sculpture, Fondation Maeght.

Fondation Maeght

The Fondation Maeght (623 chemin des Gardettes, St-Paul-de-Vence; tel: 04 93 32 81 63; www.fondation-maeght.com; daily, July–Sept 10am–7pm, Oct–June until 6pm; charge) is arguably the most interesting of all the museums on the Côte d'Azur, inaugurated in 1964 to house the fabulous modern art collection put together by Paris art dealer Aimé Maeght and his wife Marguerite. The concrete building was designed by the Spanish architect José-Luis Sert, and is beautifully integrated with both landscape and artworks, inside and out. A series of pools, terraces and sculptures include funky, colourful ceramic fountains by Miró and tiled designs by Braque. Other sculptures, among them works by Giacometti and Calder, are dotted around the pine-shaded garden. All the structural features were devised to promote an understanding of 20th-century art, and the architect worked directly with some of the artists, principally Miró and Chagall, to achieve this. A few of the holdings are sometimes on loan and the collection is rehung for themed exhibitions each summer, but with reserves this large there is always something to see.

Around a dozen families still make their living cultivating violets in Tourrettes-sur-Loup. The fragrant purple flowers are harvested between mid-October and mid-March; between May and July the leaves are picked and delivered to the perfume factories in Grasse. The end of the flower harvest is celebrated in March by the Fête des Violettes, with a Mass, dancing and a floral procession.

BELOW: playing boules in Tourrettes-sur-Loup.

been diagnosed with tuberculosis and died in the town in 1930.

Within the city walls

The medieval centre of Vence is very picturesque and, once you get away from the souvenir sellers, the lanes and alleyways are little changed from previous centuries – except that many of the lanes on the north side of town now have light and air where they end at the town ramparts; the walls have been cut down to waist height to reveal a mountain view.

There are many traces of Vence's days as a powerful bishopric. Its strategic mountain position made it a trophy for successive Ligurians, Lombards, Romans, countless Christians and Saracens, and the Germans and Italians of World War II, who all passed through here.

Begun in the 4th century, the **Ancienne Cathédrale**, in place Clemenceau on the site of a Roman temple, reflects the town's battle-torn past. The building is a patchwork of styles and eras, with its simple Baroque facade, Gothic windows, Roman tablets incorporated into the porch, fragments of the earlier Carolingian church, 15th-century carved choir stalls and a delicate 1979 mosaic by Chagall of Moses in the baptistery.

Behind here pleasant place Godeau contains an ancient Roman column and is a pleasant place to stop for a drink, while rue de l'Evêché, which has some interesting craft galleries and artists' studios, leads to place du Peyra and its restaurant terraces. On one side of the square, abutting a medieval tower, is the **Château de Villeneuve-Fondation Emile Hugues** (Tue–Sun 10am–12.30pm, 2–6pm, closed between exhibitions; charge), the 17th-century baronial residence of the powerful Villeneuve family, now used for high-quality exhibitions of modern and contemporary art. Outside the Porte du Peyra, place du Frêne contains a venerable ash tree supposedly planted by François I in 1538, and, beyond here, square du Grand-Jardin is the setting for the farmers' market (mornings daily) and Les Nuits du Sud, Vence's summer world music festival.

The Gorges du Loup

From Vence it's a scenic drive along D2210 to the attractive hilltop village of **Tourrettes-sur-Loup** ❸, dubbed the 'city of violets' *(see margin, page 220)*. Now home to the requisite Provençal clan of potters, painters and woodcarvers, Tourrettes was a Roman and subsequently Saracen stronghold. The only evocations of war today come from the 15th-century château, once marking the entrance to the village, now at its centre and occupied by the Mairie (town hall). In the main square, the church conceals a triptych by the Bréa school. On the outskirts of town, the **Bastide aux Violettes** (Quartier de la Ferrage; Tue–Sat 10am–12.30pm, 1.30–5pm; free) is a museum dedicated to the history of violets and their production.

To the west of Tourrettes, off the D2210 is the Domaine des Courmettes (route des Courmettes; tel: 04 92 11 02 32; Apr–Oct daily 9.30am–8pm, Nov–Mar Fri–Wed 10am–5pm; free), a nature reserve with three different routes of various levels of ability – L'Aigle is a three-hour trek up the Pic des Courmettes (1,248 metres/4094ft) for great views over the countryside and coast. In the same area, **La Ferme des Courmettes** (tel: 04 93 59 39 93; http://chevredescourmettes.com) is a small farm that makes organic goats' cheese and which is open to visitors for tours and tastings; their produce is sold at some of the best restaurants in the region.

The D2210 from Tourrettes descends through woodland into the river valley at **Pont-du-Loup** – home to the much publicised **Confiserie Florian** (tel: 04 93 59 32 91; www.confiserieflorian.com; daily 9am–noon, 2–6.30pm; free), an old-fashioned sweet manufacturer open to visitors; look out for the crystallised roses and violets. Also here is the **Atelier de Cuisine des Fleurs** (16 route de Grasse; tel: 04 92 11 06 94) where Yves Terrillon offers lessons in cooking with flowers for children and adults. The village, framed by mountains on either side, is dominated by the remains of a railway viaduct which was blown up by the Germans in 1944 and never repaired.

TIP

Molinard (60 boulevard Victor Hugo; tel: 04 92 42 33 21; www. molinard.com) runs 60-minute courses in perfume making. Create your own personal blend from 90 ingredients with the help of a 'nose'.

Below: hilltop Tourrettes-sur-Loup.

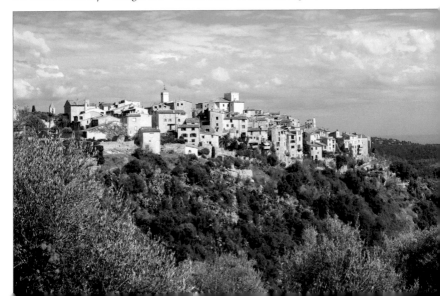

Perfumes of Provence

Although best known for making perfumes for the world's biggest fashion houses, Grasse's 'noses' also concoct fragances for use in cleaning products

The perfume industry in Grasse originated with an immigrant group of Italian glove-makers in the 16th century. They discovered the wonderful scents of the flowers in the area and began perfuming their soft leather gloves, a fashion introduced by Catherine de Medici and a favourite way to use perfume at a time when the odour of the general populace definitely required masking.

Demand for the floral perfumes steadily grew in the 18th and 19th centuries, and Grasse prospered as a perfume mecca. Local production of the raw material declined, however, after World War II due to competition from countries such as Turkey, Egypt and Bulgaria, where labour costs were much lower. On top of this, the gentle climate attracted many wealthy people to the area, pushing land prices sky-high and causing acres to be sold off as building plots.

Nonetheless, each morning you can still see vast mountains of rose petals, vats of mimosa or jonquils and spadefuls of violets and orange blossom just picked and waiting to be processed.

The flowers must be picked early in the day, when the oil is most concentrated, and delivered immediately. It takes vast quantities of blooms to produce the tiniest amounts of 'absolute' (concentrated) perfume: around 750kg (1,650lbs) of roses for just 1kg (2.2lbs) of rose absolute and about 4,000kg (8,800lbs) for 1kg of essential oil.

The art of perfume making

Various methods are used to create the absolutes and essential oils that the perfumier mixes to create a fragrance. The oldest method is steam distillation, now used mainly for orange blossom. Water and flowers are boiled in a still, and the essential oils are extracted by steam.

Another ancient, expensive, method is *enfleurage*. The flowers are layered with a semi-solid mixture of lard, spread over glass sheets and stacked in tiers. When the fat is fully impregnated with perfume, the scent is separated out by washing the *axonge* (fat) with alcohol. A more modern method is extraction by volatile solvents, leaving a final dose of concentrated essence.

The highly trained perfumiers or 'noses' can identify and classify hundreds of fragrances. In creating a fragrance, a perfumier is rather like a musician, blending different 'chords' of scent to create a harmony. The desired result is a complex perfume that will slowly diffuse around the body – a process the French call *sillage*. Nowadays, many of the raw ingredients are imported, with the exception of jasmine and may rose; others, such as musk, formerly made from animals, are chemically synthesised. But the perfumiers' know-how keeps Grasse at the forefront of the industry, not just with perfumes for the great fashion houses but with the fragrances used in household cleaning products and food-industry flavourings. ❑

LEFT: visiting the Parfumerie Fragonard factory.

You can then decide to head southwards towards Le Bar-sur-Loup or upstream on the D6 along the imposing **Gorges du Loup** ④, where the torrential Loup River has scythed its way through a gorge of grey rock. It is punctuated by some impressive waterfalls, notably the **Cascade de Courmes,** which plunges down about 50 metres (160ft) halfway along the Gorges, the smaller **Cascade des Desmoiselles**, and, further up, **Saut du Loup** (Wolf's Leap). Signs advise on sudden rises in the water level, dependent on the hydroelectric station upstream.

In the other direction, **Le Bar-sur-Loup** is a relatively ungentrified village whose church (tel: 06 59 83 52 18; visits by appointment) contains a fascinating if macabre painting of the dance of death. Outside the 16th-century château on place F. Pault are two cannons captured by Admiral François de Grasse from the British at the Battle of Chesapeake in 1781; he was born here. The village is a good centre for walking and maps in English are available from the tourist office.

Gourdon

If the term *village perché* needed a perfect example, **Gourdon** ❺ would be it. One whole side of the village teeters on the edge of a rocky cliff, obviating the need for any fortress walls to repel invaders. The views down to the coast from place Victoria are well worth the trip.

From Gourdon the D3 zigzags down to Grasse. On your way you might choose to detour to **Valbonne** ❻. Valbonne immediately stands out from its neighbours as it was laid out in the 16th century on a strict rectangular grid plan by monks from the Abbaye de Chalais, on the southern edge of the town. The abbey houses the **Musée du Vieux Valbonne** (Tue–Sat June–Sept 3–7pm, Oct–May 2–6pm, closed Jan; charge), a local heritage museum.

Another very different planned city lies east of here on the Plateau de Valbonne. Founded in the early 1970s, **Sophia-Antipolis** is southern France's answer to Silicon Valley, a brave new world of high-tech companies, research institutes and a branch of the university of Nice.

TIP

Le Domaine de Manon (36 chemin du Servan, Plascassier; tel: 06 12 18 02 69; www.le-domaine-de-manon.com) is a family-run flower farm on the outskirts of Grasse that is open to the public. Come in May–mid-June (Tue at 10am) to see Centifolia roses or Aug–mid-Oct (Tue at 9am) for jasmine.

BELOW: family stroll in Gourdon.

Carved statue representing the perfumier's art outside the Parfumerie Fragonard, one of Grasse's oldest perfume-making establishments.

BELOW: gathering jasmine, Grasse.

Grasse, the perfume capital

Literature fans may recognise **Grasse** ❼ as the setting for Patrick Süskind's novel *Perfume*. France's sprawling perfume capital is not one of Provence's most attractive towns, and the hilly geography and winding boulevards make finding your bearings difficult. But the municipality is at last making an effort to revive the rather run-down town centre through restoration and pedestrianisation.

Between 1138 and 1227 Grasse was a free city, allied to Pisa and Genoa, and governed by a consulate, like the Italian republics, before being annexed by the counts of Provence. When Provence was united with France in 1482, Grasse continued to trade with Italy, importing animal skins and selling linen and high-quality leather goods. In the 16th century, the fashion for perfumed gloves encouraged the perfume industry in Grasse, but it was not until the 18th century that tanning and perfumery began to develop as separate trades.

Perfume museum

On a still day, Grasse lives up to its reputation as a scent capital: a sweet aroma lingers in the air. Huge hoardings announce factory visits to the three big perfumiers – Fragonard, Molinard and Galimard – all actually located some way outside the town centre. The **Musée International de la Parfumerie** (MIP; 2 boulevard du Jeu de Ballontel: 04 97 05 58 00; www.museesdegrasse. com; May–Sept daily 10am–7pm, Apr daily 11am–6pm, Oct–Mar Wed–Mon 11am–6pm, closed Nov; charge) in an 18th-century mansion and its modern extension provides an imaginative introduction to the sense of smell and the art of perfumery, tracing it back to ancient Egyptian times, with displays of the assorted plants, minerals, roots and animal matter used to make perfumes. The museum has a vast collection of perfume bottles, a greenhouse containing olfactory plants and materials to sniff and touch, a reconstruction of a medieval apothecary's shop and works by contemporary artists.

Nearby is the **Musée Provençal du Costume et du Bijou** (2 rue Jean-Ossola; tel: 04 93 36 44 65; daily 10am–1pm, 2–6pm, Nov–Jan Mon–Sat; charge), where 18th- and 19th-century regional costumes and jewellery are attractively presented around the upstairs rooms of a period house, with a Fragonard perfume shop below. The perfume company's original factory, the **Usine Historique de Fragonard** (20 boulevard Fragonard; daily 9am–6pm, Nov–Jan 9am–12.30pm, 2–6pm; free), opened in 1926, is just down the hill. A few perfumes, soaps and cosmetics are still made here.

Grasse cathedral

Rue Jean-Ossola is the best way into the largely pedestrianised old town and is lined with fine façades, among them that of the Hôtel Luce at No. 14, where Alexandre Dumas's hero, the swashbuckling musketeer d'Artagnan, is said to have stayed. On place du Petit-Puy are a fortified watchtower, the Hôtel de Ville (once the bishop's palace) and the **Cathédrale Notre-Dame-de-Puy**, a much altered, rather gloomy Romanesque structure. It contains three paintings by Rubens and a rare religious subject, *The Washing of the Feet*, by Jean-Honoré Fragonard (1732–1806), who was born in Grasse. There are wonderful views across the surrounding countryside from the square at the side of the cathedral.

The Fragonard connection

Although the town makes the most of its connection with Fragonard, he actually spent most of his career in Paris or on the Grand Tour of Italy with aristocratic patrons, and it was only after the French Revolution that he took refuge in Grasse in the house of a wealthy cousin, now the **Villa-Musée Fragonard** (23 boulevard Fragonard; www.museesdegrasse.com; May–Sept daily 10am–7pm, Apr daily 11am–6pm, Oct–Mar Wed–Mon 11am–6pm, closed Nov; free). The most remarkable aspect of the house is its stairwell, decorated with grisaille frescos by Fragonard's son when he was only 13 years old. In a neighbouring building, the **Musée de la Marine** (Mon–Fri 10am–12.30pm, 2.30–6pm, closed most of Nov; free), commemorates the life of the Admiral de Grasse, who defeated the British fleet at the battle of Chesapeake during the American War of Independence.

Another fine neoclassical residence contains the **Musée d'Art et d'Histoire de Provence** (2 rue Mirabeau; May–Sept daily 10am–7pm, Apr 11–6pm Oct–Mar Wed–Mon 11am–6pm, closed Nov; free) devoted to Provençal life, with rooms furnished in period style.

Mouans-Sartoux

About 15 minutes' drive south of Grasse on the D304, the unremarkable town of **Mouans-Sartoux ❽**, two separate communes until 1858, has a couple of reasons to make it a worthwhile stop. **Les Jardins du**

Below: cradle vaulting of Grasse cathedral.

MIP (979 chemin des Gourettes; tel: 04 92 98 92 69; www.museesdegrasse. com; May–Sept daily 10am–7pm, Apr daily 11am–6pm, Oct–Mar Wed–Mon 11am–6pm; charge, combined tickets with MIP available), the gardens of the Musée International de la Parfumerie, opened in 2013 after seven months of renovation. With the aid of an audio-video guide, visitors can learn about how the local flowers including jasmine, roses and orange blossom are grown. There is also an 'olfactory trail' to discover the different plant and flower smells and a shady picnic site. If you don't have a car, you can take the No. 20 or 21 bus from Grasse.

In the town itself, the 15th-century château is now home to **L'Espace de l'Art Concret** (tel: 04 93 75 71 50; July–Aug daily 11am–7pm, Sept–June Wed–Sun 1–6pm; charge). The gallery was founded in 1990 by Gottfried Honegger and Sybil Albers to house their collection of 'concrete art', a movement that began in Paris in 1930; the name refers to art being 'real' and 'free from symbolism' – not actually made of concrete.

Grottes de St-Cézaire

Napoleon passed by Grasse after escaping from Elba. The former N85 road (now D6185/D6085), known as the Route Napoléon, roughly follows the route he took through Provence on his return to Paris for the Hundred Days. From Grasse, the route climbs over the Col du Pilon pass before reaching the hamlet of St-Vallier-de-Thiey.

From here you can continue to Castellane (see page 166) or alternatively turn off on the D5 to the **Grottes de St-Cézaire** ❾ (tel: 04 93 60 22 35; daily, June–Aug 10am–6pm, Sept–May 10am–noon, 2–5pm, closed Dec–Jan; charge), a cave complex with stalactites in extraordinary shades of dark red and pink; remember to bring sturdy shoes and warm clothes.

From St-Cézaire you can return to Grasse via the village of **Cabris** (6km/4 miles from Grasse on the D4 road), which commands a most impressive view from its castle ruins. This is also excellent walking country, as the GR51 passes through the village.   ❏

BELOW: hillside Cabris.

RESTAURANTS

Restaurants

Prices for a three-course meal without wine. Many restaurants have a less expensive lunch menu:

€ = under €25
€€ = €25–40
€€€ = €40–60
€€€€ = over €60

St-Paul-de-Vence

La Colombe d'Or
1 place du Général de Gaulle
www.la-colombe-dor.com
Tel: 04 93 32 80 02. Open L & D daily. Closed Nov–22 Dec. €€€–€€€€
Once frequented by penniless artists who persuaded the owner to accept their paintings in payment for meals and board, this legendary hotel and restaurant now displays works by Miró, Picasso, Modigliani, Matisse and Chagall for a jet-set clientele. Serves classic cuisine and has arguably the most beautiful terrace in the region.

Vence

Les Bacchanales
247 avenue de Provence
www.lesbacchanales.com
Tel: 04 93 24 19 19. Open L & D Thu–Mon. €€
Chef Christophe Dufau is based in a modern dining room in a 19th-century villa on the edge of Vence, towards the Matisse chapel (Chapelle du Rosaire). His beautifully presented regional cooking is characterised by the use of wild herbs and edible flowers in dishes. There's usually live jazz on Friday evenings.

La Litote
5 rue de l'Evêché
www.lalitote.com
Tel: 04 93 24 27 82. Open L & D Tue–Sat, L Sun. €€
This friendly bistro in the old town brings an imaginative whiff of modernity to Provençal cuisine. The outdoor tables fill place de l'Evêché. Concerts on Thursday nights.

Tourrettes-sur-Loup

Clovis
21 Grande-Rue
www.clovis-gourmand.fr
Tel: 04 93 58 87 04. Open L & D Wed–Sun. €€–€€€€
Top-quality bistro cooking in an old village house with a small streetside terrace. Chef Julien Bousseau uses seasonal produce from local suppliers and each week his menu focuses on a particular meat, fish and vegetable. Pork cheeks with chanterelle mushrooms and 'house' gnocchi is the kind of thing to expect.

Grasse

Auberge du Vieux Château
place du Panorama, Cabris
www.aubergeduvieux
chateau.com
Tel: 04 93 60 50 12. Open L & D Wed–Sun (plus Mon & Tue July–Aug). €€–€€€
Set in the former castle guardroom in a lovely village just to the west of Grasse, this place is very popular among Grasse's anglophone expats, thanks to its terrace views and a frequently changing, Mediterranean menu.

La Bastide St-Antoine
48 avenue Henri Dunant
www.jacques-chibois.com
Tel: 04 93 70 94 94. Open L & D daily. €€€€
Difficult to find but well worth the search, this restaurant is set in an old olive grove outside Grasse, and is fashionable for the gourmet cuisine of Jacques Chibois. In season, truffles and wild mushrooms are house specialities.

Café des Musées
1 rue Jean Ossola
Tel: 04 92 60 99 00. Open summer daily 8.30am–6.30pm, winter Mon–Sat. €
This stylish modern café is conveniently located between the perfume and costume museums (Musée International de la Parfumerie and Musée Provençal du Costume et du Bijou). It's ideal for a drink or a light lunch of salads, savoury tarts and home-made desserts.

RIGHT: spectacularly situated restaurant, Gourdon.

MERCANTOUR NATIONAL PARK AND THE ARRIÈRE-PAYS NIÇOIS

Away from the coast, the eastern Alpes-Maritimes is characterised by wild mountains, plunging gorges, clear sparkling rivers and Italianate villages with frescoed churches

Nice
Marseille

Main attractions
PEILLON VILLAGE
VALLÉE DES MERVEILLES
MUSÉE DES MERVEILLES, TENDE
SOSPEL
SAORGE

BELOW: ibex roam the Mercantour Massif.

The rugged, sparsely populated Mercantour Massif provides a startling contrast to the built-up coast. Ice and fast mountain torrents have cut deep gorges through the rock. Flowing roughly north to south, the rivers Cians, Tinée and Vésubie all empty into the River Var, while further east lie the Bévéra and Roya rivers. The scenery ranges from olive groves grown on the lower slopes to pines and edelweiss, mountain lakes and bare Alpine peaks, many of them over 2,000 metres (6,560ft). The area is a paradise for hikers and mountaineers in summer and skiers in winter.

In addition to its spectacular scenery, this Alpine region by the Italian border also has a little-known architectural and artistic heritage that reflects a period when it was more heavily populated, largely because of the active trade routes, notably the salt route, linking the Comté de Nice, Piedmont and Liguria. Chapels, often decorated with ornate frescos, were put up as protection against the frequent outbreaks of plague, and dur-

ing the Counter-Reformation, fine Baroque churches were constructed as the Catholic Church sought to reassert its authority against the Protestant Reformation.

The Arrière-Pays Niçois

Even a few kilometres inland from Nice or Monaco, you soon find yourself in a mountain environment studded with medieval villages. Unspoilt **Peillon**, 15km (9 miles) northeast of Nice, clings like an eagle's eyrie onto a jagged ridge above the River Paillon. Vaulted alleys and steep stairways are lined with 16th-century houses, and the Chapelle des Pénitents Blancs is decorated with dramatic 15th-century frescos of the Passion of Christ. Also in the village is an olive oil mill, Le Moulin à Huile Roger Guido (916 boulevard de la Vallée; tel: 04 93 91 24 40).

Further along steep narrow roads and hairpin bends stands the perched village of **Peille**, with some lovely Renaissance and Gothic fountains, doorways and stonework amid the cobbled alleyways. It's possible to walk to Peille from Peillon along the old Roman road (2 hours). An old stone house is the location of the Musée du Terroir (Wed–Sun 10am–noon, 1–6pm; free), a local heritage museum.

Coaraze ❶, another delightful village balancing at an altitude of 650 metres (2,100ft), calls itself *le village du soleil*. Wander through the narrow cobbled streets looking out for the sundials, which have been a feature here since Jean Cocteau decorated the town hall with one. Next to the lizard mosaic on place Félix-Giordan is a poem relating the local legend of how the villagers caught the devil, who cut off his tail to escape. (Coaraze derives from the Provençal words 'coa raza' meaning 'cut tail'.) On the edge of the village is the **Chapelle Bleue**, named after the blue murals created by Ponce de Léon in 1965. If you have the time and the energy, a four-hour hike will take you up to the ruined village of Rocasparvièra through wonderful scenery.

Parc National du Mercantour

Covering a large swathe of the region is the **Parc National du Mercantour ❷**,

Thousands of Bronze Age drawings can be seen in the Vallée des Merveilles.

BELOW: Alpine flowers.

TIP

Those with a head for heights might like to explore the park by *via ferrata* – iron ladders bolted into rocks by Italian soldiers during World War I. Local tourist offices will have details of guided outings in their area. Also see www.viaferrata.org.

a huge national park created in 1979, which joins the Parco Naturale Alpi Marittime around the Argentera Massif in Italy. It consists of two zones: the highly protected, largely uninhabited central zone, and the peripheral zone, where the villages are situated.

Botanists now believe that more than half of the 4,200 or so species of wild flowers found in France grow in the Mercantour, including 63 varieties of orchid. In 2007, work started here on Europe's largest ever inventory of flora and fauna. Wildlife includes ibex, chamois, marmots, ptarmigan, black grouse, golden eagle and rare species of owl. As well as a successful project to reintroduce ibex to the park, there has also been one to reintroduce bearded vultures; not only are they the world's largest bird of prey they are also one of the eight most threatened bird species in Europe. More controversial are the wolves that have returned to the area after crossing the border from Italy,

now a source of heated argument between environmentalists and the shepherds who claim that the wolves are killing their sheep.

Vallée des Merveilles

At the heart of the national park lies the mysterious **Vallée des Merveilles** ❸, where the mountains shelter a remarkable display of almost 36,000 prehistoric rock engravings by early Bronze Age settlers *(see page 234)*.

Some demanding hiking

There are two main points of access into the Vallée des Merveilles: from **St-Dalmas-de-Tende** in the Roya valley on the eastern side, and from **Madone de Fenestre** in the Vésubie valley to the west. The valley is accessible only in summer and only on foot (although a few all-terrain vehicles are permitted). Much of the land is really only suitable for those hikers with limbs and lungs strong enough to endure a day or two of solid walking and with

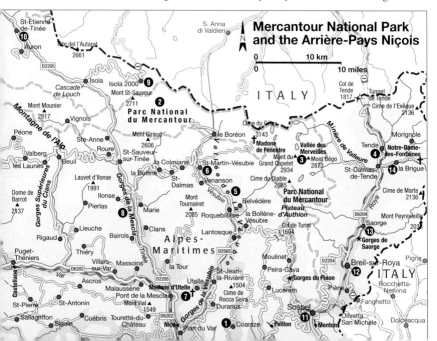

hiking gear to match. Hardened hikers can probably make do with a large-scale map – arm yourself with the IGN 1:25,000 map and a Topoguide. If an overnight stay is necessary, try one of the simple mountain refuges administered by the Club Alpin Français (tel: 04 93 62 59 99; www.cafnice.org). Often there aren't even any paths, let alone signposts if you lose your way. For the less experienced hiker, a mountain guide is essential, or join one of the regular guided walks to some of the more accessible engravings, organised by the national park (June–Sept, information from Maisons du Parc and tourist offices, *see margin right*). They last about three hours and leave from the Refuge des Merveilles or Refuge de Fontanalbe (the latter is the easiest to reach, from Castérino, west of St-Dalmas-de-Tende).

The area between **Mt-Bégo** and the 2,934-metre (9,626ft) **Mont du Grand Capelet** makes for a good, if tough, hike, with several lakes on the way. There are mountain refuges either end of the 60km (40-mile) valley. If a thunderstorm strikes, don't panic: shepherds working in the valleys below more than 3,000 years ago treated Mt-Bégo like a temple, a place where sheep were sacrificed in an attempt to appease terrifying storms. In contemporary and less superstitious times, the mountain is simply seen as an effective lightning conductor.

Tende

The main base for excursions into the Mercantour, especially the Vallée des Merveilles, is **Tende ④**. When the rest of the Comté de Nice rejoined France in 1860, this upper part of the Roya valley, the favourite hunting ground of King Vittorio Emanuele II, was granted to Italy, joining France only in 1947. The stacked houses, many of them dating from the 15th century, are built in local green-hued schist and have balconies and overhanging roofs. The 15th-century **Eglise Collégiale Notre-Dame de l'Assomption** (daily, summer 9am–6pm; winter until 5pm) has a belfry shaped like two stacked barrels and a Baroque interior with 17th-century organ loft.

The **Musée des Merveilles** (avenue du 16 septembre 1947; tel: 04 93 04 32 50; May–Oct Wed–Mon

TIP

There are Maisons du Parc providing information about the Parc National du Mercantour in St-Etienne-de-Tinée (tel: 04 93 02 42 27), St-Martin-Vésubie (tel: 04 93 03 23 15) and Tende (tel: 04 93 04 73 71). They are open in summer and during school holidays.

BELOW LEFT: the national park is dotted with refuges for hikers.
BELOW: on the trail to Pas des Ladres in the park.

The 'Route du Baroque Nisso-Ligure' (www.guide riviera. com) promotes the Baroque heritage of the Alpes-Maritimes and neighbouring Liguria. The richly decorated churches were the visible symbol of the Counter-Reformation, as the Catholic Church asserted its power against the Protestant Reformation. Many of them are in the Mercantour along the route Royale between Nice and Turin.

10am–6.30pm, July–Sept daily, Oct–Apr Wed–Mon until 5pm, closed 2 weeks in Mar, 2 weeks in Nov; free), in a striking modern building, has an exhibition devoted to the prehistory of the park, including original fragments from the rock drawings and mouldings of the most famous motifs. Also worth a visit is the **Maison du Miel et de l'Abeille** (place Lieutenant Kalck; July–Aug Wed–Sun 10am–noon, 1–5pm; free) which looks at the history and production of local honey.

Vallée de la Vésubie

Within easy reach of Nice and the coast, the glorious **Vallée de la Vésubie ❺** leads you away from a Mediterranean landscape to the fresher Alpine scenery of dark-green pines, waterfalls near Le Boréon and green pastures at Roquebillière. Le Boréon is the location of **Alpha Loup** (tel: 04 93 02 33 69; www.alpha-loup.com; daily, July–Aug 10am–6pm, June and Sept–Oct until 5pm, times vary rest of year; charge), a nature park dedicated to wolf conservation where you could spend half a day or a day following trails to view the furry

BELOW: restored mill by the Roya River.

predators. The main town, **St-Martin-Vésubie ❻** offers cool respite as a mountaineering centre in the summer. This is a sleepy and unpretentious place, disturbed only by the rush of water down a 1-metre (3ft) -wide canal. The twin torrents of Le Boréon and the Madone de la Fenestre converge in the town to form the River Vésubie.

Summer for a Vésubian inhabitant starts on 2 July, when a procession wends its way out of St-Martin carrying an 800-year-old wooden statue of Notre-Dame-de-Fenestre 12km (7 miles) east to the sanctuary at **Madone de Fenestre** (open daily). Winter begins when the procession makes the return journey in the third week of September. A few kilometres to the west of St-Martin-Vésubie is a small skiing resort at **La Colmiane**, complete with a few old chalets.

Heading south on the D2565 from St-Martin-Vésubie brings you to **Roquebillière**. The main reason to come here is to spend a couple of hours or a couple of days in the hot springs at the Thermes de Berthemont-les-Bains (tel: 04 93 03 47

Winter Sports in the Alpes-Maritimes

In winter, the 85 percent of the population of the Alpes-Maritimes resident near the coast suddenly seems to acquire a taste for the backcountry. The right bank of the Var becomes a fashionable artery as the Niçois head to the skiing resorts: Auron and Isola 2000 for the *sportif* in search of a conversation piece; Valberg and Beuil for the less pretentious or those more keen on cross-country skiing. **Valberg** (www.valberg.com) is a family-oriented resort with good facilities for children, and a snowboarding park. Its *domaine* is now linked to **Beuil** (www.beuil.com), an ancient village which was once the seat of the Grimaldis. **Auron** (www.auron.com) lines up a full range of slopes and trails for the inveterate skier, as well as a modern snowpark for snowboarders. The modern chalets, flats and ski lifts dotting the pastures are the inland equivalent of the concrete structures on the coast, although it is possible to stay in some of the more charming villages in the area. Inaugurated in 1971, **Isola 2000** (www.isola2000.com) has space-age architecture, and its 120km (75 miles) of pistes have been joined by high-thrill snowboarding and heli-skiing options.

00; Apr–Nov; charge); they are the only natural thermal springs on the French Riviera.

Further down the road, the **Gorges de la Vésubie** begin at St-Jean-la-Riv-ière; there is a spectacular panorama from above the fortified village of **Utelle**, at **Madone d'Utelle ❼**. The sanctuary here (tel: 04 93 03 19 44; daily) is on the site of an ancient shrine to a statue of the Virgin, destroyed in the French Revolution. The new church, consecrated in 1806, is still a place of pilgrimage, with sim-ple accommodation and a restaurant.

Tinée valley

The Gorges de la Vésubie end at the Plan du Var. Leaving the D6202 at the Pont de la Mescla, the D2205 heads up the Tinée valley through the **Gorges de la Mescla ❽**, where spec-tacular slabs of rock overhang both road and river. The minuscule village of **Roure** not only offers vertiginous views but is home to the **Arboretum Marcel Kroenlein** (tel: 04 93 35 00 50; daily 10am–6pm; charge), a steep garden planted with Alpine trees and flowers and dotted with sculptures

by well-known regional artists; it was created In 1988 by a former director of the Jardin exotique de Monaco. Further along the D6202, the old vil-lage of **Isola** is today largely a door-way to the modern ski resort of **Isola 2000 ❾** *(see box, page 232)*, near the Italian frontier, but it does have sev-eral of the chapels indicative of the once fervent religious life of these valleys, three *lavoirs* (wash houses) and a communal bread oven in use until 1950.

Further up the valley at 1,140 metres (3,740ft), rural **St-Etienne-de-Tinée ❿**, though largely rebuilt after a fire in the 1930s, has an important religious heritage. The walls and vault of the **Chapelle St-Sébastien** (contact tourist office for visits: St-Etienne tel: 04 93 02 41 96; Auron tel: 04 93 23 02 66) are cov-ered with paintings telling the life of the martyr saint, attributed to Jean Canavesio and Jean Baleisoni, dating from 1492. Even the nearby ski resort of **Auron** *(see box, page 232)* contains the frescoed 14th-century **Chapelle St-Erige**, unlikely survivor amid the modern apartment blocks.

TIP

Each August, the Festival International des Orgues Historiques gives people the chance to hear the historic organs housed in many of the churches of the Roya and Bévéra valleys. For details, tel: 04 93 04 22 20; www.royabevera.com

BELOW: skiing in the Mercantour.

Vallée des Merveilles

The Vallée des Merveilles is a vast open-air museum revealing thousands of prehistoric rock carvings

Cradled in a majestic circle of Alps, the Vallée des Merveilles is aptly named. It is a landscape of rock-strewn valleys, jagged peaks and eerie lakes.

Just west of the Lac des Mèsches is the Minière de la Vallaure, an abandoned mine quarried from pre-Roman times to the 1930s. Prospectors came in search of gold and silver but had to settle for copper, zinc, iron and lead. The Romans were beaten to the valley by Bronze Age settlers who carved mysterious symbols on the polished rock, ice-smoothed by glaciation. These carvings were first recorded in the 17th century but investigated only from 1879, by Clarence Bicknell, an English naturalist. He made it his life's work to chart the carvings, and died in a valley refuge in 1918.

The rock carvings are similar to ones found in northern Italy, notably those in the Camerino Valley near Bergamo. However, the French carvings are exceptional in that they depict a race of shepherds rather than hunters. The scarcity of wild game in the region forced the Bronze Age tribes to turn to agriculture and cattle-raising. Carvings of yokes, harnesses and tools depict a pastoral civilisation, and these primitive inscriptions may have served as territorial markers for the tribes in the area. Whatever their meaning, this is the largest site of rock art in Europe.

However, the drawings are also open to less earthbound interpretations. Anthropomorphic figures represent not only domestic animals and chief tribesmen but also dancers, devils, sorcerers and gods. Some are said to represent a 'divine primordial couple': the 'earth' goddess who is impregnated by the storm god, Taurus. Such magical totems are in keeping with Mont Bégo's reputation as a sacred spot *(see page 231).* Given the bleak terrain, it is not surprising that the early shepherds looked heavenwards for help. Now as then, animals graze by the lower lakes. However, the abandoned stone farms and shepherds' bothies attest to the unprofitability of mountain farming.

Seeing the carvings

The Vallée des Merveilles is accessible only by four-wheel drive or on foot, and now, due to vandalism, certain areas can only be visited with an official guide. However, there is also a signposted footpath that leads visitors to some carvings without a guide; it begins at Lac des Mèsches car park and is a seven-hour round trip. Given the mountain conditions, the drawings are only visible between the end of June and October. It is an 8km (4-mile) drive west from St-Dalmas to the Lac des Mèsches. In the nearby town of Tende, the tourist office (tel: 04 93 04 73 71) offers information on trips and guides, and you can also visit the Musée des Merveilles *(see page 231).* A signposted path can also be found on the eastern side of Mont Bégo in the Fontanalbe valley, which is again accessible to visitors without a guide; there are 280 carvings along what is called the 'sacred route'. ❑

Left: fine rock carving in the Vallée.

Sospel

On the southeastern edge of the Parc National is the charming Italianate town of **Sospel** ⓫. It's popular with the Mentonnais for a day out, for walking (the GR52 long-distance footpath runs through here) or for hunting in autumn. Successively under the rule of the counts of Ventimiglia, Provence and Nice, it was the second-most important town in the Comté de Nice in the Middle Ages, when it had a flourishing religious life. The Bévéra, a tributary of the Roya, runs through it, leaving a series of islets around the **Vieux Pont** (old bridge). The bridge is an oddity, with a toll gate in the middle for levying tax on the salt route. Today it contains the tourist office.

The oldest part of the town is a cluster of buildings with wooden balconies overlooking the river. By the river, a sheltered *lavoir* filled with water even at the height of summer still survives. On the southern side of the bridge, houses come in weathered shades of orange, yellow, ochre or red stucco, and the 17th-century Baroque **Cathédrale St-Michel** lords it over an attractive cobbled square. Inside is an altarpiece by Francesco Brea, a member of the celebrated Niçois dynasty of painters. It is an atmospheric setting for Les Baroquiales, a festival of Baroque music in July.

You can also visit the reinforced concrete **Fort St-Roch** (July–Aug Tue–Sun 2–5pm, June and Sept Sat–Sun until 6pm; charge), built as part of the Maginot Line (there's another one at Ste-Agnès, further south near Menton), the defensive system of partially underground fortresses built along the eastern border of France during the 1930s.

Northwest of Sospel, the D2566 climbs through deep pine forests to the **Col de Turini** (from where you can join the Vésubie valley or return to Nice via Lucéram), with a small ski resort and a good starting point for some relatively gentle walks. The nearby **Plateau d'Authion** was a battlefield on more than one occasion; you'll find the **Cabanes Vieilles** (ruins of Napoleonic barracks) there, destroyed during combat with retreating German troops at the end of World War II.

Botanists now believe that more than half of the 4,000 or so species of wild flower found in France grow in the Mercantour, including 63 varieties of orchid.

Below: the winding road to Sospel.

Breil is well-worn hiking country; signed walks lead to medieval watch-towers, such as La Cruella, or to isolated chapels to the west of the village. Longer hikes lead to Sospel or La Vésubie further west.

Roya Valley and Saorge

Northeast of Sospel, the D2204 takes you over the Col de Brouis (Brouis pass) to join the Roya valley just north of **Breil-sur-Roya** . On a flat expanse of valley, the wide Roya has here been turned into an artificial lake that lies along the edge of town and as a result it is a popular centre for water sports; Roya Evasion (tel: 04 93 04 91 46; www.royaevasion.com) offers a wide range of activities including kayaking and canyoning. Breil produces excellent olive oil, using a variety of olive, the *cailletier*, found only in the Alpes-Maritimes; visitors can buy olive oil, tapenade and also honey from organic producer Cédrisa at the village's Tuesday-morning market

The **Vallée de la Roya** was retained by the Italians – against local wishes – until October 1947, because it was the only link with the Mercantour and the hunting grounds of the king of Italy. The Italian influence, along with a troubled history and terrible communications, have helped to preserve the valley in its splendid isolation, and the locals' French has a distinctively Italian sound.

North of Breil, the road, which shares the valley with the railway, gets more dramatic, passing through steep gorges on the way to the spectacularly situated town of **Saorge** , which still has the appearance of a mountain stronghold. Packed into a cliff face, it takes a trek on foot to reach the centre, through some of the steepest cobbled alleyways imaginable. Tall, narrow houses tower over dark streets. Some people do still live here, but the young tend to be quick to move out to search for employment elsewhere. The contemporary exodus contrasts with ancient times, when everyone seemed to be trying to invade the fortified village – unsuccessfully. Such was its reputation for impregnability that would-be invaders eventually gave up trying.

The steepness does not rule out the existence of a fine Renaissance church, **St-Sauveur**, with a red-and-gold altar. The finely carved church organ was made in Genoa in the 19th century. Its installation, and even the building of

BELOW: Saorge.

Mountain Trains

Three scenic railway lines run into the interior of the Alpes-Maritimes. The SNCF-run Nice–Cuneo line follows the Peillon, Bévéra and Roya valleys through long, twisting tunnels and over numerous viaducts, stopping at Peillon, Sospel, Breil-sur-Roya, Saorge, La Brigue and Tende; total journey time is around 3 hours. In summer, a special tourist train, dubbed the 'Train des Merveilles', leaves Nice at around 9am, arriving at Tende at 10.45am; it provides a tourist commentary and slows down for photo opportunities. In winter the 'Train des Neiges' is a special service for skiers, consisting of a shuttle from Tende to Castérino. Another line joins this one from Ventimiglia in Italy to Breil-sur-Roya.

the church, would not have been possible without the strength and agility of the mules used to carry materials up the hill. Saorge has not forgotten the contribution the animals made (and still make) to life in the village: one of the village festivals is dedicated to St Eloi, patron saint of mules.

Saorge Monastery

Amid olive trees at the top of town, the **Monastère de Saorge** (www.monuments-nationaux.fr; May–Sept Wed–Mon 10am–noon, 2–6pm, Feb–Apr and Oct until 5pm, closed Nov–Jan; charge), founded in 1633, no longer has Franciscan monks; instead its tranquil atmosphere now serves for writers' retreats and workshops. The church is a fine example of the local Baroque style, with an elaborate master altar with barley-sugar columns surrounding a statue of the Virgin. The whitewashed two-storey cloister is painted with several ornate sundials.

La Brigue

At St-Dalmas-de-Tende, side roads lead off in one direction towards the Vallée des Merveilles, and in the other to **La Brigue** , another of those mountain villages clearly once more populated and prosperous than it is today. Until the 19th century, three quarters of the population reared the Brigasque breed of sheep and the wealth created by the wool trade attracted Jewish merchants, money lenders and goldsmiths who indulged in artistic patronage. This is evident in the finely carved lintels, Baroque churches, arcaded medieval houses and the ruins of the 14th-century Château Lascaris, which is floodlit at night.

However, the main reason to pause here lies 4km (2½ miles) further east, where the simple exterior of the isolated **Chapelle de Notre-Dame-des-Fontaines** (May–Oct daily 10am–12.30pm, 2–5.30pm; charge) does little to prepare you for the extraordinary wealth of frescos within. Attributed to Jean Baleison and Jean Canavesi, the 15th-century cycle of the life of the Virgin, the Passion and the Last Judgement has earned it the nickname 'the Sistine Chapel of the southern Alps'. ❏

The chapel of Notre-Dame-des-Fontaines, near La Brigue, is a local place of pilgrimage, renowned for its vivid frescos, painted in 1492 by Canavesi of the Niçoise school.

RESTAURANTS

Restaurants

Peillon
Auberge de la Madone
3 place Auguste Arnulf,
Peillon Village. Tel: 04 93 79 91 17. Open L & D Thu–Tue. Closed Nov–Jan, except Christmas hols. €€€
Father and son duo Christian and Thomas Millo produce imaginative regional cuisine.

Tende
Le P'tit Chez Soi
29 avenue du 16 septembre 1947
Tel: 04 93 04 68 68. Open L Tue–Sat & D Fri–Sat. €
Rustic-yet-contemporary wine bar where the Mediterranean meets Gascony in the kitchen. Highlights include the platter of local cheeses and the large selection of regional wines. There is also a terrace.

St-Martin-Vésubie
Le Boreon
Quartier La Cascade,
Le Boreon
www.hotel-boreon.com
Tel: 04 93 03 20 35. Open L & D daily. Closed Nov–Mar. €–€€€
A pretty lakeside chalet 8km (4 miles) northeast of St-Martin-Vésubie. where cooking often includes game stews and duck fillet with honey.

Sospel
Restaurant Bel Aqua
Hôtel des Etrangers,
7 boulevard de Verdun
www.sospel.net
Tel: 04 93 04 00 09. Open L & D Thu–Mon. Closed Nov–Feb. €€
This restaurant is a favourite with locals and visiting Mentonnais. Specialities include ice cream flavoured with *génépi*, the local liqueur.

La Brigue
Le Mirval
3 rue Vincent Ferrier
www.lemirval.com
Tel: 04 93 04 63 71. Open D Mon–Fri, L & D Sat–Sun. Closed Dec–Mar. €
Delightful riverside restaurant. Both Italian and Niçois dishes available.

Prices for a three-course meal without wine. Many restaurants have a less expensive lunch menu:
€ = under €25
€€ = €25–40
€€€ = €40–60

NICE

Queen of the Riviera, capital of the Côte d'Azur, Nice is a gem of a city, with a wealth of museums, lively old town markets, and enough gardens, fountains and palm trees to raise the alfresco lifestyle to an art form

France's fifth city was founded around 350 BC by the Greeks, Called "Nikaea", it was built on the hill by the waterfront. Later, the Roman settlement of Cemenelum developed further inland on the Cimiez hill. In the Middle Ages, **Nice ❶** asserted its independence from Provence as a mini-republic ruled by consuls. When Provence was incorporated into France in 1486, Nice and its hinterland remained a quasi-independent *comté*, under the protection of the dukes of Savoy, and was often a pawn between the rival ambitions of the French crown and the Holy Roman Empire. After the Revolution, Nice briefly became part of France under Napoleon, before returning to the kingdom of Piedmont-Sardinia. In 1860, the population voted to become French.

Nice's Italianate legacy can be seen in the city's culinary specialities, such as ravioli (which the Niçois claim to have invented), and in the Genoan-style painted facades in the old town. Nice was first embraced as a fashionable winter resort by English aristocrats in the late 18th century. In the 1820s and 30s, the promenade des Anglais was laid out and railways, hotels, villas and gardens were all built to serve the needs of the Riviera royalty that followed in their wake. The fashion for sun- and sea-bathing arrived in the 1920s, attracting artists and writers.

Today, the city's traditional mellow lifestyle co-exists with its business status as France's second-largest convention city after Paris; its high-tech industry is growing rapidly, rivalling tourism as the city's main revenue generator. A new business district has developed and mayor Christian Estrosi has plans for an ambitious 'Eco-Vallée'

Main attractions

COURS SALEYA MARKET, VIEUX NICE
COLLINE DU CHÂTEAU
VIEUX PORT
MAMAC
PROMENADE DES ANGLAIS
CATHÉDRALE ORTHODOXE RUSSE
MUSÉE MATISSE

LEFT: Nice's most famous hotel, the Negresco, built in 1912.
RIGHT: the market on cours Saleya.

Matisse lived in many locations in Nice before settling in Cimiez. One of his homes was in the big yellow house at the end of cours Saleya (1 place Charles Félix). Here, Matisse painted odalisques, drawing inspiration from the views of the sea and the flower market below.

with port facilities, congress centre and football stadium along the Var River on the city's western edge.

Orientation

Nice divides up neatly into old and new parts, with the medieval streets of Vieux Nice to the east, and the broad avenues and squares of the new town behind the promenade des Anglais to the west. Elegant residential districts, such as Costebelle and Cimiez, sit on the hills inland.

Vieux Nice

Vieux Nice is a maze of lively, narrow streets, where tiny grocers rub shoulders with clothes shops, art and craft galleries, souvenir outlets and quirky bars. The old town gained pretty much the appearance it has today in the 16th and 17th centuries, when the population was forced down from the medieval upper town. Look up and admire the t*rompe l'oeils* and frescos, especially the so-called 'Adam and Eve house'

in rue de la Poissonnerie; the *Pistone* building in rue du Marché; No. 27 rue Benoît Bunico; and in rue Pairolière, the Maison de la Treille (the house with a climbing vine), which was the inspiration for one of Raoul Dufy's pictures. The best place to start exploring is the **cours Saleya Ⓐ**, lined with cafés, a vibrant flower market (Tue–Sat 6am–5.30pm, Sun until 1pm) and a fruit and vegetable market every morning except Monday, when there's a flea market instead. Early risers can also hit the small fish market on place St-François (Tue–Sun mornings). A fun way to explore the culinary delights of the old town is with **A Taste of Nice** (tel: 06 19 99 95 22; www.foodtoursofnice. com) who run half-day walking tours at 10am Tue–Sun.

Between cours Saleya and quai des Etats-Unis are **Les Ponchettes**, a row of low white buildings once used by fishermen, now mostly galleries and restaurants. Nice has a thriving contemporary art scene and here you

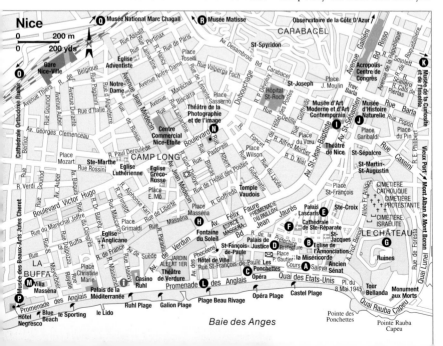

will find two municipal galleries: **La Galerie de la Marine** (59 quai des Etats-Unis; Tue–Sun 10am–6pm; free), and **La Galerie des Ponchettes** (77 quai des Etats-Unis; Tue–Sun 10am–6pm; free) which exhibit the work of emerging local artists or international artists who have links with the city. To the north the former palace of the Sardinian kings now houses the Préfecture. On rue de la Poissonnerie, a discreet facade hides the exuberantly decorated Baroque **Chapelle de l'Annonciation** (Mon–Sat 7am–noon and 2.30–6.30pm, Sun 8am–noon and 3–6.30pm), known as the Eglise Ste-Rita to locals who light candles to Rita, patron saint of lost causes. At the eastern end of the cours is the pedimented **Ancien Sénat**, which administered justice on behalf of the Dukes of Savoy.

West of the cours on rue St-François-de-Paule are Nice's town hall and the **Opéra de Nice** , a feast of Second Empire opulence, with a colonnaded marble façade. On the place du Palais de Justice is Nice's imposing law court, the **Palais de Justice** , inaugurated in 1892, and facing it, an 18th-century clocktower and the russet façade of the Palais Rusca. The pavement cafés are an ideal spot to enjoy this newly renovated square, and on Saturdays there's a market here selling pottery and books.

On rue Droite, once the town's main north–south thoroughfare, is the **Palais Lascaris** (15 rue Droite, Wed–Mon 10am– 6pm; free), a grand 17th-century mansion reflecting the city's Genoese past, with a splendid balustraded staircase, salons with painted ceilings, a collection of historical musical instruments and an 18th-century pharmacy. This street, not named for its straightness but because it directly connected the two main gates of the city, is now where many young artists have their ateliers.

The streets become darker and narrower the further in you go. Look at the lintels, some of which are inscribed with dates and incantations; *interna meliora* – 'better things inside' – hangs over a former brothel on rue de la Place Vieille.

At the heart of Vieux Nice on place Rossetti is the Baroque **Cathédrale de Ste-Réparate** (Mon–Fri 9am–noon, 2–6pm, Sat until 7.30pm, Sun 9am–1pm, 3–6pm), named after the patron saint of the city, a young virgin brought here in the 4th century from Israel in a boat pulled by angels. Her landing place is now known as the Baie des Anges (Angels' Bay). The cathedral has a dome of glazed tiles and an 18th-century belltower. The square itself is a great spot for coffee or ice cream. The elegant 18th-century arcaded **place Garibaldi**, at the north-eastern corner of Vieux Nice, is named after the popular hero of Italian unification, who was born in the city.

What is underneath the square is arguably more interesting than what is above. **La Crypte Archéologique** (guided tours Wed–Mon 10am–4pm; reserve at the Centre du Patrimoine, 75 quai des Etats Unis; charge) is a

EAT

Nice's most famous gelateria is Fenocchio (2 place Rosetti; www. fenocchio.fr), in front of the cathedral in Vieux-Nice, which has 94 flavours of ice creams and sorbets including lavender and rosemary.

BELOW: Nice's old town.

Matisse in Nice

Matisse was inspired by many places in the south of France, but it is in Nice that his presence is felt most strongly and which finally became his home

Matisse was one of the most influential artists of the 20th century yet it was only when he was recovering from appendicitis at the age of 20 that he first picked up a paint brush – 'a kind of paradise', as he described it. He initially studied in Paris under the Symbolist Gustave Moreau but discovering Impressionism in the 1890s had a major impact on his style.

He first went to Nice in 1917, staying in the Hôtel Beau Rivage (which then had a seafront facade), painting the sea and the great sweeping bay of the promenade des Anglais fringed with palm trees. He often visited the ageing Renoir at his villa in Cagnes, drawing inspiration from his determination to paint despite the infirmity of arthritis. In Nice, Matisse moved his family into an apartment at 105 quai du Midi, then to a small house on Mont Boron, from where he could watch the dawn each morning. Here his daughter Marguerite posed for him on the balcony overlooking the sea.

After returning to Paris at the end of World War I, Matisse came back to Nice, to the light and colour he craved, staying several times in the Hôtel de la Méditerranée on the promenade des Anglais. He took an apartment on place Charles Félix in the old town, where he filled the studio with the Moorish screens and rugs that would appear in his paintings for decades to come.

With his wife Amélie, he moved to a bigger apartment on place Charles Félix, with superb views from balconies on two sides, where he painted his famous odalisques, framed by shuttered windows and flowers, capturing forever the voluptuous ease of the Riviera. Apart from a long trip to Tahiti, and visits to Paris and America, where he was working on *The Dance*, he spent the rest of his life in Nice. He was sustained by visits from his long-suffering family, swimming and canoeing, and a succession of devoted models who, despite their sensuous poses, were never lovers. The most important model was Lydia, a Russian refugee who became his secretary, ultimately precipitating a permanent rift with Madame Matisse.

Matisse in Cimiez

At the start of World War II, Matisse moved to Cimiez, where he continued to paint, make sculptures, etchings and finally paper cut-outs, 'drawing with scissors'. He spent part of the war years in Vence in the Villa le Rêve, where he designed the chapel that is the most moving monument to his memory. But it represented no last-minute conversion. 'Why not a brothel, Matisse?' asked Picasso. 'Because nobody asked me, Picasso.'

At age 79, he moved back to Cimiez, where he died in 1954, his walls covered in cut-outs of flowers, birds and dancers. The Matisse Museum, a beautiful 17th-century Italianate villa in Cimiez, houses Matisse's works from every period, as well as the vases, shell furniture and Moroccan wall-hangings *(see page 246)*. ❑

LEFT: The Matisse Museum in Cimiez.

vast underground 'room' where visitors can see Nice's 15th-century city walls, which were uncovered during the building of the new tramway.

Le Château and the Vieux-Port

The old town's eastern extremity is flanked by **Le Château ⑥**, site of the original medieval hill town and the citadel demolished by Louis XIV in 1706. Today it is a pleasant park with an artificial waterfall, a playground and some scant medieval ruins, as well as three cemeteries (Catholic, Protestant, Jewish) with some splendidly melodramatic funerary monuments. Most people make the climb for the marvellous panoramic views of the city; if you don't want to walk, you can take the lift at the end of quai des Etats-Unis up to the **Tour Bellanda** – a mock fortified tower where composer Hector Berlioz lived in the 1840s – or the tourist train that leaves from the Jardins Albert 1er.

East of the castle hill, past the stirring World War I and II **Monument aux Morts** is Nice's picturesque **Vieux-Port** (old port). This departure point for cruise ships sees swish yachts moored alongside small fishing boats. It is also the location of **Trans Côte d'Azur** (quai Lunel; tel: 04 92 00 42 30; www.trans-cote-azur.com; Apr–Oct Tue–Sun; charge) who run boat trips along the coast to Monaco, Cannes and St-Tropez. Quai des Deux Emmanuel is lined with bars and fish restaurants, while on place de l'Ile de Beauté, Genoese-style *trompe l'oeil* painted facades frame the neo classical church **Eglise Notre-Dame du Port**. Behind here on rue Catherine Ségurane and rue Antoine Gauthier is a cluster of antiques dealers and arcades.

On the eastern side of place de l'Ile de Beauté, boulevard Carnot marks the start of the Basse Corniche coast road, which loops around Mont Boron past extravagant villas and mock castles towards the Italian frontier (*see page*

264). A fascinating curiosity at No. 25 (entrance on impasse Terra Amata) is the **Musée d'Archéologie de Nice – Site de Terra Amata** (Wed–Mon 10am–6pm; free), located on the spot excavated in 1966 where a nomadic tribe of elephant hunters had camped out on the beach some 400,000 years ago. Sights include a prehistoric cave and a human footprint in limestone. A little further along the coastal road is the Grotte du Lazaret (33bis boulevard Franck Pilatte; tel: 04 92 00 17 37; by reservation only), a small cave inhabited 200,000 years by hunters.

Place Masséna and the east

Symbolic heart of Nice and junction between Vieux Nice and the new town, **Place Masséna ⑪** was laid out in the 1840s as part of the grandiose town-planning schemes of King Charles-Albert of Turin. Towards the sea, the Jardin Albert 1er provide a swathe of greenery, dotted with statuary and modern sculptures, covering over what was the mouth of the River Peillon. The sculptures are part of an art trail, L'Art dans la Ville, which runs along tramway line 1 and is best expe-

TIP

If you plan to visit the main sights in Nice, Antibes and Monaco consider buying a French Riviera Pass which gives free access to certain attractions and tours for 24, 48 or 72 hours. You can buy one in the tourist office at 5 promenade des Anglais.

BELOW: the Vieux Port.

Roman ruins in Cimiez, part of the archaeological park known as Les Arènes.

rienced during a night-time guided tour (Fri 7.45pm; reserve at the tourist office; charge). Heading inland along the promenade des Arts esplanade are the modern Théâtre de Nice and the **Musée d'Art Moderne et d'Art Contemporain ❶** (MAMAC; place Yves Klein; tel: 04 97 13 42 01; www.mamac-nice.org; Tue– Sun 10am–6pm; free), a striking building of octagonal marble towers joined by glass walkways. The focus is on French and American art from the 1960s to the present, including some iconic Pop Art pieces by Andy Warhol and Roy Lichtenstein, a room devoted to local hero Yves Klein, and a large collection of Nikki de Saint-Phalle's colourful papier-mâché figures. Next to the museum is the **Louis Nucéra library**, dominated by the Tête Carrée, a monumental square head designed by Sacha Sosno. A couple of minutes' walk northeast along boulevard Rosso will bring you to the **Musée d'Histoire Naturelle ❿** (Tue–Sun 10am–6pm; free), a natural history museum devoted to the biodiversity of the region, while kids will love the **Musée de la Curiosité et de l'Insolite ❾** (39 rue Beaumont; Wed–Sun

2–7pm, daily in school hols; charge), a museum of automatons, musical toys, fairground attractions and optical illusions a few blocks away.

For the best overview of what is not a very complicated city, head southeast (you'll need a car) up to the ruined 16th-century fort of **Mont Alban**. It is approached through a municipal forest on Mont Boron, which is also the location of the **Batterie du Mont Boron** (route Forestière de Mont Boron), a 19th-century fort due to be transformed into a centre for architectural research. North of here, Mont Gros is the site of the **Observatoire de la Côte d'Azur** (tel: 04 92 00 30 11; www.ocea.eu; guided visits Wed, Sat, Sun at 2.45pm; charge), an astronomical observatory designed by Charles Garnier and Gustave Eiffel.

Promenade des Anglais and the New Town

The palm-lined **promenade des Anglais ❶**, funded in the 1820s by Nice's English colony, runs for 5km (3 miles) along the seafront. Although it's become a busy main road, the 'prom' is still *the* place for a stroll or a spot

BELOW: floats parade at the Carnaval de Nice.

Carnaval de Nice

Nice celebrates Mardi Gras with the largest pre-Lent carnival in France (www.nicecarnaval.com), culminating in a spectacular explosion of fireworks above the Baie des Anges. For two weeks around Shrove Tuesday huge papier-mâché floats proceed through the town amid bands, confetti battles and throngs of spectators. Highlights include the *bataille des fleurs*, when thousands of fresh flowers are tossed into the crowds, and the ceremonial burning of *Sa Majesté Carnaval*, the carnival king, on the promenade des Anglais at the end of the festival. If you want to join in the spectacle, make sure you book your accommodation well in advance.

of people-watching. Much of the long shingle beach is taken up with private beach concessions with sun loungers and restaurants, although there are public stretches. The other side of the road is lined with grand hotels and apartment blocks. At No. 15 the **Palais de la Méditerranée** is a modern casino and luxury hotel behind a striking Art Deco facade. Set in tropical gardens, the **Villa Masséna**  (Wed–Mon 10am–6pm; free), in a lavish villa built in 1898, has grand reception rooms and a winter garden downstairs. The museum upstairs contains portraits, costumes and memorabilia of the aristocrats and intellectuals who shaped the town's Belle Epoque glory; the 19th-century garden around the villa has been completely rejuvenated.

Next door at No. 37 is the famed **Hôtel Negresco**, which was built in 1912 and remains the crown of the promenade. It is a national monument where visiting heads of state occupy entire floors and the flamboyance of the exterior is only eclipsed by the jewels within – it has a world-class collection of art. This was here F. Scott Fitzgerald stayed and although you won't find 'a diamond as big as the Ritz', you can see a crystal chandelier by Baccarat with 16,309 stones and weighing more than a tonne, designed originally for the Tsar of Russia.

Behind the promenade des Anglais lies the new town, laid out in the late 19th and early 20th centuries with garden squares, fanciful villas and Belle Epoque and Art Deco buildings. Cutting inland from place Masséna towards the station, **avenue Jean Médecin** is a busy shopping street, now pedestrianised with the tramway running down the centre. The town's most upmarket fashions can be found on rue de Paradis, rue Alphonse Karr and avenue de Verdun.

A few blocks southeast of the station is the **Théâtre de la Photographie et de l'Image** (27 boulevard Du-bouchage; Tue–Sun 10am–6pm; free), housed in a lovely Belle Epoque theatre, which is devoted to promoting the photographic arts and whose permanent exhibition includes work by Grasse-born Charles Nègre, one of the early pioneers of photography.

A couple of blocks west of the station, the **Cathédrale Orthodoxe Russe** (boulevard Tzarewitch; Tue–Sun 9am–noon, 2–6pm; charge) is a startling reminder of Nice's once thriving Russian colony. Complete with five onion domes, precious icons and an ornate gilded iconostasis, this is more 17th-century Moscow than Belle Epoque France. Services are held here, of course, in Russian.

On the Baumettes hill, a Belle Epoque villa built for a Ukrainian princess houses the **Musée des Beaux-Arts Jules Cheret** (33 avenue des Baumettes; www.musee-beaux-arts-nice.org; Tue–Sun 10am–6pm; free). Here you can see European fine arts from the 17th to 20th centuries, with highlights from Brueghel, Fragonard, Dufy, Bonnard, Sisley, Van Dongen and Rodin, as well as pastels by poster artist Jules Cheret. In the Fabron district further west, the 1920s villa of perfum-

BELOW: the Russian Cathedral.

KIDS

Parc Phoenix is a great place to go with children. The park has parrots, an otter pool, musical fountain and stepping stones, while the vast greenhouse contains steamy tropical plants, carp, flamingos and a spider house.

ier François Coty contains the **Musée International d'Art Naïf Anatole Javovsky** (avenue Val Marie; Wed–Mon 10am–6pm; free), an exceptional collection of charming, often obsessively detailed paintings by (self-taught, often mentally ill) Naïve artists.

At the western end of promenade des Anglais, you'll come to the exotic, flower-filled **Parc Floral Phoenix** (daily 9.30am–7.30pm, until 6pm in winter; charge), with its vast glass and steel tropical greenhouse (*see margin left*). Set by a lake on the edge of the park, the **Musée des Arts Asiatiques** (tel: 04 92 29 37 00; Wed–Mon, May–mid-Oct 10am–6pm, mid-Oct–Apr until 5pm; free), in a spectacular circular building designed by architect Kenzo Tange, has a fine collection of Asian artefacts and a tea pavilion, where the tea ceremony is performed the first Sunday of each month (reservation necessary; charge).

Cimiez

In the fashionable residential area of Cimiez you'll find palm-filled gardens, Belle Epoque villas and vast former hotels (now apartments), with

BELOW: Musée Matisse.

the crowning jewel being the Hôtel Excelsior Régina (corner of boulevard de Cimiez and avenue Régina), built in 1895. A statue of Queen Victoria in front commemorates her frequent visits here. It was later converted into apartments, one of which Matisse lived in during World War II.

About halfway up the hill, the **Musée National Marc Chagall** Q (avenue du Docteur Ménard; tel: 04 93 53 87 20; www.musee-chagall. fr; Wed–Mon May–Oct 10am–6pm, Nov–Apr until 5pm; charge) contains a phenomenal collection of Chagall's works, centred around 12 vast, exuberant canvases illustrating stories from the Old Testament.

Cimiez is also the site of Roman Nice. Almost opposite the Régina are the **Arènes**, the scant remains of Nice's amphitheatre, today the venue for the city's outdoor jazz festival in July. Behind here, the **Musée d'Archéologie de Nice – Site de Cimiez** (160 avenue des Arènes de Cimiez; Wed–Mon 10am–6pm; free) preserves the remains of three Roman bath complexes.

Henri Matisse

Set amid olive groves in Les Arènes park is the **Musée Matisse** R (164 avenue des Arènes de Cimiez; tel: 04 93 81 08 08; www.musee-matisse-nice.org; Wed–Mon 10am–6pm; free but charge for guided tours at 3.30pm Mon, Wed–Fri), in a red-ochre Genoese villa and its modern underground extension. Matisse loved Nice and its 'clear, crystalline, precise, limpid' light (*see page 242*); he bequeathed many works to the city, which form the core of this fabulous collection.

Matisse and Raoul Dufy are buried in the cemetery of the Franciscan **monastery** (place du Monastère de Cimiez; tel: 04 93 81 00 04; Mon–Sat 10am–noon, 3–6pm); the adjoining church has three medieval masterpieces by Louis Bréa. The monastery's beautiful gardens have a sweeping panorama of the Baie des Anges. ❑

RESTAURANTS

Restaurants

Prices for a three-course meal without wine. Many restaurants have a less expensive lunch menu:
€ = under €25
€€ = €25–40
€€€ = €40–60
€€€€ = over €60

Bistrot Antoine
27 rue de la Préfecture
Tel: 04 93 85 29 57. Open L
& D Tue–Sat. €€
The up-and-coming address in Vieux Nice has made its mark with rejuvenated regional fare and light, market-inspired *plats du jour*.

Le Bistro Gourmand
3 rue Desboutin
Tel: 04 92 14 55 55. Open L
& D Tue–Sat. €€–€€€€
At the western edge of the old town, this stylish modern restaurant offers Michelin-star Mediterranean cuisine, with a lunch menu starting at €23. The wine list includes local AOC Bellet.

Le Casbah
3 rue Docteur Balestre
Tel: 04 93 85 58 81. Open L
Tue–Sun & D Tue–Sat.
Closed Aug. €€
A few blocks east of Nice Etoile shopping centre, this bright contemporary restaurant with touches of North Africa serves the best Moroccan food in town.

Le Chantecler
Hôtel Negresco
37 promenade des Anglais
www.hotel-negresco-nice.com
Tel: 04 93 16 64 00. Open
D Wed–Sun & L Sun. €€€€
The best restaurant in town also has the classiest surroundings. Chef Jean-Denis Rieubland's Provence-inspired dishes are works of art and the wine cellar boasts 15,000 bottles.

Comptoir du Marché
8 rue du Marché
Tel: 04 93 13 45 01. Open L
& D Tue–Sat. €
The retro dining room in the latest enterprise by Arnaud Crespo of Le Bistrot d'Antoine is usually packed to the rafters. There's a limited-but-tasty range of dishes and a good wine list. Book in advance.

Keisuke Matsushima
22 ter rue de France
www.keisukematsushima.com
Tel: 04 93 82 26 06. Open L
Tue–Fri & D Mon–Sat.
€€–€€€€
Japan meets Provence with brilliant young chef Keisuke Matsushima. Subtly lit slate tables provide a suitable setting for his artistically presented creations – think green, purple and wild asparagus with lemon froth or scallops with truffles, peas and wasabi. He also has a bistro, L'Ecole de Nice, at 16 rue de la Buffa.

La Merenda
4 rue Terasse. No phone.
Open L & D Mon–Fri. €€
This tiny bistro in the old town is considered by many to serve the best traditional Niçois cuisine, although the lack of phone (stop by in advance to reserve a table) is inconvenient.

Les Pêcheurs
18 quai des Docks
www.lespecheurs.com
Tel: 04 93 89 59 61. Open L
& D Wed–Sun. €€–€€€
Smart port-side restaurant with a canopied terrace where, unsurprisingly, fish is the speciality. The cuisine sometimes has a touch of the Far East, as in pan-seared tuna teriyaki with stir-fried vegetables.

Le Safari
1 cours Saleya
www.restaurantsafari.com
Tel: 04 93 80 18 44. Open L
& D daily. €€–€€€
This popular restaurant draws a mix of locals and visitors. Serves Niçois specialities and wood-fired pizzas.

Yuzu
35 rue du Maréchal Joffre
Tel: 04 93 85 79 87. Open L
& D Tue–Sat. €–€€€
Authentic sushi bar in the heart of the shopping district. Chef Keiji Sakaguchi previously worked at Takara, France's leading Japanese restaurant in Paris. *Wagyu* beef is also on the menu.

RIGHT: the salade Niçoise originates in, of course, Nice.

THE RIVIERA FROM CANNES TO CAGNES

This stretch of the azure coast saw the birth of the Riviera as a summer destination. Here lovely (if crowded) beaches alternate with historic Antibes and Cagnes, luxuriant secluded peninsulas and the party towns of Cannes and Juan-les-Pins

Originally a winter destination favoured by the British and Russians, the stretch of coast from Cannes to the Italian border was dubbed the French Riviera by the Italians and the Côte d'Azur by the French – the latter term coined in 1887 by French writer Stephen Liégeard, who was inspired by the deep blue of its sea.

In 1923, the Hôtel du Cap stayed open over the summer for the first time, heralding the birth of the summer season and a new era in tourism, kick-started by glamorous American visitors. Scott Fitzgerald, Ernest Hemingway and Dorothy Parker were joined by artists and writers, Colette and Picasso among them. They helped build the Riviera myth with its jazz-age images of a hedonistic lifestyle centred on the new pastimes of sunbathing, water-skiing and cocktail parties.

An even greater revolution came with the advent of paid holidays, introduced by France's first socialist government in 1936, and the continued democratisation of holiday-taking after World War II. Consequently, the coast oscillates between two extremes: the Côte d'Azur of the very rich – a privileged world of yachts and villas – versus the campsites and cheap hotels catering for backpackers and budget travellers.

Cannes

Long an insignificant fishing village, **Cannes ❷** was first put on the map in 1834 when the British Lord High Chancellor, Lord Brougham, was forced to winter here due to an outbreak of cholera in Nice. Brougham, whose statue stands on the allées de la Liberté, was so taken with Cannes

Main attractions
LA CROISETTE, CANNES
LE SUQUET, CANNES
ILE SAINTE-MARGUERITE
MARCHÉ PROVENÇAL, VIEUX ANTIBES
MUSÉE PICASSO, VIEUX ANTIBES
MARINELAND, ANTIBES
MUSÉE RENOIR, CAGNES-SUR-MER

LEFT: the Carlton hotel on the promenade of La Croisette.
RIGHT: this is the life – Cannes' seafront.

The Hôtel Martinez has the largest private beach along La Croisette.

that he had a villa built here, starting a trend for wintering in the town. Within three years, 30 new villas had been built and the shoreline avenue, now called La Croisette, was laid.

Cannes's international status was cemented with the establishment of the town's film festival *(see page 252)*, inaugurated in 1946. For ten days each May, the town becomes the centre of the film universe, thronged by movie magnates, film stars and fans. Yet for all its glamour, Cannes has a pleasantly lived-in feel. Year-round trade fairs and conferences give it a permanent population and an economy not entirely reliant on tourism.

La Croisette

Sweeping east along the seafront is **La Croisette Ⓐ**, a palm tree-lined promenade bordered by plush hotels and apartments on one side, manicured beaches and smart beach clubs on the other. It is a focus for strolling and people-watching, with a constant stream of open-topped cars in summer. At No. 1 is the **Palais des Festivals et des Congrès Ⓑ**, nicknamed 'the bunker', which since 1983 has been home to the Film Festival, celebrated for the famous climb up "les marches", its red-carpeted stairs – a great photo op for acting out your own film star fantasies. It is also used for congresses, trade fairs and rock concerts and is home to the tourist office (which organises guided tours around the Palais two–three times a month) and the Croisette Casino. Film stars and directors have left a trail of handprints in the esplanade outside.

Cannes's grandest hotels are all on La Croisette, bearing testimony to the resort's glamorous history. At No. 14, the Belle Epoque **Majestic** has kept up its palatial status with a new wing of luxurious suites added in 2010, and its own private jetty stretching towards the sand across the street.

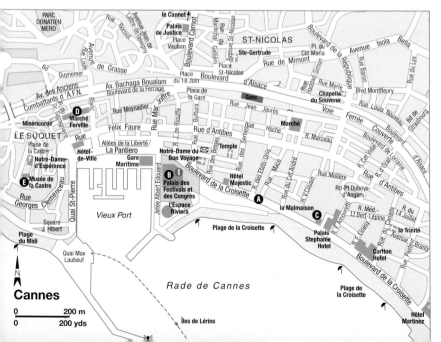

At No. 47, **La Malmaison ⊙** (July–Aug Fri–Wed 11am–8pm, Thu until 9pm, Sept daily until 7pm, Oct–Apr Tue–Sun 10am–1pm, 2–6pm, closed May–June; charge) is the only surviving part of the original Grand Hôtel – 19th-century forerunner of today's seafront giants, since replaced by a 1970s high-rise. The building now houses temporary art exhibitions.

At No. 58, the **Carlton** has a wedding-cake façade that has barely changed since it was built in 1912. The pepper-pot cupolas at each end are said to be modelled on the breasts of la Belle Otero, a celebrated dancer and courtesan. Further down the drag, at No. 73, is the Art Deco **Hôtel Martinez**, the largest hotel in France when it opened in 1929.

The Port-Vieux and Le Suquet

West of the Palais des Festivals sits Cannes' old harbour, which still has a few fishing boats among the luxury yachts, and the allées de la Liberté, with its bandstand and *pétanque* players. Behind rue Félix Faure with its fish restaurants lies pedestrianised rue Meynardier and the excellent covered food market, **Marché Forville ⊙** (Tue–Sun am). Cannes' oldest neighbourhood, **Le Suquet**, winds up the hill behind, past the 16th-century church **Notre-Dame d'Espérance**, whose parvis is used for the Nuits du Suquet classical music festival in July. At the top, on shady **place de la Castre**, the castle and watchtower were built by Lérins monks in the 11th century to guard against Saracen attack. The castle houses the **Musée de la Castre ⊙** (July–Aug Fri–Wed 10am–7pm, Thu until 9pm, Apr–June and Sept Tue–Sun 10am–1pm, 2–6pm, Oct–Mar Tue–Sun 10am–1pm, 2–5pm; charge), an eclectic ethnographic and archaeological collection, including musical instruments from around the world, plus a couple of rooms of Provençal and Orientalist paintings. In the museum courtyard, you can climb the Tour du Suquet for panoramic views.

West of Le Suquet, above the Plage de la Bocca (a good bet for bathing if you don't fancy one of the expensive private beaches), the Croix des Gardes

TIP

Boats run all year from quai Laubeuf in Cannes to the Iles de Lérins. Trans Côte d'Azur (tel: 04 92 98 71 30, www.trans-cote-azur.com) and Horizon (tel: 04 92 98 71 36) run services to Ile Ste-Marguerite. Planaria (tel: 04 92 98 71 38) runs services to Ile St-Honorat. Note that you cannot combine the two islands in one trip.

BELOW: strolling along La Croisette.

Cannes Film Festival

You can't beat the Festival de Cannes for true A-lister glamour. Film industry outsiders can join in the atmosphere at the film screenings at Cinéma de la Plage

For ten days in May, over 30,000 film producers, directors, distributors and actors, and 4,800 international journalists descend on Cannes for the Festival de Cannes (www.festival-cannes.com). The public crowds the railings in front of the Palais des Festivals in hope of autographs, while paparazzi snap stars in glamorous evening wear as they make the legendary climb up the Palais' red-carpeted steps.

Both public and media remain fascinated by the festival, debating the merits of the films, whether the stars are out in force and, of course, whether the right film has been awarded the Palme d'Or. The festival likes to arouse controversy and to spring surprises: in 2009, jury president Isabelle Huppert was accused of manipulating the jury to award the Palme d'Or to Michael Haneke; while

French-Tunisian Abdellatif Kechiche won in 2013 with his graphic lesbian drama, *Blue is the Warmest Colour*, amid claims that he had humiliated his lead actresses during filming.

The festival was originally conceived by the French government in the 1930s to provide an alternative to the Venice Film Festival, where only films meeting the approval of Mussolini's censors were shown. Cannes was elected for its 'sunny and enchanting location'. The first festival was scheduled for 1939, but plans were scuppered by World War II, and it was not until 20 September 1946 that glasses were raised at the belated inaugural festival.

The judging

Each year the festival's board of directors chooses a 10-member international jury: nine artists and a president. Past presidents range from Jean Cocteau (1953 and 1954) to the first woman president Olivia de Havilland (1965) and, more recently, Martin Scorsese (1998), Tim Burton (2010) and Steven Spielberg (2013). The jury awards the prestigious 'Palme d'Or' for Best Film, as well as prizes including Best Actor, Best Actress and Best Screenplay. Enduring past winners include Fellini's *La Dolce Vita* in 1960, Coppola's *Apocalypse Now* (1979), Mike Leigh's *Secrets and Lies* (1996) and Quentin Tarantino's *Pulp Fiction* (1994). The festival is firmly international – recent years have seen an enormous rise in the number of Asian, Middle Eastern and Eastern European films and relatively low numbers of US films.

The festival is also a major venue for the buying and selling of film rights, with some 4,000 films screened outside the competitions in the important Marché du Film.

The festival is supposed to be for industry insiders only, with tickets to screenings notoriously difficult to come by. The public do get to see some films, as the festival organises the outdoor Cinéma de la Plage (public screenings on the beach). Pick up invitations at the tourist office. ❏

LEFT: 1953 festival: Dany Robin, Kirk Douglas, Olivia de Havilland and Edward G. Robinson.

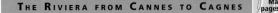
district was the first part of Cannes to be built up by foreign aristocrats. Several of their fantastical villas remain, including **Villa Rothschild** (1 avenue Jean de Noailles), now the municipal library, whose exotically planted gardens have become a public park, and the **Château de la Tour** (10 avenue Font de Veyre), a crenellated mock castle, now a hotel.

Le Cannet

Up boulevard Carnot, on the hill above Cannes, **Le Cannet ❸**, once a separate hill village now more or less engulfed by its bigger neighbour, still has a villagey appeal. Le Cannet is notable as the former home of the painter Pierre Bonnard, who lived in the Villa du Bosquet from 1926 until his death in 1947. The Belle Epoque Hôtel-Villa St-Vianney, adjoining the town hall, has been converted into the **Musée Bonnard** (16 boulevard Sadi Carnot; Tue–Sun, June–Sept 10am–6pm, Thu until 9pm, Oct–May until 6pm, Thu until 8pm; charge), a museum devoted to the artist, a founding member of Post-Impressionist movement *Les Nabis*.

The Iles de Lérins

If you want to escape the crowds, take a boat from quai Laubeuf, in Cannes' Vieux-Port, and head for the delightful **Iles de Lérins**.

At a mere 400 metres (1,300ft) in width, **Ile St-Honorat ❹**, mainly covered by eucalyptus and cypresses, is the smaller of the two Lérins islands. Although it seems like a quiet backwater, the island has an impressive ecclesiastical history, dating back to a monastery founded by St Honorat in the 5th century. For centuries it was a religious centre where many important bishops – including Ireland's St Patrick – trained. It was so powerful that it owned much of the land along the Mediterranean coast, including Cannes. But its abundant wealth meant it was subject to constant raids from pirates, as well as papal corruption, and its decline was inevitable. In 1869 it was bought by the Cistercians, who built a new monastery on the site of the old one. There is a restaurant (€€) and a snack bar (May–Sept) on the island.

Ste-Marguerite ❺, the larger island, named after Honorat's pos-

Most of the monastic buildings on Ile St-Honorat date from the 11th and 12th centuries. However, the abbey church (www. abbayedelerins.com; open daily, closed for Sun services) was built in the late 19th century by the Cistercian monks who bought the island in 1869. There's a small museum and a shop where the monks sell their own wine and a herb-based liqueur called Lérina.

BELOW: lunch in Le Cannet.

The 12th-century chapel Notre-Dame-de-Vie in Mougins.

sibly non-existent sister, is home to the impressive **Fort Royal**, begun by Richelieu in the early 17th century and occupied by the Spanish during the Thirty Years War. The keep now contains the **Musée de la Mer** (Tue–Sun, June–Sept 10am–5.45pm, Apr–May 10.30am–1.15pm, 2.15–5.45pm, Oct–Mar until 4.45pm; charge) where you can see ancient amphoras and other artefacts salvaged from shipwrecks, and the prison cells where Protestants were held after the Revocation of the Edict of Nantes in 1685. Some of the cells have been decorated with murals by artist Jean Le Gac but the most evocative is the heavily barred cell of the Man in the Iron Mask, immortalised by Alexandre Dumas. The prisoner's identity is still a mystery, although numerous, often far-fetched, suggestions include Louis XIV's twin brother, disgraced civil servant Nicolas Fouquet, playwright Molière and the son of Oliver Cromwell. The island is perfect for a day's excursion, with a small beach west of the harbour and rocky inlets for bathing, a nature reserve for waterfowl around the Etang de Batéguier, a botanical trail and plenty of picnic spots.

Mougins

Five km (3 miles) inland from Cannes, **Mougins** ❻, which overshadowed the former during the Middle Ages, has guarded its image as a pristine hill village. Its steep streets, terraces trailing flowers, concealed mansions, and some of the Côte's best restaurants make it a chic place for Cannes conference-goers to hang out. Every September, the village hosts Les Etoiles de Mougins, a food festival featuring some of the world's top chefs.

In the 1920s and 1930s, when it became the done thing to holiday on the Côte d'Azur, artists Cocteau and Man Ray arrived, and Picabia built his eccentric Château de Mai here. Picasso came too. The town's artistic connections are nowadays reflected in its numerous art and craft galleries. At the top of the village, the **Musée de la Photographie** (Porte Sarrazine; Tue–Fri 10am–12.30pm, 2–7pm, Sat–Sun 11am–7pm; free) has numerous photographs of Picasso, as well as works by master snapper Robert Doisneau.

In 2011 a new museum opened its doors, the **Musée d'Art Classique de Mougins** (MACM; 32 rue Commandeur; tel: 04 93 75 18 65; www.

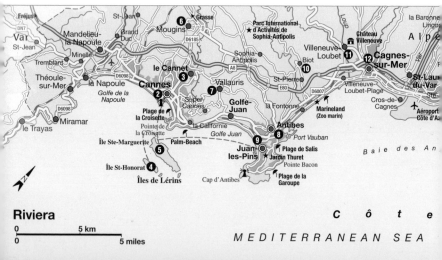

mouginsmusee.com; daily, July–Aug 10.30am–8pm, Thu until 10pm, Sept–June 9.30am–7pm; charge), in a renovated medieval building. The museum was founded by British entrepreneur Christian Levett to show how classical art has influenced modern painters and sculptors including Rubens, Dalí and Damien Hirst.

Outside the town, off the D3, is the small 17th-century chapel of Notre-Dame-de-Vie, which Picasso liked so much that he decided to stay and live here. Adjacent to the chapel, a house, called *L'Antre du Minotaure* (the Minotaur's lair), was the artist's home and studio from 1961 until his death in 1973. Today it is a private property and not visible from the road.

Vallauris

Another town with strong links to Picasso is **Vallauris** ❼, east of Cannes, where the artist turned his hand to pottery in the 1940s *(see box, page 256)*; the **Madoura Pottery** (which at the time of writing had just been acquired by the local council, who plan to turn it into a 'cultural complex') still retains the copyright to Picasso's ceramics. Ceramics have

been the mainstay of Vallauris for more than four centuries, continuing the tradition with countless pottery workshops and the Biennale de la Céramique every even-numbered year. Unfortunately the main shopping street is now clogged with tacky pottery outlets and the old town largely dwarfed by modern housing blocks. Uphill, however, visitors can experience the more highbrow side to Vallauris in the shape of the town's three museums, all housed in the largely Renaissance château.

In the chateau chapel, the **Musée National Picasso La Guerre et La Paix** (tel: 04 93 64 71 83; www.musee-picasso-vallauris.fr; July–Aug daily 10am–7pm, rest of summer Wed–Mon 10am–12.15pm, 2–6pm, until 5pm in winter; charge) contains Picasso's ode to peace, completed in 1952, with its two massive panels *War* and *Peace*, and a third panel depicting figures of the four continents around a dove. Though painted with passion, it is by no means Picasso's best work and is not improved by the fact that he neglected to prime the surface, so the dull brown of the hardboard shows through the large fields of

DRINK

Antibes has its very own absinthe bar, Balade en Provence (25 cours Masséna; open from 6pm every evening), in the basement of an olive oil shop by the covered market. Stand (or sit) at the original zinc counter and learn the traditional way of drinking the 'green fairy'. There are other alcohols available.

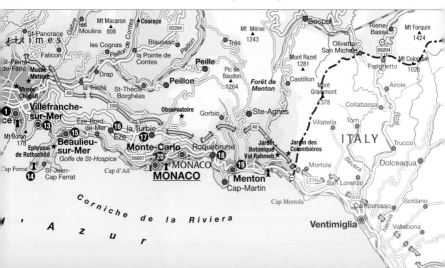

TIP

Held each July in the Pinède Gould, Jazz à Juan (www.jazzajuan.com) is one of the world's leading jazz festivals and the place to catch first-rate names in American jazz, blues and fusion, such as B.B. King, Dizzy Gillespie, Wayne Shorter and Keith Jarrett, in a stunning setting against the Mediterranean Sea.

white paint and scrubbed brush-work. Some of the pottery made by Picasso during the six years when he had his Fournas atelier (now 95 avenue Pablo Picasso) is exhibited in the **Musée de la Céramique** (same hours), also in the chateau. The collection traces the pottery heritage of Vallauris, from early domestic wares, via Art Nouveau forms by the Massier dynasty, to modern art pottery. A third museum, the **Musée Magnelli** (same hours) contains works by abstract painter Alberto Magnelli. Just outside the chateau stands Picasso's bronze of a man holding a sheep, which he presented to the town in 1949.

Antibes-Juan-les-Pins

Back on the coast, the historic port of **Antibes ➑** contrasts with the villas and tropical vegetation of the Cap d'Antibes and the indulgent party town of **Juan-les-Pins**, renowned for its clubs, expensive boutiques and casinos. Founded by the Phoenician Greeks, who named it Antipolis, Antibes was a keystone in French naval strategy. Having

been sacked twice by Emperor Charles V in the 16th century, kings Henri II and Henri III added fortifications; in 1680 Louis XIV brought in his military engineer Vauban to give it the star-shaped ramparts and bastions that line the shore. The largest yachting marina in Europe ensures that Antibes is lively all year round with a large spin-off industry of yacht brokers and ship chandlers, and a big English expat community.

Vieux Antibes

Behind the ramparts, Antibes has a splendid cobble-stoned old town with a covered food market on **cours Masséna** (Tue–Sun mornings, daily July–Aug). In summer there's a craft market here in the afternoons. Off the marketplace, the orange and yellow baroque facade of the **Eglise de l'Immaculée Conception** hides the simple, earlier structure of what was once a cathedral. Next door is the severe **Château Grimaldi**, once the bishop's palace, later residence of the Grimaldi family, the king's governor and a barracks before becoming an

BELOW RIGHT: Picasso in 1948.

Picasso's Pots

In 1946, Picasso discovered Vallauris when he visited a pottery exhibition and the Madoura workshop of Suzanne and Georges Ramié. In 1948, he settled in the town with his companion Françoise Gilot. Although he had experimented with ceramics in Paris in the 1920s, this was the start of a true fascination with clay and a burst of creativity that saw the production of some 4,000 pieces of pottery before his death in 1973. To begin with, Picasso did not make the plates and jugs himself but worked in close collaboration with the Ramiés and their craftsmen, painting the pots with wonderfully free designs of faces, fish or bullfighting scenes that often show him at his most joyful. If some items were merely series decorated by the artist (and he also licensed Madoura to produce some of his designs in limited editions), he was later to mould and pummel the damp clay to create new forms in zoomorphic vessels. His heads, owls or birds and tanagra-shaped vases are true sculptural one-offs. Long dismissed by art critics as 'not proper Picasso' and by art potters as 'not proper pottery', Picasso's pots are now seen as a true aspect of the artist's oeuvre and a contribution to the vitality of modern ceramics.

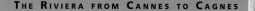

archaeological museum. In 1946, Picasso had a studio here, often using Ripolin household paint due to the scarcity of art materials after the war. The castle now houses the beautifully refurbished **Musée Picasso** (tel: 04 92 90 54 20; Tue–Sun, mid-June–mid-Sept Tue–Sun 10am–6pm, mid-Sept–mid-June Tue–Sun 10am–noon, 2–6pm; charge), which features his celebrated work *Joie de Vivre* (*Joy of Life*) and the triptych *Satyre, Centaure, Faune*, as well as several of his nudes and still lifes, including *Le Gobeur d'Oursins* (*Sea Urchin Eater*), pottery and drawings. Works by other artists who lived in Antibes are also on display, such as abstract paintings by Hans Hartung, and Russian-born Nicolas de Staël's last unfinished canvas *Le Grand Concert* (sometimes removed during temporary exhibitions). Outside on the terrace are sculptures by Miró and Arman and elongated bronze figures by Germaine Richier. The villagey streets of old Antibes' Commune Libre du Safranier form a bohemian arty district which proudly declared its 'independence' in 1960.

At the southern end of the ramparts, the gunpowder stores of the Bastion St-André contain the **Musée d'Archéologie** (Tue–Sun 10am–noon, 2–6pm, until 8pm Wed and Fri July–Aug, until 5pm in winter; charge), with remnants of ancient Antipolis, Roman stelae and mosaics, and the mysterious Galet d'Antibes, a large stone with mysterious inscriptions dating from the 5th century BC. Antibes' best public beach, the **Plage de Salis** (boulevard James Willie) is a 15-minute walk from here.

On a promontory on the port's northern side is the bastioned fortress of **Fort Carré** (Tue–Fri 12.30–4pm, Sat–Sun 10am–4pm, closed Sun outside of school hols; charge), a 16th-century fort that was enlarged by Vauban.

Juan-les-Pins and Cap d'Antibes

Wooded Cap d'Antibes is an exclusive millionaires' paradise, home to jet-setters' favourite, Hôtel du Cap-Eden-Roc, the hotel that set the trend for the summer season, and colossal villas belonging to Russian oligarchs

TIP

The Chapelle de la Garoupe (Mon–Sat 3–6pm, Sun 10am–1pm, 3–6pm) on Cap d'Antibes has been a site of pilgrimage for centuries. It's a pleasant walk up the stony chemin du Calvaire, past the stations of the Cross, from the Port de Salis.

BELOW: view towards Fort Carré from the beach.

Portrait of Auguste Escoffier at the eponymous museum.

and Arab princes. On the western side of the promontory, **Juan-les-Pins'** ❾ reputation for hedonism is well established: the F. Scott Fitzgeralds and other wealthy American socialites were swinging here as early as the 1920s. La Garoupe, the sandy beach on Cap d'Antibes, is still the place to sunbathe, and there are some public stretches between the snooty private beach concessions. It is also the starting point for the Sentier Tir-Poil coastal footpath, which leads to the **Villa Eilenroc** (460 avenue L. D. Beaumont; July–Sept Wed, Sat–Sun 3–7pm, Apr–June Wed, Sat 10am–5pm, Oct–Mar Wed, Sat 1–4pm; charge except Oct–Mar), designed by Charles Garnier of Paris and Monte Carlo opera houses fame; its gardens are the setting for the Musiques au Cœur classical music festival every July. On the top of the peninsula, **Jardin de la Villa Thuret** (90 chemin Raymond; Mon–Fri summer 8am–6pm, winter 8.30am– 5.30pm; free), with its jungle-like tangle of plants, is one of the Riviera's oldest botanic gardens. Right next door is the Villa Thenard,

BELOW: relaxing among the fishing boats in Juan-les-Pins. **BELOW RIGHT:** Golfe Juan.

where Grand Duke Nicholas of Russia died in 1929.

Biot

Heading east from Antibes, **Marineland** (www.marineland.fr; daily, July–Aug 10am–11pm, mid-Apr–June and Sept until 7pm, times vary rest of year; charge) is a huge marine theme park with afternoon whale and dolphin shows. On the same site are the aquatic fun park Aquasplash (mid-June–Aug daily 10am–7pm; charge), Adventure Golf (July–Aug daily noon–midnight, mid-Apr–June and Sept until 7pm, times vary rest of the year; charge), and Kid's Island theme park (July–Aug daily noon–8pm, times vary rest of the year; charge).

The artist Fernand Léger (1881–1955) adopted **Biot** ❿, another medieval perched village, as his outpost. At the foot of the village, the **Musée National Fernand Léger** (chemin du Val de Pome; tel: 04 92 91 50 30; www.musee-fernandleger.fr; Wed–Mon May–Oct 10am–6pm, Nov–Apr until 5pm; charge) has a vast ceramic mosaic on its exterior, and is the permanent home of nearly 400 of the

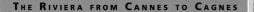

artist's paintings, tapestries, stained glass and ceramics, surrounded by a garden with giant versions of some of his sculptures.

Like Vallauris, Biot was long known for its potteries. Since 1956, however, it has been more associated with glass and the beautiful creations of the **Verrerie de Biot** (chemin des Combes; www.verrerie biot.com; Mon–Sat 9.30am–8pm, until 6pm in winter, Sun 10.30am–1pm, 2.30–7.30pm, until 6.30pm in winter) famed for its bubble glass. You can watch the master glassblowers at work in the factory located at the foot of the village; adjoining it are a shop, a small glass museum and the Galerie Internationale du Verre, exhibiting the work of international art glassmakers.

Villeneuve-Loubet

The resort of **Villeneuve-Loubet** ⑪ is often associated with the gigantic pyramidal forms of the **Marina Baie des Anges** development (contact tourist office for guided visits, tel: 04 92 02 66 16). Built in the 1970s, it was long decried as one of the monstrosities of coastal over-construction, though today its stepped-back terraces and roof gardens seem positively restrained compared to the urban sprawl that surrounds it.

Villeneuve-Loubet also has its old medieval hill town, located 3km (2 miles) inland. Above the village is the medieval **castle** where French king François I stayed for three weeks in 1538 for the signature of the Treaty of Nice. Although the castle is still privately owned, it is open for guided visits (enquire at the tourist office, 16 avenue de la Mer, tel: 04 92 02 66 16).

Lower down the hill, the **Musée Escoffier de l'Art Culinaire** (www. fondation-escoffier.org; daily, July–Aug 2–7pm, Wed and Sat 10am–noon as well, Sept–June 2–6pm, closed Nov; charge) preserves the memory of Auguste Escoffier, 'king of chefs and chef of kings', in the house where he was born in 1846. Exhibits include Escoffier's handwritten recipe book and photographs of Australian soprano Dame Nelly Melba, for whom he invented the Peach Melba.

The pyramidal Marina Baie des Anges.

BELOW LEFT: glass blower at work. **BELOW:** bubble glass (*verre à bulles*) of Biot.

Inside the Château-Musée Grimaldi.

BELOW: Musée Renoir, Cagnes.

Cagnes-sur-Mer

Cagnes-sur-Mer ⑫ splits into three parts. At the lower end, Cros-de-Cagnes is a rather downmarket modern seaside resort, with a racetrack, a pebbly beach backing onto the road and the added disadvantage of aircraft noise. Cagnes-sur-Mer, with its public park and a covered market (mornings only) occupies the middle ground. Rising up above both of them is the medieval village of **Haut-de-Cagnes**, where plentiful restaurants make it a popular night out for Niçois. Crowning the village is the crenellated tower of the **Château-Musée Grimaldi** (Wed–Mon, May–Sept Wed–Mon 10am–1pm, 2–6pm, Oct–Apr 10am–noon, 2–5pm; charge).

Originally a watchtower, it was transformed into a Renaissance residence by Jean-Henri Grimaldi. On the ground floor, a small museum pays homage to the olive tree, while upstairs are paintings of the Montparnasse cabaret singer Susy Solidor by artists such as Cocteau, and a collection of contemporary Mediterranean art. The highlight, however, is the grand ceremonial room on the first floor, whose ceiling, painted by Italian artist Giulio Benso Pietra, is a vertiginous feat.

The elderly Renoir lived in Cagnes from 1906 to 1919. The house he built at Les Collettes, just east of Cagnes-sur-Mer, is now the **Musée Renoir** (Wed–Mon, Apr–Sept 10am–1pm, 2–6pm, gardens 10am–6pm, June–Sept and Oct–Mar until 5pm; charge), reopened in 2013 following extensive renovation. It remains much as it was when the artist lived here. Paintings of his garden, of his granddaughter Coco, and a version of his *Large Bathers* reflect the high tonality of his late works. There are also several of the bronze sculptures Renoir increasingly turned to at the end of his life.

Cagnes-sur-Mer has a varied programme of festivals throughout the year. The main sporting events revolve around the Hippodrome (racecourse), the second-largest in France, with both sand and grass tracks, as well as a trotting (harness racing) track. The Fête de la Châtaigne (Chestnut Festival) in November is a more traditional option. ❑

RESTAURANTS

Restaurants

Prices for a three-course meal without wine. Many restaurants have a less expensive lunch menu:
€ = under €25
€€ = €25–40
€€€ = €40–60
€€€€ = over €60

Cannes

Aux Bons Enfants
80 rue Meynardier.
No phone. Open L & D Mon–Sat. Cash only. €
Opened in 1935 and still run by the same family, this bistro is popular for its generous home cooking. Expect starters like grilled sardines, followed by beef *daube*.

Mantel
22 rue St-Antoine, Le Suquet
www.restaurantmantel.com
Tel: 04 93 39 13 10. Open L Fri–Mon & D Thu–Tue.
€€–€€€
Ducasse protégé Noël Mantel's smart restaurant is one of the hottest addresses in town. The cuisine is local and seasonal and the desserts come in pairs.

Sea Sens
Five Seas Hotel
1 rue Notre Dame
www.five-seas-hotel-cannes.com
Tel: 04 63 36 05 06. Open L & D Mon–Fri. €€€–€€€€
Hip new restaurant on the fifth floor of an ultra-cool

hotel where Arnaud Tabarec's flavours take diners on a trip around the world. Leave room for dessert – they're made by the World Pastry Champion.

Le Cannet

Bistrot des Anges
rue de l'Ouest
Tel: 04 92 18 18 28. Open L & D daily. €€
Contemporary bistro in a lovely old farmhouse which is also home to Bruno Oger's acclaimed other restaurant Villa Archange (€€€€). There's a bar on the terrace.

Mougins

Au Rendez-Vous de Mougins
place du Commandant Lamy
www.au-rendez-vous-mougins.fr
Tel: 04 9375 8747. Open L & D daily. €€
Simple Provençal specialities in a convivial atmosphere on the village square.

La Place de Mougins
41 place du Commandant Lamy
www.laplacedemougins.com
Tel: 04 93 90 15 78. Open L & D Wed–Sun. €€–€€€€
Well-travelled chef Denis Fétisson has brought his take on market cuisine to the Côte's culinary capital, where each month he celebrates a different local product.

Antibes-Juan-les-Pins

La Passion des Mets
7 rue James Close, Antibes
Tel: 04 92 94 07 31. Open L & D Tue–Sun. €
Traditional Provençal dishes served by friendly staff in Vieux Antibes. Generous portions.

Les Pêcheurs
10 boulevard Maréchal Juin, Cap d'Antibes
www.ca-beachhotel.com
Tel: 04 92 93 13 30. Open Apr–Oct. Les Pêcheurs D, Le Cap L. €€€€
This waterside restaurant and hotel complex with private sandy beach has rejuvenated the local scene with the acclaimed cooking of Philippe Jégo. Lunch is in the simpler Le Cap on the beach.

Biot

Les Arcades
16 place des Arcades
Tel: 04 93 65 01 04. Open L Tue–Sat, D Tue–Sun. €€
This popular village inn doubles as an art gallery. Provençal cuisine is served indoors or under the medieval arcades.

Cagnes-sur-Mer

Josy-Jo
2 rue du Planastel, Haut-de-Cagnes
www.restaurant-josyjo.com
Tel: 04 93 20 68 76. Open L & D Tue–Sat, D Sat. Closed mid-Nov–mid-Dec. €€–€€€€
Josy Bandecchi serves courgette flower fritters and chargrilled steaks in the ancient village house where artists Modigliani and Soutine stayed.

RIGHT: beauty on a plate.

FANTASY LAND

Many of the spectacular buildings of the Riviera reflect the fantasy world that their wealthy creators wanted to live in

Château Grimaldi in Antibes (*left*) shows the rich medieval heritage of this coast of lordly princes, Saracens and pirates. It is part of the romance that has attracted wealthy visitors who have been able to act out their dreams here. The Monaco royal family are Grimaldis, and their own fairy-tale palace was the Hollywood dream of the actress Grace Kelly, who married into it. In the 1920s the rich and sociable American artist Gerald Murphy, whose motto was 'Living well is the best revenge', and his wife Sara built Villa America on the Garoupe beach. It had 14 bedrooms and the first rooftop sun deck on the Riviera. More spectacularly, Béatrice de Rothschild, wife of a Russian banker, Maurice Ephrussi, built villa Ephrussi de Rothschild, inspired by his cousin, Fanny Khan, who had married Theodor Reinach, creator of Villa Kérylos, a Greek fantasy.

With a plentiful supply of money and artists it was hard for them to go wrong. But the artists, too, found great settings for their work.

ABOVE: Villa Kérylos was built in 1902–8 for the French archaeologist Theodor Reinach to resemble a 2nd-century BC villa from Delos, incorporating all modern comforts. Reinach's guests had to dress in Greek *peplos* and dine lying on couches.

BELOW: Beatrice Ephrussi de Rothschild had this Venetian-style villa built and held parties mimicking the court of Marie Antoinette at Versailles. Exotic plants and animals filled the garden.

LEFT: in Cimiez, the original Roman settlement in Nice, a highly original folly with *trompe l'œil* facades was built among the ancient ruins in the Genoese style for the Consul of Nice, Jean-Baptiste Gubernatis, and completed by his grandson in 1685. Now the Villa Arènes, it houses the Matisse Museum.

ABOVE: The ruined 14th-century Château de la Napoule was bought and restored in 1918 by the eccentric American sculptor Henry Clews, who had a fanatical hatred of anything modern. Living in a complete fantasy world, he and his wife Marie loved dressing up in medieval costumes, which they designed for their servants as well as themselves. Their menagerie included pigeons with musical pipes attached to their wings.

TYPICAL FARMHOUSES

For many visitors the *mas*, or farmhouse, of southern France embodies the ideal country style. These sturdy, squat buildings are designed to be cool in summer and easy to heat in winter; their stone walls are thick and their windows small, shuttered and absent on the north side in places where the mistral wind is strong. Terracotta tiles cover the floors both upstairs and down, and the paintwork is often a lavender blue. They have hardly changed in design since Roman times and their tiles, once made using clay moulded over the tilers' thighs, are just the same. This shape is used not just on farmhouses, but on every domestic building in the region, keeping towns harmonious. Planning laws continue to insist all new houses have these terracotta roofs, pitched at a lowly 30 degrees, so the weight of the tiles keeps pressing downwards. Other embellishments typical of the region include ironwork wind vanes and spires. A farmhouse complex may include stables, lofts, cellars and dovecotes, and even an ice house built of stone and insulated with hay.

LEFT: The fishermen's chapel St-Pierre in Villefranche had a make-over by Jean Cocteau in 1957, using local masons and ceramicists. Inside, his imaginative frescos depict Christ with the local fishermen.

RIGHT: Fondation Maeght by the Catalan architect Josep-Lluis Sert is an exemplary Modernist building and a highly successful gallery space. Sert had designed Miró's Mallorca studio, which the Maeghts saw and liked.

THE RIVIERA FROM VILLEFRANCHE TO MENTON

East of Nice towards the Italian frontier, arid limestone mountains descend almost directly into the sea. Historic ports, such as Villefranche-sur-Mer and Italianate Menton, mix with exclusive residential peninsulas, while the mild climate has peppered the area with exotic gardens

Three corniche roads snake eastwards from Nice towards the Italian border. The Basse Corniche (D6098), or Corniche Inférieure, hugs the coast, winding between villas and apartment blocks and providing an overview of how heavily built-up it has become – though still interspersed by old harbours and exclusive headlands. The Moyenne Corniche (D6007) is the shortest and probably the most stylish of the three routes, while the Grande Corniche (D2564), roughly tracing the Roman Via Aurelia, is the highest of the three corniches, passing through a sparsely vegetated limestone landscape. It is also the longest route from Monaco to Nice, though not necessarily the slowest, since heavy traffic often clogs the coast road. For those in a hurry, the A8 *autoroute* runs parallel to it, slightly further inland.

Villefranche-sur-Mer

The Basse Corniche leaves the Vieux-Port of Nice climbing up round the fantastical villas of Mont Boron. First stop to the east, the town of **Ville-franche-sur-Mer ⑬** was established in the 14th century as a *villefranche* or customs-free port by Charles II d'Anjou, and was long the principal port of the Comté de Nice. In 1557, to protect the port, Philibert of Savoy built a massive **citadelle**, now home

to the town hall, congress centre and four minor museums. These include sculptures by Antoniucci Volti and the **Musée Goetz-Boumeester of modern paintings** (Wed–Mon, July–Aug 10am–noon, 3–7pm, June–Sept 9am–noon, 3–6pm, Oct–May 10am–noon, 2–5pm, closed Tue am and Nov; free), with minor works by Picasso, Picabia and Miró. Until France withdrew from NATO's integrated military command in 1966, Villefranche was used as a base by the US Navy; British and American

ships still use the sheltered harbour, which is one of the deepest in the world, as do cruise ships and a small fishing fleet.

The town is well restored but not bijou, with tall painted stucco houses and lively fish restaurants lining quai Courbet. Here you'll also find the **Chapelle St-Pierre** (Wed–Mon, summer 10am–noon, 3–7pm, winter 10am–noon, 2–6pm, closed mid-Nov–mid-Dec; charge), also known as the Cocteau Chapel, one of the most extraordinary works by Surrealist writer, artist and film-maker Jean Cocteau. He restored the medieval chapel dedicated to St Peter, patron saint of fishermen, painting it with quirky fishing scenes and episodes from the saint's life. Nearby is the famous Hôtel Welcome, where Cocteau stayed in Room 22.

The Italianate old town climbs up the hill behind the harbour, dominated by the tall campanile of the Baroque **church of St-Michel**, which contains an expressive, 17th-century figwood sculpture of the Dead Christ. Many of the houses are built on the Italian model, with large arched loggias on the ground floor, most of which have been filled in. The town seems to specialise in *trompe l'oeil* wall paintings, usually of windows. The chapel on rue de l'Eglise is entirely painted with *faux* Pisan Romanesque façade, which has what seems to be a genuine Pisan-style doorway dated to 1590. The main street of the old town is **rue du Poilu**, which leads to the tiny place du Conseil, from which there is a good view of the harbour and Cap Ferrat. The picturesque 13th-century **rue Obscure** starts here: the street is almost entirely composed of covered passageways which the residents used for shelter when the town was attacked.

Cap Ferrat

Continuing east along the bay from Villefranche, a side road leads to **Cap Ferrat ⓮**. Hideout of the seriously rich and famous, this is one of the few areas of the coast that guards its aura of exclusivity. Much of it lurks behind security fences and guard-dog warnings, but the Plage Passable is a pleasant little beach, not far from the former villa of King Leopold II

TIP

The main attraction of the Fondation Ephrussi de Rothschild is its nine themed gardens. A meandering promenade takes you past roses, exotic cacti and Provençal flora, through a French formal garden with musical fountains, a Japanese garden with gravel and little shrines, an Italian Renaissance garden, and the romantic lapidary garden with its fragments of Gothic architecture and medieval statuary.

FAR LEFT: an ideal way to travel along the coast. **BELOW:** St-Jean-Cap Ferrat.

EAT

For beach restaurants, try fashionable **Paloma Beach** (tel: 04 93 01 64 71; www.paloma-beach. com) on Cap Ferrat. It's casual at lunchtime, with grilled fish and salads, more romantic (and expensive) for candlelit dinners. At Cap d'Ail, laidback **L'Eden** (tel: 04 93 78 17 06; www.edenplagelamala. com) serves good-value traditional French cooking amid a Balinese-style tropical decor on the idyllic Plage Mala.

BELOW: the casino in Beaulieu-sur-Mer.

of Belgium, from where you can join the coastal path round the Cap.

Leopold's merciless exploitation of the Congo helped to finance his excesses, such as a large park laid out on the peninsula. In its grounds he built a palace for himself and three houses, one for each of his mistresses. With so many mistresses, Leopold became concerned that he might die without absolution, so in 1906 (three years before his death) he built another house nearby for his confessor, Monseigneur Charmeton. In 1926 W. Somerset Maugham bought this house, calling it Villa Mauresque after its Moorish style.

The pink-and-white **Fondation Ephrussi de Rothschild** (tel: 04 93 01 33 09; www.villa-ephrussi.com; Feb–Oct daily 10am–6pm, July–Aug until 7pm, Nov–Jan Mon–Fri 2–6pm, Sat, Sun and school hols 10am–6pm; charge) was built in 1905–12 to house the art collection of Baroness Ephrussi de Rothschild (1864–1934). Around a Venetian Gothic central courtyard, panelled rooms are laden with 18th-century French furniture, a ceiling painted by Tiepolo, and pre-

cious Sèvres and Vincennes porcelain, but its greatest attraction is its 7 hectares (17 acres) of exotic gardens: they spread along the crest of the Cap with gorgeous views on all sides (*see margin, page 265*). The views are equally lovely from the quaint café-restaurant.

Towards the tip of the Cap is **Villa Santo Sospir** (14 avenue Jean Cocteau; tel: 04 93 76 00 16; daily visits by appointment; charge), where Jean Cocteau lived in the 1950s and which he decorated in frescoes inspired by Greek mythology. Around the corner is the super-luxurious **Grand Hotel du Cap Ferrat**, where it's (just about) more affordable to have a drink in the bar than book a room.

The village of **St-Jean-Cap-Ferrat** consists of little more than a beautiful yacht harbour with some food shops, exclusive boutiques and smart restaurants. There is a one-way system in and out of the village and parking is often difficult.

Beaulieu-sur-Mer

Across the bay from St-Jean you can spot another glamorous mansion. On the water's edge at **Beaulieu-sur-Mer**,

the **Villa Kerylos** (tel: 04 93 01 01 44; www.villa-kerylos.com; Feb–Oct daily 10am–6pm, July–Aug until 7pm, Nov–Jan Mon–Fri 2–6pm, Sat, Sun and school hols 10am–6pm; charge) is a 1902–8 reconstruction of an ancient Greek villa by wealthy German scholar Theodor Reinach. Together with architect Emmanuel Pontremoli he created what is not so much a replica villa as an idealised version, with marble columns and cool courtyards open to the sea and sky, which houses a large collection of mosaics, frescos and furniture. If you're coming from Cap Ferrat, walk here(about 15 mins) along the waterside **promenade Maurice Rouvier**, which will take you past walled gardens and villas including the late actor David Niven's beautiful former home, La Fleur du Cap.

Beaulieu-sur-Mer ⓑ itself is a genteel retirement town with a Belle Epoque casino, luxury hotels and elegant rest-homes reclining in the sheltered climate. However, the harbour is lined with lively restaurants and there's a funky private beach, **Zelo's** (tel: 04 93 01 11 00; www.zelos beach.com; charge), with four-poster beds and sets from well-known DJs. From here the Basse Corniche passes through the sprawling resort of Eze-Bord-de-Mer and Cap d'Ail before reaching Monaco.

Eze

Impaled on a rocky spike some 400 metres (1,300ft) above the sea is picturesque **Eze Village** ⓰, with its cluster of pantiled medieval houses and Baroque church. Access is from the Moyenne Corniche or by donkey track from the coast, and its entrance, through a small hidden archway, comes after a short winding climb from the main road – the village is closed to motor vehicles. If you're fit enough, you can walk up the narrow **chemin de Nietzsche** (about 1 hour), named after the philosopher

Friedrich Nietzsche, who walked the path to get his creative juices flowing, from the unremarkable seaside town of **Eze-sur-Mer**.

Few other *villages perchés* command the popularity of Eze, and pushing through the crowded narrow streets at the height of summer can be trying. However, the village's current prosperity belies its troubled past. Eze began as a Ligurian settlement and was later fortified by the Phoenicians, then developed by the Romans. After the Romans came the Lombards, who in AD 578 murdered the inhabitants and burnt the town to the ground. The Lombards held Eze until 740, when the Saracens appeared. Eze was one of the their last strongholds; they were not driven from Provence until 980 and they razed the town when they left. After the Saracens, Eze was taken and retaken over and over. In the 14th century, it was finally bought by Amadeus of Savoy, whose family retained control until the entire area was ceded to France in 1860.

During the Middle Ages, Eze became a centre of piracy. A massacre

The Trophée des Alpes was built by the Roman Senate as a reward to Emperor Augustus for his successful campaign against the remaining 44 rebellious Alpine tribes.

BELOW: the hilltop village of Eze.

Le Corbusier's unconventional grave.

BELOW: breathtaking view over Roquebrune Village.

took place in 1543, when the French army of François I, aided by the Turkish fleet under the command of the corsair Barbarossa, launched an attack. Street by street the inhabitants were slaughtered and the town looted.

A new Eze slowly grew from the ruins but was struck again, this time by the 1887 earthquake, which did more damage to the town and split what remained of the town walls. The village was abandoned and by the 1920s was more or less empty.

These days, one undoubtedly flourishing aspect is the **Jardin Exotique** (daily July–Aug 9am–7.30pm, June and Sept until 7pm, Apr–May until 6pm, Oct until 5.30pm, Feb–Mar until 5pm, Nov–Jan until 4.30pm; charge), a fine collection of cacti and succulents, interspersed with terracotta sculptures. This garden was planted in 1950 around the ruins of the chateau, which had been dismantled in 1706. Below the garden the amber-coloured **Eglise Notre-Dame de l'Assomption**, which has an ornate Baroque interior, was built in 1765. No less than 18 sun motifs signify the presence of God, and also

perhaps the cult of Isis – according to popular legend, Eze gets its name from Isis, goddess of life and eternity, to whom the Phocaeans had erected a temple on the site of the village.

La Turbie

High up on the Grande Corniche east of Eze, the white marble columns of the ruined Roman monument at **La Turbie** ⓱ stand out against the sky. The village derives its name from the Latin *tropaea*, meaning trophy, after the vast monument **la Trophée des Alpes** (18 avenue Albert I; tel: 04 93 41 20 84; www.monuments-nationaux. fr; daily, mid-May–mid-Sept 9.30am–1pm, 2.30–6.30pm, mid-Sept–mid-May 10am–1.30pm, 2.30–5pm; charge). It was erected here in 6 BC in honour of Emperor Augustus's victory over 44 Alpine tribes, whose names are inscribed inside.

The Trophy dominates the narrow streets of the medieval village, which still has its fortified gateways. The **Eglise St-Michel** is an 18th-century Baroque offering, full of gaudy red marble that might befit a film star's villa in St-Tropez.

Roquebrune Cap-Martin

Between Monaco (*see page 275*) and Menton lies **Roquebrune Cap-Martin ⓲**. The Cap is an exclusive millionaire's haunt: Empress Eugénie, wife of Napoleon III, and Winston Churchill stayed here, as did some less desirable characters, Emperor Bokassa (head of state of the Central African Republic 1966–79) among them. Much of it is off-limits, although you can walk round the Sentier du Littoral, which hugs the sea edge, with opportunities for bathing from the rocks. Just west of the Cap, within easy reach of Roquebrune Cap-Martin station, the pleasant beach of Cabbé sits under the gardens of the elegant Villa Mangano. It is largely pebble, but has some sand at low tide, unlike the busier shingle beach of more downmarket suburb, Carnolès (on the Menton side).

Up on the coast path sits the **Cabanon** (visits Tue and Fri 9.30am; reserve several days ahead with tourist office, tel: 04 93 35 62 87; charge), the tiny log cabin constructed by Le Corbusier in 1951–2. It's not the only avant-garde building here: Eileen Gray's groundbreaking Villa E-1027 was designed by the Irish-born decorator and architect in 1929. After being abandoned for several years, it is currently being restored.

Perched high up above Carnolès is old **Roquebrune Village**, a picturesque tangle of alleys and houses built into the rock, with terraces offering superb views over the skyscrapers of Monte-Carlo below. Its **Château** (tel: 04 93 35 07 22; daily, June–Sept 10am–1pm, 2.30–7pm, Feb–May 10am–12.30pm, 2–6pm, Oct–Jan until 5pm; charge) dates back to the 10th century when Conrad I, count of Ventimiglia, built it to keep out the Saracens. In the cemetery next to the village, Le Corbusier, who drowned while swimming in the sea in 1965, is buried alongside his wife in a tomb of his own design.

Roquebrune's other popular landmark, along the steep footpath that runs down to the lower town, is the wonderfully gnarled **Olivier Millénaire**, an ancient olive tree that is probably even older than its name (1,000-year-old olive tree) claims.

The Trophée des Alpes was built by the Roman Senate as a reward to Emperor Augustus for his successful campaign against the remaining 44 rebellious Alpine tribes.

BELOW: Roquebrune Village is a tangle of lovely alleys.

Walking the Caps

Although the Riviera's exclusive headlands can seem like the preserve of the rich and famous, everyone has the right to walk along the French seashore, a right increasingly enforced by the local authorities as they maintain and improve the signposting on the Sentier du Littoral (coastal path). The path takes you around three of the region's most beautiful headlands: Cap Ferrat (footpath from Plage Passable to Port St-Jean), Cap d'Ail (footpath from Plage Mala to Plage Marquet), and Cap Martin (along the Sentier Corbusier, between the Plage du Cabbé and Carnolès). At times the path hugs the water or crosses beaches, with opportunities for bathing from the rocks or in surprisingly wild coves, inaccessible from the road and surrounded by Mediterranean vegetation and azure seas – or with surreal views of Monaco's tower blocks. At other times, steps climb up the cliffs and the path skirts the rear of private grounds, offering glimpses of Belle Epoque villas, tropical gardens and the lifestyle of the privileged few. The Conseil Général des Alpes Maritimes publishes a Randoxygène guide, *Rando Pays Côtier*, available from tourist offices. Also try www.randoxygene.org for more details.

TIP

The attractive town of Ventimiglia just across the Italian border from Menton is a popular hop for locals thanks to its vast food and general goods market every Friday. Beware the fake designer handbags sold here: people are regularly stopped at the border customs post and may incur large fines for smuggling.

Below Left: the Italianate Menton old town. **Below Right:** Menton lemons.

Menton: lemon capital

Sheltered by mountains, **Menton** ⑲ basks in an enchanted setting with 300 days of sun a year and a climate at least two degrees warmer than that of Nice. Mexican and North African vegetation, as well as citrus fruit, flourish in this subtropical greenhouse.

In the second half of the 19th century, Menton was renowned as a winter sanatorium, thanks to Dr Bennet, an English doctor, who promoted Menton's mild climate as perfect for invalids. As a result British and Germans flocked here in winter, as did Russians, who added another of the Riviera's Russian Orthodox churches to the town. Royal visitors such as Queen Victoria helped the town acquire a reputation as the most aristocratic and anglophile of all the resorts on the Riviera. Along the seafront and in the hills surrounding the Italianate old town, grand hotels and romantic villas were built.

Nowadays, most of the grand hotels have been demolished or converted into apartments, and the mild climate has given Menton the reputation of a cosy retirement home.

However, the town has been rejuvenated since 1993 when Menton and Ventimiglia together became the European Union's first joint urban community, combining frontier posts and municipal and business activities *(see margin left)*.

Jean Cocteau

Surrealism fans will be interested to learn that the Salle des Mariages, where marriage ceremonies are held in Menton's **Hôtel de Ville** (town hall) was decorated with murals by Jean Cocteau in the 1950s (reservation advised tel: 04 92 10 50 00; visits Mon–Fri 8.30am–noon, 2–4.30pm; charge). A tiny bastion on quai Monléon, by the harbour, contains the **Musée du Bastion** (Wed–Mon 10am–6pm; charge), which Cocteau designed as a memorial to himself, with his own quirky pebble mosaics by the entrance, on the floors and around the window frames on the first floor; the displays change regularly. In 2011 a new museum devoted to the artist, the **Musée Jean Cocteau Collection Séverin Wunderman** (2 quai Monléon; tel: 04 89 81 52

50; www.museecocteaumenton.fr; Wed–Mon 10am–6pm; charge) opened its doors in an exciting new building designed by Bandol-based architect Rudy Ricciotti, who also designed the new MuCEM in Marseille and the Département de l'Art Islamique at the Louvre. Wunderman was a Belgian-born American businessman who donated his private collection of 1800 artworks (990 of them by Cocteau) to the town; the works are shown chronologically. Also on show are photographs of Cocteau and his cohorts by Arles-based photographer Lucien Clergue, who was introduced to the artist, writer and filmmaker by his friend Picasso.

Nearby are the excellent **covered market** and the place du Marché with its flower stalls. Running behind them, pedestrianised rue St-Michel and avenue Félix-Faure hum with shops and restaurants.

The old town

The Italianate old town occupies the hill, all narrow shady streets stacked with houses. Flights of steps decorated with black-and-white pebble mosaics lead up from quai Bonaparte to Baroque **Basilique St-Michel Archange** (daily 10am–noon, 3–5.15pm, closed Sat am and Sun am), which has a pink-and-orange campanile and sculptures on its facade. The square in front is the main venue for Menton's prestigious chamber music festival each August. A second Baroque church stands across the square, the **Chapelle de la Conception**, its walls ringed by life-size statues of saints.

Built in tiers where the castle once stood, the **Cimetière du Vieux-Château**, at the top of the hill, holds the tombs of many of the Russian and British families who settled here from the end of the 19th century, including those of illustrator Aubrey Beardsley and William Webb Ellis, creator of the modern game of rugby.

At the western end of the town, behind the seafront apartments and hotels of the promenade du Soleil, is the 18th-century pink-and-white **Palais Carnolès**, the former summer residence of the Monaco royal family, still with its fine staircase and some of its original panelling and painted ceilings. Today it contains the **Musée des**

Menton celebrates its little yellow lemons with a flamboyant annual festival starting in mid-February and continuing into March. Over two weeks, lemons and oranges are piled high into incredible sculptures in the Jardin des Biovès, and on the Sundays, floats and bands parade along the seafront. For details, contact www.feteducitron.com

Below Right: sweeping view over the Baie de Garavan.

Once endemic on Easter Island, the Sophoro toromiro tree species died out, leaving just one specimen – now long gone – growing inside a volcano crater. Thankfully, explorer Thor Heyerdahl was able to take some seed pods back to Sweden with him in 1956, hence the trees now growing in Menton.

Beaux Arts (3 avenue de la Madone; Wed–Mon 10am–noon, 2–6pm; free), including a Madonna by Louis Bréa, Flemish and Dutch paintings, and works by Suzanne Valadon, Raoul Dufy and Graham Sutherland. Surrounding it, the **Jardin des Agrumes**, run by INRA (the state agricultural research institute), has many different species of citrus tree.

A horticulturalist's paradise

Menton boasts a remarkable number of exotic gardens – two of these are easily accessible to the public. The **Jardin Botanique Exotique Val Rahmeh** (avenue St-Jacques; tel: 04 92 41 76 76; Wed–Mon, Apr–Sept 10am–12.30pm, 3.30–6.30pm, Oct–Mar 10am–12.30pm, 2–5pm; charge), arranged around a 1920s villa, proves that everything can indeed grow in Menton. A winding trail leads between magical and medicinal plants, dry and wet environments, towering palms, dank tropical ferns, forests of bamboo and exotic cocoa, avocado, banana, guava and citrus fruits, tea bushes and spice trees. This

garden is also one of the institutions cultivating the *Sophoro toromiro* tree in the hope of introducing it back into the wild *(see margin left)*.

The **Serre de la Madone** (route de Gorbio; tel: 04 92 41 76 76; www.serredelamadone.com; Tue–Sun, Apr–Oct 10am–6pm, Dec–Mar until 5pm, closed Nov; charge) is a romantic garden designed in the 1920s by Lawrence Johnson, creator of the garden at Hidcote Manor in England. It is laid out with geometrical pools, terraces, fountains and classical statues that create different perspectives and environments for irises, acanthus, camellias, water plants, toxic daturas and flora from all over the globe.

Interesting gardens that can only be visited on tours organised by the Service du Patrimoine (tel: 04 92 10 33 66, *see page 215*) include the **Jardin des Colombières** (July–mid-Aug daily at 4pm), inspired by classical mythology, the **Jardin de la Fontana Rosa** (Mon and Fri 10am), which has ceramic motifs paying tribute to Don Quixote, and the grounds full of tropical and subtropical plants at **Villa de la Maria Serena** (Tue 10am). ❑

BELOW: the Serre de la Madone garden.

RESTAURANTS

Restaurants

Prices for a three-course meal without wine. Many restaurants have a less expensive lunch menu:

€ = under €25
€€ = €25–40
€€€ = €40–60
€€€€ = over €60

Villefranche-sur-Mer
Le Bistrot de la Rade
15 rue du Poilu
Tel: 04 54 59 18 82. Open L & D daily. €€
In the bustling main street of the old town, this buzzy Franco-Italian restaurant has something for all tastes, from salad to pizza.

St-Jean-Cap Ferrat
Le Sloop
Port de Plaisance
Tel: 04 93 01 48 63. Open L Thu–Tue & D Mon, Thu–Sat. Closed mid-Nov–mid-Dec. €€–€€€
Fish, shellfish and French classics are served in a maritime-themed dining room or on the terrace overlooking the yachting marina. A favourite of Lord Lloyd-Webber and the late Michael Winner.

Eze
Château de la Chèvre d'Or
rue du Barri
www.chevredor.com

Tel: 04 92 10 66 61. Open L & D daily. €€€€
Luxurious dining with spectacular views. As well as the gastronomic restaurant, in summer you can also eat on the terrace (light, regional specialities at lunch, Asian-inspired cuisine at dinner) and in the informal Café du Jardin.

La Turbie
Café de la Fontaine
4 avenue du Général de Gaulle
www.hostelleriejerome.com
Tel: 04 9328 5279. Open L & D daily. €€
Bruno Cirino of the Hostellerie Jérôme has brilliantly revived the village café as a casual but chic bistro, with a superb-value blackboard menu of homely specials, such as marinated sardines, Nice-style rabbit and home-made fruit tarts. Open for breakfast or afternoon drinks as well.

Roquebrune Cap-Martin
Les Deux Frères
place des Deux Frères
www.lesdeuxfreres.com
Tel: 04 93 28 99 00. Open L Wed–Sun & D Tue–Sat. €€–€€€€
The old village school is now a pleasant small hotel and restaurant.

Attractive southern dishes might include artichoke salad or red mullet in a herb crust.

Menton
A Braijade Meridionale
66 rue Longue
www.abraijade.fr
Tel: 04 93 35 65 65.
Open L & D daily. €€–€€€
The only restaurant in the old town is famous for its flambéed meat skewers and local *mentonnais* cuisine. The *P'tit Citron de Menton* menu (for two people) includes the famous lemons in every course as well as wine and coffee.
Mirazur
30 avenue Aristide Briand
www.mirazur.fr

Tel: 04 92 41 86 86. Open July–Aug L Thu–Sun & D Tue–Sun, Feb–June and Sept–Oct L & D Wed–Sun. Closed Nov–Jan. €€€€
In the hands of adventurous young Argentine chef Mauro Colagreco, staid Menton now has one of the most exciting restaurants on the coast, with two Michelin stars. Daring combinations of the finest ingredients, including fruit and vegetables from his kitchen garden, meet impeccable technique in specialities like low temperature pigeon. The dining room offers panoramic views over the bay. Make a reservation to secure a table.

RIGHT: superb presentation at Mirazur.

MONACO

Monaco is Europe's second-smallest independent country after the Vatican, with a huge concentration of wealth and sky-high property prices to match. The Principality has a busy cultural and sporting season and a legendary casino, plus all the trappings of a mini state

S een from across the bay, Monaco ⑳ is a surreal sight with its cluster of skyscrapers against a backdrop of mountains, like Hong Kong on the Mediterranean. Indeed, comparisons with Hong Kong are not unjustified: a tiny, densely populated state squeezed between coast and mountains, a mix of modernity and Belle Epoque splendour and an important banking centre.

Of the 36,000 residents, only 8,000 are Monégasque citizens, and of the 40,000 people who work in Monaco to serve its tax exiles, gamblers and holidaymakers, many don't actually live in the state itself but commute in from more affordable lodgings in surrounding towns. High property prices are due not only to the rich residents and high-income tourists, but also because Monaco is bursting at the seams. One of the quandaries for the royal oligarchy is how to extend the city, not just building upwards but through continued projects of land reclamation over the sea or through colonisation of neighbouring France: the swanky Monte-Carlo Country Club at the end of avenue Princesse Grace is actually in Roquebrune-Cap Martin, while the Monte-Carlo Golf Club is at La Turbie.

A new Grimaldi

In 2005 Prince Albert II *(see box, page 276)* acceded to the throne, on the death of his father, Prince Rainier III, after 56 years as head of state. In theory Monaco is a constitutional monarchy, with a Minister of State who heads a cabinet of four ministers and a legislature of 24 elected by Monégasque citizens, but in practice the Prince remains enormously powerful. The Minister of State is chosen by the prince and approved by the French government. Albert is the latest

Main attractions
PALAIS PRINCIER
MUSÉE OCÉANOGRAPHIQUE
JARDIN EXOTIQUE
MARCHÉ DE LA CONDAMINE
PORT HERCULE
CASINO DE MONTE-CARLO
NOUVEAU MUSÉE NATIONAL DE MONACO

LEFT: the skyscrapers of Monaco. RIGHT: a Monte Carlo status symbol.

Princess Grace, formerly American film star Grace Kelly, who married Prince Rainier in 1956 and died in a car crash in 1982, is buried in the cathedral cemetery, along with numerous other members of the Grimaldi dynasty.

BELOW: Princess Charlene and Prince Albert II.

ruler in the Grimaldi dynasty, which has been running the principality since 1297, when François Grimaldi sneaked in disguised as a Franciscan monk (there's a bronze statue of him in the place du Palais) and seized the fortress that had been built up on the rock by the Genoese. In 1612, Honoré II took the title of Prince. Although temporarily annexed by France from 1789 to 1814 during the French Revolution and under Napoleon – when the prince was put in prison and and the palace temporarily used as a hospital – Monaco's independence was formally recognised by France in 1861. The principality's relationship with France is not always an easy one: in 1962 President Charles de Gaulle, trying to stop French citizens settling in Monaco to avoid paying French taxes, sealed off Monaco's borders until Rainier conceded the issue. More recently, an official report criticised Monaco for money laundering.

Orientation

Monaco is split into six districts: medieval Monaco-Ville or the old town, La Condamine port area,

glamorous Monte-Carlo, the Larvotto beach district further east, La Fontvieille west of the Rocher, and residential Monaghetti on the hill behind. Although the state is tiny, it's very hilly. If you're on foot, there's a system of lifts and stairways, as well as five bus routes for getting around.

Le Rocher

Monaco-Ville, the core of Monaco, is often referred to as 'Le Rocher' (the Rock), since it sits on a precipice which juts into the sea between Port Hercule and the modern port of Fontvieille. To reach the top, take the footpath from places des Armes (10 mins) or catch bus 1 or 2 to Monaco-Ville. Le Rocher is crowned by the royal palace, the **Palais Princier** Ⓐ (place du Palais; www.palais.mc; Apr–Oct daily 10am–6pm; charge). The salmon-pink palace was pale yellow until it was redesigned by Princess Grace, the Hollywood star who became the wife of Rainier III in 1956. When a red-and-white diamond-spangled banner is flying, the prince is in residence and the palace is closed to the public. The audioguided

Albert II

The year 2005 saw the arrival of a new head of Europe's second-smallest but richest state with the coronation of Albert II, hitherto best known for his sporting achievements (a member of Monaco's Olympic bobsleigh team) and succession of glamorous female companions, including Claudia Schiffer, Naomi Campbell and Brooke Shields. Would it be a new style of monarchy? Prince Rainier III had done much to transform the Monaco economy in his 56-year reign but was increasingly surrounded by octogenarian councillors. Fifty-three-year-old Prince Albert II has brought in a younger team of ministers and advisers, is actively engaged against climate change and for sustainable development – and female staff are now being allowed to wear trousers for the first time. He has also involved Monaco more deeply in humanitarian causes, giving financial aid to countries in the wake of natural disasters, such as Haiti and Pakistan. As to the important question of an heir to the throne, Albert only married his long-term girlfriend, former South African swimming champion Charlene Wittstock, in July 2011. He has two illegitimate children but by law they cannot succeed him.

visit takes in the Cour d'Honneur, where HSH Prince Albert II married Charlene Wittstock in July 2011, and sumptuous 17th- and 18th-century state apartments, including the Salon Louis XV and the Throne Room. You can also watch the changing of the guard that takes place on the square outside each day at 11.55am; this is performed by the prince's French *carabinieri* as the Constitution forbids the use of Monégasque guards, a precaution devised to prevent a coup d'état. An adjacent entrance leads to the **Musée des Souvenirs Napoléoniens** (daily, Apr–Oct 10am–6pm, Dec–Mar 9.30am–5pm, closed Nov; charge), a collection of Napoleonic memorabilia, including Napoleon's cradle and famous black hat, as well as an exhibition of documents from Monaco's history.

The old town is a labyrinth of covered passageways, tiny squares and tangerine-coloured façades. Rue Basse has several old porticoed houses with carved lintels and vaulted cellars. But in the height of summer it is hard to appreciate the architecture since the quarter is given over to tawdry tourist trinkets. The neo-Byzantine **Cathédrale** (4 rue Colonel Bellando del Caste; open daily 8.30am–7pm, until 6pm in winter), which was built in white stone from La Turbie during the 19th century, contains tombs of the Grimaldis, including Prince Rainier and Princess Grace; every Sunday at 10am from September to June mass is sung by the cathedral choir. Nearby, the **Musée de la Chapelle de la Visitation** (place de la Visitation; Tue–Sun 10am–4pm; charge) houses a collection of Baroque religious paintings, including works by Rubens and Ribera. Also worth a look is the **Chapelle de la Miséricorde** (daily 10am–6pm), which has a stripey marble interior and a painted wood sculpture of the Dead Christ, attributed to 18th-century local sculptor François-Joseph Bosio,

TIP

Monaco has a different dialling code to France. If you're calling Monaco from abroad – including the surrounding Côte d'Azur – you'll need to use the international dialling code (00 377). To call France from Monaco, dial 00 33 and leave off the 0 at the start of French phone numbers.

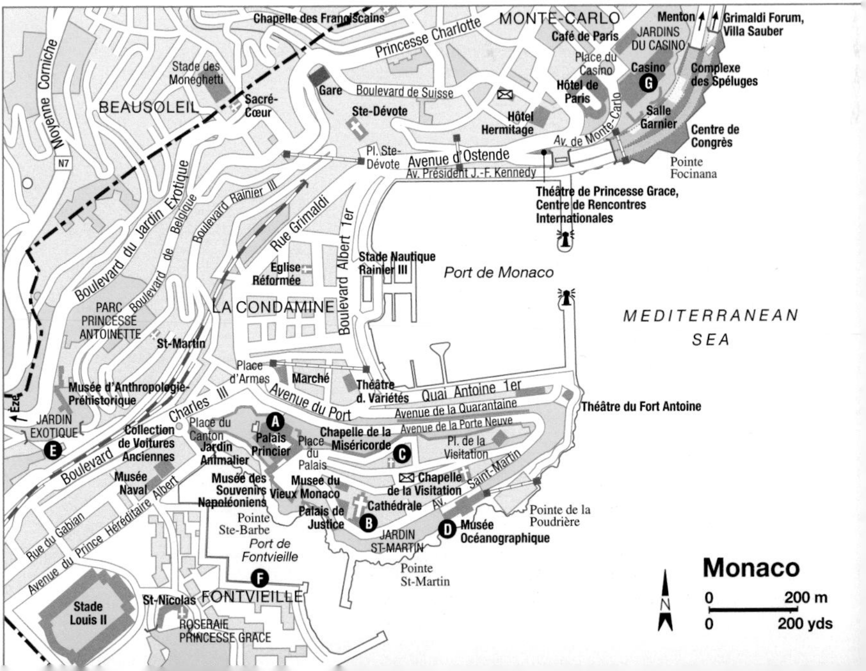

Monaco

0   200 m
0   200 yds

The statue of François Grimaldi (see page 276) at the palace shows him disguised a monk with a sword hidden beneath his cloak.

Below: the changing of the guard at the Palais Princier.

that is paraded through town on Good Friday. To find out more about the history and traditions of Monaco visit the **Musée du Vieux Monaco** (2 rue Emile de Loth; June–Sept Wed, Fri 11am–4pm; free).

On the edge of the Rock, the **Musée Océanographique** (avenue St-Martin; www.oceano.mc; daily July–Aug 10am–8.30pm, Apr–June and Sept until 7pm, Oct–Mar until 6pm; charge) was founded in 1910 by Prince Albert I. Known as the Navigator Prince, Albert is the best loved of the previous sovereigns. He dedicated his life to the oceans and this 'temple of the sea' is his memorial. The undoubted star is the aquarium, home to some weird and wonderful species. One of the most startling sights is a section of live coral reef taken from the waters off Djibouti. Children are drawn to the huge tank of catsharks and black-tip reef sharks, which constantly circle a wrecked boat alive with yellow-and-blue fish.

Climbing up the cliffside in the Moneghetti district behind Le Rocher, the **Jardin Exotique** (boulevard du Jardin Exotique; www.

jardin-exotique.mc; daily, 15 May–15 Sept 9am–7pm, 16 Sept–14 May until 6pm; charge) is a display of prickly cacti and succulents from deserts and other dry zones. Landscaping the cliffs was a mammoth feat of engineering, taking 20 years to complete. The result is breathtaking: tiered gardens are interlinked by high footbridges and canopies of vegetation; secluded spots are formed by pergolas and arbours. At the foot of the garden is the **Grotte de l'Observatoire** (35-minute guided tour included in the entry price), a cave complex with stalactites and stalagmites. Prehistoric finds from here and other caves in the region are displayed in the adjacent **Musée d'Anthropologie Préhistorique** (same times as garden, admission included with garden entry). Nearby, the 1920s Villa Paloma is one of two Belle Epoque villas (see **Villa Sauber** in Monte-Carlo) that have become Monaco's new fine art museum, the **Nouveau Musée National de Monaco** (56 boulevard du Jardin Exotique; www.nmnm.mc; daily, June–Sept 11am–7pm, Oct–May 8am–6pm; charge). Exhibitions

here are always on the theme of 'art and territory', how the landscape inspires and features in art.

The harbours

La Condamine district is Monaco's old harbour area and site of a daily food market on place d'Armes. In 2002, Port Hercule was expanded with a huge new semi-floating jetty. The port is lively with bars and restaurants, has an outdoor salt-water Olympic-sized swimming pool (ice rink in winter) on quai Albert Ier and is a prime vantage point for the Monaco Grand Prix. A market takes place on place d'Armes every morning.

Fontvieille Ⓕ was a new residential district created on reclaimed land in the 1980s around a modern marina. Just back from the port, constructed rather bizarrely over a shopping centre on the Terrasses de Fontvieille, is a cluster of small museums: the **Collection de Voitures Anciennes** (www.palais.mc; daily 10am–6pm; charge), the late Prince Rainier's collection of vintage cars and carriages, the **Musée des Timbres et des Monnaies** (Stamp and Coin Museum;

daily July–Sept 9.30am–6pm, Oct–June until 5pm; charge); the **Musée Naval** (www.musee-naval.mc; daily 10am–6pm; charge), and the **Jardin Animalier** (daily, June–Sept 9am–noon, 2–7pm, Mar–May 10am–noon, 2–6pm, Oct–Feb until 5pm; charge), a small zoo with around 250 animals of 50 different species who have all been rescued or donated.

You'll also find the **Roseraie Princesse Grace** (Princess Grace Rose Garden), laid out with 4,000 rose bushes planted amid Mediterranean pine and olive trees, a lake and a collection of modern sculpture. The nearby Stade Louis II (3 avenue des Castelans; www.asm-fc.com; guided visits Mon–Fri 10.30am, 11.30am, 2.30pm, 4.30pm; charge), is home to Monaco's football team.

Monte-Carlo

For most people the district that epitomises Monaco is Monte-Carlo – or more particularly the ensemble of the Casino, Café de Paris and the Hôtel de Paris – with its ornate Second Empire architecture, luxury boutiques and swarms of Ferraris and Rolls-Royces.

Spiky Echinocactus grusonii *cling to the terraces and hill landscape of the Jardin Exotique.*

Below: Port de Fontvieille.

The Monaco Grand Prix is the most glamorous on the F1 circuit and involves 78 laps around the Principality's hairpin bends at the end of May. Book many months in advance to secure grandstand places.

BELOW: a Ferrari draws up outside Monte-Carlo's Casino.

This is the area that made the Principality's fortune when Prince Charles III built the casino on a hill (hence Monte Carlo) previously used for cultivating lemons. You can visit the chocolate-box **Casino** (place du Casino; tel: +377 98 06 23 00; www.casinomontecarlo.com; Mon–Fri 2pm until late, Sat–Sun noon until late for gaming, smart dress, open to over 18s only, ID required; visits 9am–12.30pm; tel: +377 98 06 21 75; charge), built in the late 19th century, awash with gilt and cherubs. Today, the casino retains much of its old glamour and strict rules: a sign forbids ministers of religion or Monégasques to enter the *salles de jeux*. Opera and ballet are performed in the Casino's painstakingly restored **Salle Garnier**, named after its architect, Charles Garnier, who was also responsible for the Opéra in Paris. The *salle* was added to the casino building in 1879 to provide musical entertainment for gamblers and to bring cultural kudos to the city state. It has a prestigious history, with first-rate singers and adventurous programming: Diaghilev's acclaimed Ballet Russes performed here regularly in 1911–14 and 1920–24.

Next door the domed Café de Paris – where great chef Auguste Escoffier once held sway – also has a casino, while its brasserie terrace offers perfect opportunities to watch the clientele of the **Hôtel de Paris** coming and going. Built in 1864, this inspirational hotel was designed with unbridled extravagance. Exquisite details include the rotunda with a fan-shaped portico, the curvaceous cupolas and the caryatids adorning the reception rooms. In 1943, the hotel was occupied by the Gestapo. In theory, Monaco was neutral but Albert's great-grandfather supported the Vichy regime. The hotel manager feared for his finest wines and cognacs so he concealed them in a crypt at the bottom of the cellar. It is still the deepest hotel wine cellar in the world, with a 'champagne alley' containing bottles dating back to 1805. If you really want to blow your budget, visit überchef Alain Ducasse's Louis XV restaurant on the ground floor of the hotel or go shopping on the avenue des Beaux-Arts.

Along the seafront below the Casino, accessible by a series of lifts, the ornate stucco **Villa Sauber** is used for art shows as part of the **Nouveau Musée National de Monaco** (17 avenue Princesse Grace; daily, June–Sept 11am–7pm, Oct–May 8am–6pm; charge; *see page 278*). Exhibitions here are always on the theme of 'art and spectacle', especially theatre arts.

Almost opposite is a modern **Japanese garden** and the angular, glass-sided **Grimaldi Forum** (10 avenue Princesse Grace; www.grimaldiforum.com; tel: +377 99 99 20 00), used for exhibitions, concerts and dance. Further along the avenue are Monaco's man-made beach at Larvotto, and the famous Sporting Club d'Eté complex, home to Jimmy'z nightclub.

In 2013, a €1 billion project to build a new residential area near the forum, increasing Monaco's territory by 3 percent, had just been announced; the work is to be completed in 2024. ❑

RESTAURANTS

Restaurants

Prices for a three-course meal without wine. Many restaurants have a less expensive lunch menu:

€ = under €25
€€ = €25–40
€€€ = €40–60
€€€€ = over €60

Beefbar
42 quai Jean-Charles Rey, Fontvieille
www.beefbar.com
Tel: +377 97 77 09 29.
Open L & D daily. €€–€€€€
On the western side of Fontvieille harbour, this contemporary 'bar' serves cuts of some of the world's finest beef but chicken, fish and salad are also available. The two-course lunch menus (€17–25) are excellent value and include a glass of wine.

Le Café de Paris
place du Casino, Monte-Carlo
www.casinocafedeparis.com
Tel: +377 98 06 76 23.
Open daily 8am–2am. €€€
Completely renovated in 1920s style, the place where the crêpe Suzette was supposedly invented by accident for Edward VII (and named after one of his mistresses) is one of the sights of Monte-Carlo. Classic brasserie food and great terrace for people-watching.

Joël Robuchon Monte-Carlo
Hôtel Metropole, 4 avenue de la Madone, Monte Carlo
www.metropole.com
Tel: +977 93 15 15 10.
Open L & D daily. €€€€
After Paris, Robuchon has brought his contemporary global tapas concept to Monte-Carlo in the hands of chef Christophe Cusset, with a succession of inventive dishes and sometimes daring combinations of flavours, although there is also a more conventional rotisserie menu.

Loga
25 boulevard des Moulins, Monte-Carlo
www.leloga.com
Tel: +377 93 30 87 72.
Open L Mon–Sat & D Thu–Tue. €–€€€
A busy, convivial Italian bistro and tea room in the heart of the shopping district. Specialities include *escalope milanaise* (fried breaded veal cutlet) and homemade tiramisu, and there also are *barbajuans*, a local speciality which is a kind of deep-fried spinach and ricotta pasty, on the menu.

Le Louis XV
Hôtel de Paris, place du Casino, Monte-Carlo
www.alain-ducasse.com
Tel: +377 98 06 88 64.
Open L & D Thu–Mon (plus Wed D mid-June–Aug).
Closed Dec and 2 weeks in Feb. €€€€
The flagship of the Ducasse empire, in the hands of Franck Cerruti, a native of Nice, serves lavish seasonal Mediterranean cuisine in the palatial dining room of the Hôtel de Paris. Smart dress and reservations required.

Polpetta
2 rue Paradis, Monte-Carlo
www.restaurantpolpetta.com
Tel: +377 93 50 67 84. Open L & D Sun–Fri, D only Sat. €€
Once frequented by Frank Sinatra, this bistro offers hearty Italian food, and is among the best value for money in Monaco.

St-Benoît
10 ter avenue de la Costa
Tel: +377 93 25 02 34.
Open L Tue–Sun & D Tue–Sat. €€–€€€€
A favourite with locals, in a rooftop position with views over the marina. The emphasis is on classic fish and shellfish.

Stars and Bars
6 quai Antoine 1er
www.starsnbarsmonaco.com
Tel: +377 97 97 95 95.
Open daily 11am–midnight. €€
Burgers and Tex-Mex are the name of the game at this hugely popular American restaurant, which has racing cars hanging from the ceiling. A huge terrace overlooks Port Hercule. There's a friendly welcome for all, and service all day.

RIGHT: ice cream sundaes at Le Café de Paris.

INSIGHT GUIDES TRAVEL TIPS
PROVENCE AND THE FRENCH RIVIERA

TRANSPORT

Getting There and Getting Around

Getting There

By Air

The main gateway to the south of France is Nice-Côte d'Azur Airport (NCE; tel: 0820 423 333; www.nice. aeroport.fr), France's second airport, which has two terminals served by numerous international airlines. There are also airports in Marseille (MRS; tel: 04 42 14 14 14; www.marseille.aeroport.fr), Toulon-Hyères (TLN; tel: 0825 018 387; www.toulon-hyeres.aeroport.fr), Avignon (AVN; tel: 04 90 81 51 51; www.avignon.aeroport.fr) and Nîmes (FNI; tel: 04 66 70 49 49; www.aeroport-nimes.fr).

From the UK and Ireland

Online bookings often provide the cheapest rates. As well as booking direct with different airlines (listed below), well-established ticketing sites include www.expedia. com (UK and US sites), www.cheapflights.com (UK and US sites), www. cheaptickets.com (US), www.lastminute. com (UK) and www.opodo.co.uk (UK); www.travelsupermarket.com and www. skyscanner.net are a price-comparison websites.

British Airways tel: 0844 4930 787 (UK); 800 247 9297 (US); 0825 825 400 (France); www.brit ishairways.com operates flights to

Nice and Marseille from several UK airports.

Cityjet tel: 0871 66 33 777 (UK); 0818 776 057 (Ireland); 3654 (France); www.cityjet.com flies from Dublin, Edinburgh and London City to Avignon and Toulon-Hyères.

EasyJet tel: 0843 104 5000 (UK); 0820 420 315 (France); www. easyjet.com operates flights from Belfast, Bristol, Edinburgh, Newcastle, Liverpool, London Gatwick, Luton and Stansted to Nice, and from Bristol and London Gatwick to Marseille.

Flybe tel: 0871 700 2000 (UK); + 44 1392 268 529 (from abroad), www.flybe.com goes from Aberdeen, Belfast, Birmingham, Edinburgh, Jersey and Southampton to Avignon, and from numerous UK and Irish airports to Nice.

Jet2 tel: 0871 226 1737 (UK); 08 21 23 02 03 (France); www.jet2. com flies from East Midlands, Leeds and Manchester to Nice.

Monarch tel: 08719 40 50 40 (UK); www.monarch.co.uk flies from Birmingham to Nice.

Ryanair tel: 0871 246 0000 (UK); 1520 444 004 (Ireland); 08 92 56 21 50 (France); www.ryanair.com flies from East Midlands, Edinburgh and Stansted to Marseille, from Dublin to Nice, from Liverpool and Luton to Nîmes, and from Stansted to Toulon-Hyères.

Aer Lingus tel: 0871 718 5000

(UK); 0818 365 000 (Ireland), 08 21 23 02 67 (France), www. aerlingus.com flies from Dublin to Marseille and Nice, and from Cork to Nice.

From the US

Delta tel: 800 221 1212 (US); 08 11 64 00 05 (France); www. delta.com has a daily flight from JFK-New York to Nice. Otherwise flights from the US go via Paris. To reach Provence from Paris, **Air France** tel: 0871 6633 777 (UK); 800 237 2747 (US); 3654 (France); www.airfrance.fr flies from Paris to Nice, Marseille, Avignon and Toulon-Hyères, and from Cork to Nice.

Getting from the Airport

Nice-Côte d'Azur Airport. The 20-minute taxi ride to the centre of town can be expensive (€20–30), but there is a vast network of bus services covering the entire region as far as Marseille and Genoa. Useful routes include 98 to Nice town centre, 99 to Nice train station, 110 express line to Monaco and Menton, 210 to Cannes, and 250 to Golfe-Juan/Vallauris via Antibes. **Héli Air Monaco**, tel: 00 377 9205 0050; www.heliairmonaco.com runs regular helicopter services between Nice airport and Monaco with prices prices starting at €130 one way per passenger.

Marseille Provence Airport is at Marignane and has regular buses to Marseille Gare St-Charles (25 mins, €8), as well as direct buses to Aix-en-Provence (30 mins, €7.60), Manosque, Digne, St-Maximin and Brignoles. A shuttle bus runs to Vitrolles Aéroport train station (15 mins, €4.80) for destinations including Marseille, Arles, Nîmes, Avignon, Cavaillon and L'Isle-sur-la-Sorgue. A taxi to Marseille will cost about €50.

Toulon-Hyères Airport is actually located at Hyères, and is convenient for St-Tropez. Bus No. 7803 runs from the airport to St-Tropez via Le Lavandou, Bormes-les-Mimosas, La Croix Valmer, Gassin and Cogolin. Bus No. 102 runs from the airport to Hyères and Toulon town centres. For a taxi tel: 04 94 00 60 00 or see www.taxi-hyeres.com.

Avignon Airport is at Montfavet on the eastern edge of the city; taxis to the centre cost around €22. Alternatively you can take bus No. 3 from the airport to Thiers then bus No. 9 to Avignon train station (about 45 mins, €1.30) and vice versa on the return journey.

Nîmes Airport is located between Nîmes and Arles. A shuttle bus (navette) timed to coincide with flights runs to Nîmes train station (buy the €5 ticket on the bus). Prepare to pay around €25 for a taxi to Nîmes, around €30 to Arles.

By Rail

The TGV high-speed track has now reached Marseille and Nîmes, reducing the journey time from Paris Gare de Lyon to only around 3 hours. There are between 10 and 12 TGVs per day from Paris to Marseille, 9 per day to Nice (around 6 hours) and 15 a day to Avignon (approx. 3 hours). Other stations served include Orange, Aix-en-Provence TGV, Toulon, St-Raphaël, Cannes and Menton.

From the UK, Eurostar trains run to Lille and Paris Gare du Nord; it is possible to book through tickets from all over the UK to stations

ABOVE: local train on the way to Marseille.

in Provence on www.eurostar.com or tel: 08432 186 186, making London to Marseille, for example, a journey of 6 hours 30 minutes with a change at Lille. From mid-July to mid-September there is also a direct train between London St Pancras and Avignon Centre every Saturday.

Tickets

In the UK, tickets for journeys in France can be booked at the Rail Europe Travel Centre (193 Piccadilly, London, W1J 9EU; tel: 08448 484 064) or online at www.rail europe.co.uk. As well as individual journeys, a variety of passes are available including InterRail passes for use in up to 29 European countries. and InterRail France passes for 3 to 8 days within France only.

In the US, call Rail Europe at 1-800 622 8600 or book online at www.raileurope.com. Non-Europeans and non-North Africans can buy a **Eurailpass** (www.eurail.com). Assorted options allow first- or second-class travel in France only, in 2 to 5 countries or in up to 20 other participating countries, but must be purchased before your arrival in Europe.

By Bus

Eurolines (tel: 08717 818178 (UK); 08 92 89 90 91 (France); www.eurolines.com) runs a daily overnight service from London Victoria to Avignon, Aix-en-Provence, Marseille and Nîmes. Return tickets start at £119 to Avignon and £126 to Aix, Marseille and Nîmes.

By Car

If you don't mind a long drive, and want to have a car to tour when you get to Provence, then driving from the UK is a good option. However, note that in July and August – particularly on Saturdays around the 14 July and 15 August public holidays – the motorways get extremely busy. Traffic bulletins on Autoroute FM (107.7FM) are useful, with hourly bulletins in English in summer.

Road distances to the South are as follows:
• Calais–Nice: 1,167km (725 miles)
• Caen–Nice: 1,161km (721 miles)
• Dieppe–Avignon: 854km (531 miles)
• Calais–Avignon: 965km (600 miles)

The fastest route to Provence is from Calais via Paris, the A6 Autoroute to Lyon and the A7 down the Rhône valley. All autoroutes have péage toll booths.

Another option is to drive to Paris and then put your car on the train. The SNCF has an Auto Train service from Paris to Avignon, Marseille, Toulon, Fréjus/St-Raphaël and Nice (see www.raileurope.co.uk; tel: 08448 484 050), though note that you do not travel on the same train as your car.

Car Ferry Operators

The following companies operate across the English Channel:
Brittany Ferries sails from Portsmouth to Caen, Cherbourg, Le Havre and St-Malo; from Plymouth to St Malo and Roscoff;

TRANSPORT

ACCOMMODATION

ACTIVITIES

A – Z

LANGUAGE

from Cork to Roscoff; and, May–Oct only, from Poole to Cherbourg. Tel: 0871 244 0744 (UK); 0825 828 828 (France), 021 4277 801 (Ireland); www.brittany-ferries.com
DFDS Seaways sails from Dover to Dunkerque and Calais; from Newhaven to Dieppe; and from Portsmouth to Le Havre. Tel: 0871 574 7235 (UK); 02 32 14 68 50 (France); www.dfdsseaways.com
MyFerryLink sails from Dover to Calais. Tel: 0844 2482 100 (UK); 0811 654 765 (France); www.myferrylink.com.
P&O sails from Dover to Calais in 90 minutes. Tel: 08716 64 21 21 (UK); 0825 120 156 (France); www.poferries.com

Eurotunnel

Eurotunnel carries cars and their passengers from Folkestone to Calais on a simple drive-on-drive-off train system (journey time 35 minutes). Payment is made at toll booths (which accept cash, cheques or credit cards). For the best prices and to avoid queues, it is best to book ahead (tel: 08443 35 35 35 (UK); 0810 630 304 (France); www.eurotunnel.com).

GETTING AROUND

Although it is possible to get around Provence by train and bus, a car (or, if you're energetic, a bicycle) is essential to explore the region independently.

Public Transport

Public transport within larger towns is fairly efficient but can be limited between towns and in rural areas.

By Bus

Details of routes and timetables are available from tourist offices and bus stations (gares routières). Both should also be able to give details of coach tours and sightseeing excursions.
For information on bus routes and timetables between towns,

visit the site www.lepilote.com for the Bouches-du-Rhône département, www.vaucluse.fr for the Vaucluse, www.varlib.fr for the Var, www.lignesdazur.com for the coastal zone of the Alpes-Maritimes. Many bus services are geared towards transporting teenagers to school and frequency may be reduced during the summer holidays. Expect to pay around €1.50 per bus journey; it's normally cheaper to buy a carnet (booklet) of tickets if you plan to travel extensively

By Train

There is a reasonably good SNCF rail network in the south of France, especially in the Rhône Valley and along the coast. You can pick up free local timetables from railway stations (gares SNCF) or visit www.voyages-sncf.fr.
Services range from the high-speed TGV lines, which stop only at main stations, to the local TER services, which run along the Côte d'Azur, stopping at all stations between Marseille and Ventimiglia, and the scenic line along the Côte Bleue west from Marseille to Martigues; the Pass Bermuda (€6 for one person or €10 for two people) allows unlimited travel along the Côte Bleue for one day throughout August. See www.tersncf.com for timetables. Out-of-town stations usually (but not always) have a connecting navette (shuttle bus) to the town centre. Sometimes the SNCF runs a connecting bus service (indicated as 'Autocar' in timetables) to stations where the train no longer stops or along disused lines; rail tickets and passes are valid on these routes. Children under 4 years old travel free, those from 4 to 12 have reduced rates; a Pass Isabelle Famille (€35) allows four adults and two children aged under 16 to have unlimited travel in the region for one day. Before boarding the train remember to composter (validate) your ticket at a machine in the station.
Two scenic mountain lines depart from Nice. The **Roya Valley line** aka the 'Train des Merveilles' runs from Nice to Tende through

the Peillon and Roya-Bévéra valleys. The privately operated **Train des Pignes** (tel: 04 97 03 80 80; www.trainprovence.com) has four return journeys from Nice Gare de Provence that run up the Var valley to Digne-les-Bains. Vintage steam trains run on Sundays in summer.

By Car

Between cities: roads to and around the main resorts get completely choked up during July and August, and you can spend as much time getting to the beach as you spend on it.
Motorways (autoroutes) are designated 'A' roads, National Highways (routes nationales) 'N' or 'RN' roads. Local roads are known as 'D' routes and very small 'C' communal roads. Note that many roads have recently been renumbered, as former N roads have come under local control and have been renumbered as D routes.
Parking in the main resorts is often costly; parking meters have been replaced by horodateurs, (pay-and-display machines), which take coins and/or special parking cards that can be bought at a tobacconist (tabac).
British, US, Canadian and Australian licences are all valid in France. You should always carry your vehicle's registration document and valid insurance. Addi-

BELOW: cycling past the Pont St-Bénézet in Avignon.

tional insurance cover, in some cases including a 'home-return' service, is offered by a number of organisations, including the AA (tel: 0800 072 3279; www.theaa.com) and Aria-Assistance (tel: 0844 338 5533; www.aria-assistance.co.uk).

Speed Limits

Speed limits are as follows, unless otherwise indicated: 130kph (80mph) on motorways; 110 kph (68mph) on dual carriageways; 90kph (56mph) on other roads, except in towns where the limit is 50kph (30mph) and occasionally 30kph (20mph); there are a growing number of speed radars. Speed limits are reduced by 20kph (12mph) on motorways in wet weather and during periods of high pollution.

Rules of the Road

- Drive on the right.
- The minimum age for driving in France is 18. Foreigners may not drive on a provisional licence.
- If you are driving your own car it must be fitted with a GB sticker.
- Dipped headlights must be used in poor visibility and at night. Beams must be adjusted for right-hand-drive vehicles.
- The use of seat belts (front and rear) is compulsory.
- Children under 10 are not allowed to ride in the front seat unless there is no rear seat or the rear seat is already occupied by children under 10.
- Carry a red triangle to place 50 metres (165ft) behind the car in case of a breakdown or accident, a fluorescent yellow jacket and two breathalysers carrying an 'NF' number. In an accident or emergency, call the police (dial 17) or use the free emergency telephones (every 2km/1 mile) on motorways. If another driver is involved, lock your car and go together to call the police. It is useful to carry a European Accident Statement Form (obtainable from your insurance company), which will simplify matters in the event of an accident.

Traffic on major roads generally has priority, with traffic being halted on minor approach roads by one of the following signs: *Cédez le passage* – give way *Vous n'avez pas la priorité* – you do not have right of way

If an oncoming driver flashes their headlights it is to indicate that he or she has priority – not the other way around.

Car Hire

To hire a car you need to be at least 21 years old and must have held a driving licence for at least a year. Some hire companies will not rent to people under 26 or over 60. Expect to pay about €245 a week for a small car with insurance and 1,700km (1,056 miles) included. Watch out for cheaper companies that may balance a low hire cost with high charges in the event of damage to the vehicle. Fly-drive packages, or arranging car hire in advance, can work out slightly cheaper than hiring once you arrive; to compare prices see www.travelsupermarket.com. The SNCF offers 20 percent discount for train-plus-car rental packages with AVIS (www.voyages-sncf.com).

Avis, tel: 08 21 23 07 60 www.avis.com
Budget, tel: 08 25 00 35 64 www.budget.com
Easycar, www.easycar.com
Europcar, tel: 08 25 35 83 58 www.europcar.com
Hertz, tel: 08 25 86 18 61 www.hertz-europe.com

By Boat

A good way to avoid traffic jams on the French Riviera is to take a boat to your destination. Trans Côte d'Azur (www.trans-cote-azur.com) runs day trips from Nice and Cannes to Monaco and St-Tropez. Les Bateaux de St-Raphael (tel: 04 94 95 17 46, www.bateauxsaintraphael.com) run day trips from St-Raphael to St-Tropez while Les Bateaux Verts (tel: 04 94 49 29 39, www.bateauxverts.com) link St-Tropez with

Cogolin, Port Grimaud, Ste-Maxime and Les Issambres; they also organise day trips to Cannes from St-Tropez, Ste-Maxime and Les Issambres. On the Rhône, Mireio (tel: 04 90 85 62 25; www.mireio.net) runs day trips including lunch from Avignon to Arles and Tarascon.

Bicycles

If you're planning to bring your own bike, most long-distance trains have special areas designated for bicycle transport. You must reserve in advance and pay a small fee. Alternatively, if you partially dismantle your bicycle and put it in a carrier (available at most bicycle shops) you can carry it on as luggage for no extra fee. Most regional trains also make provisions for bicycles, as does the Eurostar.

Within the region, Aix, Avignon, Marseille and Nice all have inexpensive municipal bike hire schemes, where you pick up the bike at one spot and leave it at another; ask at your local tourist office for details. To hire a bike by the half-day, day or longer, try Holiday Bikes (tel: 01 41 27 49 00; www.holiday-bikes.com).

Taxis

Taxis are normally available at railway stations and official taxi ranks in city centres. Outside the cities, hotels and tourist offices should have information on local companies or check the *pages jaunes* telephone directory.

Aix tel: 04 42 27 71 11, www.taxisradioaixois.com
Avignon tel: 04 90 82 20 20, www.taxis-avignon.fr
Cannes tel: 0890 712 227, www.taxicannes.fr
Marseille: tel: 04 91 02 20 20, www.taximarseille.com
Monaco tel: 0820 209 898, www.taximonacoprestige.com
Nice: tel: 04 93 13 78 78, www.taxi-nice.fr
Nîmes tel: 04 66 29 40 11, www.taxinimes.fr
Toulon: tel: 04 94 93 51 51, www.taxis-region-toulonnaise.fr.

TRANSPORT

ACCOMMODATION

ACTIVITIES

A – Z

LANGUAGE

A CCOMMODATION

WHERE TO STAY

Hotels

All hotels in France carry star ratings, set down by the Ministry of Tourism, ranging from one star to extremely luxurious five stars. Even the simplest hotels may be perfectly clean and acceptable, though you shouldn't expect much in the way of room service or facilities such as air conditioning or lifts. Grand five-star establishments will have spacious rooms, restaurants and bars, spas and sports facilities and often literally hundreds of staff ready to cater to every whim. Don't rely too heavily on the star system, however – it depends on criteria such as room size, presence of a lift, business centres and languages spoken at reception, rather than the quality of welcome or good taste. Country hotels and grand hotels will often have a restaurant.

Hotel Associations

As well as international groups such as Accor (www.accor.com), which has hotels ranging from budget Formule 1 and Etap, via Ibis, Mercure and Novotel to the luxury Sofitel brands, and Kyriad (www.kyriad.com), there are associations of independent hotels, to which several of the hotels in this guide belong. Most offer centralised booking services. These include:

Best Western www.bestwestern. com. Mid-range independently owned hotels.
Châteaux & Hôtels Collection tel: 0811 741 740 (France); +33 1 72 72 92 02 (outside France); www.chateauxhotels.com. Mid- to high-end hotels, restaurants and rooms in private chateaux.
Exclusive Hotels +33 825 131 020; www.exclusive-hotels.com. Two hundred stylish, urban boutique hotels, including several in the PACA region, with good internet booking rates.
Logis de France www.logishotels. com. Federation of over 3,000 private hotels, mainly in the budget to mid-range category in villages and small towns. Many have good restaurants.
Relais & Châteaux tel: 0825 825 180 (France); 00 800 2000 00 02 (UK), +1 800 735 2478 (US/Canada); www.relaischateaux. com. Luxury hotels, often with gourmet restaurants.
Relais du Silence tel: +33 1 70 23 81 63; www.relaisdusilence.com. Mid- to high-end hotels 'de charme' in particularly peaceful settings.

Prices and Reservations

Paradoxically for an area that boasts some of the most expensive hotels in the world, Provence and the Côte d'Azur has many remarkably inexpensive decent hotels: it is quite possible to spend anything from €45 for a night in a double room to well over €1,000. In tourist destinations rates are often highest in July and August, while in more business-oriented cities, such as Marseille and Toulon, you may find that rates are actually lower in August and at weekends. Some places shoot up prices for special events such as the Monaco Grand Prix, Nice Carnaval, Cannes Film Festival and the *féria* in Nîmes. Note that prices are charged per room not per person, and generally do not include breakfast. Details of room prices should be visible either outside the hotel or in reception, as well as on the back of bedroom doors. Supplements may be charged for an additional bed or a cot *(lit bébé)*. Some seaside hotels try to insist on *demi-pension* or a minimum of two or three nights in summer.

When reserving, the hotel may ask for your credit card number; some will demand a non-refundable *arrhes* (deposit). Try to book ahead for the peak summer season, key events or the Easter and May public holidays. If you arrive without a reservation, the tourist office should be able to tell you which hotels have rooms available for the night and may even have a hotel reservation service.

Before booking, it's always a good idea to compare prices at a price comparison website such as www.travelsupermarket.com, www.trivago.com or www.kayak.co.uk.

Bed and Breakfasts

Bed and breakfast *(chambres d'hôtes)* accommodation is increasingly widely available in Provence and can be anywhere from a working farm or simple village house to a sumptuous château – with correspondingly large variations in price. Home-cooked evening meals, often eaten at a communal *table d'hôte*, are sometimes available. Under French regulations, *chambres d'hôtes* have a maximum of five bedrooms and fifteen people, with breakfast included in the price.

Fleurs de Soleil (tel: 09 51 67 79 80 (France); www.fleursdesoleil. fr), **Chambre d'Hôtes de Charme** (tel: 04 94 72 55 48; www.chambresdhotedecharme.com) and **iGuide Hotels** (www.iguide-hotels.com) list charming B&B accommodation throughout the region.

Gîtes, Villas and Flat Rentals

Self-catering accommodation can be a good way to holiday in the south. *Gîtes* are found in rural areas, mostly away from the coast, sometimes on working farms or in converted farm buildings. On the coast, accommodation can vary from modern apartment complexes to luxury villas. There are several national networks of *gîtes*, the largest of which is **Gîtes de France** (www. gites-de-france.fr), whose members are regularly inspected by the national federation and rated between one and five 'épis' (ears of corn). The organisation also has **Gîtes Panda** (www.gites-panda.fr), which offers traditional accommodation in France's regional parks, including the Lubéron, Verdon and Mercantour. The other main network is **Clévacances** (www.clevacances.com), which has furnished seaside apartments, country cottages and B&Bs, with its own system of key ratings. Many tourist

offices also have details of rental accommodation. Rentals generally run Saturday to Saturday, although it may be possible to rent for a weekend in low season.

At the luxury end of the market, **Balfour France** (tel: 0845 222 0057 (UK), +33 494 754 085 (outside UK); www.balfourfrance.com) concentrates on luxury villa rentals, generally with pools and often with maid and chef service thrown in, with properties in Provence, on the Var coast around St-Tropez and around Grasse and Cannes. **Côte d'Azur Collection** (tel: 0844 576 0176 (UK); www.cotedazurcollection. co.uk) offers mid-range to luxury villas and apartments throughout Provence. In recent years, websites such as **AirBnB** (www.airbnb.com) and **Housetrip** (www.housetrip. com) allow individuals to advertise their own (budget) accommodation for renters to book direct.

Falling between hotel and apartment are apart-hotels (rooms with kitchenette), such as **ApparCity** (www.appartcity.com) and **Citadines** (www.citadines.com), and holiday apartment complexes such as **Pierre et Vacances** (tel: 0870 0267 145 (UK), 0892 702 180 (France); www.pv-holidays.com).

Various UK-based tour operators also offer a range of self-catering accommodation as part of a package holiday. Try: **Allez France**, www.allezfrance.com **Chez Nous**, www.cheznous.com **Cottages4You**, tel: 0845 268 0760 (UK); www.cottages4you.co.uk

Gîtes d'Etape

Gîtes d'Etape offer basic accommodation for walkers or cyclists, often in remote mountain areas; expect communal dorms, bunk beds and shared bathrooms. You will need to make reservations, especially in busy periods.

Mountain refuges *(refuges)* offer similar accommodation and some also provide meals. Many refuges are open from June to September only, and they should always be booked in advance. Lists of refuges are available from local tourist offices.

Youth Hostels

To stay in most youth hostels *(auberges de jeunesse)* you need to be a member of the Youth Hostel Association (YHA) or the **Fédération Unie des Auberges de Jeunesse** (FUAJ), tel: 01 44 89 87 27; www.fuaj.org, which is affiliated to the International Youth Hostel Federation (www.hihostels.com), although it is possible to take up temporary membership for the night.

Camping

French campsites *(campings)* are often remarkably well appointed. Look for those with the Camping Qualité label, which adhere to a national quality charter, with 151 adherent sites in the PACA region (see www.campingqualite.com). The **French Federation of Camping and Caravanning** (FFCC) website www.campingfrance.com contains a bilingual listing of campsites.

Most campsites open between March or April and September or October. Prices range from around €15–30 per night for two people with a car, caravan or tent. On the coast during high season the campsites can be very crowded. Although camping rough *(camping sauvage)* is not permitted, it may be worth asking the owner of the land for permission if there is nowhere official to pitch up nearby. Fire is an ever-present risk in the region, so be careful when cooking.

Campsites are graded from one-star (minimal comfort, water points, showers and sinks) to four-star luxury sites (more space and offer above-average facilities, such as pools and restaurants). For something more rural, look out for signs designated *Aire naturelle de camping* and *Camping à la ferme* .

The following offer camping holiday packages with ferry transport and tent or mobile home pitch: **Canvas Holidays** (UK), tel: 0845 268 0827; www.canvasholidays.co.uk **Select Site** (UK), tel: 0844 406 0127; www.select-site.com **Vacansoleil**, tel: 0333 700 5050, www.vacansoleil.ie

TRANSPORT

ACCOMMODATION

ACTIVITIES

A – Z

LANGUAGE

AVIGNON

Avignon

Bed and Breakfast A
Le Limas
51 rue du Limas
Tel: 04 90 14 67 17
www.le-limas-avignon.com
Very stylish four-bedroom accommodation in an 18th-century house where the contemporary décor enhances its character. Breakfast includes homemade *pâtisseries* and there's a roof terrace with views over to the palace. **€€–€€€**

Hôtel de Blauvac B
11 rue de la Bancasse
Tel: 04 90 86 34 11
www.hotel-blauvac.com
A lovely budget option on a narrow street in the heart of town. The 17th-century former residence of the Marquis de Blauvac is simple but alluring. The 16 rooms have exposed stone walls and modern bathrooms. **€**

Hôtel Boquier C
6 rue du portail Boquier
Tel: 04 90 82 34 43
www.hotel-boquier.com
Beautiful hotel in an 18th-century townhouse just off the cours Jean-Jaurès and 5 minutes' walk from the station. Each of the 12 rooms is individually decorated in Provençal style on the theme of one of the five conti-

PRICE CATEGORIES

Price categories are for an average double room in high season:
€ = under €100
€€ = €100–180
€€€ = €180–300
€€€€ = more than €300

nents. Conveniently, parking is available. **€**

Hôtel Cloître St-Louis D
20 rue du Portail Boquier
Tel: 04 90 27 55 55
www.cloitre-saint-louis.com
Set around a pleasant cloister, the Cloître St-Louis combines a characterful wing of a former monastery with a dramatic, modern steel-and-glass wing, with a swimming pool on top. The modern wing was designed by French architect Jean Nouvel, who designed the iconic Torre Agbar building in Barcelona . **€€€–€€€€**

Hôtel d'Europe E
14 place Crillon
Tel: 04 90 14 76 76
www.heurope.com
Set at the rear of a lovely courtyard, in an antique-filled 16th-century mansion, this elegant hotel has modern, comfortable rooms with soundproofing and very welcoming staff. Guests have ranged from Napoleon, Lamartine, Victor Hugo and John Stuart Mill to more recent politicians and actors. **€€€–€€€€**

La Ferme F
chemin des Bois, Ile de la Barthelasse
Tel: 04 90 82 57 53
www.hotel-laferme.com
A beautiful farm in a peaceful spot on an island, yet within easy reach of the city centre. Pleasant rooms, fresh, simple cuisine, and a swimming pool. **€**

Mercure Cité des Papes G
1 rue Jean Vilar
Tel: 04 90 80 93 00
www.mercure.com

If you are determined to stay next door to the lovely Palais des Papes, consider the modern 73-roomed Cité des Papes. Request one of the quiet back rooms with palatial views. **€€**

Hôtel Mignon H
12 rue Joseph Vernet
Tel: 04 90 82 17 30
www.hotel-mignon.com
This sweet little hotel with 16 colourful rooms is surprisingly adequate for its category and price. It's not luxurious and the rooms are small, but the location is central and the bathrooms sparkle. Breakfast included. **€**

Hôtel de la Mirande I
4 place de la Mirande
Tel: 04 9014 2020
www.la-mirande.fr
The faultlessly decorated Mirande offers 20 personalised rooms in the 17th-century Hôtel de Vervins, situated just behind the Palais des Papes. The salons and glazed-in courtyard still have the feel of a private house and you can take cookery courses in the old kitchens. **€€€€**

La Péniche J
chemin île Piot
Tel: 04 90 25 40 61
www.chambrepeniche.fr
This barge, moored just 10 minutes' walk from the city centre, has been converted into a cosy four-bedroom B&B. On one side is the greenery of Ile Piot and on the other great views over the old town. There is even a small pool and sun-deck on board. **€**

Villeneuve-lès-Avignon

Cube Hôtel K
impasse du Rhône
Tel: 04 90 25 52 29
www.cubehotel.fr
Modern hotel with colourful contemporary décor and great views over the Rhône and Avignon from the terrace and waterside rooms. There is a bar, free Wi-Fi and a concierge service. **€**

Hôtel-Restaurant La Magnaneraie L
37 rue Camp de Bataille
Tel: 04 90 25 11 11
www.magnaneraie.najeti.fr
If you're having trouble finding somewhere to stay in Avignon, you could consider staying in Villeneuve. This hotel is housed in a 15th-century silk farmhouse built of honey-coloured stone, and is set in large gardens with ponds, palms and ancient oaks. More contemporary facilities include a large swimming pool and tennis courts; you can also hire bicycles. **€€–€€€**

Hôtel La Suite M
65-67 rue de la République
Tel: 04 90 21 51 07
www.hotellasuite.fr
It took two years to renovate and turn this 17th-century mansion into a hotel and the results were worth it. The contemporary interior sits comfortably with the original features and the young team works hard to ensure a smooth stay. There is also a secluded garden with a pool. **€€€**

ORANGE AND THE MONT VENTOUX

Orange

Hôtel Le Glacier
46 cours Aristide-Briand
Tel: 04 90 11 40 40
www.le-glacier.com
An attractively furnished hotel in a good location on the edge of the old town. Very friendly staff. No restaurant. €€

Hôtel Arène
place des Langes
Tel: 04 90 11 40 40
www.hotel-arene.fr
Central hotel on a quiet square with Provençal-style rooms and modernised 'executive' rooms. Good restaurant and a coffee bar with internet access. €€

Châteauneuf-du-Pape

La Garbure
3 rue Joseph Ducos
Tel: 04 90 83 75 08
www.la-garbure.com
Cosy eight-room village hotel renowned for its regional cuisine. Good value all round. €

La Sommellerie
route de Roquemaure
Tel: 04 90 83 50 00
www.la-sommellerie.fr

In the heart of the famous vineyards, 4 km (2.5 miles) from the village centre, this restored 17th-century farm has pleasant rooms with rustic furnishings. Dining room serves regional cuisine. Has a swimming pool. €€

Carpentras

Le Fiacre
153 rue Vigne
Tel: 04 90 63 03 15
www.hotel-du-fiacre.com
An interesting old town house and an excellent choice if you want to stay somewhere central. €€

Château du Martinet
Route de Mazan
Tel: 04 90 63 03 03
www.chateau-du-martinet.fr
An impressive château which has been turned into a romantic luxury hotel. The owners offer table d'hôte on Tuesdays and Fridays. Breakfast included. €€€

Séguret

Domaine de Cabasse
route de Sablet
Tel: 04 90 46 91 12

www.cabasse.fr
A must for wine lovers, this 21-room hotel is surrounded by its own vineyards and tastings are regularly organised. There is also a very nice restaurant and a swimming pool. €–€€

Vaison-la-Romaine

Hostellerie le Beffroi
rue de l'Evêché
Tel: 04 90 36 04 71
www.le-beffroi.com
Le Beffroi is a delightful 16th-century hostelry in two adjoining houses. Located in the medieval upper town with period decor and a good restaurant (open from April to October). The terrace swimming pool has lovely views. €€

Bed and Breakfast
Les Tilleuls d'Elisée
1 avenue de Jules Mazen (chemin du Bon Ange)
Tel: 04 90 35 63 04
www.vaisonchambres.info
Very pretty B&B in a 19th-century village house decorated in Provençal style and surrounded by

olive trees. Great views over the surrounding countryside. Homemade jams at breakfast. €

Crillon-le-Brave

Hôtel Crillon-le-Brave
place de l'Eglise
Tel: 04 90 65 61 61
www.crillonlebrave.com
Perched on a cliff, with wonderful views over the countryside, this 23-room luxury hotel is perfect for a romantic break. Expect Vi-spring beds, L'Occitane products, three restaurants and a swimming pool. €€€€

Sault

Hostellerie du Val de Sault
route de St-Trinit
Tel: 04 90 64 01 41
www. valdesault.com
This is an elevated modern hotel with gardens and a swimming pool looking out onto Mont Ventoux. There are rooms with terraces, and the cuisine served is typical of the region and tasty. Closed Nov–Mar. €€€

THE LUBERON

Lourmarin

Le Mas de Guilles
route de Vaugines
Tel: 04 90 68 30 55
www.guilles.com
A quiet and relaxing *mas*, set amid vineyards at the end of a long avenue of olive trees, just outside Lourmarin. Most rooms are spacious and attractive

with big old Provençal wardrobes. Swimming pool and tennis courts in the grounds. Dinner is served either in a vaulted dining room or on the terrace. €€–€€€

Vaugines

Hostellerie du Luberon
Tel: 04 90 77 27 19
www.hostellerieduluberon.com

A simple, Provençal *mas* with a friendly, family-run atmosphere. The restaurant looks out onto the pretty gardens and a pool. €€

Ménerbes

Hostellerie Le Roy Soleil
route des Beaumettes, D103

Tel: 04 90 72 25 61
www.roy-soleil.com
A relaxed hotel in an 18th-century manor amid vineyards beneath the village, with flamboyantly decorated rooms and a pool. As well as the gastronomic restaurant, there's a simpler bistro for weekday lunch. Closed mid-Nov–mid-Mar. €€–€€€€

TRANSPORT
ACCOMMODATION
ACTIVITIES
A – Z
LANGUAGE

Bonnieux

Bastide de Capelongue
Les Claparèdes, chemin des Cabanes
Tel: 04 90 75 89 78
www.capelongue.com
Beautiful modern stone *mas* in the midst of the *garrigue* plateau above the village, with spacious rooms, two pools and a first-rate restaurant in the hands of top chef Edouard Loubet. There are also stylish apartments to rent at the Ferme de Capelongue. €€€€

Apt

Domaine des Andéols
St-Saturnin-lés-Apt
Tel: 04 90 75 50 63
www.andeols.com
This painstakingly restored hamlet has brought conceptual design to deepest Provence. The 10 achingly hip 'houses' are furnished with modern design classics and contemporary artworks. There's an immaculate garden and a restaurant overseen

by Paris chef Guy Martin. Dine al fresco by candlelight in the summer. Stylish indoor and outdoor pools, library and hamman. Closed from Nov–Mar. €€€€

Sainte Anne
62 place du Faubourg du Ballet
Tel: 04 90 74 18 04
www.apt-hotel.com
Perfectly placed to explore the Luberon regional park, this renovated hotel in a 19th-century townhouse has seven stylish rooms. Breakfast is delicious and homemade. There's no restaurant but it's a short walk into town. €–€€

L'Isle-sur-la-Sorgue

La Maison sur la Sorgue
6 rue Rose Goudard
Tel: 06 87 32 58 58
www.lamaisonsurlasorgue.com
Truly stunning four-bedroom B&B in a 17th-century townhouse with a loggia and a courtyard with a pool. There is also an art

gallery and interior decoration shop here. A special place. €€€€

Mas de Cure Bourse
120 chemin de la Serre
Tel: 04 90 38 16 58
www.masdecurebourse.com
Set in orchards 3km (2 miles) from the town, this former 18th-century coaching inn has pleasant, traditionally decorated rooms, a restaurant, large garden and swimming pool. €€

Fontaine-de-Vaucluse

Hôtel du Poète
Tel: 04 90 20 34 05
www.hoteldupoete.com
Charming hotel next to the river in an old watermill with 24 bright rooms. There isn't a restaurant but there is an attractive garden and swimming pool. €€

Gordes

La Bastide de Gordes
route de Combe
Tel: 04 90 72 12 12
www.bastide-de-gordes.com
A fine Renaissance building on the ramparts with elegant rooms, wonder-

ful views and many modern facilities, including a salubrious spa, solarium and sauna. Visits to local vineyards can be arranged. Has 29 rooms and two suites. €€€€

Le Mas des Romarins
Route de Sénanque
Tel: 04 90 72 12 13
www.masromarins.com
There are just 12 bright, traditionally furnished rooms in this stone farmhouse on the outskirts of Gordes. The small restaurant specialises in regional cuisine and wine and there is a lovely flower-filled garden and pool. €€

Roussillon

Le Close de la Glycine
place de la Poste
Tel: 04 90 05 60 13
Tel: 04 90 72 25 61
www.luberon-hotel.fr
Hotel-restaurant in the heart of one of the most beautiful villages in Provence with great views over the surround-ing countryside. The eight rooms are traditionally furnished and some have a terrace. €€

MARSEILLE AND THE CALANQUES

Marseille

Hôtel Alizé
35 quai des Belges
Tel: 04 91 33 66 97
www.alize-hotel.com
This much-loved budget address has Provençal-style rooms and a prime position on the Vieux-Port. €€

Au Vieux Panier
13 rue du Panier
Tel: 04 91 91 23 72
www.auvieuxpanier.com

Arty, hip B&B in a 17th-century former grocery store. Each of the five bedrooms has been decorated by a different local artist. Unsurprisingly, the place also hosts exhibitions and there are great views over the rooftops down to the sea from the roof terrace. €€

Hôtel Le Corbusier
280 boulevard Michelet
Tel: 04 91 16 78 00

www.gerardin-corbusier.com
The hotel in the Cité Radieuse is a cult address for architecture fans. Rooms range from simple monastic cabins with shared bathrooms right up to mini-suites for four. There's also the original bar, an adventurous restaurant, and the use of the Cité's rooftop gym and paddling pool. €€

Hôtel Dieu
1 place Daviel
Tel: 04 13 42 42 42
www.ihg.com
Opened in 2013, the

PRICE CATEGORIES

Price categories are for an average double room in high season:
€ = under €100
€€ = €100–180
€€€ = €180–300
€€€€ = more than €300

latest member of the Intercontinental Group is Marseille's flagship luxury hotel. Located in the Panier district, the former 18th-century hospital has 194 contemporary rooms and suites. There is a spa, an indoor pool, two restaurants and a bar with great views over the port. €€€€

Hôtel Lutétia
38 allée Léon Gambetta
Tel: 04 91 50 81 78
www.lutetia-marseille.com
Smart budget hotel a few blocks east of Gare St-Charles, just off La Canebière. Rooms have flat-screen TVs and free Wi-Fi. If it's full, try its sister hotel, Hermès (2 rue de la Bonneterie, tel: 04 96 11 63 63) just off the port. €

Mama Shelter
64 rue de la Loubière
Tel: 04 84 35 20 00
www.mamashelter.com
The hip Parisian institution has opened a branch down south a few blocks east of cours Julien. Rooms are minimalist and white with iMacs, free in-room movies and free Wi-Fi. There's a canteen-style restaurant and a bar with DJs at the weekends. They even

have a private beach over on Prado. €–€€

Radisson Blu Marseille Vieux Port
38-40 quai du Rive Neuve
Tel: 04 88 44 52 00
www.radissonblu.com/hotel-marseille
An airy modern hotel spread over two buildings on either side of an outdoor pool and sunbathing deck. 189 rooms come with Provençal or African-inspired minimalist decoration. Bar, Mediterranean restaurant and a brasserie. €€€

Résidence du Vieux-Port
18 quai du Port
Tel: 04 91 91 91 22
www.hotel-residence-marseille.com
This 1950s hotel has great views to Notre-Dame-de-la-Garde. The spacious balconied rooms have been redecorated in a reinterpretation of their original 50s style with high-tech bathrooms. A neo-50s brasserie is downstairs. €€€

Le Ryad
16 rue Sénac de Meilhan
Tel: 04 91 47 74 54
www.leryad.fr
A little piece of Morocco in Marseille. Not only are the nine rooms decorated in chic North African style but there's a

tea room with mint tea and sweet pastries open every afternoon. In the evening, tagine or couscous is available by request. €€

Hôtel Vertigo
42 rue des Petites Maries
Tel: 04 91 91 07 11
www.hotelvertigo.fr
Hip hostel with retro furnishings where rooms sleep two to six people. This one is near St-Charles train station and they've just opened another branch at the Vieux-Port. €

Villa Monticelli
96 rue du Commandant Rolland
Tel: 04 91 22 15 20
www.villamonticelli.com
Away from the hustle and bustle near Prado, this terracotta-painted villa has five individually decorated rooms named after local historical personalities. Breakfast, served on the terrace in summer, includes 18 different homemade jams. There is also an iPad available to guests. €€

Cassis

Les Jardins de Cassis
avenue Auguste Favier
Tel: 04 42 01 84 85
www.hotel-lesjardinsde-cassis.com
A lovely Provençal-style

hotel situated on the hillside above the town centre, sitting in a palm tree-filled garden. The rooms are clean and well maintained. Nineteen of the 36 rooms have balconies or private terraces. Also has a pool. €€

Hôtel du Joli Bois
route de la Gineste
Tel: 04 42 01 02 68
www.hotel-du-joli-bois.com
In the heart of the Calanques, this budget hotel offers basic, inexpensive accommodation for walkers, climbers and bikers in rooms sleeping two to five people. There is free secure parking and a free lock-up for bikes. No restaurant. €

Maison No.9
9 avenue du Docteur Yves Bourde
Tel: 04 42 08 35 86
www.maison9.net
Surrounded by Cassis vineyards, this 19th-century wine producer's farmhouse has been turned into a luxury four-bedroom B&B by its interior decorator owner. There are charming uninterrupted views across to Cap Canaille from the pool. €€€

AIX-EN-PROVENCE

Hôtel Artéa
4 boulevard de la République
Tel: 04 42 27 36 00
www.hotel-artea.com
This 18th-century town house near La Rotonde was once home to composer Darius Milhaud. It has undergone substantial

refurbishment but remains good value, with smart new decoration and bathrooms. No lift. €€

Hôtel Cardinal
24 rue Cardinal
Tel: 04 42 38 32 30
www.hotel-cardinal-aix.com
A charming budget hotel near the Musée Granet,

in an 18th-century building cluttered with antique furniture. €

Hôtel Cézanne
40 avenue Victor Hugo
Tel: 04 42 91 11 11
www.hotelaix.com
The Cézanne has been transformed into a lovely modern boutique hotel with a relaxing down-

stairs bar with neo-Baroque armchairs, individually decorated rooms and king-size beds. Helpful staff. €€€

Hôtel des Augustins
3 rue de la Masse
Tel: 04 42 27 28 59
www.hotel-augustins.com
Housed in a building that was an Augustine

TRANSPORT
ACCOMMODATION
ACTIVITIES
A – Z
LANGUAGE

convent until the French Revolution of 1789, it became a hotel in the 1890s. Conveniently located near the cours Mirabeau, this place has comfortable rooms and an imposing vaulted reception area. €€–€€€

Hôtel des Quatre Dauphins
54 rue Roux Alphéran
Tel: 04 42 38 16 39

www.lesquatredauphins.fr
Overlooking the dolphin fountain in the Quartier Mazarin, this small hotel has lots of fans. It is inexpensive but not without character and comfort. No lift. €

L'Epicerie
12 rue du Cancel
Tel: 06 08 85 38 68
www.unechambreenville.eu
Four spacious rooms

decorated in Provençal style make up this B&B in a lovely 18th-century house in the old town. The breakfast room looks like a 1950s grocery store but you can eat outside on fine days. €€

Le Pigonnet
5 avenue du Pigonnet
Tel: 04 42 59 02 90
www.hotelpigonnet.com

This historic bastide is a luxurious and tranquil retreat just a short walk from the city centre. It has an upmarket restaurant, swimming pool and loungers, rose garden and shady, verdant grounds in which Cézanne once painted a view of the Montagne Ste-Victoire. €€€€

Sᴛ-Rᴇ́ᴍʏ ᴀɴᴅ ʟᴇꜱ Aʟᴘɪʟʟᴇꜱ

St-Rémy-de-Provence

Le Château des Alpilles
route du Rougadou
Tel: 04 90 92 03 33
www.chateaudesalpilles.com
Sophisticated 19th-century chateau in its own park includes accommodation in restored farmhouse and chapel. Has a pool, and restaurant serving excellent regional dishes. €€€€

Hôtel de l'Image
36 boulevard Victor Hugo
Tel: 04 90 92 51 50
www.hotel-image.fr
Occupying a former music hall, this is a very stylish hotel. Particularly lovely is the Japanese-inspired garden with its pools and pathways. The

hotel also offers a modern restaurant, a cocktail bar and a spa. €€€

Sous les Figuiers
3 avenue Taillandier
Tel: 04 32 60 15 40
www.hotel-charme-provence.com
Tastefully decorated country house where the artist owner offers painting lessons. There is a small pool and a terrace 'under the fig trees'. Breakfast consists of seasonal and locally made products. €€

Hôtel Canto Cigalo
8a chemin de Canto Cigalo
Tel: 04 90 92 14 28
www.cantocigalo.com
Attractive country house hotel in a rural location a 10-minute walk from the town centre. The 20 rooms are simply furnished in Provençal

style and the gravel-covered garden boasts a swimming pool. No restaurant. €

Les Baux-de-Provence

L'Oustau de Baumanière
Route d'Arles
Tel: 04 90 54 33 07
www.oustaudebaumaniere.com
A legendary luxury hotel in a superbly renovated 16th-century farmhouse outside Les Baux, with a magnificent view and celebrated gastronomic restaurant (see page 139). Closed Jan–Feb. €€€€

Fontvieille

Hôtel La Peiriero
36 avenue des Baux

Tel: 04 90 54 76 10
www.hotel-peiriero.com
Constructed in the 1970s in old stone quarries in the Alpilles and sitting in lovely gardens, La Peiriero has 43 rooms, a pool, sauna and mini-golf. €€

Salon-de-Provence

Abbaye de Sainte-Croix
route de Val de Cuech
Tel: 04 90 56 24 55
www.hotels-provence.com
This secluded luxury hotel outside Salon has a unique setting in a former Benedictine abbey, complete with medieval chapel and 25 rooms and suites occupying former monks' cells. Closed Nov–Mar. €€€

Aʀʟᴇꜱ ᴀɴᴅ ᴛʜᴇ Cᴀᴍᴀʀɢᴜᴇ

Arles

Hôtel Le Belvedere
5 place Voltaire
Tel: 04 90 91 45 94
www.hotellebelvedere-arles.com
Between the station and the arena, this 17-room contemporary hotel

offers 'minimalist Baroque' style on a budget. Some rooms have a balcony overlooking the square. There's free Wi-Fi throughout. €

Hôtel Calendal
5 rue Porte de Laure
Tel: 04 90 96 11 89

www.lecalendal.com
Welcoming hotel with Provençal-style rooms in a cluster of old houses set around a pretty courtyard. Good location behind the Arena; some rooms have views of the Théâtre Antique. There's

Pʀɪᴄᴇ Cᴀᴛᴇɢᴏʀɪᴇꜱ

Price categories are for an average double room in high season:
€ = under €100
€€ = €100–180
€€€ = €180–300
€€€€ = more than €300

a restaurant, tea room and spa. €€

Grand Hôtel Nord-Pinus
place du Forum
Tel: 04 90 93 44 44
www.nord-pinus.com
This luxury hotel with its fashionable bar is an Arles institution. The stairway decorated with *féria* bullfighting posters and Peter Beard photos shows the town's dual interests. €€€

Hôtel du Musée
11 rue du Grand Prieuré
Tel: 04 90 93 88 88
www.hoteldumusee.com.fr
A 17th-century mansion tucked away on a winding street near the

Rhône, with a pretty courtyard for breakfast, vaulted lounge and its own art gallery. €

Hôtel Particulier
4 rue de la Monnaie
Tel: 04 90 52 51 40
www.hotel-particulier.com.
Paris meets Arles in this very chic townhouse where (almost) everything is white. There is a spa and hammam in the basement. €€€€

Stes-Maries-de-la-Mer

Les Arcades
5 rue Paul Herman
Tel: 04 90 97 73 10
www.lesarcades.camargue.fr

Excellent-value budget hotel in the centre of the village. The décor is 'modern Camargue' and of the 19 rooms only 11 have air conditioning. There's free Wi-Fi but no restaurant. €

Mas de Calabrun
route de Cacharel
Tel: 04 90 97 82 21
www.mas-de-calabrun.fr
About 6 km (3 miles) north of the village in the middle of the marshes, this is a typical Camargue hotel with traditional décor. There's on-site horse riding, bike hire and a pool. Regional dishes are served in the restaurant. €€

Etang de Vaccarès

Le Mas de Peint
Le Sambuc, D36, between Arles and Salin-de-Giraud
Tel: 04 90 97 20 62
www.masdepeint.com
This elegant period farmhouse offers the full rural Camargue experience, with 11 rustic chic bedrooms, and delicious Provençal meals *à la table d'hôte* (by reservation only). Bulls and horses roam the 1,300-acre (526-hectare) estate. Relax by the pool or take a ride to view the wildlife. €€€

NÎMES AND THE PONT DU GARD

Nîmes

Hôtel de L'Amphithéâtre
4 rue des Arènes
Tel: 04 6667 2851
www.hoteldelamphitheatre.com
On a side street behind the Roman arena, this excellent budget hotel's main selling points are its location and friendly staff. Rooms have been renovated and have all mod cons including free Wi-Fi. No restaurant. €

Hôtel Imperator Concorde
quai de la Fontaine
Tel: 04 66 21 90 30
www.hotel-imperator.com

The low-key façade hides comfortable, traditional rooms, a good restaurant, a vintage lift and a luxuriant garden. This is where toreadors have traditionally stayed – and bullfighting fan Ernest Hemingway. €€€

Le Pré Galoffre
route de Générac
Tel: 04 66 29 65 41
www.lepregaloffre.com
About 6 km (3 miles) to the south of Nîmes where the *garrigue* meets the Cévennes, this tastefully renovated stone farmhouse with a lovely garden and pool

offers excellent value for money. Delicious breakfast with local produce but no restaurant. €

Royal Hôtel
3 boulevard Alphonse Daudet
Tel: 04 66 58 28 27
www.royalhotel-nimes.com
The Royal Hôtel is a cult address with its artfully casual boho decor, worn leather armchairs, wood floors, modern art and friendly staff. Most rooms overlook the place d'Assas, where its trendy tapas bar, La Bodeguita, has tables on the pavement. It can

get noisy at the weekend. €–€€

Pont du Gard

Hostellerie Le Castellas
30 Grande Rue, Collias
Tel: 04 66 22 88 88
www.lecastellas.com
Better known for its Michelin-starred restaurant, this ancient stone village house about 5 kms (3 miles) from the Pont du Gard, also has 13 quirky bedrooms; one bath looks like a water trough. The swimming pool is particularly lovely. €€–€€€

THE GORGES DU VERDON

Moustiers-Ste-Marie

La Bastide de Moustiers
chemin de Quinson

Tel: 04 92 70 47 47
www.bastide-moustiers.com
This beautifully restored ancient *bastide* was the first of Alain Ducasse's country *auberges*,

with just 12 gloriously romantic rooms exuding luxury and rural calm, and an excellent restaurant *(see page 169)*. It has

extensive grounds with lawns and a terrace, kitchen garden, swimming pool and its own helicopter pad. €€€–€€€€

La Bonne Auberge
Le Village
Tel: 04 92 74 66 18
www.bonne-auberge-moustiers.com
A reasonable inexpen-
sive hotel in the village.
Features a rustic res-
taurant serving regional
dishes, and a pool.
Closed Nov–Mar. €

BELOW: Moustiers-Ste-Marie.

Trigance

Château de Trigance
route du chateau
Tel: 04 94 76 91 18
www.chateau-de-trigance.fr
This lovely 11th-century
fortress towers over
the hilltop village of
Trigance just south of
the Gorges. It has
appropriately medieval-
themed bedrooms
with four-poster beds
and a good restaurant
in the vaulted arms
room. Closed Nov–
Mar. €€

Castellane

**Nouvel Hôtel de
Commerce**
18 place Marcel Sauvaire
Tel: 04 92 83 61 00
www.hotel-du-commerce-verdon.com
Reasonably priced
rooms in a 19th-century
building and its modern
extension, plus an
excellent restaurant in
the hands of a former
student of Alain
Ducasse. There's also a
very nice pool and sun
terrace. €

DIGNE AND THE SOUTHERN ALPS

Digne-les-Bains

Hôtel le Grand Paris
19 boulevard Thiers
Tel: 04 92 31 11 15
www.hotel-grand-paris.com
This 17th-century
former convent is *the*
place to stay in Digne.
The hotel has 16 rooms,
three suites, an
excellent restaurant and
a tree-shaded patio. €€

Mane

Couvent des Minimes
chemin des Jeux de Maï
Tel 04 92 74 44 44
www.couventdesminimes-
hotelspa.com
A warm, golden stone
17th-century
monastery just south
of Forcalquier has been
turned into a swish
hotel by the Occitane
beauty group, with
elegant, pared-back
rooms, a restaurant
and a spa. The terraced
gardens contain a
swimming pool, tennis
court and a typically
Provençal *pétanque*
pitch. €€€

TOULON AND THE WESTERN VAR

Toulon

**Le Grand Hôtel
Dauphiné**
10 rue Berthelot
Tel: 04 94 92 20 28
www.grandhoteldauphine.com
For a hotel in such a
central location by place
Puget in the old town, it
offers good value. Has
55 air-conditioned
rooms, and friendly
staff. €

La-Seyne-sur-Mer

Kyriad Prestige
1 quai du 19 mars 1962
Tel: 04 94 05 34 00
www.kyriad-prestige-toulon-la-
seyne-sur-mer.fr
A striking modern hotel
right on the harbour at La
Seyne with views across
the bay to Toulon. 94
rooms with balconies and
an outdoor pool. €€

Sanary-sur-Mer

**Hostellerie La
Farandole**
140 chemin de la Plage
Tel: 04 94 90 30 20
www.hostellerielafarandole.com
Opened in 2011, this
contemporary luxury
hotel and restaurant
overlooking the bay has
27 bright rooms, a gour-
met restaurant, a
rooftop bar, a pool and a
spa. €€€€

Hôtel de la Tour
24 quai General de Gaulle
Tel: 04 94 74 10 10
www.sanary-hoteldelatour.com
The best-placed hotel in
Sanary, located next to
the Saracen tower, with
most rooms overlooking
the port. The hotel has
24 pretty rooms and
friendly owners, plus a
restaurant specialising
in seafood. €€

Bandol

L'Ile Rousse
25 boulevard Louis-
Lumière, Plage de
Renecros
Tel: 04 94 29 33 00
www.ile-rousse.com
This waterfront hotel
and thalassotherapy
centre was totally
renovated in 2010, and
has 67 comfortable
rooms, most with a sea
view and direct access

BELOW: cookery course.

to its two private beaches. Refined cuisine served in the restaurant. €€€
Key Largo
19 corniche Bonaparte
Tel: 04 94 29 46 93
www.hotel-key-largo.com
Only eight of the 18 rooms in this Belle

Epoque villa have sea views but the location on the eastern side of Renécros beach and the fact that breakfast is included in the room price make up for it. There's a free municipal car park in front of the hotel. €

St-Maximin la-Sainte-Baume

Hôtellerie Le Couvent Royal
place Jean Salusse
Tel: 04 94 86 55 66
www.historic-hotels.com
Occupies a royal monastery founded in 1295

adjoining the finest Gothic church in Provence. The former monks' cells have been converted with good taste into 67 bedrooms. Meals are served in the vaulted chapterhouse or in the cloister. €€–€€€

INLAND VAR HILL VILLAGES

Les-Arcs-sur-Argens

Logis du Guetteur
Place du Château
Tel: 04 94 99 51 10
www.logisduguetteur.com
Pleasant, atmospheric hotel with romantic rooms in part of the 11th-century castle dominating the village. Good restaurant and swimming pool. €€

Tourtour

Auberge Saint-Pierre
Route d'Ampus
Tel: 04 94 50 00 50
www.aubergesaintpierre.com
Surrounded by fields, this is an idyllic place to make your base. As well

as 16 traditionally furnished rooms, there's a gypsy caravan available to guests. And then there's an indoor and an outdoor swimming pool, a spa and a restaurant serving dishes made with local farm produce. A real find. €€
La Bastide de Tourtour
route de Flayosc
Tel: 04 98 10 54 20
www.bastidedetourtour.com
Palatial 25-room hotel built in 1967 in traditional tufa stone, set in a park with fabulous views over the Var and beyond. The facilities include a heated pool, billiard room, tennis court and a good restaurant. €€€–€€€€

Villecroze

Auberge des Lavandes
place Général de Gaulle
Tel: 04 94 70 76 00
A small, good-value *auberge* with Norwegian owners, plus a good restaurant. Closed mid-Oct–Mar. €

Fayence

Moulin de la Camandoule
Chemin de Notre-Dame des Cyprès
Tel: 04 94 76 00 84
www.camandoule.com
This ancient olive mill in the valley below Fayence has been elegantly converted into a small, peaceful hotel with a

good restaurant serving traditional Provençal fare. Nine bedrooms and two duplex suites, all have an en suite bathroom. Lunch and dinner are served on the terrace in summer. Swimming pool. €–€€

Seillans

Hôtel des Deux Rocs
place Font d'Amont
Tel: 04 94 76 87 32
www.hoteldeuxrocs.com
This converted 18th-century residence is set in a lovely spot at the top of the town and is complete with 14 beautifully decorated rooms, a good restaurant and lovely terrace. €€

ST-TROPEZ AND THE MAURES

Hyères

Hôtel BOR
T3 allée Emile Gérard, Hyères Plage
Tel: 04 94 58 02 73
www.hotel-bor.com
A warm Provençal *mas* right on the beach, this is a stylish, modern hotel with a restaurant and bar. BOR stands for 'Beautiful, Original, Rare', which is a fair description. €€

Hôtel Europe
45 avenue Edith Cawell
Tel: 04 94 00 67 77
www.hotel-europe-hyeres.com
This 19th-century hotel was completely renovated in 2010 and the result is white walls, pale wood and splashes of colour here and there – in other words, a fairly standard contemporary hotel interior. There are 42 rooms sleeping 2 to 5 people and a roof ter-

race-cum-sundeck with great views. Free parking is available nearby. No restaurant. €€

Ile de Porquerolles

Mas du Langoustier
Tel: 04 94 58 30 09
www.langoustier.com
A warm Provençal *mas* that is luxurious if a bit precious, surrounded by

gardens. Fabulous restaurant. Free transport from the port to the hotel. Closed Oct–Easter. €€€

PRICE CATEGORIES

Price categories are for an average double room in high season:
€ = under €100
€€ = €100–180
€€€ = €180–300
€€€€ = more than €300

Hôtel-Résidence Les Mèdes
rue de la Douane
Tel: 04 94 12 41 24
www.hotel-les-medes.fr
A contemporary hotel with modern décor which offers apartments for 2 to 6 people as well as rooms. Breakfast is included in the price. €€€

Ile de Port Cros

Le Manoir
Tel: 04 94 05 90 52
www.hotel-lemanoirportcros.com
The only hotel on the no-smoking, no-car island of Port Cros. Rooms in the colonial-style 19th-century building are cosy and some have balconies. The room price includes breakfast and dinner. Large garden with a pool. Closed Nov–Mar. €€€

Bormes-les Mimosas

Hôtel Bellevue
14 place Gambetta,
Bormes Village
Tel: 04 94 71 15 15
www.bellevuebormes.com
A hotel-restaurant set on the lively main square of the old village. Most of the twelve rooms are decorated with Provençal print fabrics. Closed mid-Nov to mid-Jan. €

Hôtel de la Plage
boulevard de la Plage,
La Favière

PRICE CATEGORIES

Price categories are for an average double room in high season:
€ = under €100
€€ = €100–180
€€€ = €180–300
€€€€ = more than €300

Tel: 04 94 71 02 74
www.hotelbormes.com
This family-oriented hotel in Bormes' beach resort of La Favière has been run by the same family since it opened in 1939. Most of the 45 air-conditioned rooms have balconies or terraces, and there's a restaurant serving dinner if desired. *Pétanque* and ping pong outside. Closed Oct–Easter. €–€€

Le Lavandou

Hôtel Baptistin
quai Baptistin Pins
Tel: 04 98 00 44 51
www.baptistin-hotel-lavandou.com
Modern hotel with just 14 stylishly decorated rooms opposite the port. The waterside rooms all have balconies. No restaurant. €€–€€€

Le Rayol-Canadel

Le Bailli de Suffren
Tel: 04 98 04 47 00
www.lebaillidesuffren.com
The curved 1960s building – all rooms with balconies or terraces and sea views – is set on the beach below the gardens of the Domaine de Rayol. Pool, private beach, bar, restaurant and hire boats to explore the St-Tropez peninsula without the traffic jams. €€€€

La Croix-Valmer

La Pinède Plage
Tel: 04 94 55 16 16
www.pinedeplage.com
Comfortable hotel set amid parasol pines on the Plage de Gigaro. Great for sporting types: you can step almost straight onto the sand, where there are free

ABOVE: Les Roches, Le Lavandou.

kayaks, pedalos and windsurfers, and the chance to jet- and water-ski. €€€€

Grimaud

Le Verger Maelvi
route de Collobrières
Tel: 04 94 55 57 80
www.hotel-grimaud.com
On the edge of the village, this traditional Provençal house was completely renovated in 2011. The 14 rooms have contemporary décor and there's a lovely swimming pool. No restaurant. Closed mid-Nov–Mar. €€–€€€

La Boulangerie
route de Collobrières
Tel: 04 94 43 23 16
www.hotel-laboulangerie.com
A small but comfortable and friendly hotel situated in the quiet of the Massif des Maures. The hotel's amenities include a pool and tennis courts but no restaurant. Closed mid-Oct–Easter. €€

St-Tropez

Hôtel Ermitage
avenue Paul Signac
Tel: 04 94 81 08 10
www.ermitagehotel.fr

Ultra-hip hotel with funky retro décor up behind place des Lices. The 27 rooms have been individually designed by an eclectic bunch including Christian Louboutin and Marc Newson. Terry Richardson's photographs are part of the erotic theme and there are usually artists in residence. The restaurant is typically 'French bistro'. €€–€€€€

Kube Hotel Saint-Tropez
route de Saint-Tropez (D98),
Gassin
Tel: 04 94 97 20 00
www.kubehotel.com
The offshoot of the trendy Paris Kube has kept the trademark glass-and-steel reception cube and ice bar but has more of a resort feel. A gorgeous minimalist marble pool stretches between shady lawns where you can eat in summer. There's also a smaller heated pool, outdoor cocktail bar and rooftop champagne bar. €€€€

Hôtel Lou Cagnard
18 avenue Paul Roussell
Tel: 04 94 97 04 24
www.hotel-lou-cagnard.com
This attractive old

Provençal house is the best of the 'budget' accommodation in St-Tropez. Its 19 rooms are simply decorated and breakfast under the fig trees in the garden is a delight. €–€€

Hôtel Les Palmiers
26 boulevard Vasserot.
Tel: 04 94 97 01 61
www.hotel-les-palmiers.com
Proof that good-value, no frills accommodation exists even in St-Tropez, Les Palmiers has a great location by place des Lices, though the hotel itself is set back in a tropical garden. Rooms are simple but clean. €€

Hôtel Pastis
75 avenue du Général Leclerc
Tel: 04 98 12 56 50
www.pastis-st-tropez.com
This is more like a dream home than a hotel. The nine individually decorated rooms overlook a courtyard with a swimming pool; each boasts artworks from the owners' Pop Art collection, one has a copper bathtub. A special place. €€€€

La Ponche
3 rue des Remparts
Tel: 04 94 97 02 53
www.laponche.com
Discreet, exclusive

retreat conjured out of a group of old fishermen's cottages next to the Port des Pêcheurs. Some bedrooms have private roof terraces and sea views. Good regional cooking in the restaurant. Private garage. Closed Nov–mid-Feb. €€€€

Hôtel Sube
Port de St-Tropez
Tel: 04 94 97 30 04
A long-established hotel right on the port where all the action is (though it can be noisy). Best rooms have views of the port. The hotel bar is a favourite meeting place for yachtie types. €€–€€€

Ramatuelle

La Ferme d'Augustin
Plage de Tahiti
Tel: 04 94 55 97 00
www.fermeaugustin.com
This lovely old farmhouse is set in vineyards next to Tahiti Beach. The 46 bedrooms overlook the gardens, and many have balconies and sea views. The restaurant (for hotel guests only) favours produce from the hotel's kitchen garden. Heated swimming pool. Most guests are regulars so reserve

well ahead. Closed mid-Oct–Mar. €€€–€€€€

Hostellerie Le Baou
avenue Gustave Etienne
Tel: 04 98 12 94 20
www.hostellerie-le-baou.com
This big upmarket hotel just below the village has good-sized modern rooms with balconies or private garden terraces. Restaurant. €€€

Kon-Tiki Village
Plage de Pampelonne
www.riviera-villages.com
Not strictly camping, but Tahitian-style huts which sleep up to six people and some chalets right on the beach. There are several restaurants, a spa and a whole host of activities so it's a great place for families. The company also has two other parks in the area, Prairies de la Mer and Toison d'Or. €€€€

La Réserve Ramatuelle
chemin de la Quessine
Tel: 04 94 44 94 44
www.lareserve-ramatuelle.com
This ultra-modern hotel is one of the finest on the Riviera and has prices and service to match. The nine rooms and 19 suites each have their own terrace or garden. The spa uses

Crème de la Mer products and the restaurant focuses on tasty, healthy dishes. For a real treat, book one of the villas dotted around the grounds. Closed Nov–Mar. €€€€

Plan-de-la-Tour

Mas des Brugassières
1.5km (1 mile) south of the village
Tel: 04 94 55 50 55
www.masdesbrugassieres.com
In the Maures hills, 10km (6 miles) from Ste-Maxime, this intimate hotel was modelled on a Provençal *mas*, or farmhouse. The large garden includes a small pool; many rooms open onto a semi-private terrace. Closed mid-Oct–Mar. €€

Fréjus

Hôtel L'Aréna
145 boulevard Général de Gaulle
Tel: 04 9417 0940
www. hotel-frejus-arena.com
Situated in the old town with 39 Provençal-style rooms, a pool, a pleasant garden and an excellent regional restaurant. €€

ST-PAUL, VENCE AND THE GORGES DU LOUP

St-Paul-de-Vence

Les Cabanes d'Orion
2436 chemin du Malvan
Tel: 06 75 45 18 64
www.orionbb.com
Kids will love this place as accommodation is in well-equipped tree houses. When you're not exploring the grounds, relax in the sauna or

enjoy a massage. In summer, the minimum stay is Mon–Fri or Fri–Mon. €€€

La Colombe d'Or
place des Ormeaux
Tel: 04 93 32 80 02
www.la-colombe-dor.com
The 16-roomed Colombe d'Or was once frequented by unknown, penniless

artists who persuaded the original owner, aul Roux, to accept their paintings in payment for meals and board. As a result, works by Miró, Picasso, Modigliani, Matisse and Chagall can now be viewed by guests of the hotel and restaurant. €€€€

Hostellerie des Remparts
72 rue Grande
Tel: 04 93 32 09 88
www.hostellerielesremparts.com
A cheap, slightly eccentric option right in the heart of the old village. Friendly staff and a restaurant. Closed mid-Nov–mid-Dec and Jan. €–€€

Vence

Château St-Martin
route de Coursegoules
Tel: 04 93 58 02 02
www.chateau-st-martin.com
True luxury in the former castle of the Knights Templar, on the hills above Vence with views to the coast. Rooms are classic and the restaurant has an ever-growing reputation. Extensive grounds include tennis court and infinity pool. €€€€

Le 2
2 rue des Portiques
Tel: 04 93 24 42 58
www.le2avence.fr
Another stylishly decorated B&B in an old stone house but in this one the dominant colours are white, black and grey. All four rooms are air conditioned and have free Wi-Fi; the loft room has its own roof terrace. There's also a small bistro, often with live music in the evenings. €€

La Maison du Frêne
1 place du Frêne
Tel: 04 93 24 37 83
www.lamaisondufrene.com
This imposing 18th-century house has been turned into a temple of contemporary art where bright colours reign supreme and copies of Warhol and Picasso adorn the walls. The four rooms are very stylishly decorated and it's unlikely you'll want to leave. €€–€€€

Mas de Vence
539 avenue Emile Hugues
Tel: 04 93 58 06 16
www.azurline.com
A 10-minute walk from the old town, this neo-Provençal mas has comfortable if functional air-conditioned rooms and a decent restaurant; what really stands out are the pleasant outdoor pool and friendly staff who will go out of their way to help. €–€€

La Villa Roseraie
14 avenue Henri Giraud
Tel: 04 93 58 02 20
www.villaroseraie.com
This pretty Belle Epoque villa has a lovely garden, pool and 12 rooms (some small). A five-minute walk from the old town of Vence. No restaurant. €€

Tourrettes-sur-Loup

Le Mas des Cigales
Tel: 04 93 59 25 73
www.lemasdescigales.com
This traditionally decorated five-room B&B was opened in 2011 by a Belgian couple. Guests can enjoy the pool, the tennis court or a game of pétanque and table d'hôte is offered a couple of times a week. €€

Courmes

La Cascade
62 chemin de la Cascade
Tel: 04 93 09 65 85
www.gitedelacascade.com
A five-room gîte in a stunning rural location between Gourdon and Tourrettes-sur-Loup. As well as a delicious breakfast, evening meals are available on request and organic produce is used where possible. After a hard day's walking, relax by the pool or have a game of pétanque. €

Grasse

La Bastide Saint-Antoine
48 avenue Henri Dunant
Tel: 04 93 70 94 94
www.jacques-chibois.com
This 18th-century bastide has stark but chic, modern rooms and offers wonderful views of the mountains and sea. It has a pool, olive grove and organises regular art exhibitions. It's best known for its gastronomic restaurant (see page 227). €€€€

Moulin Ste-Anne
9 chemin des Près
Tel: 04 92 42 01 70
www.moulin-sainte-anne.com
Beautifully renovated 18th-century olive mill with five rooms: Mouliniers has an amazing Jacuzzi/steam bath while Aile Sud is split level with a small kitchen and overlooks the field where the donkey and the ewe live. The pool is particularly inviting and you'll need a car to get into Grasse. €€

Le Patti
place du Patti
Tel: 04 93 36 01 00
www.hotelpatti.com
Attractive hotel in an 18th-century building on the edge of the old town. The 73 rooms are generally small but prettily decorated in Provençal style. Dinner is served beneath the olive trees on the terrace in summer. €

PARC DU MERCANTOUR AND ALPINE VALLEYS

Peillon

Auberge de la Madone
3 place Auguste-Arnulf
Tel: 04 93 79 91 17
www.auberge-madone-peillon.com
Located at the gates of the village, this auberge offers a flowery terrace with a wonderful view, a one-star Michelin restaurant and gorgeous rooms fitted with antiques. The hotel also owns a smaller (and cheaper, €) hotel, Lou Portail, with six TV-free rooms. €€

St-Dalmas-sur-Tende

Le Prieuré
rue Jean Médecin
Tel: 04 93 04 75 70
www.leprieure.org
Three-star hotel with a pleasant restaurant, set in a lovely valley. Has a policy of employing people with disabilities. The hotel organ summer trips to the Vallée des Merveilles within Mercantour Park. €

Tende

Le Chamois d'Or
Hameau de Casterino
Tel: 04 93 04 66 66
www.hotelchamoisdor.net
A traditional mountain chalet on the threshold of the Vallée des Merveilles. The large, comfortable rooms are furnished in a contemporary, montagnard style. Regional cuisine served in the restaurant. 22 rooms. €€

Colmiane

Le Green Ecolodge
route de télésiège
Tel: 04 93 03 00 00
www.greenecolodge.com
Quirkily decorated six-room mountain lodge where recycled wood is the main theme; there even appears to be a tree growing out the bar. The restaurant serves local, seasonal cuisine and there is a small spa. €€

Sospel

Hôtel des Etrangers
9 boulevard de Verdun
Tel: 04 93 04 00 09
www.sospel.net
A Sospel institution with popular restaurant and a pool overhanging the river. English is spoken, and the proprietor is an expert on local history. Closed Nov–Feb. €

La Brigue

Hôtel Mirval
place St Martin
Tel: 04 93 04 63 71
www.lemirval.com
Comfortable 18-room hotel at the entrance to the medieval village. The owners organise 4x4 tours of the Mercantour as well as outings by Segway. €

Breil-sur-Roya

Hôtel Le Roya
place Bianchéri
Tel: 04 93 04 48 10
www.hoteleroya.com
A simple pink stucco hotel next to the village car park (market here on Tuesdays) offering B&B for those on a budget. €

NICE

Hôtel Aria A
15 avenue Auber
Tel: 04 93 88 30 69
www.aria-nice.com
This renovated 19th-century hotel overlooks an attractive garden square amid the Belle Epoque and Art Deco buildings of the new town. The 30 rooms are light and high-ceilinged, decorated in sunny colours. Good value. €–€€

Hôtel Beau Rivage B
24 rue St François-de-Paule
Tel: 04 92 47 82 82
www.nicebeaurivage.com
Matisse, Nietzsche and Chekhov all stayed at the 118-room Beau Rivage, located near the opera in the old town. It's been given a suave, minimalist refurbishment by architect Jean-Michel Wilmotte. Also has a fashionable private beach. €€€€

PRICE CATEGORIES

Price categories are for an average double room in high season:
€ = under €100
€€ = €100–180
€€€ = €180–300
€€€€ = more than €300

Boscolo Exedra C
12 boulevard Victor Hugo
Tel: 04 97 03 89 89
www.boscolohotels.com
A Belle Epoque hotel on one of the city's main shopping streets has been given a 21st century makeover with chic white décor and original works of contemporary art. As well as an Italian restaurant, there's a futuristic gym and spa. Design-conscious guests will love it. €€€€

Hôtel Grimaldi D
15 rue Grimaldi
Tel: 04 93 16 00 24
www.le-grimaldi.com
A lovely intimate hotel with 46 prettily furnished rooms in two Belle Epoque houses in the new town. There is a delicious breakfast buffet. €€–€€€

Hi Hotel E
avenue des Fleurs
Tel: 04 97 07 26 26
www.hi-hotel.net
The colourful trendy Hi aims to make you reconsider the way you stay at a hotel with nine different bedroom concepts for music-lovers, computer nerds, movie fans and so on. There's a garden courtyard, DJ bar and rooftop sundeck with minuscule swimming pool. €€€

Hôtel Negresco F
37 promenade des Anglais
Tel: 04 93 16 64 00
www.hotel-negresco-nice.com
This flamboyant Belle Epoque hotel is an opulent vestige of Nice's golden era. The 150 rooms and apartments are magnificently furnished with antiques, priceless paintings and tapestries. The celebrated Chantecler restaurant (see page 247) is acknowledged as one of the best tables in the region. €€€€

Nice Garden Hôtel G
11 rue du Congrès
Tel: 04 93 87 35 62
www.nicegardenhotel.com
A family-run hotel with nine tastefully decorated rooms, each overlooking the verdant Mediterranean garden – there are even orange trees. Children over the age of six are welcome and it's only 10 minutes' walk from the train station and the beach. €–€€

Hôtel du Petit Palais H
17 avenue Emile Bieckert
Tel: 04 93 62 19 11
www.petitpalaisnice.com
One of the few hotels still up in Cimiez in the former villa of actor-playwright Sacha Guitry. It has friendly staff and attractive rooms, some with small terraces or balconies giving rooftop views to the Baie des Anges. €€–€€€

Hôtel Suisse I
15 quai Raubà Capèù
Tel: 04 92 17 39 00
www.hotel-nice-suisse.com
Behind a period facade virtually built into the cliff face of castle hill, the Hôtel Suisse has been stylishly modernised with an airy ground-floor salon and breakfast room and a different colour scheme on each floor. Most rooms have a sea view and balcony. €€–€€€

Villa Saint-Exupéry Gardens J
22 avenue Gravier
Tel: 04 93 84 42 83
www.villahotels.com
In the hills above the city, housed in a converted monastery with a beautiful garden, this hostel with a mix of rooms and dorms has been voted one of the world's best. Breakfast and a walking tour of Nice are included

in the price. They've recently opened another hostel, Villa Saint-Exupéry Beach, in the centre of town. **€**

Hôtel Wilson K
39 rue de l'Hôtel des Postes
Tel: 04 93 85 47 79
www.hotel-wilson-nice.com

Budget boho hotel with eclectic décor. The 16 rooms have different themes: there's Matisse, Africa and flowers amongst others. But you'll need to be fit – the hotel is on the third floor of a 19th-century build-

ing and there's no lift. On the plus side, it's a mere 5-minute walk to the beach. **€**

Hôtel Windsor L
11 rue Dalpozzo
Tel: 04 93 88 59 35
www.hotelwindsornice.com
From the outside it looks

like a 19th-century hotel, but inside this boho arty establishment boasts a hammam, aviary, exotic garden, and rooms commissioned by different contemporary artists. **€€–€€€**

THE RIVIERA FROM CANNES TO CAGNES

Cannes

Hôtel 7 Art
23 rue du Maréchal Joffre
Tel: 04 93 68 66 66
www.hotel-7art.com
Bright and breezy budget boutique hotel which pays homage to the '7th art' – that is, cinema. Rooms are small but include free Wi-Fi and it's a short walk to the train station. If it's full, try their other property, Hôtel Alnea (tel: 04 93 68 77 77, www.hotel-alnea.com, **€**). Breakfast included in the room price. **€€**

Hôtel Canberra
120 rue d'Antibes
Tel: 04 97 06 95 00
www.hotel-cannes-canberra.com
A smart, comfortable boutique hotel with 30 rooms and 5 suites. There is a pleasant outdoor pool and Le Café Blanc, a 1950s-style lounge bar, serves snacks from Tue to Sat. **€€–€€€€**

Carlton Intercontinental
58 La Croisette
Tel: 04 93 06 40 06
www.intercontinental-carlton-cannes.com
The legendary palace hotel where the jury always stays during the film festival has sumptuous suites. However, it helps to have film-star

means as standard rooms can be disappointingly small. Avoid those at the rear without sea views. Includes two restaurants, a health club, swimming pool and private beach with watersports facilities. **€€€€**

Le Cavendish
11 boulevard Carnot
Tel: 04 97 06 26 00
www.cavendish-cannes.com
Attractive Belle Epoque building on the big boulevard that descends towards La Croisette. The comfortable period town-house style was conceived as in homage to the English lords who once frequented the coast, with some wonderful circular rooms in the corner turret. **€€€**

Five Seas Hotel
1 rue Notre Dame
Tel: 04 63 36 05 05
www.five-seas-hotel-cannes.com
The latest addition to Cannes' collection of luxury boutique hotels doesn't disappoint. The 45 rooms and suites have achingly hip design; the presidential suite has a terrace jacuzzi. There is also a fashionable restaurant, a Carita spa, a rooftop pool and a yacht available for guests to book. **€€€€**

Hôtel Florian
8 rue du Commandant André
Tel: 04 93 39 24 82
www.hotel-leflorian.fr
On the hippest shopping street, this is one of the best budget options in town. There are 20 rooms and 15 apartments sleeping up to four people. With plenty of bars in the vicinity, it's reassuring that there is double glazing and aircon. **€–€€**

Hotel Martinez
73 La Croisette
Tel: 04 92 98 73 00
www.hotel-martinez.com
A glitzy Art Deco extravaganza. When it opened, it was France's largest hotel. A major facelift in 2003 saw the creation of two vast rooftop suites and a luxurious Givenchy spa, and renovation of the splendid facade, grand staircase and hall. **€€€€**

Le Mistral Hôtel
13 rue des Belges
Tel: 04 93 39 91 46
www.mistral-hotel.com
This is a stylish budget discovery just a couple of streets back from the Palais des Festivals. The eleven rooms, named after different winds (chinook, scirocco, etc), are decked out in warm colours and stripey wood; larger ones can accommodate three

people and have well-lit bathrooms. No lift. **€€€**

Hôtel Molière
5 rue Molière
Tel: 04 93 38 16 16
www.hotel-moliere.com
There's a relaxed mood at this small hotel, set at the rear of a long garden between La Croisette and rue d'Antibes. Rooms sport modern minimalist tones, and most have good-sized balconies. **€€**

Hôtel Splendid
4–6 rue Félix-Faure
Tel: 04 97 06 22 22
www.splendid-hotel-cannes.fr
A sparkling white Belle Epoque edifice in the heart of the action, virtually opposite the Palais des Festivals. Rooms have been comfortably updated while retaining period flourishes; breakfast is served on a large sunny terrace. **€€–€€€**

Mougins

Le Mas Candille
boulevard Clément Rebouffel

PRICE CATEGORIES

Price categories are for an average double room in high season:
€ = under €100
€€ = €100–180
€€€ = €180–300
€€€€ = more than €300

TRANSPORT

ACCOMMODATION

ACTIVITIES

A – Z

LANGUAGE

ABOVE: a suite with a stunning sea view.

Tel: 04 92 28 43 43
www.lemascandille.com
A luxurious hotel on the edge of the old village. Choose the rooms in the main *mas*, decorated with light Provençal colours and antique furniture, rather than the rather dark Asian-themed rooms in the modern *bastide* annexe. Spacious gardens, a lovely pool and a Shiseido spa. Good modern Provençal cooking in the restaurant. €€€€

Antibes–Juan les-Pins

Belles Rives
boulevard Edouard-Baudoin, Juan-des-Pins

Tel: 04 93 61 02 79
www.bellesrives.com
Close enough to town to enjoy the lively atmosphere, yet sufficiently far away from the noise and crowds. The Belles Rives has retained all the attraction of the stylish Art Deco period, when it was the home of Zelda and F. Scott Fitzgerald. It has a gourmet restaurant, piano bar and beach restaurant. €€€€
Grand Hôtel du Cap-Eden-Roc
boulevard Kennedy, Cap d'Antibes

Tel: 04 93 61 39 01
www.hotel-du-cap-eden-roc.com
A jet-setters' destination in wooded grounds, this

is the ultimate in Riviera glamour and a favourite with Hollywood actors. A serious splurge. €€€€
La Jabotte
13 avenue de Max Maurey, Antibes

Tel: 04 93 61 45 89
www.jabotte.com
Adorable – and affordable – lodgings with bright decor just up the street from the Plage de Salis. The original artwork in the rooms is the work of one of the owners. Not all rooms en suite. Closed Nov and Christmas week. Ten rooms. €€
Hôtel des Mimosas
rue Pauline, Juan-des-Pins

Tel: 04 93 61 04 16
www.hotel-mimosas.fr
A large, early 20th-century house set in quiet gardens just a 5-minute walk from the beach. Attractive bedrooms, swimming pool. No restaurant. Closed Oct–Apr. €€
Relais du Postillon
8 rue Championnet, Vieux Antibes

Tel: 04 93 34 20 77
www.relaisdupostillon.com
It's hard to find a bargain in high season on the

Côte d'Azur, but the Relais du Postillon in the old town of Antibes comes pretty close, with 15 characterful rooms and a homely bar. €–€€
Hôtel Royal Antibes
16 boulevard Maréchal Leclerc, Antibes

Tel: 04 83 61 91 91
www.hotelroyal-antibes.com
On the waterfront towards Cap d'Antibes, this modern luxury hotel, beach and spa opened its doors in 2011. The 63 rooms, suites and apartments offer the latest contemporary comforts and the New York-style Café Royal res-taurant serves Mediterranean cuisine for breakfast, lunch and dinner. €€€

Biot

Hôtel des Arcades
16 place des Arcades

Tel: 04 93 65 01 04
www.hotel-restaurant-les-arcades.com
Quirky, antique-filled hotel with large rooms in a 15th-century mansion. The restaurant is also an art gallery. €

THE RIVIERA FROM VILLEFRANCHE TO MENTON

Villefranche-sur-Mer

La Fiancée du Pirate
8 boulevard de la Corne d'Or

Tel: 04 93 76 67 40
www.fianceedupirate.com
In a residential area above the bay, 'the Pirate's Girlfriend' has a beach house feel. Some rooms have sea views, some open onto the garden and there are bungalows too. The pool

means you don't have to trek to the beach. €€–€€
Hôtel Welcome
3 quai Amiral Courbet

Tel: 04 93 76 27 62
www.welcomehotel.com
With the best location in Villefranche, it's hardly surprising that this historic hotel has welcomed many illustrious guests. The spacious rooms nearly all have balconies overlooking

the port, and there's a stylish wine bar. Closed mid-Nov–Christmas. €€–€€€€

St-Jean-Cap Ferrat

Brise Marine
58 avenue Jean Mermoz

Tel: 04 93 76 04 36
www.hotel-brisemarine.com
An authentic late 19th-century villa with fairly small but immaculate rooms, some with sea

view, and a steeply terraced garden that leads down to the sea. Closed Nov–Jan. €€
Grand Hôtel du Cap Ferrat
71 boulevard Général de Gaulle

Tel: 04 93 76 50 50
www.grand-hotel-cap-ferrat.com
This Riviera grand dame was brought up to date in 2009. Bedrooms in the main building boast vast beds and walk-in

dressing rooms, while ground-floor suites in the modern annex each have a private spillover pool. There's also a new spa, although it's hard to beat the beauty of the original pool. €€€€

Beaulieu-sur-Mer

La Réserve de Beaulieu
5 boulevard du Général Leclerc
Tel: 04 93 01 00 01
www.reservebeaulieu.com
A grand Riviera dowager, opened in 1905, with luxurious rooms, spa and billiards room, a swimming pool in the garden and a private beach and harbour. Located right on the seafront. Closed mid-Oct–mid-Dec. €€€€

Eze

La Bastide aux Camélias
23 route de l'Adret

Tel: 04 93 41 13 68
www.bastideauxcamelias.com
Gorgeous B&B in a renovated 16th-century farmhouse on the outskirts of the village, with amazing views over the coast. The four bedrooms all have a romantic air and there's a lovely garden and pool. Book an aromatherapy massage if you still need to destress. €€

Château de la Chèvre d'Or
rue de Barri
Tel: 04 92 10 66 66
www.chevredor.com
Staying at the Golden Goat is an unforgettable experience. The 28-room hotel, created out of old village houses, combines a warm provincial elegance with Riviera élan, and the Michelin-starred restaurant (see page 273) has magnificent coastal views. €€€€

Roquebrune-Cap-Martin

Les Deux Frères
Roquebrune Village
Tel: 04 93 28 99 00
www.lesdeuxfreres.com
A hotel and restaurant occupying the old schoolhouse, it has 10 differently decorated rooms, ranging from veiled bridal room to Moorish-inspired. €–€€

Menton

Hôtel Aiglon
7 avenue de la Madone
Tel: 04 93 57 55 55
www.hotelaiglon.net
A 19th-century white stucco mansion converted into an atmospheric hotel. The Belle Epoque bar/salon is a delight; rooms are less elaborate, with old-fashioned charm. Set in large gardens, there's an outdoor pool and a play area and ping pong for children. €€

Hôtel Lemon
10 rue Albert 1er
Tel: 04 93 28 63 63
www.hotel-lemon.com
Eco-aware contemporary budget hotel in a Belle Epoque villa. Rooms are light and airy with 'breatheasy' paint; breakfast is made with local and organic produce. A breath of fresh air in staid Menton. €

Hôtel Napoléon
29 Porte de France
Tel: 04 93 35 89 50
www.napoleon-menton.com
This modern seafront hotel is near Val Rahmeh gardens. Bedrooms at the front have balconies overlooking Garavan Bay, while those at the rear have mountain views. There's a bar, garden with banana trees and outdoor pool and gym. Also owns the Plage Napoléon across the street, with a beach restaurant serving Italian cuisine and delicious ice creams. €€€

MONACO

Columbus
23 avenue des Papalins
Tel: +377 92 05 90 00
Tel: +377 9330 2464
www.columbushotels.com
In Fontvieille, this was Monaco's first boutique hotel and a favourite with racing drivers as it was once owned by David Coulthard.

PRICE CATEGORIES

Price categories are for an average double room in high season:
€ = under €100
€€ = €100–180
€€€ = €180–300
€€€€ = more than €300

Accommodation is in stylish rooms, suites and an apartment, and there is a pool. The restaurant serves Asian-Fusion cuisine. €€€

Hôtel de France
6 rue de la Turbie, La Condamine
Tel: +377 93 30 2 464
www.monte-carlo.mc/france
A rare bargain option, located on a side street near the train station and convenient for the port and palace, with 26 bright rooms. €–€€

Hôtel Normandy
6 allée des Orangers, Cap d'Ail
Tel: 04 93 78 77 77

www.hotelnormandy.no
Just outside Monaco, this 16-room arty hotel offers plenty of charm and great views over the coast. It's also a short walk from Plage Mala, one of the loveliest beaches on the Riviera. €–€€

Le Méridien Beach Plaza
22 avenue Princesse Grace, Monte-Carlo
Tel: +377 93 30 98 80
www.lemeridienmontecarlo.com
The huge modern Méridien Beach is very popular with the new fortunes from Russia and eastern Europe.

Contemporary art in the lobby and a 24-hour restaurant where you can watch the chefs cooking. Outdoor and indoor pools, plus private beach. €€€€

Hôtel de Paris
place du Casino, Monte-Carlo
Tel: +377 98 06 30 16
www.montecarloresort.com
This palatial hotel is the most magnificent and glamorous place to stay in Monaco, and boasts Alain Ducasses's three-star restaurant, the Louis XV. It. Direct access to the Thermes Marins spa. €€€€

ACTIVITIES

FESTIVALS, THE ARTS, NIGHTLIFE, OUTDOOR ACTIVITIES AND SHOPPING

FESTIVALS

Festivals abound in Provence, especially in summer, when world-class music, theatre and dance are staged here, such as the Avignon theatre festival, jazz in Nice and Juan-les-Pins, and opera in Aix-en-Provence and Orange. All year round you'll find traditional celebrations of everything from bullfighting and patron saints to lemons. Pick up the annual booklet *Terre des Festivals* at tourist offices or download it at www.terre-desfestivals.fr.

January

Isola 2000: *Trophy Andros*. Car-racing tournament on ice.
Monaco: Monte-Carlo Rally; International Circus Festival (www.montecarlofestival.mc)

February

Avignon: *Les Hivernales*. Contemporary dance (www.hivernales-avignon.com).
Bormes-les-Mimosas: *Corso Fleuri*. Mimosa festival with flower-decorated floats.
Marseille: *Fête de la Chandeleur*. Candlemas procession and blessing of *navettes* biscuits at the Abbaye St-Victor.

Menton: *Fête du Citron*. Carnival-time lemon festival with parade, bands and incredible citrus fruit sculptures (www.feteducitron.com).
Nice: *Carnaval*. Decorated floats parade behind the Roi du Carnaval; flower battles on the promenade des Anglais (www.nice-carnaval.com).
Villefranche-sur-Mer: *Combat Naval Fleuri*. Flower jousting on traditional *pointu* fishing boats.

March

Monte-Carlo: *Les Printemps des Arts*. Biennial of dance and classical music (odd years) until mid-April (www.printempsdesarts.com).
Vallauris-Golfe-Juan: *Fête Napoléon*. First weekend in March locals re-enact Napoleon's landing at Golfe Juan on 1 March 1815.

April

Antibes: *Salon des Antiquaires*. Antiques fair by the Port Vauban (www.salon-antiquaires-antibes.com).
Arles: *Féria de Pâques*. Easter *féria* bullfighting and festivities in the Roman arena (www.feriaarles.com).
Monaco: *Tennis Masters*.

May

Banon: cheese fair – celebration of the local Banon goat's cheese.

Cannes: Film Festival (see page 252).
Fréjus: *Bravade St-François*. Festival in honour of the patron saint of Fréjus.
Grasse: *Expo Roses*. Rose show.
Monaco: Formula 1 Grand Prix.
Nîmes: *Féria de Pentecôte*. Bull-fighting, music and *bodegas*.
St-Tropez: *Bravades* (16–18) with costume parades to celebrate the town's patron saint and military history.
Stes-Maries-de-la-Mer: *Pèlerinage de Mai*. France's biggest gypsy gathering.

June

France: *Fête de la Musique* on 21 June sees free concerts held on midsummer's day. *Fête de la Saint-Pierre* on 27 June is the festival of the patron saint of fishermen, celebrated in ports.
Antibes: International Young Soloist Festival.
Monte-Carlo: *Fête de la St-Jean* (23 and 24 June). Traditional *fêtes* of St-John the Baptist.
Nice: *Festival du Musique Sacré*. Religious music in Vieux Nice churches. *Ironman France*. Triathlon.
Tarascon: *Fête de la Tarasque*. Celebrating the legend of the monster that terrorised the town.
Vaucluse: *Fête de la Vigne et du Vin*. Wine festival.

July

France: Bastille Day (14 July). Fireworks and dancing commemorate the French Revolution.
Aix-en-Provence: *Festival d'Art Lyrique*. International opera *(see page 125)*.
Antibes-Juan-les-Pins: *Jazz à Juan*. International jazz. *Musiques au Coeur*. Opera.
Arles: *Les Rencontres d'Arles*. Prestigious international photography festival with exhibitions until September *(see page 146)*; *Suds à Arles*. World-music festival (www.suds-arles.com).
Avignon: *Festival d'Avignon* and *Le Off*. International theatre festival and its fringe offshoot *(see page 70)*.
Cannes: *Les Nuits Musicales du Suquet* classical concerts (www.nuitsdusuquet-cannen.com).
Hyères: *Design Parade*. Modern design competition and debates at the Villa Noailles. Exhibitions last until September.
Lacoste: *Festival de Lacoste*. Opera, dance and theatre in a Luberon hill village (until early August).
Ménerbes: *Les Musicales du Luberon*. Classical concerts in the village church.
Marseille: *Mondial du Pétanque*. Over 12,000 competitors enter the world *pétanque* championships.
Monte-Carlo: Concerts in the courtyard of the Palais Princier; spectacular Fireworks Festival; *Les Nuits de la Danse*; Monte-Carlo Sporting Summer Festival.
Nice: Nice Jazz Festival. Eclectic jazz in the Roman arena and Jardin des Arènes in Cimiez (www.nicejazzfestival.fr).
Orange: *Les Chorégies d'Orange*. First-rate lyric opera in the Théâtre Antique (until mid-August) *(see page 76)*.
Pont-du-Gard: Nocturnal light show on the aqueduct until late August.
La Roque d'Antheron: *Festival International de Piano*. Leading pianists perform in the château gardens and Luberon churches (www.festival-piano.com).
La Seyne-sur-Mer: Jazz festival in the Fort Napoléon.
Vaison-la-Romaine: *Vaison Danses*. Contemporary dance in the Roman theatre (www.vaison-danses.com).
Vallauris: *Biennale Internationale de Céramique*. Pottery Festival, until October, even years.
Vence: *Les Nuits du Sud*. World music until early August (www.nuits dusud.com).

August

Brignoles: *Festival de Jazz*.
Cannes: *Festival Pantiero*. Electronic music and DJs (www.festivalpantiero.com).
Digne-les-Bains: *Corso de la Lavande*. Lavender festival.
Fréjus: *Fête du Raisin*. Wine-tasting and feasting.
Grasse: Festival of Jasmine.
Menton: International Chamber Music Festival by the quayside (www.musique-menton.fr).
Nice: *Fierà de la San Bertoumieu*. Craft and regional-produce fair, with traditional music and games.
Ramatuelle: theatre and comedy festival.
Salon-de-Provence: *Musique à l'Emperi*. Chamber music at the Château de l'Empéri (www.festival-salon.fr)
St-Rémy-de-Provence: *Féria Provençale*. Bull-running and music.

September

Antibes: *Festival d'Art Sacré*. Religious music in the old cathedral.
Arles: *Fêtes des Prémices du Riz*. Rice festival and bullfighting.
Cassis: *Ban des Vendanges*. Wine harvest celebration.
Cavalaire-sur-Mer: *Grand Prix de France Jet Offshore*. Jet-skiing.
France: *Journées du Patrimoine*. Third weekend in September when historic monuments and official buildings are open to the public free.

October

Collobrières: *Fêtes de la Châtaigne*. Chestnut harvest festival on three Sundays in October.
Marseille: *Fiesta des Suds*. World music festival in the Dock des Suds (www.dock-des-suds.org).
Roquebrune-sur-Argens: *Fête de Miel*. Honey festival.

November

Arles: *Salon International des Santonniers* (until mid-Jan). Exhibition of Christmas crib figures; *Marché de Noël*.
Carpentras: *Foire St-Suffrein*. Food and horse fair.
Marseille: *Foire-aux-Santons* (late Nov until mid-Jan). Provençal Christmas crib figures market dating back to 1803.
Monte-Carlo: 19 Nov, National Holiday: parades and spectacles (fireworks the previous evening).

WHAT'S ON AND TICKETS

César (www.cesar.fr), a weekly listings magazine, is distributed free in the Gard, Vaucluse and Bouches-du-Rhône *départements*.

Friday editions of newspapers are a good source of information on the local nightlife: see *La Provence* and *La Marseillaise*. Also visit www.nicematin.fr and www.laprovence.com. The major cities produce brochures of the main events –enquire at the tourist office.

Tourist offices may also have ticket offices for local music, theatre or cultural events. Many theatre and opera box offices accept credit card telephone or internet bookings. In major cities, FNAC (www.fnac.com) and Virgin stores are ticket agents for local gigs. Tickets can also be bought via **France Billet** (tel: 0892 692 694; www.francebillet.com).

December

Bandol: *Fêtes du Millésime.* Tastings of the new Bandol wine vintage.
Fréjus: *Foire aux Santons.* Provençal crib figures and Christmas market.
Nice: *Crèche vivante.* Living Christmas nativity scene on place Rossetti.
St-Raphaël: *Fêtes de la Lumière.* Involves fireworks and street theatre.

THE ARTS

Outside the summer festival season, performing arts are largely found in the main cities, such as Marseille, Nice, Avignon, Aix, Arles, Toulon or Monte-Carlo, where you will find opera, theatre and cinema venues. Respected resident companies include the Théâtre de Nice, Ballets de Monte-Carlo and the Ballet Preljocaj in Aix. In summer, you'll also find touring circuses, outdoor rock concerts and film screenings all along the coast.

Venues

Aix-en-Provence

Ballet Preljocaj–Pavillon Noir, 530 avenue Mozart; tel: 04 42 93 48 00; www.preljocaj.org. Exciting contemporary dance from international visiting companies and the resident Ballet Preljocaj.
Cinéma Renoir, 24 cours Mirabeau; tel: 0892 68 72 70; www.lescinemasaixois.com. One of three cinemas showing films in their original language.
Grand Théâtre de Provence, 380 avenue Max Juvenal; tel: 04 42 91 69 70; www.lestheatres.net. Opera, classical and orchestral performances.
Théâtre des Ateliers, 29 place Miollis; tel: 04 42 38 10 45; www.theatre-des-ateliers-aix.com. Contemporary theatre.

Antibes

Théâtre Antibea, 15 rue Georges Clemenceau; tel: 04 93 34 24 30; www.theatre-antibea.com. Small theatre with a varied repertoire. Some English-language plays.

Arles

Cargo de Nuit, 7 avenue Sadi-Carnot; tel: 04 90 49 55 99; www.cargodenuit.com. Venue for world music and jazz concerts.
Patio de la Camargue, 51 bis chemin Barriol; tel: 04 90 49 51 76; www.patio.chico.fr. Dinner-cabaret from the former frontman of the Gypsy Kings.

Avignon

AJMI, 4 rue des Escaliers Ste-Anne; tel: 04 90 86 08 61; www.jazzalajmi.com. Improvisational jazz in a small venue.
Opéra-Théâtre d'Avignon, 20 place de l'Horloge; tel: 04 90 82 42 42; www.opera-avignon.fr. The main permanent theatre in Avignon. Stages ballet, chamber music and comedy.
Théâtre des Carmes, 6 place des Carmes; tel: 04 90 82 20 47. Avignon's oldest theatre company, based in a restored Gothic cloister.
Utopia, 4 rue des Escaliers Ste-Anne; tel: 04 90 82 65 36; www.cinemas-utopia.org. Avignon's main 'VO' or *version-originale* (original-language) cinema, with a bohemian bistro and café.

Cannes

Cinéma Les Arcades, 77 rue Felix Faure; tel: 04 93 39 10 00. Shows some films in English.
Palais des Festivals et des Congrès, 1 boulevard de la Croisette; tel: 04 92 99 84 00; www.palaisdesfestivals.com. The official venue for the Film Festival is also used for plays, ballets and concerts.
Théâtre Alexandre III, 19 boulevard Alexandre; tel: 04 93 94 33 44; www.theatredecannes.com. A former cinema, this theatre stages plays, including classics and modern interpretations.

Cavaillon

Théâtre de Cavaillon, rue du Languedoc; tel: 04 90 78 64 64; www.theatredecavaillon.com. A state-subsidised theatre putting on theatre, dance, music and multi-disciplinary projects, as well as nomadic pieces and events in nearby Luberon villages.

Marseille

Cité de la Musique, 4 rue Bernard Dubois; tel: 04 91 39 28 28; www.citemusique-marseille.com. Music, dance and art exhibitions.
Espace Julien, 39 cours Julien; tel: 04 91 24 34 10; www.espace-julien.com. Hip venue with an eclectic programme.
L'Intermédiaire, 63 place Jean-Jaurès; www.lintermediaire.fr. Rock, reggae, jazz and African music.
Opéra Municipal de Marseille, 2 rue Molière; tel: 04 91 55 11 10. Opera, ballet and classical music.
Pelle Mêle, 8 place aux Huiles; tel: 04 91 54 85 26. Atmospheric jazz club by the port.
Le Silo, 35 quai du Lazaret; www.silo-marseille.com. New arts venue in the redeveloped docklands.
Théâtre du Gymnase, 4 rue du Théâtre-Français; tel: 04 91 24 35 24; www.lestheatres.net. Vintage theatre staging innovative drama.
Théâtre National de Marseille, 30 quai Rive Neuve; tel: 04 91 54 70 54; www.theatre-lacriee.com. Renowned theatre in the old fish market.

Monaco

Grimaldi Forum, 10 avenue Princesse Grace; tel: +377 99 99 20 00; www.grimaldiforum.com. Musicals, concerts, ballet and art exhibitions.
Open-air cinema, chemin des Pêcheurs; www.cinema2monaco.com. Nightly screenings (June–Sept), mainly in English, in a stunning seaside location.
Salle Garnier, place du Casino, Monte-Carlo; tel: +377 98 06 28 00 www.opera.mc. Glamorous opera.
Théâtre de Princesse Grace, 12 avenue d'Ostende; tel: +377 93 25 32 37. Concerts, spectacles and classic theatre.

ABOVE: Monaco aquarium.

Nice

Acropolis, esplanade Kennedy; tel: 04 93 92 83 00; www.nice-acropolis.com. Venue for ballet and music concerts.

Cinémathèque de Nice, Acropolis, 3 esplanade J.F. Kennedy; tel: 04 92 04 06 66, www.cinematheque-nice.com. A cinema screening classic and recent movies in VO (*version originale* with subtitles).

Cinéma Rialto, 4 rue de Rivoli. Shows VO films.

Opéra de Nice, 4 rue St-François-de-Paule; tel: 04 92 17 40 00; www.opera-nice.org. Classic venue for concerts, ballet and opera.

Théâtre National de Nice, promenade des Arts; tel: 04 93 13 90 90; www.tnn.fr. Theatre premiering new drama by its own troupe and visiting companies.

Wayne's Bar, 15 rue de la Préfecture; tel: 04 93 13 46 99; www.waynes.fr. Live music every night from up-and-coming young bands.

Nîmes

Théâtre de Nîmes, 1 place de la Calade; tel: 04 66 36 65 00; www.theatredenimes.com. Hosts a varied programme of theatre as well as visiting contemporary dance companies.

Toulon

Opéra de Toulon, place Victor Hugo; tel: 04 94 92 70 78; www.operadetoulon.fr. Ornate municipal opera house staging opera and Baroque and classical concerts.

Zénith Omega, boulevard Commandant Nicolas; tel: 04 94 22 66 77; www.zenith-omega-toulon.com. Arena-style venue for rock concerts.

Provence has a magnificent legacy of art, and many major art museums. There are also numerous smaller museums and galleries offering a variety of art and crafts. Most museums charge an entrance fee (although municipal museums in Nice are now free), but look out for discounts for families, or off-peak periods. As a rule, national museums are closed on Tuesday, while municipal museums shut on Monday. Opening times vary. Most museums close from noon to 2 or 2.30pm, although major sites are often open continuously, especially in summer.

NIGHTLIFE

The Côte d'Azur is famed for its nightlife, in particular its legendary casinos, which nowadays often incorporate nightclubs, cabarets and restaurants. The larger cities have a variety of late-night bars and clubs. Several Parisian clubs migrate to Cannes for the Cannes Film Festival, and in high summer special events are hosted all along the coast. St-Tropez and Juan-les-Pins are legendary party destinations, but in smaller towns and villages there is usually little going on at night unless a festival is taking place. Most will have a bar or café that stays open until midnight or later though.

Casinos and Cabaret

Roulette and black jack are all part of the Riviera's glamorous image. As well as the fashionable casinos listed here, there are also lower-key casinos with a variety of table

games and slot machines at other resorts including Bandol, Beaulieu, Menton and Cavalaire, and inland at Aix-en-Provence and Grasse. You have to be over 18 to enter a casino (bring ID).

Cannes

Casino Barrière Les Princes, 50 boulevard de la Croisette; tel: 04 92 97 06 18 50, www.lucienbarriere.com. Casino, restaurant and two bars.

La Croisette – Casino Barrière, 1 Espace Lucien Barrière; tel: 04 92 98 78 00; www.lucienbarriere.com. Casino, restaurant and bar.

Palm Beach Casino, 57 boulevard F. Roosevelt; tel: 04 97 06 36 90; www.casinopalmbeach.com. Casino, restaurant and piano bar (noon–4am).

Monte-Carlo

Casino de Monte-Carlo, place du Casino; tel: +377 92 16 23 00; www.casinodemontecarlo.com. The original and still the most famous casino on the Côte d'Azur. Formal dress is required. Open all year: main salon from 2pm, private rooms from 4pm. Has a separate cabaret and several restaurants.

Nice

Casino Ruhl, 1 promenade des Anglais; tel: 04 97 03 12 22; www.lucienbarriere.com. Glitzy casino with gaming tables, slot machines and a cabaret at weekends.

Nightclubs, pubs and bars

Aix-en-Provence

Le Mistral, 3 rue Frédéric Mistral; www.mistralclub.fr. House and techno club with a young clientèle.

Antibes–Juan-les-Pins

La Siesta, rte du Bord de Mer, Antibes; tel: 04 93 33 31 33, www.lasiesta.fr. Seafront complex with restaurant, bar, casino and club.

Le Sens, 10 rue Sade, Antibes; tel: 04 93 74 57 06. By day, a wine shop and by night, a fashionable wine bar.

Avignon

Le Bokao's, 9 bis boulevard du quai St-Lazare; tel: 04 90 82 47 95; www.bokaos.fr. Big trendy dance club.

Le Cid Café, 11 place de l'Horloge, tel: 04 90 82 30 38. Seventies-style café with DJs in the evening.

L'Esclave, 12 rue du Limas; tel: 04 90 85 14 91; www.lesclavebar.com. Predominantly gay bar and disco. Popular during the summer theatre festival.

Red Sky, 21-23 rue St-Jean-le-Vieux; tel: 04 90 85 93 23. Irish pub with draught Guinness.

Cannes

Le Bâoli, Port Canto, La Croisette; tel: 04 93 43 03 43; www.lebaoli.com. Glamorous all-night restaurant, sushi bar and discothèque in a tented Arabian Nights setting.

Gotha Club, Palm Beach, place Franklin Roosevelt; tel: 04 93 45 11 11; www.gotha-club.com. Hip new club attracting top DJs and stars.

Les Marches, Palais des Festivals, tel: 04 93 39 77 21. Chic new club with great views from the terrace bar.

Morrison's Pub, 10 rue Tesseire. Irish pub with live music and sport on big screens.

Le Night, 52 rue Jean-Jaurès; tel: 04 93 39 20 50. The top gay club in town.

Marseille

The New Cancan, 3 rue Sénac-de-Meilhan; tel: 04 91 48 59 76; www.newcancan.com. The most popular gay club in Marseille.

Le Trolleybus, 24 quai de Rive Neuve; tel: 04 91 54 30 45; www.letrolley.com. Huge club in old port buildings offering techno, salsa, jazz, rock, DJs and concerts.

Monaco

Black Legend, quai Albert Ier; tel: +377 93 30 09 09; www.black-legend.com. Seventies-style club specialising in 'black' music (soul, funk, disco etc).

La Rascasse, quai Antoine; tel: +377 93 25 56 90; www.larascasse montecarlo.com. All-night pub with

an outdoor terrace and a restaurant. Plays jazz and rock.

Le Sporting d'Eté, avenue Princesse Grace; tel: +377 92 16 22 77. Fashionable Euro-trash rendezvous, with restaurants, Jimmy'z nightclub, concerts and the Summer Casino. Open during summer season only.

The Living Room, 7 avenue des Spélugues; tel: +377 93 50 80 31; www.mcpam.com. Chic Latin club that attracts a sophisticated older crowd.

Zelo's, 10 avenue Princesse Grace; www.zelosworld.com. Ultra-hip bar and club in the Grimaldi Forum.

Nice

L'Abat-Jour, 25 rue Benoît Bunico. Fashionable bar with retro sofas, art exhibitions and DJ sets.

La Civette du Cours, 1 cours Saleya. The best place for people watching over an apéritif.

L'Effervescence, 10 rue de la Loge; tel: 04 93 80 87 37. Champagne bar.

Le Ghost, 3 rue de la Barillerie; tel: 04 93 92 93 37; www.leghost-pub.com. A cool Vieux Nice bar-club with good cocktails and thumping electro DJs.

Snug and Cellar, 22 rue Droite and 5 rue Rossetti; tel: 04 93 80 43 22; www.snugandcellar.com. English gastropub with a happy hour (8–10pm) and moreish cocktails.

Le Six, 6 rue Raoul Bosio. The city's most popular gay bar.

St-Tropez

Bleu, 33 rue Portail Neuf. New cocktail bar by the citadel.

Les Caves du Roy, Hôtel Byblos, avenue Paul Signac; tel: 04 94 56 68 00; www.byblos.com. Legendary jet-set club in Hôtel Byblos. Closed Nov–Mar.

L'Esquinade, 5 rue du Four; tel: 04 94 97 87 44. Gay-friendly club playing dance, techno, disco and world music.

Le Papagayo, Résidence du Port; tel: 04 94 97 95 95; www.papagayo-st-tropez.com. Opened in the 1960s and still the place for party people.

OUTDOOR ACTIVITIES

Provence offers a huge range of opportunities for sports enthusiasts, whether you're after a bucolic cycle ride or serious rock-climbing. Golf is very popular, as is tennis, and even fairly small villages often have tennis courts, though you may have to become a temporary member to use them. First port of call for finding out about facilities should be the *départemental* tourist board websites *(see page 321)* and local tourist offices, which can provide information on boat and bike hire facilities, tennis courts and horse-riding. Several UK travel firms offer holidays tailored to specific activities *(see page 321)*.

BELOW: canoe trip on the Gardon river under the Pont du Gard's arches.

Cycling

Cycling is a wonderful way to enjoy Provence *(see page 287 for advice on transporting your own bike)*. If you don't have a bike, you can rent cycles locally. You could consider a package cycling holiday, with accommodation booked in advance and your luggage transported for you. The Luberon and the Alpilles are particularly popular cycling areas, while the Mont Ventoux ascent is a famed Tour de France challenge. For the Vaucluse, www.provence-cycling.co.uk is an excellent English-language website providing information on itineraries, short breaks, cycle hire and bike-friendly hotels and restaurants.

The IGN (Institut Géographique National) 906 Cycling France map gives details of routes, clubs and places to stay. Information is also available from the Touring Department of the **Cyclists Touring Club** (tel: 0844 736 8450; www.ctc.org.uk). Its service to members includes competitive cycle and travel insurance and free detailed touring itineraries, whilst its tours brochure lists trips to the region, organised by members. The club's French counterpart is **Fédération Française de Cyclotourisme**, www.ffct.org; tel: 01 56 20 88 94.

Birdwatching

The Camargue is the main location in Provence for birdwatching and is well known for its flamingo colonies. The best places to see them and their friends is at the Parc Ornithologique du Pont de Gau, La Capelière and the Marais du Vigueirat. The tourist office in Les-Stes-Maries-de-la-Mer will have details of guided tours.

Diving

The Iles de Lérins, the Iles d'Hyères and the Calanques offer some of the best diving in the Mediterranean. Diving centres in Marseille, Cassis, Nice and Cannes offer diving courses and initiation sessions for beginners as well as trips for experienced divers.

Fishing

Here you have a choice of sea- or freshwater fishing. The season opens around the second Saturday in March. For freshwater fishing you will need to be affiliated to an association. For general information and addresses of local fishing associations contact local tourist offices.

Golf

Provence has many excellent golf courses, and the Mediterranean climate means golf can be played all year round. Most clubs offer lessons. First-rate 18-hole courses include: Royal Mougins Golf Club (tel: 04 92 92 49 69; www.royalmougins.fr) near Cannes; Golf Terre Blanche at the Four Seasons Resort Provence (tel: 04 94 39 90 00; www.terre-blanche.com), near Fayence, and the Monte-Carlo Golf Club (tel: 04 92 41 50 70) at La Turbie.

Hiking and Climbing

There is a vast network of signposted footpaths, including several long-distance footpaths *(sentiers de grande randonnée)*, as well as opportunities for rock-climbing, notably in the regional and national parks, such as the Parc du Mercantour, the Gorges de Verdon, the Calanques and the Luberon, and in the Massif des Maures and the Estérel ranges. Ensure you are suitably equipped with water, warm clothing, good boots and a map. There are also stretches of scenic coast path (*Sentier du Littoral* or *Sentier des Douaniers*). In high summer, footpaths in some of the massifs may be closed due to fire risk.

Some local tourist offices or ramblers' organisations put on guided walks of local sights, plants or wildlife; for example the Office National des Forêts organises walks in the Maures (information at the tourist office in Bormes-les-Mimosas), the Maison de Gorges de Verdon at La Palud-sur-Verdon organises walks in the Gorges de Verdon and the Nice branch of the Club Alpin Français (www.cafnice.org) organises walking, climbing and skiing trips in the Mercantour National Park. For specialised guides who can take you walking in the Mercantour contact the tourist office or Maison du Parc in Tende.

Maps/Walking Guides

The French Ramblers' Association (**Fédération Française de la Randonnée Pédestre**; FFRP; www.ffrandonee.fr) in Paris publishes **Topo-guides** (guide books in French incorporating IGN 1:50,000 scale maps) to France's footpaths, including guides to the *grandes-randonnées* and guides to different areas with walks of varying lengths and difficulties. These are available from map retailers (high-street stores or online) and from all good bookshops in the region.

IGN Blue series (*Série Bleue*) maps at a scale of 1:25,000 are ideal for walkers; IGN also publish maps of the national parks and produce walking maps on CD-ROM under the **IGN Rando** logo – the *Série Bleue* and the Top 25 are for walkers.

Horse-riding

Horse-riding and pony-trekking are popular activities in Provence, with *centres équestres* (equestrian centres) all over the region, in rural areas, the mountains, less inhabited parts of the coast, and especially in the Camargue.

Skiing

The Alpes-Maritimes are very popular for skiing, with several large resorts, such as Auron, Valberg and Isola 2000 in the Mercantour (www.stationsdumercantour.com) for downhill skiing (*see page 232*). Smaller Val Casterino and Le Boréon are more geared to cross-country skiing. They are only a few hours from the coast, and at certain times of the year you can combine the beach and skiing in one day. Other small stations include Gréolières-les-Neiges north of Grasse and Mont Serein on Mont Ventoux in the Vaucluse.

Watersports

Sailing and Windsurfing

Antibes and Cannes are major yachting centres, while Juan-les-Pins is said to have been the birthplace of water-skiing. If you're interested in yacht or speedboat hire, all the main marinas have yacht brokers and ships' chandlers. Many private beaches have a good range of equipment for hire, such as dinghies, catamarans, sea kayaks, and surfing and water-skiing equipment. There are dinghy sailing schools at Bormes-les-Mimosas, Mande-lieu-la Napoule and Menton; the Base Nautique (50 boulevard Franck Pilatte) near the Vieux Port in Nice is home to assorted rowing, sailing and diving clubs and schools. Noted windsurfing spots include Six-Fours-les-Plages, west of Toulon, and the Plage de l'Almanarre at Hyères.

Inland, you'll find sailing clubs and boat hire on several lakes, such as the Lac de St-Cassien, near Montouroux, and the Lac de St-Croix and Lac d'Esparron in the Gorges de Verdon.

Canoeing and Kayaking

Several companies, mainly based in Castellane, organise canoeing, canyoning and white-water rafting trips in the Gorges de Verdon. There is also gentler kayaking on the Sorgue River at Fontaine-de-Vaucluse and L'Isle-sur-la-Sorgue. Many beaches also hire out sea kayaks.

Spectator Sports

Equestrian Events

The major horse-racing venue is the Côte d'Azur Hippodrome at Cagnes-sur-Mer, where meetings are held during the day from December to May and in the evenings in July and August. There are also racetracks at Hyères (Hippodrome de la Plage, for flat racing, steeplechasing and trotting) and Marseille (Hippodrome Borély for flat racing and trotting). There are international show-jumping competitions in Cannes in May and Monaco in June, and an international polo event at St-Tropez in July.

Football and Rugby

Marseille (Olympique Marseille), Nice and Monaco all have premier division football teams, as does AC Arles-Avignon team, which plays in Avignon. Toulon rugby team is one of Europe's most successful.

Motor Sports

Motor racing's big social and sporting event is the **Monaco Grand Prix** in May, one of the most decisive contests in the Formula 1 championship, which takes place around the streets and tight bends of the principality; hotels and the best grandstand views are booked up months ahead. In January, the Monte-Carlo Car Rally, first staged in 1911, takes in the region's snowy mountains before finishing in Monte-Carlo. The Trophy Andros, car racing on ice, takes place in Isola 2000 in January.

Sailing and Windsurfing

Les Voiles d'Antibes in June starts off the classic yacht racing season, followed by the Régates Royales at Cannes in September. This coincides with the Cannes International Boat and Yacht Show and **Les Voiles de St-Tropez** (late September-early October), a spectacular gathering of vintage and modern sailing yachts. The

Plage de l'Almanarre near Hyères often hosts major windsurfing competitions.

Tennis

The Monte-Carlo Open men's tournament is held in April, with the Nice Tennis Open in May.

Wildlife

The Mercantour National Park is the place to go for wildlife, with more than 100 species of animal, some quite rare, including wolves. Contact the Maison du Parc in Barcelonnette, St-Etienne-de-Tinée, Valberg, St-Martin-Vésubie or Tende for details of tours.

SHOPPING

Shopping Areas

Over the years, many French towns have kept the town centre for small boutiques and individual shops. Large supermarkets, furniture stores and DIY outlets are often grouped on the outskirts of the town, mostly designated as a *centre commercial*. This laudable intent is somewhat marred by the horrendous design of some of these centres – groups of garish functional buildings that make the town's outskirts very unattractive. In the case of Nice, for example, there are vast hypermarkets

SPAS & THALASSOTHERAPY

More luxury hotels now have spas offering a variety of beauty treatments and massages. Historic spa towns offering the benefits of natural warm water springs include Aix-en-Provence, Digne-les-Bains and Gréoux-les-Bains. Along the coast, some resorts have thalassotherapy centres offering saltwater treatments, notably at L'Ile des Embiez, Bandol, Hyères, Fréjus, Antibes and Monaco. For information see www.france-thalasso.com.

beyond the airport to the west of town at St-Laurent-du-Var.

Centres commerciaux are fine for bulk shopping, self-catering or finding a selection of wine to take home at reasonable prices, but it is in the town centres that you will find the individual souvenirs that give a taste of the region.

What to Buy

Local crafts: There are countless opportunities to buy local crafts, although be aware that some of the garish 'Provençal' fabrics and mass-produced pottery may well have been imported. Among specialities to look out for are *santons* (clay Christmas crib figures in various sizes depicting typical Provençal villagers and pastimes – the baker, the shepherd, the fishwife, etc), pottery and faience (famous centres include Vallauris, Apt and Moustiers-Ste-Marie), printed fabrics and table linen, hand-woven baskets, soaps and toiletries, olive wood bowls and utensils. Some towns are linked with particular products, such as hand-blown glass from Biot, earthenware in Vallauris, leather goods and bullfighting costumes in Arles and the Camargue, and perfumes in Grasse.

Antiques and Collectables

Antiques can be another good buy in the south. The flea market at L'Isle-sur-la-Sorgue *(see page 98)* has the largest concentration of antiques dealers outside Paris. Also worth a look are the antiques district of Nice behind the Vieux-Port, the streets between the Préfecture and the Palais de Justice in Marseille, and the Quartier Mazarine and streets around place des Trois-Ormeaux in Aix-en-Provence. Monaco has upmarket antiquaires along boulevard des Moulins and branches of the international auction houses. Particularly southern articles are 'Beaucaire' mirrors carved with

grapes and vines, antique printed fabrics and quilts and faience from Apt, Marseille and Moustiers.

Books

Due to its sizeable Anglophone community, Provence has its fair share of English-language bookshops. In Aix-en-Provence, Book in Bar (4 rue Joseph Cabassol) also has a tearoom as does Cami-Li Books and Tea (155 rue de la Carreterie) in Avignon. In Marseille there's the Librairie Internationale Maurel (95 rue de Lodi). On the Riviera, there's Antibes Books (24 rue Aubernon), Castle Bookshop (1 rue St-Pierre) in Fayence, the English Bookcentre (12 rue Alexis Julien) in Valbonne and Cannes English Bookshop (11 rue Bivouac Napoléon). Most FNAC stores also have a section in English.

Fashion and Accessories

Aix-en-Provence, Avignon, Marseille, St-Tropez, Cannes, Nice and Monaco are all major fashion shopping destinations. In Marseille, head to the Centre Bourse on cours Belsunce for 'high street' shops while rue St-Ferréol has more upmarket boutiques. In Nice, you'll find everything from mainstream to designer to new-agey organic wear in Vieux Nice; the main shopping area is around rue de France and in Nice Etoile mall on avenue Jean Médecin. In Cannes, La Croisette and rue d'Antibes are where to find glitzy evening wear and jewellery. St-Tropez is the place for summer party wear – as well as the famous tropézienne sandals from Atelier Rondini and mens' swimming trunks at Villebrequin. There are branches of Galeries Lafayette department store in Avignon, Marseille, Toulon, Cannes, Nice and Menton.

Food and Wine

Foodie treats to take home include olive oil and jars of *tapenade*, dried

herbs and *saucisson sec*, mountain honey and sweets such as the *calissons* of Aix *(see page 49)*.

With wines varying from celebrated Châteauneuf-du-Pape and sweet Beaumes-de-Vénise to the pale pink rosés from Côtes de Provence, Provence offers numerous opportunities to buy direct from vineyards. Good sources of information for visiting wine producers, tastings and wine courses include: Maison des Vins des Côtes de Provence (Les Arcs; tel: 04 94 99 50 20), Maison des Vins de Châteauneuf-du-Pape (8 rue Maréchal Foch, Châteauneuf-du-Pape; tel: 04 90 83 70 69; www.vinadea.com), and Maison de la Truffe et du Vin in Ménerbes (tel: 04 90 72 38 37).

Toys

Museum shops tend to have an interesting selection of playthings for children, including dressing-up outfits of knights and princesses. Le Nain Rouge (47 rue Espariat) in Aix-en-Provence has old-fashioned wooden toys as does Les Minots de Marseille (26 place aux Huiles). Also in Marseille, the toys, costumes and puppets at Atelier Imago (5 rue St-Bruno) are made by a theatre designer. Les Féeries d'Emilie in Toulon (72bis cours Lafayette) and St-Maximin (8

SIZE CONVERSION CHART		
WOMEN		
France	**UK**	**US**
38	10	8
40	12	10
42	14	12
44	16	14
46	18	16
48	20	18
MEN		
France	**UK**	**US**
32	32	42
34	34	44
36	35	46
38	36	48
40	37	51
42	38	54

MARKET ETIQUETTE

In a market all goods by law have to be marked with the price. Prices are usually by the kilo or by the *pièce*, that is, each item priced individually. Usually the stallholder *(marchand)* will select the goods for you. Sometimes there is a serve-yourself system – observe what everyone else is doing to see whether this is the case or not. With some foods, you may be offered a taste to try first: *un goûter*.

ABOVE: the flower market on cours Saleya, Nice.

boulevard Jean-Jaurès) are a treasure trove of dolls and puppets, as is O Lutin in Nice (18 rue Barla). Nature et Découverte stores (Aix, Avignon, Marseille, Nice and Toulon) have a good selection of eco-friendly and outdoorsy toys.

Tax Refunds (Détaxes)

A refund (average 19.6 percent) of value-added tax (TVA) can be claimed by non-EU visitors if they spend over €175 on the same day in any one shop. The shop will supply a *détaxe* form, which you will need to have stamped by customs on leaving the country. Send a copy back to the shop, which will refund you by bank transfer or through your credit card. However, *détaxe* does not cover food, drink, antiques or works of art.

Markets

Virtually every town and village in Provence will have its open-air market, which is both a social rendezvous and the place where chefs stock up. In smaller towns and villages, the market will usually be one or two mornings a week, in larger towns there may be a daily morning market or covered market open morning and afternoon. Expect to find locally produced vegetables, fruit, herbs, goat cheese, dried sausages,

meat and poultry, fish, honey, olives and olive oil; you may also find household goods, kitchenware and clothing. Below are some of the best.

Alpes-de-Haute-Provence

Castellane: Wed, Sat
Colmars-les-Alpes: Tue
Digne-les-Bains: Wed, Sat
Forcalquier: Mon
Manosque: Sat
Moustiers-Ste-Marie: Fri
Sisteron: Wed, Sat

Alpes-Maritimes

Antibes: Tue–Sun; daily in summer
Cannes Marché Forville: Tue–Sun; daily in summer
Grasse: Tue–Sun
Menton Halles Municipales covered market: daily
Nice Cours Saleya: Tue–Sun
St-Etienne-de-Tinée: Fri
Sospel: Thur, Sun
Tende: Wed
Vallauris: Tue, Sun
Vence: Tue, Fri

Bouches-du-Rhône

Aix-en-Provence: main market daily; flower market Mon, Wed, Fri, Sat
Arles: Wed, Sat
Cassis: fish market daily; food and general market Wed, Fri
Fontvieille: Mon, Fri
La Ciotat: Tue, Sun
Marseille: Vieux Port fish market daily; avenue du Prado food and general market Mon–Sat.
St-Rémy-de-Provence: Wed, Sat

Stes-Maries-de-la-Mer: Mon, Fri
Salon-de-Provence: Wed, Fri
Tarascon: Tue

Gard

Aigues-Mortes: Sun
Nîmes Les Halles covered market: Tue–Sun

Monaco

Marché de la Condamine: daily

Var

Collobrières: Sun, Thu
Draguignan: Wed, Sat
Fayence: Tue, Thu, Sat
Hyères: Tue, Sat
La Londe-des-Maures: Sun
Le Lavandou: Thu
Salernes: Sun
St-Tropez: Tue, Sat
Ste-Maxime: covered market Tue–Sun; farmers' market Thu
Sanary-sur-Mer: Wed
Toulon Cours Lafayette: Tue–Sat

Vaucluse

Apt: Sat, farmers' market Tue
Avignon Les Halles covered market: Tue–Sun; produce and flea market Sat and Sun
Cadenet: Mon
Carpentras: Fri
Cavaillon: Mon
Châteauneuf-du-Pape: Fri
Coustellet farmers' market: Sun, except Jan–Feb, and Wed evening June–Aug
Cucuron: Tue
Roussillon: Wed
Vaison-la-Romaine: Tue; farmers' market Sat, plus Thu summer.

A – Z

A Handy Summary of Practical Information, Arranged Alphabetically

A dmission Charges

Entrance fees for museums and galleries generally fall between €4 and €8 per adult, with free admission for children – check on the qualifying age, since for some places it is under 18 and others under 12 or 7 years of age. Look out for special rates for students and over 60s. Municipal museums in Nice are free. National museums and monuments, including the Musée Chagall in Nice, Musée Léger in Biot and Musée Picasso in Vallauris are free to all European Union nationals aged under 26, although there may be a charge for temporary exhibitions.

Various passes, such as City Pass Marseille, Passion in Avignon, Pass Monuments in Arles, Pass

Sites Var, French Riviera Pass and the ticket Nîmes Romaine, provide discounts to museums and monuments, and sometimes reduced prices on guided tours and transport as well. Most tickets can be bought at the local tourist office or the museums themselves.

Age Restrictions

Minimum ages: consent 15, marriage 18, buying alcohol 16, drinking wine or beer in a bar 16, drinking spirits in a bar 18, driving 18, entering a casino 18.

B udgeting for your Trip

Expect to pay:
25cl (un demi) of draught lager €3.50; glass of house wine €4–7;

main course in a budget (€8–12), moderate (€15–25) and expensive (€30–50) restaurant, although there are often good-value fixed price menus, especially at lunch. Expect prices to be higher along the coast than in inland villages. Allow the following for a double room in a cheap (€60–80), moderate (€120–160) and deluxe hotel (€300+) in high season, not including breakfast. A taxi from Nice airport into the city centre will cost around €25 and a bus/metro/tram ticket will be about €1.50 or €5 for a day pass.

C hildren

Sightseeing with children is only likely to be difficult in steep hill villages with lots of steps, which

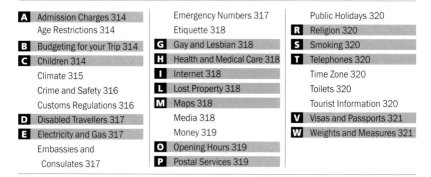

can be difficult to negotiate with a pushchair.

A wide range of activities can be found to suit children of all ages, from riding, cycling and river-bathing to exploring castles. Most towns and villages have swimming pools, tennis courts and playgrounds.

The beach and the sea are the easiest way to amuse children, and private beach concessions with sun-loungers and parasols are the easiest of all. Inflatables are often provided, and there are sometimes also bouncy castles.

Many seaside resorts have children's clubs on the beach, where, for a fee, children can be left under supervision for a few hours to take part in organised sports and fun events. At some resorts you'll be able to find swimming lessons and sailing courses (usually in Optimists).

Circuses often tour the seaside resorts in summer, while the Cirque Alexis Gruss takes up summer quarters at Piolenc, north of Orange. Look out also for summer fireworks festivals in Cannes and Monaco.

When hiring a car, be sure to book any baby seats in advance, although larger hire companies do usually have a few ready to go.

Hotels and Restaurants

Most hotels have family rooms (chambre triple ou quadruple) or can often add an extra bed (lit supplémentaire) in a double room so that children do not have to be separated from their parents. A cot (lit bébé) can also often be provided, sometimes for a small supplement, although it is a good idea to check this in advance. Most upmarket hotels and villa companies can arrange babysitting.

Eating out is easy, especially during the day, as going out for a meal is a quintessential part of French culture and all but the poshest restaurants welcome young children. Many restaurants offer a children's menu, will split a prix-fixe menu between two children, or even give you an extra plate to share your own meal.

Shopping

French shops are well provided with all child necessities. Disposable nappies (couches jettable) are easy to find, and French baby food is often of gourmet standard, though watch out for added sugar.

Children's Attractions

Museums and Monuments

The Egyptian collections and African sculptures at the Vieille Charité in Marseille, Matisse's colourful paintings and cut-outs at the Musée Matisse in Nice, the Musée d'Art Moderne et Contemporain in Nice, the medieval siege instruments at the Château des Baux in Les Baux-de-Provence,

BELOW: summer fun on L'Isle-sur-la-Sorgue.

the Arènes (Roman amphitheatre) in Nîmes, the Musée de la Préhistoire at Quinson in the Gorges de Verdon, the Musée International de la Parfumerie in Grasse and the Collection de Voitures Anciennes (vintage cars) in Monaco all have plenty to interest children.

Zoos, Parks and Aquariums

Child-friendly zoos and nature parks include the Musée Océanographique in Monaco, Zoo de la Barben near Salon-de-Provence, and the Zoo de Mont Boron (plus the ride up in the téléferique) at Toulon. There are children's trails at the Marais de Vigueirat nature reserve in Camargue and the Parc Floral Phoenix in Nice, but the most popular attraction is likely to be the Marineland complex just east of Antibes, with its whale and dolphin displays, and adjoining water fun park, crazy golf and wild west park.

Boat Trips

Enjoyable boat trips include the Ile Ste-Marguerite from Cannes, Ile de Porquerolles and Port-Cros from the Presqu'île de Giens, Hyères and Le Lavandou to the Iles de Frioul and Calanques from Marseille and Cassis, around the port de Toulon. Several companies also offer marine viewing trips in glass-bottomed boats.

Climate

Provence and its Côte d'Azur are renowned for their sunshine. Each year there are typically more than 300 sunny days and less than 850mm (33.5ins) of rain. When it does rain, however, it pours. Average temperatures range from 48°F (8°C) in winter to 84°F (26°C) in summer – however, maximum temperatures in summer can easily reach the high 30°Cs, so it is advisable to keep in the shade between noon and 3pm. If walking outside during the hottest hours, wear a hat and carry plenty of drinking water, and apply sunscreen regularly. Winters are usually mild and sunny, and summers are typically hot

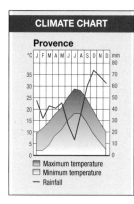

CLIMATE CHART

Provence

◼ Maximum temperature
◻ Minimum temperature
— Rainfall

and dry. Inland, the plains around Carpentras and Aix-en-Provence have a more continental climate, which means that summers can be stiflingly hot, but be prepared for the drop in temperature in high mountain areas such as Mont Ventoux and the Mercantour.

Climate varies between the high country and low country. However, the whole region experiences the sporadic virulence of the legendary northwest wind, the mistral, from late autumn to early spring. There have also been violent storms in the area in recent years, causing major floods and damage.

When to Visit

The tourist season starts around Easter and continues to the end of October. Many restaurants and hotels close at the end of the season, especially along the coast. During the peak period from 15 July to the end of August reservations are essential. Other popular times to come are during Nice Carnaval and Menton lemon festival in February and the Monaco Grand Prix in May. Always reserve in advance if you're visiting the ski resorts in winter, especially at weekends and during French school holidays.

What to Wear

The clothing you bring depends on your destination and when you travel; you will only need to dress

up for chic restaurants in the cities or casinos. Bring plenty of light clothing in summer but dress appropriately for visiting churches and synagogues; a scarf or shirt are always useful cover-ups. Try not to wander around the streets in swimwear – in Monaco it is formally forbidden. Even in summer, a sweater, wrap or light jacket is useful for cooler evenings, and a waterproof coat or jacket will be needed from October to April. Comfortable shoes are advisable for sightseeing.

Weather Information

For weather information visit www. meteofrance.com

Temperatures are always given in Celsius (centigrade). To convert to Fahrenheit, see below:

0°C = 2°F	20°C = 68°F
10°C = 50°F	25°C = 77°F
15°C = 59°F	30°C = 86°F

Crime and Safety

Incidents of violent crime against visitors are rare, but you should apply the usual precautions when wandering about late at night. Try not to carry large amounts of cash, never leave valuables in your car, and be on the lookout for pickpockets, especially in crowds. In Nice and Marseille, be aware there have been incidents of bags

BELOW: the beach at Cannes.

and watches snatched through open car windows when waiting at traffic lights. Any loss or theft should be reported immediately to the nearest *commissariat de police* in main towns and *gendarmerie* in rural areas.

Customs Regulations

You may take any quantity of goods into France from another EU country as long as they are for personal use and you can prove that tax has been paid on them in the country of origin. Customs officials still have the right to question visitors.

Quantities accepted as being for personal use are as follows:
• 800 cigarettes, 400 small cigars, 200 cigars or 1 kg of loose tobacco.
• 10 litres of spirits (more than 22 percent alcohol), 90 litres of wine (under 22 percent alcohol) or 110 litres of beer.

For goods brought in from outside the EU, the recommended quantities are:
• 200 cigarettes or 100 small cigars, 50 cigars or 250 g of loose tobacco.
• 1 litre of spirits (over 22 percent alcohol) and 2 litres of wine and beer (under 22 percent alcohol).
• 50 g of perfume.

Visitors may also carry up to

€10,000 in currency.
If you go to the very popular Friday street market in Ventimiglia just across the border in Italy, be careful about buying counterfeit goods. Customs checks are frequent at the Menton border post and you could be prosecuted.

D isabled Travellers

Disabled access is often difficult in historic buildings or the stepped streets of old hill towns, but many of the south's recently renovated museums do have wheelchair access. All hotels built since 1978 should have at least one specially adapted bedroom, while public buildings, such as town halls, museums and hospitals built since 1978 should also be accessible, though it's always wise to check beforehand exactly what is meant by this. The Association des Paralysés de France (www.apf.asso.fr) publishes an annual *Guide Vacances*. A new label Tourisme & Handicap (www.tourisme-handicaps.org) is gradually being introduced to indicate tourist facilities accessible for physically, visually, aurally or mentally handicapped travellers, with information about labelled hotels, gîtes, campsites, restaurants, tourist sights and local transport on the different *départemental* websites *(see tourist information, page 321)*. There is also wheelchair access to some beaches – designated *handiplages*.

Disabled parking places are widespread and are indicated with a wheelchair sign. The international blue disabled parking disc scheme is recognised in France. To hire a wheelchair or other equipment enquire at the local pharmacy.

For further information in the UK contact: Tourism for All UK, tel: 0845 124 9971; www.tourismforall.org.uk. In the US contact sath, tel: (212) 447 7284; www.sath.org

Transport

Eurotunnel (UK tel: 08443 35 35

EMERGENCY NUMBERS

The following services operate 24 hours daily:
Police: 17
Fire (Sapeurs-Pompiers): 18
Ambulance (samu): 15
European Emergency
Number: 112

Other Useful Numbers
SOS Médecins: 3624 Medical assistance.
SOS Helpline: 01 46 21 46 46 (3–11pm) in English

35; France tel: 0810 63 03 04) – the Channel Tunnel car-on-a-train service – allows disabled passengers to stay in their vehicle. Eurostar trains (tel: 08432 186 186; www.eurostar.com) give special-rate wheelchair-user fares and a reduced rate for one travelling companion.

Most ferry companies offer facilities for disabled travellers if they are contacted in advance.

For rail travel, the SNCF runs the Service Accès Plus (tel: 0890 640 650, then press 1; www.accessplus.sncf.com, or with reservations on www.voyages-sncf.fr) to help disabled voyagers. For help boarding the train, reservations should be made at least 48 hours in advance. *Le Guide du Voyageur à Mobilité Réduite SNCF* is available free in train stations. Reduced tolls are charged on *autoroutes* for vehicles fitted to accommodate disabled people.

E lectricity and Gas

220-volt, 50-cycle AC is universal, generally with a three-pin plug. British visitors should buy an adaptor (*adaptateur*); American visitors will need a transformer (*transformateur*).

In many rural areas butane gas is used for cooking and heating water. Campers and caravanners needing replacement gas canisters will find them on sale at local shops, garages and supermarkets (return the empty one).

Embassies and Consulates

Australia: (Embassy) 4 rue Jean-Rey, 75015 Paris; tel: 01 40 50 33 00; www.france.embassy.gov.au
Canada: (Consulate) 35 avenue Montaigne, 75008 Paris; tel: 01 44 43 29 02; www.international.gc.ca
Ireland: (Embassy) 12 avenue Foch, 75116 Paris; tel: 01 44 17 67 00; www.embassyofirelandparis.com
New Zealand: (Embassy) 7er rue Léonard da Vinci, 75116 Paris; tel: 01 45 01 43 41; www.nzembassy.com/france
South Africa: (Embassy) 53 quai d'Orsay, 75343 Paris Cédex 7; tel: 01 53 59 23 23; www.afriquesud.net
UK: (Consulate) 24 avenue du Prado, 13006 Marseille; tel: 04 91 15 72 10; http://ukinfrance.free.gov.uk
US: (Consulate) 7 avenue Gustave V, 06000 Nice; tel: 04 93 88 89 55; http://france.usembassy.gov/consulara.html
Place Varian Fry, 13006 Marseille; tel: 04 91 54 92 00; www.amb-usa.fr/marseille
7 avenue Gustave V, 06000 Nice; tel: 04 93 88 89 55; www.amb-usa.fr/marseille/nice

French Embassies Abroad

Australia: 6 Perth Avenue; Yarralumla ACT 2600, Canberra; tel: 02 6216 0100; www.ambafrance-au.org
Canada: 42 promenade Sussex, Ottawa; tel: 613 789 1795; www.ambafrance-ca.org
Ireland: 36 Ailesbury Road, Ballsbridge, Dublin 4; tel: 01 277 50 00; www.ambafrance-ie.org
New Zealand: Sovereign House, 34-42 Manners Street, Wellington 6142; tel: 04 384 25 55; www.ambafrance-nz.org
South Africa: 250 Melk Street, New Meuckleneuk, 0181 Pretoria; tel: 012 425 1600; www.ambafrance-rsa.org
UK: 58 Knightsbridge, London, SW1X 7JT; tel: 0207 073 1000; www.ambafrance-uk.org
US: 4101 Reservoir Road NW,

Washington DC 20007; tel: 202 944 6000; www.ambafrance-us.org

Etiquette

Madame/Mademoiselle and Monsieur are widely used in French. Unless you know someone well or are talking to children, use the formal *vous* rather than *tu* form. It is polite to shake hands when meeting someone. Don't kiss cheeks with someone you don't know, unless they propose to *"donne la bise"* – a polite peck on either side. Note that topless bathing has gone totally out of fashion. See also What to Wear, under Climate.

G ay & Lesbian Travellers

France is generally gay tolerant, although gay bars and clubs are mainly restricted to the larger towns, such as Nice, Cannes, Avignon, Toulon and Marseille. Coco Beach east of Nice's Vieux Port is a popular gay beach, and there are lively Gay Pride parades in July in Nice and Marseille. The brochures *Nice Practical Guide* and *www. Cannes*, published by the respective tourist offices, list gay and gay-friendly bars and hotels. See also www.gay-provence.com for details of gay-friendly accommodation.

H ealth & Medical Care

French healthcare is of a high standard and the Côte d'Azur has the highest concentration of specialist doctors in France outside Paris. There are no compulsory vaccinations or particular health risks. Tap water is safe to drink, unless marked *eau non potable*. However you should be careful to avoid sunburn: wear sunhats and avoid exposure to the powerful midday sun. Other potential hazards are mosquitoes at night and, some years, invasions of jellyfish (*méduses*) in the sea, usually indicated at the entrance to beaches.

EU nationals staying in France are entitled to use the French social security system, which refunds up to 70 percent of medi-cal expenses. British residents should obtain a European Health Insurance Card before leaving the UK. These are available online at www.ehic.org.uk. This is not a substitute for insurance though, and does not cover repatriation in case of an accident. If you're ill, your hotel can probably recommend an English-speaking doctor or dentist; make sure it is a *médecin conventionné* (affiliated to the social security system). The main cities have hospitals with 24-hour casualty departments (*Urgences*). Consultations and prescriptions have to be paid for in France and are reimbursed, in part, on receipt of a completed *fiche* (form).The doctor will give you a prescription and a *feuille de soins* (statement of treatment), allowing you to claim back part of the cost when you return home.

Nationals of non-EU countries should take out travel and medical insurance before leaving home.

Pharmacies

Pharmacies in France are good but expensive. The staff are well qualified and should be able to advise on many minor ailments. All pharmacies can be identified by a neon green cross. Most open from 9 or 10am until 7 or 8pm Monday to Saturday.

If the pharmacy is closed there will be a sign – or the police station should be able to provide information – giving details of a *pharmacie de garde*, which will offer a night-time or Sunday service. All-night pharmacies can be found in Nice at 7 rue Masséna and 66 avenue Jean Médecin.

I nternet

Most hotels now have internet access. Wi-Fi is widespread and often, though not always, free (check at reception), otherwise hotels may have a computer in the lobby with internet access for use of guests. Wi-Fi hotspots can also often be found at airports, train stations and some cafés and brasseries. Tourist offices should be able to supply addresses of internet cafés.

L ost Property

To report a crime or loss of belongings, go to the local police station (*gendarmerie* or *commissariat de police*). Telephone numbers can be found at the front of local telephone directories. If you lose your passport, you should report it firstly to the police and then to your consulate or embassy. The SNCF (French railways) has its own lost property system.

M aps

Hotels and tourist offices can usually supply a town street map (*un plan*). For driving, a 1:200,000 or 1:250,000 scale road atlas or sheet map (*carte routière*) of Provence Côte d'Azur is useful. If you're planning to do any serious hiking, buy 1:25,000 scale maps published by IGN.

Stockists of French maps in the UK include Stanfords (www.stanfords.co.uk), which has stores London and Bristol. Online, try www.mapkiosk.com or www.amazon.co.uk

Media

Newspapers and Magazines

The French press is very regional. Popular papers in the south include *Nice-Matin*, *La Provence*, *Var-Matin*, *Le Dauphiné Vaucluse* and *La Marseillaise*, though for more weighty news you'll need to look at the national dailies *Le Monde*, *Le Figaro* and *Libération*. Foreign newspapers are widely available in the main cities and resorts. The local English-language magazine *Riviera Reporter* (www.rivierareporter.com) and newspaper *Riviera Times* (www.rivieratimes.com) are good for regional information and local politics.

Television

France has six terrestrial TV channels (TF1, France 2, France 3,

Above: Le Café de Paris, Monaco.

Arte, M6 and the subscription channel Canal+). Most hotels will also have cable, satellite or TNT channels, which often include some foreign channels, such as CNN and BBC World.

Radio

The following is just a selection of what is available (wavelengths are given in MHz):
87.8 France Inter. A state-run, middle-of-the-road channel offering music and international news.
91.7–92.1 France Musique. Another state-run channel, offering classical music and jazz.
93.5–93.9 France Culture. High-brow state culture station.
BFM. Business and economics news. Aix-en-Provence 93.8, Cannes and Nice 104.4, Hyères 87.9, Marseille 93.8.
93.4 Radio FG FM. Gay station with music and lonely hearts: www.radiofg.com
RTL. A popular mix of music and chat. Avignon 107.2, Cannes and Nice 97.4, Marseille 101.4.
Europe 1. News, press reviews and sports. Avignon 94.6, Cannes and Nice 101.4, Marseille 104.8.
105.5 France Info. Tune in for 24-hour news, economic updates and sports news.
106.5 Riviera Radio. English-language radio with a mix of music and chat.
107.7 Radio Trafic. Gives regular traffic bulletins in English.

BBC World Service. This can be received in France on FM between 88.4 and 106.5.

Money

Currency

France is part of the euro (€) zone. Banknotes are available in denominations of 500, 200, 100, 50, 20, 10 and 5 euros; avoid the largest denominations as many shops will not accept €200 and €500 notes. There are coins for 2 and 1 euros and for 50, 20, 10, 5, 2 and 1 cent. ATMs are the simplest, and usually cheapest, way of obtaining cash in euros. They are plentiful in large cities, though may be scarce in rural areas. Travellers' cheques are rarely used in France.

Credit cards (cartes de crédit)

Credit cards are widely accepted, especially Visa and Mastercard. There may be a minimum sum (often €15).
For lost and stolen credit cards: Groupement des Cartes Bancaires tel: 0892 70 57 05; American Express tel: 01 47 77 72 00; Diners Club tel: +32 (0)2 540 8760; Mastercard tel: 0800 90 1387; Visa tel: 0800 90 1179.

Tipping

A 10–15 percent service charge is included in hotel and restaurant bills, so any further tip is optional, although you may want to round off bills with a few coins. Taxis also include service charges but it is common to round up to the nearest 5 or 10. It is also the done thing to hand hotel porters, tour guides, etc, a euro or two for their services.

pening Hours

Shops generally open Mon–Sat 9.30 or 10am to 7pm; small shops often take a long lunch break, closing at noon and re-opening at 3 or 4pm. Bakeries generally open 8am–8pm and may open on Sunday, closing one other day a week; some supermarkets remain open until 9 or 10pm.
Restaurants usually serve noon–2 or 2.30pm, 7.30 or 8pm–9.30 or 10pm, and may close one or two days a week; cafés and brasseries often open from early morning until late.
Banks generally open Mon–Fri 9am–noon, 2–5pm; some open Saturday morning and close on Monday.
Museums usually open 10am–5 or 6pm (sometimes later in summer) and often close on either Monday or Tuesday; smaller museums often close for lunch.

P ostal Services

Post offices (www.laposte.fr) open Mon–Fri 9am–noon and 2–6pm, Sat 9am–noon. In large towns they may not close for lunch, but in small villages they may only open in the morning.
In larger post offices, each counter has specific services, so check you are in the right queue (look for 'Timbres' if you only want stamps) or use one of the self-service machines. You can also buy stamps at tobacconists (bureaux de tabac) and some shops selling postcards. Letter boxes are yellow. You should use Monaco stamps to send letters from Monaco.
Urgent post can be sent par exprès. The Chronopost system is also fast but is expensive.

TRANSPORT

ACCOMMODATION

ACTIVITIES

A – Z

LANGUAGE

Poste Restante

Mail should be addressed to you at: Poste Restante, Poste Centrale (for the main post office) plus the town postcode and name. There's a small fee and you will need to show your passport to collect your post.

Public Holidays

Banks, post offices, offices and many museums and shops close on public holidays (jours fériés); public transport often runs on Sunday schedules. If a public holiday falls on a Thursday or Tuesday it is common for French businesses to faire le pont ('bridge the gap') and take the Friday or Monday as a holiday as well.

The most strongly respected jours fériés are l January, 1 May, 14 July, 15 August and 25 December. While the shops may be shut, there will often be a fête on 14 July and 15 August. Foreign embassies and consulates observe French public holidays as well as their own.

1 January Nouvel An
New Year's Day
March/April Lundi de Pâques
Easter Monday
1 May Fête du Travail
Labour Day
8 May Fête de la Victoire 1945
VE Day
May Ascension
May/June Lundi de Pentecôte
Whit Monday
14 July Fête Nationale/le Quatorze juillet Bastille Day
15 August Assomption
(Assumption)
1 November Toussaint (All Saints' Day)
11 November Fête de l'Armistice (Armistice Day)
25 December Noël (Christmas)

R eligion

The French Republic is officially a lay state and does not have an established religion. However, the church calendar determines most of the public holidays and the majority of the population is nomi-

nally Roman Catholic, with substantial minority Protestant, Muslim and Jewish communities. Non-Catholic services are called cultes; Protestant churches are known as temples. Roman Catholicism is the established religion in Monaco.

There are Anglican churches with regular services in English in Nice, Cannes, Menton, Monaco and Vence.

S moking

Smoking is prohibited in all state-owned buildings and public places, including public transport, and in restaurants, bars, cafés, discothèques and casinos, except in specially ventilated sealed-off fumoirs or outside on café terraces. Smoking is banned in the public areas of hotels, but not in hotel bedrooms unless they are designated non-smoking rooms.

T elephones

French phone numbers are all 10 figures including two-digit regional prefixes as follows: numbers in southeast France all start with 04 (when dialling from outside France, omit the initial zero). They are always written and spoken in two-digit numbers (eg 01 25 25 25 25). Mobile phone numbers start 06 and 07. 08 numbers have special rates varying from 0800 freephone numbers to premium rates such as 0836. Directory enquiries are available from various providers, including 118000, 118007, 118008 and 118218.

Public Phones

Many public telephones only accept télécartes (phone cards), available from post offices and tobacconists. A surcharge will

France is always one hour ahead of the UK (ie Greenwich Mean Time +1 in winter, and GMT+2 in summer).

TOILETS

Anyone may use the toilet in a bar or café, whether they are a customer or not, unless there is a sign specifying that this is not allowed, but it is polite to at least order a coffee at the bar. (Ask for les toilettes or le WC, which is pronounced 'vay-say').

usually be added for calls made from your hotel room.

Mobile Phones

Check with your network provider that your phone will work in France (UK phones do). If so, check that your phone is set up for international roaming and buy bundles of minutes to use in Europe to keep costs down. For longer stays you can buy a French SIM card for your own phone or a pay-as-you-go (sans abonnement) mobile phone from Orange (www.orange.fr), SFR (www.sfr.fr) or Bouygues Telecom (www.bouyguestelecom.fr), all of whom have shops on the high street.

International Calls

When dialling France from abroad, dial the French country code 00 33 and omit the 0 at the start of the 10-digit number. To dial overseas from France, dial 00, followed by the country code (Australia: 61; Ireland: 353; New Zealand: 64; South Africa: 27; UK: 44; Canada & US: 1; Monaco: 377) and then the number, usually omitting the initial zero. International directory enquiries: 3212.

Tourist Information

Every town and city, and almost every small village, has its own office de tourisme, sometimes also referred to as the maison (or bureau) de tourisme. These are usually located on or near the main square, and sometimes also at main stations. In smaller villages, where the tourist office is only open for limited hours, it may be called the syndicat d'initiative,

TRANSPORT
ACCOMMODATION
ACTIVITIES
A–Z
LANGUAGE

often located at the *mairie* (town hall). Tourist offices can usually supply good town plans and local maps, as well as information about restaurants, accommodation, sights, festivals and events, guided tours and sporting facilities. Tourist office staff should be able to give you impartial advice or point you to the piles of free advertising leaflets, which are left by hotels, shops, museums and the like. Some bigger tourist offices, such as Aix and Nice, offer efficient hotel booking services if you arrive without accommodation, and ticket booking services.

Before you travel, you may want to get hold of information from the Maison de France in your country (see www.franceguide.com for addresses). See also the useful bilingual tourist board websites for the Alpes-de-Haute-Provence (www.alpes-haute-provence.com), Alpes-Maritimes (www.cotedazur-tourisme.com), the Bouches-du-Rhône (www.visitprovence.com), Var (www.visitvar.fr), Vaucluse (www.provenceguide.com) and PACA regional tourist board (www.tourismepaca.fr).

ABOVE: antiques for sale on L'Isle-sur-la-Sorgue.

Principal tourist offices

Aix-en-Provence 300 avenue Giuseppe Verdi; tel: 04 42 16 11 61; www.aixenprovencetourism.com
Antibes 11 place du Charles de Gaulle; tel: 04 97 23 11 11; www.antibes-juanlespins.com
Arles esplanade Charles de Gaulle, boulevard des Lices; tel: 04 90 18 41 20; www.arlestourisme.com
Avignon 41 cours Jean Jaurès; tel: 04 32 74 32 74; www.avignon-tourisme.com
Cannes Palais des Festivals, La Croisette; tel: 04 92 99 84 22; www.cannes-destination.fr
Grasse place de la Buanderie; tel: 04 93 36 66 66; www.grasse.fr
Marseille 4 La Canebière; tel: 0826 500 500; www.marseille-tourisme.com
Menton Palais de l'Europe, 8 avenue Boyer; tel: 04 92 41 76 76; www.tourisme-menton.fr
Monaco 2a boulevard des

Moulins, Monte Carlo; tel: +377-92 16 61 16; www.visitmonaco.com
Nice 5 promenade des Anglais, tel: 08 92 70 74 07; www.nicetourisme.com; branches at Nice train station (avenue Thiers) and Aéroport Nice Côte d'Azur (T1).
Nîmes 6 rue Auguste; tel: 04 66 58 38 00; www.ot-nimes.fr
St-Tropez quai Jean Jaurès; tel: 08 92 68 48 28; www.ot-saint-tropez.com
Toulon 12 place Louis Blanc, Bas Cours Lafayette; tel: 04 94 18 53 00; www.toulontourisme.com
Vence 8 place du Grand Jardin; tel: 04 93 58 06 38; www.ville-vence.fr

Tour Operators
The following organise holidays to Provence.
The Barge Company, tel: +33 561 59 20 07; www.bargecompany.com. Luxury barging holidays in the Camargue.
British Airways Holidays, www.britishairways.com. Short breaks and fly-drive to Nice and Marseille.
Cresta, tel: 0844 800 7019; www.crestaholidays.co.uk. Short breaks and holidays by plane or train.
French Travel Service, tel: 0844 84 888 43; www.f-t-s.co.uk. Short breaks and holidays by train.
Francophiles, tel: 01603 418849; www.travelensemble.co.uk. Escorted coach holidays.
Great Rail, tel: 01904 521936; www.greatrail.com. Tours by train.

Kirker, tel: 0207 593 1899; www.kirkerholidays.com. Tailor-made short breaks and cultural tours.
Noble Caledonia, tel: 0207 752 0000; www.noble-caledonia.co.uk. Luxury cruises on the Rhône.
Real Provence, tel: 01491 413660; www.real-provence.com. Self-guided tours.
Riviera Travel, tel: 01283 742300; www.rivieratravel.co.uk. Escorted tours by train.
Siblu, tel: 0871 911 2288; www.siblu.com. Family-friendly mobile home holidays in Fréjus.

Visas and Passports
European Union visitors do not need a visa to enter France, but should have a valid passport or identity card. Citizens of the US, Canada, Australia or New Zealand and certain other countries only need a visa for stays of more than three months. Check with the French consulate in your country.

Non-European Union nationals who intend to stay in France for more than 90 days should apply for a *carte de séjour* (or *titre de séjour*).

Weights and Measures
The metric system is used in France for all weights and measures. For a handy reckoning, bear in mind 80km equals 50 miles, 1kg is about 2lbs, and 50cl about 1 pint.

L ANGUAGE

KEY FRENCH WORDS AND PHRASES

Greetings

hello *bonjour* ('allo' on phone)
goodbye *au revoir*
good evening *bonsoir*

Useful Words and Phrases

yes/no *oui/non*
OK *d'accord*
I'm sorry *Excusez-moi/Pardon*
please *s'il vous/te plaît*
thank you (very much) *merci (beaucoup)*
excuse me *excusez-moi*
here/**there** *ici/là*
big/small *grand(e)/petit(e)*
good/bad *bon(ne)/mauvais(e)*
today *aujourd'hui*
yesterday *hier*
tomorrow *demain*
this morning *ce matin*
this afternoon *cet après-midi*
this evening *ce soir*
What is your name? *Comment vous appelez-vous?*
My name is... *Je m'appelle…*
Do you speak English? *Parlez-vous anglais?*
I am English/American *Je suis anglais(e)/américain(e)*
I don't understand *Je ne comprends pas*
Please speak more slowly *Parlez plus lentement, s'il vous plaît*
Can you help me? *Pouvez-vous m'aider?*
I'm looking for… *Je cherche…*

Where is…? *Où est…?*
I don't know *Je ne sais pas*

At the Hotel

I'd like a (single/double) room…
Je voudrais une chambre (simple/double)…
….with shower *avec douche*
….with a bath *avec bain*
Does that include breakfast?
Est-ce que le petit déjeuner est compris?
washbasin *le lavabo*
key *la cléf*
elevator *l'ascenseur*
air-conditioned *climatisé*
swimming pool *une piscine*

On the Road

Where is the nearest garage?
Où est le garage le plus proche?
Our car has broken down
Notre voiture est en panne
I want to have my car repaired
Je veux faire réparer ma voiture
left/right *gauche/droite*
straight on *tout droit*
roundabout *rond-point*
far/near *loin/près d'ici*
on foot *à pied*
by car *en voiture*
road map *la carte*
street *la rue*
give way *céder le passage*
motorway *l'autoroute*

toll *péage*
speed limit *la limitation de vitesse*
petrol *l'essence*
unleaded *sans plomb*
diesel *le gasoil*
water/oil *l'eau/l'huile*
puncture *un pneu crevé*

Shopping

Where is the nearest bank/post office? *Où est la banque/Poste la plus proche?*
I'd like to buy/try on... *Je voudrais acheter/essayer…*
How much is it? *C'est combien?*
Do you take credit cards?
Prenez-vous les cartes de crédit?
Have you got…? *Avez-vous…?*
cheap *bon marché*
expensive *cher*
a piece of *un morceau de*
each *la pièce* (eg ananas, 0.5 la pièce)
bill/receipt *la note/le reçu*

Travelling

airport *l'aéroport*
train station *la gare (SNCF)*
bus station *la gare routière*
Métro stop *la station de Métro*
bus/coach *l'autobus/le car*
bus stop *l'arrêt*
platform *le quai*
ticket *le billet*
return ticket *aller-retour*
toilets *les toilettes/les WC*

NUMBERS

0 *zéro*	11 *onze*	30 *trente*
1 *un, une*	12 *douze*	40 *quarante*
2 *deux*	13 *treize*	50 *cinquante*
3 *trois*	14 *quatorze*	60 *soixante*
4 *quatre*	15 *quinze*	70 *soixante-dix*
5 *cinq*	16 *seize*	80 *quatre-vingts*
6 *six*	17 *dix-sept*	90 *quatre-vingt-dix*
7 *sept*	18 *dix-huit*	100 *cent*
8 *huit*	19 *dix-neuf*	1000 *mille*
9 *neuf*	20 *vingt*	1,000,000
10 *dix*	21 *vingt-et-un*	*un million*

I want to get off at…
Je voudrais descendre à…
Is there a bus to…?
Est-ce qui'il y a un bus pour …?
Which line do I take for…? *Quelle
ligne dois-je prendre pour…?*
Validate your ticket
Compostez votre billet

Eating Out

Prix fixe or **menu** are fixed-price
menus. **A la carte** means indivi-
ual dishes from the menu are
charged separately.
breakfast *le petit déjeuner*
lunch *le déjeuner*
dinner *le dîner*
meal *le repas*
first course *l'entrée*
main course *le plat*
drink included *boisson compris*
wine list *la carte des vins*
the bill *l'addition*
plate *l'assiette*
glass *le verre*

Basics

beurre **butter**
confiture **jam**
crêpe **pancake**
croque-monsieur **ham-and-
cheese toasted sandwich**
croque-madame **ham-and-
cheese toasted sandwich with
a fried egg on top**
fromage **cheese**
fromage de chèvre **goat's cheese**
galette **savoury pancake**
oeuf **egg**
oeuf à la coque **boiled egg**
oeuf sur le plat **fried egg**
oeufs brouillés **scrambled eggs**
pain **bread**

poivre **pepper**
sel **salt**
sucre **sugar**

L'Entrée (Starters)

anchoïade **sauce of olive oil,
anchovies and garlic, served
with raw vegetables**
rillettes **rich fatty paste of shred-
ded duck, rabbit or pork**
soupe/potage/velouté **soup**
tapenade **olive and anchovy
paste**

Viande (Meat)

bleu **extremely rare**
saignant **rare**
à point **medium**
bien cuit **well done**
agneau **lamb**
blanquette **stew of veal or lamb
with a creamy egg sauce**
…à la bordelaise **with red wine
and shallots**
…à la bourguignonne **cooked in
red wine, onions and mushrooms**
boeuf en daube **Provençal beef
stew with red wine, onions and
tomatoes**
brochette **kebab**
canard **duck**
carré d'agneau **rack of lamb**
cassoulet **stew with beans, sausages, pork and duck, from
southwest France**
cervelle **brains**
confit **duck or goose preserved
in its own fat**
coq au vin **chicken in red wine**
côte d'agneau **lamb chop**
dinde **turkey**
entrecôte **beef rib steak**
escargot **snail**

faisan **pheasant**
faux-filet **sirloin**
foie **liver**
foie gras **fattened goose/duck
liver**
gardiane de boeuf **rich beef stew
with olives and garlic**
cuisses de grenouille **frog's legs**
gibier **game**
grillade **grilled meat**
hachis **minced meat**
jambon **ham**
lapin **rabbit**
lardons **small pieces of bacon**
lièvre **hare**
oie **goose**
porc **pork**
poulet **chicken**
ris de veau **veal sweetbreads**
rognons **kidneys**
rôti **roast**
sanglier **wild boar**
saucisse **fresh sausage**
saucisson sec **dried cured
sausage (salami)**
veau **veal**
volaille **poultry**

Poisson (Fish)

Armoricaine **cooked with white
wine, tomatoes, butter and
cognac**
anchois **anchovies**
bar (or loup) **sea bass**
bouillabaisse **Provençal fish**

EMERGENCIES

Help! *Au secours!*
Stop! *Arrêtez!*
Call a doctor *Appelez un
médecin*
Call an ambulance *Appelez
une ambulance*
Call the police *Appelez la
police*
Call the fire brigade *Appelez
les pompiers*
**Where is the nearest
telephone?** *Où est le
téléphone le plus proche?*
**Where is the nearest
hospital?** *Où est l'hôpital le
plus proche?*
I am sick *Je suis malade*
**I have lost my passport/
purse** *J'ai perdu mon
passeport/porte-monnaie*

soup, served with grated
cheese, garlic croutons and
rouille, a spicy sauce
calmars **squid**
coquillage **shellfish**
coquilles St-Jacques **scallops**
crevette **prawn (UK), shrimp (US)**
daurade (or dorade) **sea bream**
espadon **swordfish**
fruits de mer **seafood**
homard **lobster**
huître **oyster**
langoustine **large prawn**
lotte **monkfish**
moule **mussel**
moules marinières **mussels in
white wine and onions**
mulet **grey mullet**
raie **skate**
rascasse **scorpion fish**
rouget **red mullet**
saint-pierre **John Dory**
saumon **salmon**
thon **tuna**
truite **trout**

Légumes (Vegetables)

ail **garlic**
artichaut **artichoke**
asperge **asparagus**
aubergine **aubergine (eggplant)**
avocat **avocado**
champignon **mushroom**
courgette **courgette (zucchini)**
chips **potato crisps**
chou **cabbage**
chou-fleur **cauliflower**
crudités **raw vegetables**
fenouil **fennel**
frites **chips, French fries**
gratin dauphinois **sliced potatoes baked with cream**
haricot **bean**
navet **turnip**
oignon **onion**
panais **parsnip**
petits farcis **stuffed vegetables**
poireau **leek**
pois **pea**
poivron **bell pepper**
pomme de terre **potato**
salade niçoise **salad with egg,
tuna, olives, onions and
tomato**
tomate **tomato**

Miscellaneous

biologique **organic**
pâte **pastry**

pâtes **pasta**
tarte **open tart or quiche**
tourte **closed/double tart**

Fruits (Fruit)

ananas **pineapple**
cerise **cherry**
citron **lemon**
citron vert **lime**
figue **fig**
fraise **strawberry**
framboise **raspberry**
mangue **mango**
noix **walnut**
noisette **hazlenut**
pamplemousse **grapefruit**
pêche **peach**
poire **pear**
pomme **apple**
raisin **grape**
prune **plum**
pruneau **prune**

Sauces (Sauces)

aioli **garlic mayonnaise**
béarnaise **sauce of egg, butter,
wine and herbs**
forestière **with mushrooms**
hollandaise **egg, butter and
lemon sauce**
lyonnaise **with onions**
meunière **fried fish with butter,
lemon and parsley sauce**
pistou **Provençal sauce of basil,
garlic and olive oil; vegetable
soup with pistou sauce**
à la provençale **with tomatoes,
garlic, white wine and olives**

Dessert (Puddings)

clafoutis **baked pudding of bat-
ter and cherries**
coulis **purée of fruit or
vegetables**
gâteau **cake**
île flottante **meringue in custard**
crème anglaise **custard**
poire Belle Hélène **pear with ice
cream and chocolate sauce**
tarte Tatin **upside-down tart of
caramelised apples**
crème caramel **caramelised
egg custard**
crème Chantilly **whipped cream**

In a Café

coffee *café*
...with milk/cream *au lait/crème*

TABLE TALK

**I would like to reserve a
table** *Je voudrais réserver
une table*
I am a vegetarian *Je suis
végétarien(ne)*
I am on a diet *Je suis au
régime*
What do you recommend?
*Qu'est-ce que vous
recommandez?*
**Do you have local
specialities?** *Avez-vous des
spécialités locales?*
I'd like to order *Je voudrais
commander*
That is not what I ordered
*Ce n'est pas ce que j'ai
commandé*
Is service included? *Est-ce
que le service est compris?*
May I have more wine?
Encore du vin, s'il vous plaît?
Enjoy your meal *Bon appétit!*

...decaffeinated *déca/
décaféiné*
...black/espresso *noir/express*
tea *thé*
herb infusion *tisane*
hot chocolate *chocolat chaud*
milk *lait*
mineral water *eau minérale*
still/fizzy *plat/gazeux*
jug of tap water *carafe d'eau*
**fresh lemon juice served with
sugar** *citron pressé*
freshly squeezed orange juice
orange pressé
fresh or cold *frais, fraîche,
froid(e)*
beer *bière*
...bottled *en bouteille*
...on tap *à la pression*
with ice *avec des glaçons*
neat *sec*
red *rouge*
white *blanc*
rosé *rosé*
dry *sec, brut*
sweet *doux*
house wine *vin de maison*
local wine *vin de pays*
pitcher *carafe/pichet*
...of water/wine *d'eau/
de vin*
cheers! *santé!*

Further Reading

Former English adman Peter Mayle could be credited as the man who introduced the Luberon to most foreigners with **A Year in Provence**, in 1991, his enjoyable and often spot-on account of his first year in the Luberon doing up a house in Ménerbes, later followed up by *Encore Provence* and *Toujours Provence*.

Non-Fiction

Côte d'Azur: Inventing the French Riviera by Mary Blume. Excellent account of *emigré* Riviera.

The Discovery of France by Graham Robb. Quirky anecdotes tell the history of France.

France in the New Century: Portrait of a Changing Society by John Ardagh. Weighty tome on modern France.

France on the Brink: A Great Civilization Faces the New Century by Jonathan Fenby. Controversial account of French politics and life.

The French by Theodore Zeldin. Irreverent, penetrating analysis of the French character. Although written in the 1980s, it has become a classic.

The French Riviera: A Literary Guide for Travellers by Ted Jones. Writers in the south of France.

The Identity of France by Fernand Braudel. Unputdownable analysis, weaving major events with everyday life, by one of France's best historians.

The Most Beautiful Villages of Provence by Michael Jacobs and Hugh Palmer. Lovely photos of Provençal villages.

Operation Dragoon: The Invasion of Southern France 1944 by Anthony Tucker-Jones. Account of the Allied landings.

Picasso: A Biography by Patrick O'Brian. The artist's life, including his time in Provence.

The Yellow House by Martin Gayford. Van Gogh goes mad in Arles.

Food

At Home in Provence by Patricia Wells. Recipes from the American food critic's Provençal farmhouse.

A Table in Provence by Leslie Forbes. Recipes.

Lunch in Provence by Rachel McKenna and Jean-André Charial. Recipes from the chef at Oustau de Baumanière.

Fiction

The Avignon Quintet by Lawrence Durrell. Classic travel writing from Durrell.

Bonjour Tristesse by Françoise Sagan. A teenager and her father live the hedonistic Riviera life.

Caravan to Vaccarès by Alistair MacLean. It's murder in the Camargue.

The Count of Monte-Cristo by Alexandre Dumas. Gripping account of prison life (at the Château d'If) and revenge.

The Horseman on the Roof by Jean Giono. Provence in the 1830s.

Jean de Florette and **Manon of the Springs** by Marcel Pagnol. Peasant struggles in rural Provence. Novels that inspired award-winning films.

Perfume by Patrick Süskind. Sinister but gripping tale of an 18th-century Grasse perfumier.

The Rock Pool by Cyril Connolly. Satirical novel set in the 1930s.

Super-Cannes by J.G. Ballard. A futuristic thriller set in a gated business park, loosely inspired by Sophia-Antipolis.

Tender is the Night by F. Scott Fitzgerald. Wealth and decadence on the Riviera.

Total Chaos by Jean-Claude Izzo. The first of Izzo's Marseille crime trilogy featuring cop Fabio Montale (followed by **Chourmo** and **Solea**).

Other Insight Guides

Insight Step by Step and Explore Guides are self-guided walks and tours produced by local writers; presently available are *Explore Paris* and *Step by Step Nice & the French Riviera*. **Insight Fleximaps** are durable, laminated maps and cover the *French Riviera*.

Send Us Your Thoughts

We do our best to ensure the information in our books is as accurate and up-to-date as possible. However, some mistakes and omissions are inevitable and we are reliant on our readers to put us in the picture.

We would welcome your feedback on any details related to your experiences of using the book 'on the road'. The more details you can give us (particularly with regard to addresses, emails and telephone numbers), the better.

We will acknowledge all contributions, and we'll offer an Insight Guide to the best letters received.

Please write to us at:
   **Insight Guides
   PO Box 7910
   London SE1 1WE
   United Kingdom**
Or email us at:
   insight@apaguide.co.uk

Art and Photo Credits

123RF 82, 152
akg-images 21, 115B
Alamy 6C, 24B, 53, 102CL, 106, 115T, 126B, 136T, 137B, 176T, 229T, 262/263
Ardea 102CR
The Art Archive 23, 39
AWL Images 33, 48, 87, 102/103T
La Bastide 296B
Bigstock 92, 215TR
Bridgeman Art Library 27, 38, 42, 43, 46L
Chez Fonfon 5TR, 119
Corbis 28, 40, 41, 47, 78, 80, 95B, 100, 144, 155CL, 187B, 206, 214/215, 215BL, 231R, 262BR, 263BL
Dreamstime 6BL, 64, 86, 117, 118, 123, 143T, 145B, 153, 171, 174B, 193, 262BL, 276B
Mary Evans Picture Library 25, 26, 34
FLPA 102/103B, 103BR
Fotolia 9TR&CL, 74, 81T, 83, 95T, 98, 102BL, 137T, 138T&B, 155BC, 163, 176B, 181, 202, 208, 211B, 226, 228, 229B, 233
Getty Images 45L&R, 46R, 154CR&BL, 234, 256
Images France 102TL, 235T
iStock 7TL, 65, 67B, 81B, 84, 93, 103TR, 136B, 143B, 147B, 235B, 262TL, 263TR&BR, 274, 275, 285
Wadey James/Apa Publications 6BR, 7CL, 8T, 10/11, 12/13,

58/59, 62, 63L&R, 88, 89, 94, 96, 99T, 105, 111T, 113B, 116, 120, 121, 122, 125L&R, 126T, 127, 128T&B, 130, 131, 133, 134, 135, 140, 147T, 149T&B, 150, 162, 165L&R, 166B, 167, 170, 173, 180, 183B, 185, 190, 191, 199, 201B, 209B, 210, 211T, 221, 236, 254, 282, 284, 296T, 314
Leonardo 298, 303
Library of Congress 35
LOTUS PR 52, 273
Monaco Press Centre Photos 279B
Nature Picture Library 102BC
Nice CVB 154C, 239, 244B, 247, 305
OTCM 8C&BR, 104, 109L&R, 110, 111B, 113T, 114T&B
le Petit Maison 101
Pictures Colour Library 154TL&BR, 155TR
Sylvaine Poitau/Apa Publications 3B, 5TL&B, 6T, 7CTR&B, 9BR, 18, 19L&R, 22, 32, 44, 49, 50L&R, 51, 54, 56/57, 70, 72T, 79(all), 97, 99B, 145T, 152T, 156, 157, 158, 159, 160, 161, 194, 205B, 214TL, CR&BL, 215CL, C, CR&BR, 238, 241, 242, 243, 245, 246, 248, 249, 250, 251, 253B, 257, 258T, 259(all), 265, 266, 267T&B, 268T&B, 269B, 270L&R, 271, 272L&R, 278B, 279T, 280T&B, 281, 286, 288, 308, 309, 313, 315, 316,

319, 321, 322
Rex Features 154/155, 252
Clémence Rodde/Avignon Tourisme 67T, 73
SuperStock 155CR
Topfoto 20, 29, 30, 31
Villa Kerylos 262CR
Bill Wassman/Apa Publications 24T, 68, 141, 142, 244T
Gregory Wrona/Apa Publications 1, 2/3, 4T&B, 7CBR, 14, 15, 16, 17L&R, 55, 69, 71, 73B, 75, 76, 77, 82T, 85, 86T, 91L&R, 92T, 93T, 97T, 108&T, 117T, 129, 139, 146, 151, 166T, 168T&B, 174T, 175, 177T&B, 178, 179, 183T, 184, 186T&B, 187T, 188, 189, 192, 194L&R, 195, 196T&B, 197, 200, 201T, 203, 204, 207, 209T, 212, 216, 217, 218, 219, 220, 222, 223, 224T, 225, 227, 231L, 232, 237, 240, 253T, 258BL&R, 260T&B, 264, 269T, 278T
Public domain 7TR, 36, 37, 124, 132, 276T

Map Production: Apa Cartography Department

© 2014 Apa Publications GmbH & Co. Verlag KG, Singapore Branch

Production: Tynan Dean and Rebeka Davies

Cover Credits
Front Cover: Eze, Getty images
Back Cover: (top) Cassis, Dreamstime;
(middle): Simian, Sotonde, Fotolia.

Front Flap: (from top) Cassis bay, Dreamstime;
Courtyard of the Hospital at Arles Dreamstime, Vignobles de Bédoin, Fotolia; Avignon, iStockphoto

Spine: Lavender, iStockphoto

GENERAL INDEX